A TABLE *of* Sharing

A TABLE *of* Sharing

Mennonite Central Committee and the Expanding Networks of Mennonite Identity

edited by
Alain Epp Weaver

Foreword by
Robert S. Kreider

Cascadia
Publishing House
Telford, Pennsylvania

Cascadia Publishing House orders, information, reprint permissions:
contact@CascadiaPublishingHouse.com
1-215-723-9125
126 Klingerman Road, Telford PA 18969
www.CascadiaPublishingHouse.com

Library of Congress Cataloguing-in-Publication Data
A table of sharing : Mennonite Central Committee and the expanding networks
of Mennonite identity / edited by Alain Epp Weaver ; foreword by Robert S.
Kreider.
     p. cm.
Includes index.
Summary: "Over twenty scholars explore in this volume how Mennonite Cen-
tral Committee has served as a vehicle for inter-Mennonite collaboration from
1920 until the present." "[summary]"--Provided by publisher.
ISBN-13: 978-1-931038-78-2 (6 x 9 trade pbk. : alk. paper)
ISBN-10: 1-931038-78-3 (6 x 9 trade pbk. : alk. paper)
  1. Mennonite Central Committee--History. 2. Mennonites--Charities--History.
I. Weaver, Alain Epp. II. Title: Mennonite Central Committee and the expanding
networks of Mennonite identity.

BX8128.W4T33 2011
289.7--dc22

2010050209

18 17 16 15 14 13 12 11   10 9 8 7 6 5 4 3 2 1

In memory of MCC elders Elfrieda and Peter Dyck

Contents

Foreword

Now in its ninetieth year, the Mennonite Central Committee is one of the oldest relief organizations. Born in 1920 of an urgency to meet the needs of Mennonites and others in the Ukraine suffering from famine and civil war, MCC has grown global in its outreach. Arguably, MCC is now the most beloved of Mennonite institutions. As Mennonites became engaged in the work of MCC—sometimes hesitantly and reluctantly—once divided Mennonite groups have been drawn into patterns of amicable cooperation. The title, *A Table of Sharing*, intimates the presence of a Eucharistic spirit around the table of MCC service.

In his introduction, Editor Alain Epp Weaver offers a compact overview to this absorbing book. He has assembled a score of gifted scholars to contribute insightful and thoughtful essays on the story and program of an institution grappling with some of the most critical issues of the twenty-first century. All who have shared in the ministries of MCC will find essays that stimulate critical thought, stretch sensitivities, and inspire support. Invited to this table for rigorous discussion are not only Mennonites but all who are deeply concerned how the global affluent can relate with care and respect to the less affluent.

Two former executive secretaries of MCC, John A. Lapp and Ronald Mathies, lead off with a call to envision an MCC from an Anabaptist-nurtured global perspective, seeking close bonds to the evolving Mennonite World Conference and beyond to a wider circle of faith communities. Esther Epp Tiessen and James Juhnke correct MCC's master narrative in recalling the perilous steps of cautious and separatist Mennonite groups edging their way into collaborative inter-Mennonite relationships and into larger ecumenical linkages.

In a contemporary climate of negative attitudes toward institutions, Donald Kraybill reports as "mystery" a study that reveals an incredibly broad-based commitment among differing Mennonite groupings for the work of MCC.

Checking temptations to self-congratulations, writers remind us that MCC is an unfinished enterprise. Stanley Green and James Krabill raise the question whether good deeds are good enough. They encourage a continued search on how MCC is and can be a part of a winsome missional journey.

Steven Nolt describes how MCC has related to its "plain people" constituents and the need for nuanced understanding and responsiveness to the concerns and sensitivities of the Old Orders. Perry Bush reviews the salutary tension and complimentarity of the relationship between MCC and Christian Peacemaker Teams with the latter's more confrontational stance toward principalities and powers.

Tobin Miller Shearer challenges MCC to extricate itself from embedded racial bias that continues to be unresolved. In a parallel way, Beth Graybill describes how in a male-dominated world MCC has slowly, awkwardly, imperfectly begun to include women in positions of leadership.

Nancy Heisey observes how in the twentieth century MCC has helped to make Mennonites a traveling people. In the context of globalization, how does one travel with the perceptivity, humility, and anticipation of a pilgrim? Malinda Berry invites us to the table as she reviews the amazing response to the *More with Less Cookbook* with sales of more than 800,000, perhaps the most "missional" of any Mennonite book. Three Colorado State University scholars examine, the venture of SELFHELP crafts/Ten Thousand Villages in the context of the fair trade movement.

In concluding essays, time-honored ways of "doing good" are subjected to thoughtful scholarly analysis. Robb Davis poses for testing a series of paradigms of MCC's development strategies. Is development largely an economic undertaking of moving resources from the haves to the have-nots or are there other priorities? William Reimer and Bruce Guenther wrestle in development planning with the use of Western rational models, which may be in tension with the cultivation of nuanced community relationships.

Thinking of Somalia, Rwanda, and Kosovo, Ted Koontz examines "just war" arguments used by those calling for military force to protect the innocent. If "relationships are the most important part of MCC's work," Terrence Jantzi calls for a theoretical framework for relationship building. A variety of ingredients emerge: focus on local community, low budget, simple living, multiple relationships, continuity of presence.

I read the final essay by MCC Executive Director Arli Klassen as an invitation to come to the table to join in reviewing thoughtfully the mission and mandate of MCC. In responding to this call, we are invited to come as pilgrims seeking to serve the hungry, hurting, and fallen in a global community—this with the mind and spirit of Christ.

—*Robert S. Kreider*
  North Newton, Kansas
  President Emeritus, Bluffton University and
  Bethel College

Acknowledgments

Many people deserve credit and thanks for making this volume a reality. Pakisa Tshimika, Karen Klassen Harder, and Nathan Funk proved invaluable in helping to make decisions about how the book should be structured. Janet Martens Janzen, Joe Manickam, Elizabeth Soto Albrecht, Neil Janzen, Marla Pierson Lester, and Tina Mast Burnett all helped in planning a June 2010 conference in Akron, Pennsylvania, marking MCC's ninetieth anniversary at which most of this book's chapters were first presented. All of the presenters at that conference contributed to the vital task of critical reflection on MCC's history and current practice, a task this collection of essays attempts to carry forward.

Finally, MCC is distinguished by its support of and openness to critical reflection on its practice. Judy Zimmerman Herr, Bob Herr, Bert Lobe, Arli Klassen, and Ron Flaming exemplified this commitment by championing this project from its inception through to publication. As MCC moves into a period of organizational restructuring and toward its centennial mark, may it continue this commitment to open self-criticism.

Introduction: A Table of Sharing

ALAIN EPP WEAVER

Much of Mennonite Central Committee's work takes place around tables. Around the world, in homes in varied locations ranging from Appalachia, Kinshasa, Jerusalem, Port au Prince, Kolkata, and First Nations communities in Canada, MCC workers have been graciously hosted around tables (or sometimes on floors) for meals by partners, neighbors, and the so-called "beneficiaries" whom we had come to serve—but who instead gave us the gracious gift of welcome. Country representatives and program officers gather around tables with church leaders from countries like Ethiopia, Indonesia, Syria, and Bolivia and with staff from MCC's partner organizations to discuss projects and to discern future directions. MCC governance boards bring together the wide diversity of Anabaptist-Mennonite reality in Canada and the United States, from Old Order Amish to Conservative Mennonites to "granola" Mennonites, around board tables to do the business of the inter-Mennonite experiment that is MCC.

At annual relief sales people sit down at tables to indulge in all-you-can-eat pancake-and-sausage breakfasts and feasts of traditional ethnic foods, all with the justification that money is being raised for the good cause that is MCC. Around these tables, Mennonites, Brethren in Christ, and Amish from diverse theological and ethnic backgrounds have joined together to share gifts in the name of Christ with persons in need in scores of countries around the globe; through this sharing they have in turn received the fruits of bounteous sharing from inter-Mennonite, ecumenical, and interfaith partnerships. This mutual sharing, flowing not unilaterally from "donor" to "benefici-ary" but instead circulating in the economy of God's overflowing love, is rooted, moreover, in the excessive grace received and shared in thanksgiving at God's table, the table around which MCCers have routinely gathered with one another and with Mennonites and other Christians around the world.

Through participation in this Eucharistic communion, MCCers have also taken part in the ongoing expansion of Mennonite identity, the construction of what might be called the imagined Mennonite community. In his account of the rise of European nationalism, histo-rian Benedict Anderson describes nations as "imagined communi-ties," created through specific practices and media. In a similar way MCC has been a key, and perhaps the primary, vehicle for the con-struction of broader Mennonite identities. From its inception in 1920, MCC has brought together groups in the United States and Canada that otherwise had minimal interaction with one another; in the process, a sense of being part of a larger Mennonite community has been fostered. Over the decades MCC has contributed to the further expansion of Anabaptist-Mennonite identity through partnerships with churches in countries like the Democratic Republic of the Congo, India, and Zimbabwe.

MCC has also helped expand Mennonite identity beyond Men-nonite circles. While MCC's constituent denominations in Canada and the United States typically have shied away from joining ecu-menical coalitions and umbrella organizations, MCC became an ac-tive partner of ecumenical groupings such as the Middle East Council of Churches and the All Africa Conference of Churches and has hired Christians of various denominations, from Baptists to Anglicans to Coptic Orthodox; hundreds if not thousands of MCC service workers have come from non-Mennonite denominations. Service workers have worshiped in Pentecostal, Lutheran, Catholic, and Syrian Or-thodox churches. Through MCC non-Christian institutions and indi-viduals have become part of the Mennonite story: the universities be-hind the Iron Curtain at which MCC students and professors were placed during the Cold War; government councils in countries like Laos, Vietnam, and Cambodia; Shi'a religious scholars in Qom, Iran; Israeli Jewish and Palestinian Muslim peace activists; and the scores of Muslims, Hindus, and Buddhists who have worked for MCC.

The essays in this book all describe different ways how MCC has contributed to expanding networks of Mennonite identity. The chapters in the first section examine aspects of how MCC has served as a means of inter-Mennonite collaboration. John A. Lapp looks at how MCC, dependent on an inter-Mennonite ecclesial mandate, has moved out into a wide array of global partnerships. In distinctive yet complementary ways, Esther Epp-Tiessen and James Juhnke contest standard narrations of MCC's beginnings. Through an account of MCC Canada's origins, Epp-Tiessen describes how MCC has served for ninety years as an institutional space through which the efforts of different Canadian Mennonite communities and organizations came together. Juhnke, for his part, counters what he describes as a Swiss/South German bias in MCC origin accounts centered on Orie Miller, arguing that such accounts leave out or underplay Dutch-Russian-Low German narratives of MCC's beginnings. Ron Mathies then proceeds to analyze the intertwined histories of MCC and Mennonite World Conference, arguably the two major institutional players in the construction of a global Anabaptist-Mennonite identity.

The second section pays attention to how MCC has helped to shape and has been shaped by Mennonite and other Anabaptist communities in Canada and the United States. Analyzing statistical data gathered from opinion surveys, sociologist Donald Kraybill explores the phenomenon of what he terms the "mystery" of the broad-based support for MCC on the part of Mennonites and Brethren in Christ in the United States. Historian Steve Nolt, meanwhile, narrates and analyzes Old Order Amish and Mennonite interactions and engagements with MCC. Nancy Heisey in turn brings critical theory about travel to bear on a discussion of how MCC travel has shaped Mennonite identities as world-travelers, whether such travel is framed as tourism, work, or pilgrimage. Missiologists Stanley Green and James Krabill proceed to consider how MCC has been an inter-Mennonite means of sharing the good news, assessing the multiple missiologies animating MCC's work.

The essays in section three underscore that the expansion of Mennonite identity has never been a straightforward, uncontested process, but that such expanding identity has also been accompanied by exclusions of different sorts, exclusions that have only been faced when challenged by those who have been marginalized. Historian Tobin Miller Shearer draws on whiteness theory to describe how black and white racial experience within MCC has often been rendered invisible, arguing that the regime of whiteness at play in the organization only becomes visible to the beneficiaries of white privilege through conflict, i.e. through the challenges to the whiteness regime by people of color. Beth Graybill next undertakes the task of writing women back into MCC's narrative, offering an account of the polity and politics of MCC's gender history.

MCC has been a key player in and a catalyst for the creation and establishment of numerous other inter-Mennonite institutions and ventures which have helped to shape Mennonite identity, including Mennonite Economic Development Associates, Menno Travel Service, Mennonite Mutual Aid, and much more. Section four focuses on three such examples. Jennifer Keahey, Douglas Murray, and Mary Littrell, all of Colorado State University's Center for Fair and Alternative Trade Studies, place the MCC-initiated SELFHELP Crafts/Ten Thousand Villages venture within the broader history, tensions, and challenges of the fair trade movement. Theologian Malinda Berry offers a theological analysis of the MCC-sponsored World Community Cookbooks series; perhaps more than any other twentieth-century publication, these cookbooks, in particular the *More-with-Less Cookbook*, have "extended the table" of Mennonite identity and community. Historian Perry Bush next examines the intertwined histories of MCC and Christian Peacemaker Teams, probing their points of convergence and tension.

In the book's final section authors consider MCC within the framework of the broader humanitarian world. Robb Davis describes the multiple development paradigms at play within MCC. Willie Reimer and Bruce Guenther examine the integrated character of MCC's "relief" responses over the past nine decades, noting the essential place of relationships in those efforts. Theologian Ted Koontz offers a critique of the "responsibility to protect" doctrine which has become increasingly influential in policy circles in Canada, the United States, and the United Nations. Through an analysis of MCC's work in two Bolivian villages, sociologist Terry Jantzi offers a theoretical framework for understanding how MCC's emphasis on relationships arguably helps to build social capital and social density.

MCC Executive Director Arli Klassen concludes this volume with a reflection on MCC's future. In 2009 the MCCs in Canada and the United States adopted a shared mission and priority document, known popularly as the "New Wine" document, which provides a common basis for all MCC work. Over the coming years MCC will be engaged in a process of structural reorganization designed in part to strengthen MCC's engagement with and accountability to the global Anabaptist-Mennonite church. These structural changes, begun in

MCC's ninetieth anniversary year, will, God willing, carry MCC forward to its hundredth anniversary in 2020 and beyond. May these changes leave MCC well-positioned to continue expanding the networks of Mennonite identity.

—*Alain Epp Weaver, Akron, Pennsylvania*
  Director, Program Development Department
  Mennonite Central Committee

About the Contributors

Malinda Elizabeth Berry teaches theology and is director of the MA program, Bethany Theological Seminary, Richmond, Indiana. She is completing a PhD in theology from Union Theological Seminary in New York City. She is a member of Mennonite Church USA.

Perry Bush is Professor of History, Bluffton (Oh.) University, where he has been teaching since 1994. He is the author of two books and numerous articles on Mennonite history and related subjects, and is currently working on a scholarly biography of C. Henry Smith.

Robb Davis has worked in maternal and child health for nearly twenty-five years with a focus on dialogue-based health education in child nutrition and infectious diseases like malaria. He is Adjunct Faculty at Eastern University and consults and writes on issues related to monitoring and evaluation of development programs.

Esther Epp-Tiessen has worked with MCC in the Philippines, Ontario, and Manitoba and currently serves as Peace Program Coordinator of MCC Canada. She has MA's in Canadian history and theology and has authored two books on Canadian Mennonite themes.

Beth Graybill received her PhD in American Studies in 2009. She has published scholarly articles on "bonnet fiction" and on conservative Mennonite and Amish women. She is director of the Women's Center at Franklin and Marshall College in Lancaster, Pennsylvania, where she lives with her son and attends Community Mennonite Church.

Stanley Green is Executive Director of Mennonite Mission Network. He has served as the chair of the Council of International Ministries and is a doctoral candidate with the University of South Africa.

Bruce Guenther is Program Coordinator for MCC's Food, Disaster and Material Resources department and Sessional Instructor, Canadian Mennonite University. Guenther's most recent research has explored various dimensions of social protection, including its role in promoting climate change adaptation and reducing disaster risk and its linkages with agricultural growth and the politics of social protection.

Nancy Heisey is Vice President, Undergraduate Academic Dean, and Professor of Biblical Studies and Church History at Eastern Mennonite University. She served with MCC in Zaire (Democratic Republic of the Congo), Burkina Faso, and Akron, Pennsylvania.

Terrence Jantzi is currently an Associate Professor of International Development at Eastern Mennonite University. Since the late 1980s, he has served as a practitioner and consultant with the Mennonite Central Committee and similar organizations engaged in international development. His areas of expertise include both Latin America and eastern and southern Africa.

James C. Juhnke is Emeritus Professor of History, Bethel College, in North Newton, Kansas. He served in MCC-PAX in Germany 1958-60 and as director of the MCC program in Botswana 1971-73. He has written books and articles about Mennonite denominational history and biography.

Jennifer A. Keahey is a PhD Candidate in the Sociology Department at Colorado State University. Her interests include globalization; political economy; social movements and social change; and gender, race, and ethnicity.

Arli Klassen is Executive Director, Mennonite Central Committee. She has served with MCC in Africa, Canada, and the United States over the past twenty years.

Theodore J. Koontz is Professor of Ethics and Peace Studies, Associated Mennonite Biblical Seminary. He was Executive Secretary of MCC's Peace Section from 1972 to 1976 and served with MCC in the Philippines for two years in the 1980s.

James Krabill is Senior Executive for Global Ministries, Mennonite Mission Network, Elkhart, Indiana. For fourteen years he served in West Africa as a Bible and Church History teacher among African Initiated Churches (AICs). Krabill has authored or co-edited a number of publications, including: *Is It Insensitive to Share Your Faith?* (2005); *Evangelical, Ecumenical and Anabaptist Missiologies in Conversation* (2006); *Music in the Life of the African Church* (2008); *Jesus Matters: Good News for the Twenty-First Century* (2009); and *Mission from the Margins* (2010).

Donald B. Kraybill is Distinguished Professor and Senior Fellow in the Young Center for Anabaptist and Pietist Studies, Elizabethtown (Pa.) College. He is the author of numerous books on Anabaptist groups including *Concise Encyclopedia of Amish, Brethren, Hutterites & Mennonites* (Johns Hopkins, 2010).

John A. Lapp was Executive Secretary of the MCC Peace Section 1969-1972, member of the Executive Committee 1980 to 1984, and Executive Secretary of MCC 1985 to 1996. He taught history at Eastern Mennonite University, Goshen College (where he was also dean and provost), Elizabethtown College, and Bishop's College in Calcutta. He is coordinator and co-editor of the *Global Mennonite History* for Mennonite World Conference.

Mary Littrell is Professor and Head of the Department of Design and Merchandising, Colorado State University, where she is also a Faculty Associate of the Center for Fair and Alternative Trade Studies. She has been involved in fair trade research for the past fifteen years and is co-author of *Social Responsibility in the Global Market:Fair Trade of Cultural Products* (Sage, 1999) and of the forthcoming *Artisans and Fair Trade: Crafting Identity* (Kumarian, 2010).

Ron Mathies served Mennonite Central Committee as Executive Director and representative and educator in Africa in addition to contributing many years in governance at the provincial, national, and binational levels. He was Director of the Peace and Conflict Studies program, Conrad Grebel University College, Kitchener, Ontario, and Senior Fellow at the Center for International Governance Innovation.

Douglas Murray is Professor of Sociology and Co-Director of the Center for Fair and Alternative Trade Studies, Colorado State University. His scholarly work includes several books and numerous articles on the interface of development, social justice, and environmental sustainability. He has also worked for many years as a development adviser for governments and other organizations, including CARE, the Government of Denmark, OECD, and the World Bank, among others.

Steven M. Nolt is a Professor of History, Goshen (Ind.) College. His books on the Amish include the co-authored volumes *The Amish Way: Patient Faith in a Perilous World* (2010) and *Plain Diversity: Amish Cultures and Identities* (Johns Hopkins, 2007).

Linda Gehman Peachey is Women's Advocacy Director, Mennonite Central Committee U.S., and a member of the East Chestnut Street Mennonite Church. She and her husband, Titus Peachey, live in Lancaster, Pennsylvania, and have two adult daughters. In addition to her current role, Peachey worked with MCC in Laos and as Co-Director with Titus of MCC U.S. Peace and Justice Ministries.

William Reimer worked in several African countries with Mennonite Central Committee. He is currently the director of MCC's Food, Disaster, and Material Resources Department.

Tobin Miller Shearer is Assistant Professor of History, University of Montana, Missoula, where he also coordinates the African-American Studies Program. His most recent book is *Daily Demonstrators: The Civil Rights Movement in Mennonite Homes and Sanctuaries* (Johns Hopkins, 2010). With Regina Shands Stoltzfus, he is the cofounder of the Damascus Road anti-racism program.

Alain Epp Weaver is Director of Mennonite Central Committee's Program Development Department.Previously he served with MCC in the Middle East for eleven years, most recently as the representative for Palestine, Jordan, and Iraq. He is the author of *States of Exile: Visions of Diaspora, Witness, and Return* (2008) and co-editor of *Borders and Bridges: Mennonite Witness in a Religiously Diverse World* (2007).

Part I
MCC and Patterns of Inter-Mennonite Collaboration

Chapter 1

The Character of MCC: Remembering Our Dependence

JOHN A. LAPP

In the 1870s the Americans had helped the Russians immigrate. In the early 1700s the Dutch had helped the persecuted Swiss. . . . So in the 1920s Mennonites saw their giving as a renewal of their own mutual aid tradition.[1]

The human response to this theological impulse has been to create an agency or institution in the light of a vision of what the mission of God is calling us to do in a particular place and time. Inescapably agencies and institutions are the products of their particular historical and sociopolitical context in which they are created.[2]

This essay is an exercise in remembering the Mennonite Central Committee past, a past for decades deeply embedded in Mennonite, Amish, and Brethren in Christ corporate memory. This memory includes dramatic tales, steadfast survivors, heroic characters, creative programs, large-scale communal mobilization, the sights and sounds of relief sales, and more—all of which provide a rich repertoire of stories which get shared from venues as diverse as thrift store counters to pulpits on Sunday mornings. This memory by

which the MCC story lives and is transmitted far surpasses the
archives and narratives preserved by institutional guardians. This
memory extends to the embodied experiences of communities who
can meat for distribution to the hungry, of women who quilt comforters to warm refugees facing cold winters, of customers who
bought Palestinian needlework out of Edna Ruth Byler's trunk and
who now shop at Ten Thousand Villages. This memory is further carried in the lives of thousands of refugee survivors in villages, towns,
and cities on virtually all continents, in the recollections of people
who have suffered through twentieth-century wars around the
globe. For these people, MCC is remembered as a sustainer and de-
liverer in times of great turmoil as well as a bearer of good news.

MCC is also remembered by more than 15,000 individuals as a
significant life experience, one of ministering "In the Name of
Christ." For one-third of these workers, MCC assignments provided
an alternative to conscription in the United States military during the
Second World War as well as the subsequent Korean and Vietnamese
conflicts. For most workers, their years with MCC ranged from one to
six years. Some served for longer periods, with a few serving through
to retirement. Hundreds of administrators, staff, and board members
recall with considerable satisfaction a dynamic program and an almost bewildering set of diverse projects stretching across nine
decades in more than seventy countries.

With so much informal memory and a variety of substantial historical records, one could ask what more needs to be said—indeed,
what more can be said. Surveying the complex, mind-boggling diversity and breadth of the MCC story, however, one can identify at least
three recurring themes essential for understanding MCC's history
and contemporary reality. This overview explores these three themes
in turn: 1) the inter-Mennonite impulse that undergirds MCC; 2) the
historical situation to which MCC responds and the context in which
it works; and 3) the pattern of partnership intrinsic to the manner in
which MCC serves. Reflecting on each of these dimensions helps us
understand MCC as a dependent organization: dependent on an ecclesial mandate, on historical events, and on local and global partners. Above all, MCC is dependent on the One who sends and sus-
tains this ministry of the church.

It is a cliché to call MCC a complex organization. Nevertheless it
is true. MCC history is far richer than the three broad themes by
which I will narrate MCC's nine decades. MCC is as much a movement as an institution. MCC's ninety years also have to be understood as part of the broader history of Mennonite and Brethren in

Christ churches in the United States and Canada and the development of these churches over the course of the twentieth century. However, as historians begin to look ahead to MCC's centenary in 2020, a recognition of MCC's multifaceted dependence—on its Mennonite ecclesial context, on the dynamism of historical events, and on partner churches and organizations—will prove essential for a nuanced recounting of this variegated history.

THE INTER-MENNONITE IMPULSE

Historians recognize July 1920 as MCC's date of birth. But, as the opening quotation above from James Juhnke suggests, MCC's long gestation can be traced back to inter-Mennonite assistance in the sixteenth century. Furthermore, the origins of MCC can also be found in what Quaker economist Kenneth Boulding sixty years ago labeled "the organizational revolution," a revolution which transformed the ecclesial landscape in Canada and the United States, including the Mennonite landscape. Between 1870 and 1940 denominations organized, businesses became corporations, and a plethora of affinity and interest groups formed locally and nationally. MCC's pre-history consists of diverse Mennonite groupings in the United States and Canada coming together during this period to develop new forms of ecclesial partnership and to establish a variety of institutional structures to further inter-Mennonite activities.

Over the centuries, Mennonite groups have consistently been drawn into relations with one another, accepting or ignoring significant differences among themselves in the process. In the United States context, the formation of the General Conference Mennonites in 1860 injected a purposeful emphasis on Mennonite unity. This first institutionalized North American Mennonite conference, aimed at creating new relations within the Mennonite world, was joined by the organization of Mennonite Brethren and Brethren in Christ constituent bodies in 1879. The Mennonite Church General Conference in turn first met in 1898 as a binational entity encompassing Mennonite churches in Canada and the United States. None of these simple ecclesial structures had a paid staff. Publishing and mission committees, alongside the first Mennonite colleges, were the first church institutions with paid staff.

Already in the 1870s, inter-Mennonite conference committees formed in Eastern Pennsylvania, Indiana-Michigan, Kansas, and Ontario to help with the immigration of Russian and Prussian Mennonites to the United States and Canadian great plains. Inter-Mennonite

committees in Kansas, Illinois, and Indiana established the Mennonite Board of Guardians in December 1873. Guardian leaders
Christian Krehbiel, David Goertz, John F. Funk, and Bernhard
Warkentin developed some of what became long-term patterns of
inter-Mennonite cooperative work.

A second chapter of inter-Mennonite cooperation occurred in the
late 1890s with the formation of the Home and Foreign Relief Com-
mittee (HFRC), chaired by the Canadian A.B. Kolb. Centered in
Elkhart, Indiana, the committee had representatives from the Evan-
gelical Mennonite Brethren, Mennonite Brethren, several General
Conference and Mennonite Church districts, and the Mennonite
Brethren in Christ. In 1897 the HFRC sponsored the first major inter-
Mennonite fundraising and food relief effort responding to famine in
India.

Early in the twentieth century the inter-Mennonite movement
was overshadowed as the several Mennonite conferences founded
their own separate mission boards and colleges. The HFRC passed
from the scene. Inter-Mennonite energies took a further blow, meanwhile, as the Mennonite Church in particular was torn by ecclesial
conflicts nurtured by the growing fundamentalist-liberal divide intensifying in American Protestantism.

During World War I, however, Mennonites in the United States
and Canada discovered anew their minority status as peace churches,
a discovery which stimulated a new round of inter-Mennonite cooperation in dealing with the imperatives of compulsory national service. Conference relief committees supported one another in searching
for positions where draft age men could perform service of "national
significance." Even as they organized to address the needs of draft
age Mennonite men, these relief committees also heard of tragic developments in Russia and the effects of those developments on Mennonite communities in Russia and tried a variety of means of getting
assistance and personnel to Eastern Europe to respond.

All the major Mennonite as well as the Brethren in Christ
churches placed workers with the newly formed American Friends
Service Committee (established in 1917). The Mennonite Church Relief Commission for War Sufferers also placed workers with the Pres-
byterian-sponsored Near East Relief. These workers, many of them
college graduates, became forceful advocates of greater inter-Mennonite unity. A meeting of fifty AFSC-related Mennonite workers
held in Clermont-en-Argonne, Meuse, France, in June 1919, called for
"a relief and service organization ready to deal effectively with emergencies such as wars and natural disasters."[3]

Amid all this activity by relief committees and the inter-Mennonite "Young Peoples Movement," a study commission of four from Russia toured Western European Mennonite communities and North America seeking sustained and major support. This delegation suggested a cooperative program of all the relief committees. Already the conferences of Dutch-Russian background had formed an Emergency Relief Commission. Now in summer 1920 the (Old) Mennonite Relief Commission became part of a new body called the Mennonite Central Committee (MCC). As James Juhnke has observed, "for Mennonite ecumenical relationships, MCC's birth was a high moment."[4]

Parallel to the inter-Mennonite movement that birthed MCC was another inter-Mennonite conversation that gave rise to Mennonite World Conference (MWC).[5] This conversation began in correspondence among Mennonites in Germany, Holland, Russia, Canada, and the United States and culminated in an "All-Mennonite Convention" held in Berne, Indiana, in summer 1913. The keynote speaker, Christian Neff of the Weierhof, Germany, later issued a call for what became the first Mennonite World Conference which met in Basel, Switzerland, in June 1925. For most of its history, MCC has had close connections with Mennonite World Conference. While MCC supported the growth of MWC, MWC has in turn become the most conspicuous global expression of the inter-Mennonite impulse reflecting the growing impact of the worldwide Mennonite and Brethren in Christ movement. MWC has become a major vehicle for enlarging the notion of what it means to be inter-Mennonite around the globe. MWC now serves as an advocate of what it means to be inter-Mennonite across six continents and is a voice increasingly heard at the MCC table.

The inter-Mennonite impulse continued to be the driving force within MCC well beyond its inception. During the 1930s several Mennonite conference peace committees began to work together in developing a common front for dealing with the impending Second World War. Together these committees participated with Quakers and Church of the Brethren in convening an Historic Peace Church Conference in Newton, Kansas, in 1935. Then in 1939 the Mennonite and Brethren in Christ committees formed the "Mennonite Central Peace Committee." A year later in 1940 this inter-Mennonite committee, which later developed into the MCC Peace Section, asked MCC to assume responsibility for Mennonite draftees.

The experience of alternative service in both Canada and the United States without a doubt served as the most intense and extensive incubator for inter-Mennonite sentiments and convictions. Individuals learned to know one another across conference boundaries. They served under leaders frequently from conferences other than their own, and urged leaders to think more systematically in inter-Mennonite terms. During the postwar years, the enthusiasm and leadership of these personalities and those engaged in overseas service became the driving force for an expanding MCC.

The same inter-Mennonite energies which fueled MCC's expansion after World War II also led to the founding of inter-Mennonite ventures in mutual aid (Mennonite Mutual Aid, or MMA), mental health (Mennonite Mental Health Society, or MMHS), domestic disasters (Mennonite Disaster Services, or MDS), and economic development (Mennonite Economic Development Associates, or MEDA). By the end of the 1950s most conference mission boards and MCC were coordinating efforts through the Council of Mission Board Secretaries (COMBS; inter-Mennonite mission board coordination now takes place through the Council of International Anabaptist Ministries, or CIM).

One of the lessons I learned as a young administrator with MCC in 1969 from the MCC Executive Secretary, Orie O. Miller, and his successor, William T. Snyder, was that although deeply rooted, the inter-Mennonite impulse requires conscious and constant attention and practice. From the moment of MCC's foundation onward, all Mennonite groups with a stake in the new organization's mission needed to be at the table with a respectful recognition of differences. (More recently such balancing at MCC tables has appropriately considered whether or not gender, ethnic, and national differences are adequately represented).

Conscious inter-Mennonite practice has become routine through the years. MCC is now but one of several dynamic inter-Mennonite bodies. As the churches of the Mennonite, Brethren in Christ, and Amish spectrum in North America worked together in MCC, these separate groups have tended to become more and more inter-Mennonite as well. To be sure, some newer Mennonite groupings, not having had the experience of inter-Mennonite cooperation, have adopted a strongly independent and separatist stance. Most Mennonite conferences and institutions have incorporated this impulse into their own ecclesial practice. Today perhaps the most authentic inter-Mennonite impulse is found in local MCC activity. Relief sales, thrift shops, and Ten Thousand Villages stores are so thoroughly inter-Mennonite that long-established conference differences have become largely irrelevant.

MOLDED BY EVENTS

If MCC was inspired by inter-Mennonite aspirations, its activities have been usually triggered and molded by particular events. Events are rarely singular and momentary but are rather the product of deeper historical forces. MCC did not and does not exist in an historical vacuum but instead has participated in and been shaped by broader historical trajectories.

As already noted, World War I had a dramatic impact on nearly everyone in Canada and the United States, through heightened demands for food production, a drive for greater industrial production to support the war effort, increased taxation, and the conscription of young men for military service. The peace churches and many other peace-minded people were swept along by the ideology and practice of "total war" in Europe and North America. MCC emerged from this milieu as representative of the Mennonite churches' search for alternative ways to serve society other than military participation.

The search for a meaningful alternative to military service dated back decades. Mennonites in Russia had pioneered a military alternative Forestry Service in the 1880s. During the First World War, Mennonites in Canada and the United States pressured by a militant war spirit worked hard to keep young Mennonites (alongside Hutterites, Quakers, Church of the Brethren, Pentecostals, Adventists, and others) out of military camps. Some were furloughed as farm labor. The Quakers developed medical and relief programs for service as a pacifist witness in regions of war, programs in which the major Mennonite groups placed young men.

Formal hostilities ended in November 1918 except in Russia, where German troops remained in place. The Russian Revolution and the ensuing civil war broke out in 1919. Mennonites in the Ukraine were victims of both war and revolution and sent out calls for assistance to Europe and North America in 1920. MCC's first initiative, lasting from 1920 to 1926, of providing food and clothing to Mennonites in Russia and the Ukraine thus represented a response to an inter-Mennonite need but within the context of global events (the end of the First World War and the aftermath of the Bolshevik Revolution).[6]

Due to North American Mennonite conflicts, especially the fundamentalist-modernist clash within the Mennonite Church, MCC ceased operation between 1926 and 1929. MCC was reactivated, however, when a new appeal from Mennonites in Russia arrived, asking for assistance to emigrate from the tyranny of Soviet rule. MCC's executive committee met several times that year to determine a course of action. The second convention of Mennonite World Conference in Danzig in June 1930 ignited a Euro-American effort to help Mennonite refugees from Russia who had made their way to Germany to relocate. Neither Canada nor the United States, both amid depression and nativistic sentiments, would accept a new round of refugees. The Mennonites from Russia and their German hosts discovered openings for resettlement in Brazil and Paraguay. MCC, building on the experience of the newly established Menno Colony of Canadian Mennonites in Paraguay, bought extensive land in the Paraguayan Chaco from New York owners, for the purposes of building another colony, later called Fernheim. Over one thousand of these Mennonite refugees from Russia traveled to the Chaco from Germany, while several hundred more headed to southern Brazil.

Several books would be required to narrate the full story of how MCC responded to postwar events by facilitating the resettlement of Mennonite refugees to South America. The significance of this large-scale project for our analysis here is simply that it illustrates how MCC's identity and program have been and continue to be shaped through response to specific historical events. The intersection of historical events and MCC program is aptly symbolized by the names Mennonite colonists helped in Paraguay by MCC gave to the main streets of the town of Filadelphia: Paul von Hindenburg Strasse (named after the then-president of Germany, who had taken substantial interest in fate of the Mennonite refugees) today stands alongside Orie O. Miller Strasse, Harold S. Bender Strasse, and B. H. Unruh Strasse, roads named in honor of three MCC leaders at the forefront of MCC assistance to this new immigrant community.

MCC once more lapsed into inaction in 1932. Then in 1938, with World War II looming on the horizon, the newly formed Mennonite Central Peace Committee (later to become the MCC Peace Section) joined Quakers and Brethren in negotiating an alternative service program with the U.S. government. The Historic Peace Churches of Canada, meanwhile, worked to secure similar agreements with the Canadian government. Over the course of the war, alternative service in both countries constituted the focus of major inter-Mennonite efforts.

The runup to the Second World War also saw an expansion of other MCC activities. MCC became operational supporting the work of the Mennonite Church Relief Committee in Spain, assuming administrative responsibility in fall 1939. Then, as Germany invaded Poland in September 1939, MCC decided to respond to wartime suffering by sending workers to France and Germany in cooperation with the Russian Mennonite B. H. Unruh, who resided in Germany and who had already served as a pivotal person for MCC during its in 1920-26 and 1930-31 interventions. Beginning in 1936 Unruh operated as the part-time staff person for what was called the "Central Bureau for Mennonite Relief."

World War II represents a watershed for MCC. Before the war MCC was ad hoc and occasional. During the war MCC became a major administrative body to administer Civilian Public Service camps. MCC gained experience in raising large operational funds and in administering a sizable staff to direct program. During the war Orie Miller, the MCC Executive Secretary, kept exploring how Mennonites and Brethren in Christ could prepare themselves for postwar relief and reconstruction. He corresponded with the emerging World Council of Churches executive secretary Visser t'Hooft on how European churches expected to respond to this crisis. Along with his Historic Peace Church friends he encouraged the formation of an even broader ecumenical relief body called Church World Service in the United States in 1943. Despite some objections from MCC members, Miller participated in the formation of the American Council of Voluntary Agencies for Foreign Service in 1944, which later provided a base for MCC work in occupied Germany and with the United Nations relief agencies in China and the Middle East.

MCC's large postwar relief operations in Holland, Belgium, France, and Germany grew out of these war-time experiences. Postwar relief also paved the way for additional program expansion: Working in UNRRA Yugoslav refugee camps in Egypt created an entrée into Palestine (first in the Egyptian-ruled Gaza Strip and then in the Jordanian-controlled West Bank) at the end of the 1948 Arab-Israeli war. Another major postwar activity for MCC was to help refugees from Prussia and Russia now in Germany, Denmark, and Holland. This included assistance to resettle large numbers in West Germany, Canada, Uruguay, and Paraguay.

The largest MCC postwar project began in Western Germany with the arrival of C. F. Klassen, who had played pivotal roles in MCC's work in Russian in the 1920s and in facilitating the movement of refugees from Germany to Brazil and Paraguay in 1930, as MCC Commissioner for Refugees. Postwar Europe was a tragic place; Germany especially suffered massive food shortages. MCC responded to the postwar devastation by shipping ton upon ton, container upon container, of food and clothing from 1946 to 1950. The scope of MCC's response can be measured by the fact that in 1947 MCC sent more postwar assistance than any other external relief agency.

MCC's concern with suffering peoples in postwar contexts and in situations of violent conflict extended beyond the devastated Europe of the mid-1940s. Already during the war in 1942, MCC responded to the call of Mennonite missionaries in India for assistance. Little did they realize that MCC workers from their Calcutta base would soon become involved with answering the needs of refugees from the Pakistan-India conflict; nor could they have been aware that this initial MCC response in India would be the beginning of MCC's longest, continuous program right down to the present. In 1944, meanwhile, Mennonite missionaries in China invited MCC to consider program there after a visit by J. D. Graber and Sam Goering. A large relief program in China lasted for only three years from 1946-1949. With China unstable, workers moved on to the Philippines, Taiwan, and Hong Kong.

By the early 1950s MCC had become well established as the relief arm of the Mennonite and BIC churches, recognized as "a compassionate, compelling witness." During the war years and through postwar responses, MCC had gained considerable experience and credibility in relief, reconstruction, and local community development. New voices began to encourage an enlarged vision for MCC. Robert S. Kreider, an MCC Europe administrator from 1946 to 1949, represented one such new voice. After the 1953 annual meeting of MCC, he wrote an insightful letter to Orie Miller suggesting that "MCC should continuously be extending sensitive fingers out into areas of need to determine where there is urgent need for aid and where MCC is uniquely qualified and called to serve."

After noting "the nationalistic, anti-colonial racial struggles of the Middle East" and the important work in Palestine among Arab refugees, he observed that Egypt and Iran "often exhibited bitter attitudes toward the western colonial powers. Perhaps there is a ministry of service and reconciliation which ought to be done in one of these areas." He said that Indo-China might be "a good project for a PAX unit," perhaps "in cooperation with French Mennonites." He asked "whether there is not some unique mission of service for us as an MCC in Africa." Could there be a "demonstration project in reconciliation. Something like a Point 4 Program [U.S. government assistance], only MCC staffed and administered."[7]

Kreider's perceptive letter clinched directions already under way in MCC and provided a rationale for expanding program with an emphasis on reconciliation work in conflictual situations. Within a decade MCC was immersed in areas of civil conflict in Algeria and Vietnam and later in Bangladesh, southern Africa, and Central America. Kreider himself designed the Teachers Abroad Program (TAP), through which hundreds of draft-age men (and often their spouses) served as educators beginning in 1962.[8]

The examples above of MCC responses to local and global events are far from exhaustive. As the decades passed, MCC often expanded its program in ways that allowed it to help victims of conflict and natural disaster. A 1950s-era MCC reconstruction program called PAX, initiated in Europe and targeted primarily at draft-age single men, expanded into broad-based development work in Greece, Paraguay, India, South Korea, and Vietnam. In nearly every decade since, natural disasters as recent as the 2004 Southeast Asia tsunami have reminded MCC of the need for emergency assistance. And in Canada and the U.S., MCC was challenged by the Native Peoples, civil rights, and antiwar movements, leading MCCs in those contexts to develop innovative programs in peace education (e.g. the long-term MCC U.S. focus on banning "bombies") and programs of solidarity with persons denigrated by systems of oppression and discrimination (e.g the Aboriginal Neighbors program of MCC Canada and the provincial MCCs as well as the anti-racism Damascus Road program).

In sum, wherever MCC has worked, it has done so in response to a significant context. It is exhilarating to contemplate how a church agency is able to recognize "the fullness of time." It is also troubling to observe the limitations of the church's ministry. Despite the work and witness of MCC and many other church and public agencies, food shortages, civil conflict, war, and social injustice continue to be ever present. Nearly fifty years ago the famed preacher of Harvard University George A. Buttrick suggested that "history is a dialogue between God and man on pilgrimage in the language of events."[9] MCC has in a modest way been and continues to be one of the participants in this story of the ages.

THE PATTERN OF PARTNERSHIP

My final thematic observation from this survey of MCC's ninety years is that none of MCC's activities has been a singular involvement. Long before partnership became a missiological imperative, it was intrinsic to MCC patterns of service. The Gospels report that Jesus "came to serve and not to be served." MCC has tried to take that model seriously by not being in charge. This is by no means easy for an agency in a North American success-oriented culture. Large budgets, staff experience, and networks of linkages provide MCC with a significant power base. Service can exude power.

MCC workers from the beginnings have established a pattern of taking up residence, working with local churches and other organizations in a cooperative manner. MCC work is never done alone. That fact has meant giving up some autonomy and allowing others to determine priorities and shape program. Such partnerships require respectful relationships. Not all of them are successful. The vision is not always clear. To quote Atlee Beechy, a longtime MCC leader, "Service requires servanthood."

There is no one way to be a partner. From the perspective of some member conferences, MCC itself is a partnership. First it was relief committees, later mission agencies, most recently conference or denominational bodies. Partners in program may seem an appropriate continuation of partners in governance. This commitment to partnership is stated in an early document that MCC was formed "to function with and for the several relief committees of the Mennonites."[10]

The first type of partnership MCC formally engaged in was with Mennonite and other churches. In Russia these partners were the Colony Relief Committee (Chortitza) and Mennozentrum representing all Mennonites. Local partners supplied workers for food distribution and individuals to work with local and national governing authorities. A full list of church partners since 1920 would cover several pages. Until the l960s MCC partnered in a variety of countries with almost all North American Mennonite and BIC mission boards. In the 1960s MCC partnered with European Mennonite mission agencies in South America and Central Africa. MCC worked closely with the Dutch mission board in Indonesia. By the 1960s churches on most continents were operating independently; accordingly, MCC's partnerships with churches expanded still further, as MCC began to work with newly independent churches in countries ranging from India to Indonesia, Ethiopia to Zimbabwe, and Paraguay to Nicaragua.

In some settings MCC joined local churches in working together in service ministries. MCC helped in the organizing of Mennonite Christian Service Fellowship of India (MCSFI), the Association of Indigenous-Mennonite Cooperative Services (ASCIM) in Paraguay, the Congo Mennonite Agricultural Service (COMAS), and more recently China Educational Exchange (CEE, now Inter-Mennonite Partners in China).

Nor have MCC partnerships been limited to Mennonite churches and agencies. The most prominent ecumenical partners through the years have been the Quakers. As noted above, Mennonite workers served in France in 1918 with American Friends Service Committee. This partnership grew through joint work on the National Service Board for Religious Objectors during World War II. The Canadian Historic Peace Churches included joint Quaker and Mennonite participation. In postwar Europe and later in Vietnam, Mennonite and Quaker efforts frequently intersected. In Nigeria-Biafra in 1969-1970 MCC and AFSC formed Quaker-Mennonite Service which worked cross-border with the World Council of Churches and the International Committee of the Red Cross.

Ecumenical partnerships have not been restricted to the Quakers, however. During the 1950s and 1960s MCC worked closely with the Greek Orthodox Church in Macedonia and Crete. MCC has enjoyed decades-long relationships with numerous regional communions like the Coptic Orthodox and Coptic Evangelical Churches in Egypt, the Syrian Orthodox in Syria and Iraq, the Anglican diocese of Calcutta, and the Evangelical Church of Vietnam (Tin Lanh).

Another group of church partners consists of other church agencies. MCC joined its efforts with those of Church World Service and Lutheran World Relief in Vietnam Christian Service from 1966 to 1972. More recently MCC partnered again with Church World Service in a major humanitarian response called All Our Children following the U.S.-led invasion of Iraq. In a variety of locations MCC has shared a common agenda with Christian Reformed World Relief. During the Cold War MCC worked closely with the Russian Baptists who provided connections with Mennonites who had remained in the USSR. In addition to providing hundreds of Bibles and hymnals through the Baptists, MCC supported the translation of Barclay Bible commentaries into the Russian language for evangelical churches in Russia.

MCC in many places worked under an ecumenical umbrella, such as the Middle East Council of Churches and the South Africa Council of Churches. In the 1940s MCC operated under the Church Committee for China Relief. In Nigeria, Sudan, Mozambique, Pakistan, and other places MCC has nurtured close programmatic links to national church councils. In almost every location it works, MCC has sought out and has been nurtured through such ecumenical partnerships.

MCC peace-oriented activities provided numerous rich partnerships, first with the International Mennonite Peace Committee formed at the 1936 Mennonite World Conference in Amsterdam. Following World War II, MCC, the Church of the Brethren, the Quakers, and the Fellowship of Reconciliation worked closely together in a consultative committee with European churches to organize Eirene, a European Christian service agency in 1957. Beginning in 1955 this ecumenical, peace-oriented partnership sponsored a series of groundbreaking theological conversations, with the first held in Puidoux, Switzerland. These so-called Puidoux conversations renewed contacts between Christians in western and eastern Europe, gave rise to the Christian Peace Conference and Christians Associated for Relations with Eastern Europe (CAREE), and served as venues in which Mennonites vigorously represented theological convictions about nonresistance, nonviolence, and peace in ecumenical conversations.

One important word for MCC, particularly since the 1960s, was the term *secondment*. It means providing workers for a local church, mission, school, college, etc. Sometimes these workers have earned a very nominal salary or room and board with MCC covering other costs. The Teachers Abroad Program (TAP) placed several hundred teachers seconded to schools of numerous denominations in Central and Southern Africa.

A significant dimension of the partnership motif has been the growing number of MCC workers from other Christian traditions. The ecumenical character of MCC workers began in Civilian Public Service camps operated by MCC in the U.S., in which Quakers, Brethren, Baptists, Lutherans, Methodists, Church of God, Roman Catholics, and others worked alongside Mennonites. Since then MCC has always been a welcome place to non-Mennonite workers who affirm the Christian faith and who embrace MCC's commitment to nonviolent peacemaking.

If MCC has enjoyed close and intimate partnerships with churches over the decades, its ties to governments were inevitably more formal but just as persistent. From its work in the 1920s with the American Relief Administration under the leadership of the Quaker Herbert Hoover right down to the present, MCCs in both the U.S. and Canada have had to work with their governments for travel and shipping purposes. Furthermore, in countries around the world MCC was dependent on a variety of governments for permission to work locally: for permits for office operations and for visas for MCC workers.

In refugee camps in postwar Germany and Denmark and later in Egypt, Palestine, and Jordan MCC partnered in large governmental or United Nations-run programs. Resettling refugees in Canada, the U.S., or Paraguay brought MCC into close cooperation with a variety of governments. Sometimes MCC became part of the governing system, as when it joined the Council of Relief Agencies Licensed for Operation in Germany (CRALOG) immediately after World War II.[11]

By the 1950s and 1960s both U.S. and Canadian governments became increasingly concerned with mutual security and economic development. Governments quickly discerned that the religious sector had advantages in being locally connected in many countries. In the early 1950s MCC was attracted to working with the U.S. government's Point 4 Program in rural development. These funds became a significant resource for the building of the Trans-Chaco Highway in Paraguay. MCC PAX men became major players in constructing the highway in a partnership of Chaco Mennonites, the Paraguayan and American governments, and MCC. However, during the Vietnam war workers on location became concerned how USAID development assistance was incorporated into the American military effort. At that point MCC determined that accepting American government assistance had become too costly for MCC. Indeed, in the Middle East and Central America MCCers were only welcomed on the ground since they were not funded by the U.S. government.

In contrast, the Canadian International Development Agency (CIDA) has been welcomed in most countries. This Canadian government development agency also chose to put even greater emphasis than did the U.S. in working through the religious sector. Accordingly, MCC Canada has had access to major grants for international programming via CIDA. Closely linked to MCC Canada is the Canadian Food Grains Bank, an ecumenical partnership which grew out of the MCC-initiated Food Bank. A recipient in its own right of CIDA matching funds, CFGB represents a major connector between public and private assistance for impoverished people. Both CIDA and CFGB have become integral partners for much MCC overseas work.

Indeed, MCC does not work alone. It is a partnership of the church that in turn partners with churches and other agencies around the world. This is a vital dimension of MCC.

This overview of MCC's ninety years has focused on only three dimensions of the MCC story. Rather than emphasize the core programmatic character or recall the MCC underlying theological impulse, I have highlighted the contextual dimension of MCC performance. Other aspects of MCC's identity, including economic, technological, and interreligious themes, would have to be explored to present a fuller picture of MCC's history and contemporary reality.

Some contemporary thinkers suggest that context is everything. That surely overstates its significance. MCC begins dependent on the Word and a community which has strived to minister "In the name of Christ." Context is the environment in which the Word is incarnated and embodied. For MCC the mode of bearing witness is inextricably part of the content of the witness. Amid the richness of creation and the diversity of humanity, the kingdom of God is lived and demonstrated. Jesus came to bear witness in a particular time and place. Ever since, the message of restoration and reconciliation has burst forth in numerous contexts. In a world that exhibits more alienation than reconciliation, the work of the church continues to be that of bearing witness to a loving God. That was MCC's calling in 1920. It is also its calling in 2010.

NOTES

1. James C. Juhnke, *Vision, Doctrine, War: Mennonite Identity and Organization in America, 1890-1930* (Scottdale, Pa.: Herald Press, 1989), 255.

2. Wilbert R. Shenk, *Changing Frontiers of Mission* (Maryknoll, N.Y.: Orbis Books, 1999), 177.

3. Quoted in Guy F. Hershberger, "Historical Background to the Formation of the Mennonite Central Committee," *The Mennonite Quarterly Review* 44/3 (July 1970): 234.

4. Juhnke, 250.

5. See chapter 4 in this volume by Ron Mathies for a more detailed account of MWC's emergence and its interconnectedness with MCC.

6. The most comprehensive account of this early MCC work is found in P. C. Hiebert and Orie O. Miller, *Feeding the Hungry, Russia Famine 1919-1925: American Mennonite Relief Operations under the Auspices of Mennonite Central Committee* (Scottdale, Pa.: Mennonite Central Committee, 1929).

7. Robert S. Kreider letter to Orie O. Miller, January 5, 1954, reprinted in C. J. Dyck, ed. *The Mennonite Central Committee Story, Vol. II: Responding to Worldwide Needs* (Scottdale, Pa.: MCC, 1980), 26-27.

8. A prototype of such an educational program began already in 1954 in Newfoundland, Canada.

9. George A. Buttrick, *Christ and History* (New York: Abingdon, 1963), 13.

10. From a July 27, 1920 resolution, included in John D. Unruh, *In the Name of Christ: A History of Mennonite Central Committee* (Scottdale, Pa.: Herald Press, 1952), 15.

11. See chapter 5, "Amidst the Debris at War's End: Germany," in Robert S. Kreider and Rachel Waltner Goossen, *Hungry, Thirsty, a Stranger: The MCC Experience* (Scottdale, Pa.; Herald Press, 1988).

Chapter 2

New Wine for New Wineskins: MCC and the Formation of MCC Canada

ESTHER EPP-TIESSEN

The world had changed, and the demise of CMRIC, CMRC, NRRO, CHPC, and HPCCC was the end of an era. New wine had to be put into new wineskins; old wineskins could not contain the new wine.
—J. M. Klassen, 2001

As recently as September 2009, the MCC website's history section included the following claim: "Canadian Mennonites joined MCC in 1963." This statement is false. A truer statement would be, "MCC Canada was established in 1963 to work cooperatively with MCC." But even that assertion, without elaboration, is misleading because it denies the rich history of Canadian Mennonite and Brethren in Christ involvement with MCC before 1963.[1] The truth is that Canadian Mennonites actively supported MCC from its beginnings in 1920, and especially after 1939, through a variety of their own inter-Mennonite relief, immigration, and peace organizations. From the beginning, however, the relationship between the Canadian organizations and MCC was an evolving one. That relationship took a significant shift when in 1963 these Canadian organizations amalgamated to form an entity called Mennonite Central Committee

Canada.[2] It has continued to evolve until the present. The current New Wine/New Wineskins process tells us that the story is not yet over.

The purpose of this paper is not to address the entire ninety-year partnership of Canadian and U.S. Mennonites in and through MCC. Rather, it is to outline the developments that led to the formation of MCC Canada in 1963 and to explore some of the critical questions surrounding those developments. My hope is that this chapter will shed light on Canadian self-identify within the larger entity of MCC, even while it explores how Canadian perspectives were often far from homogeneous. Similarly, I hope it will illuminate some of the ongoing irritants in the Canada-U.S. relationship, even as it communicates the overwhelming desire of Canadians to share in the ministry of MCC.

Before launching into the story, I wish to identify the bias I bring to this undertaking. I grew up as the daughter of parents, Frank and Helen Epp, who were keenly interested in the development and well-being of MCC Canada. As a history student I wrote a thesis on the formation of the organization,[3] and later I served as an MCC Canada board member. For the last ten years I have served on the staff of MCC Canada. Because of these experiences, I can hardly conceive of MCC Canada not serving as the umbrella under which Canadian Mennonites and Brethren in Christ work together in relief, service, and peace witness. Consequently, I believe that the formation of MCC Canada in 1963 was a critically important development.[4] My bias necessarily influences the analysis which follows, even while I attempt to identify different perspectives.

ORGANIZATIONAL
ANTECEDENTS TO MCC CANADA

The story of MCC Canada's formation is a rich and complex narrative that spans nearly fifty years. It begins with World War I and the formation of the Non-Resistant Relief Organization (NRRO) in Ontario. The NRRO was created by Ontario Swiss Mennonites in 1918 to collect relief monies as an expression of their gratitude to the federal government for honoring their refusal to perform military service; the money was to relieve suffering caused by the war. Members of the NRRO included (Old) Mennonites, Brethren in Christ, Mennonite Brethren in Christ, Amish, and Old Order Mennonites. Initially, NRRO contributions went to a variety of non-Mennonite organizations, but in 1921 NRRO began to contribute funds to MCC for assistance to suffering Russian Mennonites. The NRRO went into dormancy in the early 1930s but was revived in 1939 as war again engulfed the world.

A second organization was the Central Relief Committee, formed as a result of the visit of members of the Russian Mennonite *Studienkommission* to western Canada in fall 1920. These men had arrived earlier that summer in the U.S. to solicit aid for Mennonites in the Soviet Union suffering from famine and the violence of the revolution. U.S. Mennonites had organized a Mennonite Central Committee (MCC) for the purpose of coordinating the efforts of their own conferences and relief committees. On October 18, 1920, at a meeting in Regina, Saskatchewan, Mennonites from Saskatchewan, Alberta, and Manitoba formed a Central Relief Committee (CRC) to channel contributions of Mennonites from those provinces to MCC for Russian relief. By the time the CRC folded in 1924, it had contributed some $57,000 to MCC, in addition to sending clothing and several freight car loads of flour to south Russia through the Save the Children Fund.[5]

A much bigger initiative in Canada, however, involved the immigration of Russian Mennonite refugees. The *Studienkommission* had come to North America, not only to solicit relief assistance for their people but to find ways of enabling them to escape the Soviet Union. In 1922 Mennonites in Canada established the Canadian Mennonite Board of Colonization (Board) to help the enormous task of transporting and re-settling their co-religionists in Canada. The Board involved the Conference of Mennonites of Central Canada, the Mennonite Brethren Conference, as well as the (Old) Mennonites and other smaller groups. Between 1923 and 1930, it helped the immigration of 20,000 Mennonites to Ontario and the western provinces. The Board worked closely with MCC throughout the immigration process. After 1924 it also effectively took on the work of CRC in collecting relief aid for Russian Mennonites.

By the late 1930s the NRRO's relief work had gone dormant, while the Board's work had shifted to collecting the *Reiseschuld* (travel debt) of recent immigrants. But the beginning of World War II initiated a new period of tremendous activity. The war also resulted in the creation of several new inter-Mennonite organizations involved in war-related ministries. The Ontario churches, including the Swiss Mennonites, Brethren in Christ, as well as new Russian Mennonite immigrants (often referred to as *Russlaender*), formed the Conference of Historic Peace Churches (CHPC) to attend to military-service-related concerns and to represent these concerns before the federal government. Western Mennonites established the Mennonite Central Relief Committee (MCRC) to prepare, collect, and ship relief goods to war sufferers; MCRC functioned as a partner organization to the Board, with very similar membership and leadership. Westerners also formed the Western Service Committee (WSC) which represented them on military-service-related questions; CHPC and WSC worked closely together, as did the NRRO and MCRC.

Manitoba Mennonites who descended from the 1870s immigration from Russia (informally referred to as *Kanadier*) were unhappy with how WSC represented them on the question of alternative service. The CHPC and the WSC had determined that it was necessary for Mennonites to offer to do alternative service to the federal government, even before the government requested this of them. But the Manitoba *Kanadier* felt that *offering* to perform alternative service was unnecessary and inappropriate; the government had, after all, honored their convictions in World War I and would do so again, they felt. Because of this significant difference of approach on alternative service, the leaders of the *Kanadier* groups decided to establish their own *Aeltestenkomitee* to represent them in negotiations with government. They also subsequently formed their own relief committee and named it the Canadian Mennonite Relief Committee (CMRC).[6] Ironically, all three separate relief committees—NRRO, MCRC, and CMRC—contributed their money and material aid to MCC's war relief effort.

Virtually all of these organizations remained active in the postwar period and into the early 1950s. Relief needs in Europe and elsewhere, another wave of refugee immigration from Europe, followed by the Cold War and the threat of another round of military service, meant that that the relief committees, the immigration board, and the various military-service-related organizations remained active. But by the end of the 1950s, changing times prompted shifts in the inter-Mennonite organizational landscape.

Once the threat of military service passed, the Western Service Committee and *Aeltestenkomitee* eventually disbanded, though the Conference of Historic Peace Churches in Ontario continued with an expanded peace mandate. At the same time, Mennonite Disaster Service units emerged in response to the federal government's new Civil Defence program, which trained civilians for rapid response in the event of a nuclear attack.[7] Additionally, Canadian Mennonites, Brethren in Christ, and Quakers joined to form a new national peace organization in 1958 with the mandate of representing their diverse communions before the federal government on issues of peace, alternative service, and Civil Defence. The new Historic Peace Church Council of Canada (HPCCC) brought together Mennonites from Ontario and the west, those from Russian and Swiss descent, as well as both those who had supported and opposed the offer of alternative service twenty years earlier. Its formation represented the achievement of an ideal sought, but not attained, during World War II, namely, a body that could speak with authority for all Canadian Mennonites and Brethren in Christ before the federal government. As such, it was a major building block toward the formation of MCC Canada several years later.

On the relief front, the Canadian Mennonite Board of Colonization and the Mennonite Central Relief Committee amalgamated into one body called the Canadian Mennonite Relief and Immigration Council (CMRIC); their respective provincial chapters joined together as well.[8] CMRIC made some overtures to CMRC (the relief committee of the *Kanadier* Manitoba-based conferences) to set aside the divisions of the past and join forces, but a full reconciliation would not happen until the formation of MCC Canada. In Ontario, the NRRO continued as the relief arm of the CHPC.

CANADIAN ORGANIZATIONS AND MCC

By the late 1950s, a movement to create a Canadian organization similar to MCC had emerged, and within five short years all the existing inter-Mennonite bodies would be dismantled to create this new body. Before describing the developments of those years, however, it is necessary to describe the relationship of the varied Canadian organizations to MCC.

As indicated previously, Canadian Mennonites had supported MCC with financial contributions in the 1920s, but it was the onset of World War II that strengthened and solidified this relationship. The November 1939 Canadian visit of MCC leader Orie O. Miller, at the invitation of Ontario Mennonites, was a key factor in establishing this cooperative foundation. Miller had just returned from Europe and reported on the growing needs there. He invited the Ontario Mennonites to identify a Canadian Mennonite who could serve as MCC's "commissioner" in England.[9] He also encouraged the western Mennonite leaders present, David Toews and B. B. Janz (chairperson and vice-chairperson of the Board, respectively), to establish a committee in the west similar to the NRRO to solicit support for MCC's war relief. Toews and Janz spearheaded the formation of the Mennonite Central Relief Committee (MCRC) in early 1940.[10] The

MCRC, as well as the CMRC (the relief committee of the *Kanadier* Mennonites of Manitoba), contributed to MCC during the war. The relief effort of Canadian Mennonites consisted of the collection of cash donations but also the preparation and shipment of large quantities of material aid. Significantly, women were at the helm of the material aid operation. Indeed, while the men were busy dealing with issues related to military service and conscientious objection, women took up the call to relieve the suffering of war by raising money, canning and drying food, and sewing clothing, layettes, and bandages.

As historian Lucille Marr has noted, through this relief effort Canadian Mennonite women gave witness to their own commitment to peace and loving nonresistance.[11] Congregationally based sewing circles provided the context in which the women's work took place; during the war these circles came together to form denominationally based women's organizations. In Ontario Mennonite women from several conferences formed a larger coordinative body called the Non-Resistant Relief Sewing Committee (Sewing Circle Committee). The contributions of the Sewing Circle Committee, as well as that of western women, were shipped directly from Ontario to support MCC's relief program in England. Between 1941 and 1944, Canadian Mennonite women contributed $71,000 worth of clothing toward this effort.[12]

MCC greatly appreciated the support of the Canadian Mennonite organizations and during the course of the war took a number of steps to draw them into a closer orbit. In 1943 the MCC Executive Committee traveled to Winnipeg to meet with representatives of the NRRO, CHPC, MCRC, and CMRC to inform them of plans for post-war reconstruction and to invite the nomination of another Canadian commissioner who, together with an American, would advise MCC on European relief needs.[13]

Later that year, Orie Miller broached the subject of establishing an MCC office in Canada, and in January 1944 this office opened in Kitchener, Ontario. This office served multiple functions: to coordinate the clothing collection program in Canada; to provide bilingual information to churches (many of the Russian-Mennonite churches in Canada still functioned primarily in German); to represent Mennonite relief interests to the federal government; and to select the growing number of Canadian MCC relief workers bound for Europe.[14] C. J. Rempel, a member of the Mennonite Brethren conference, was the first manager of this MCC office. In 1948 MCC established a smaller branch office in Winnipeg with a focus on the emerging Voluntary Service program; its functions later moved to the Kitchener office in 1952.[15]

In 1944 MCC invited each of the various Canadian organizations to appoint a representative to serve on the MCC board. Nominated individuals included C. F. Klassen for the MCRC, Julius G. Toews for the CMRC, Oscar Burkholder of the NRRO, and J. B. Martin for the CHPC. A few years later J. J. Thiessen joined as a representative of the Board of Colonization (he had replaced David Toews as chairperson).[16] With significant Canadian representation on its board, MCC increasingly began to identify itself as an international, and not only American, organization.[17] For at least some Canadians, however, it would take more than these measures to demonstrate that MCC was truly "international."

The relationship of Canadian Mennonites and MCC deepened as a result of these measures, though there were some bumps along the way, and the intimacy of the relationship varied somewhat from place to place. The closest and warmest connection was undoubtedly with the Ontario groups, namely, the NRRO, the Sewing Circle Committee, and their Ontario constituents. Initially, Oscar Burkholder, chairperson of the NRRO, stood somewhat aloof upon the opening of the MCC office in Kitchener; evidently, the matter had not been adequately processed with him.[18] But he quickly became an enthusiastic supporter. Eventually, Orie Miller's successor, William Snyder, identified the NRRO community as one of the most active and dependable of MCC's constituent bodies.[19]

The women of the Sewing Circle Committee were eager supporters of the new MCC office from the start. MCC manager Rempel strategically invited Clara Snider, president of the Sewing Circle Committee, to supervise the new MCC Food and Clothing Depot. The new depot quickly became a place for women to "can dried peas and beans, jam, jellies, apple butter, strained fruits and vegetables for infants, pork and beans, and fruits and vegetables grown in their gardens" and to store clothing in preparation for shipment.[20]

The Sewing Circle Committee maintained its separate "Cutting Room"—where a staff person cut fabric for women to sew at home—but when the Cutting Room moved next to the MCC depot, the relationship between MCC and the Sewing Circle operations grew even closer. Later on, Alice Snyder supervised both the MCC depot and the Cutting Room. At one point, C. J. Rempel reported to Orie Miller that most people in the area believed that the Cutting Room was in fact an MCC cutting room.[21] Eventually the Sewing Circle Committee provided a loan to MCC for the construction of a new office building.[22]

The Conference of Historic Peace Churches (CHPC), also represented on the MCC board, was also supportive of the MCC office,
though it related more closely to the newly formed MCC Peace Section (based in Akron) than it did to the relief program of MCC. Beginning in 1946, CHPC began to appoint a representative to the Peace
Section and to make regular contributions. The fact that C. J. Rempel,
manager of the MCC office, also served as the secretary of the CHPC,
strengthened the relationship between MCC and CHPC. Subsequent
managers would continue the strong connections between MCC and
CHPC.

The Canadian Mennonite Relief Committee (CMRC) of the Manitoba *Kanadier* churches also developed a warm relationship with
MCC. It contributed significantly both to MCC's relief program and
the Peace Section. In the 1950s the CMRC sponsored the first Canadian participant under MCC's new PAX program. When C. J. Rempel
resigned from his position as Kitchener office manager in 1951, he
was succeeded by Julius G. Toews of Steinbach, Manitoba, former
secretary of the CMRC. Eventually, Toews's son Harvey (who angli-
cized the spelling of his surname to Taves) succeeded his father in the
role. This personal connection between Kitchener and Steinbach
helped to cement the positive relationship between MCC and
CMRC.[23]

Where tensions existed between MCC and the Canadian organizations, they emerged within the Mennonite Central Relief Committee (MCRC) and the Canadian Mennonite Board of Colonization
(Board). The Board, it will be remembered, was founded in the 1920s
to help the immigration of Russian Mennonites to Canada, while the
MCRC was established in 1940 to help the raising of funds and gathering of material aid for relief. Although both organizations had
begun with broad denominational representation, by the late 1940s
they were essentially owned by two conferences, the Conference of
Mennonites in Canada and the Mennonite Brethren Conference.
Moreover, they represented almost exclusively Mennonites who had
arrived in Canada in the 1920s (the *Russlaender*). Furthermore, despite representation among 1920s immigrants in southern Ontario,
the two organizations were perceived to be "western Canadian" and
distinct from the Ontario groups.

Several things about MCC troubled members of the MCRC and
Board. The chief irritant was MCC's approach to Paraguay. In the
wake of World War II, Canada acted slowly in accepting Russian
Mennonite refugees from Europe; consequently, MCC helped resettle
several thousand in eastern Paraguay. *Russlaender* Mennonites in

Canada were deeply grateful to MCC for the extent to which it assisted these co-religionists, many of whom were their relatives and friends and many of whom had experienced significant trauma in the Soviet Union.

But their appreciation soured quickly when MCC began to reduce its support, much too soon in their view. First of all, they were angered when they learned that the funds that they were raising and providing to MCC for transportation and resettlement costs of the "Paraguayans" were being treated by MCC as loans. In the minds of the donors, these funds were intended as gifts to brothers and sisters in need. C. J. Rempel in Kitchener quickly learned of the disaffection of western Mennonites. In 1948, just after MCC had sold rather than donated a large shipment of flour to the Paraguay settlers, he wrote to Orie Miller: "The feeling is quite strong in certain sections of Canada particularly in the West, that the M.C.C. has a heart and also goods for everyone else, but when it comes to giving something on a contributory basis to Paraguay, then there always seems to be a reason for charging them with the goods rather than making it an outright gift."[24]

When MCC began to actually reduce funds for Paraguay and initiate new aid projects in others countries, outspoken Board and MCRC leaders J. J. Thiessen and B. B. Janz were incensed. They wrote letters to MCC officials. They sent official resolutions from their organizations. They raised their concerns repeatedly at the MCC board table. Quoting Galatians 6:10, they insisted that the *Glaubensgenossen* (the household of faith) should have priority over new projects in parts of the world where no Mennonites existed. J. J. Thiessen wrote to his colleague, B. B. Janz, "We in western Canada will always stand up for our brethren [sic] in the South, even if this means being misunderstood in Akron."[25]

Orie Miller responded to the frank and direct concerns of Thiessen and Janz with tact and sensitivity. He pointed out that MCC's actions with respect to gifts and loans were in keeping with fundamental policies identified at the outset of the Paraguay resettlement; he apologized for not communicating those more clearly.[26] Evidently MCC had developed these policies with the intent of ensuring that the Paraguay settlers did not develop a long-term dependence, as an earlier group had.[27] From MCC's Kitchener office, C. J. Rempel wrote that it behooved MCC to serve those in deepest need, and not only or even primarily the *Glaubensgenossen*. Rempel insisted that serving the neediest, without regard to race or creed, demonstrated "true Christian giving." Such ministry was also the reason that the Canadian federal government held MCC's world-wide ministry in high regard.[28]

Things came to a head for the MCRC and Board in 1951, when MCC tabled a budget which, because of a financial crunch, allocated only $12,000 out of $180,000 of its Aid Section for Paraguay. At the next annual meeting of MCRC meeting, chairperson B. B. Janz suggested that MCRC begin its own relief program in Paraguay. He suggested that MCRC continue to support the Aid Section with about half of its receipts but send the remainder directly to Paraguay. MCRC had in fact sent some funds, equipment, and material aid directly to Paraguay in the past.[29] But the 1951 decision marked the beginning of the official policy of MCRC. This was the first time that one of the Canadian inter-Mennonite relief organizations ran its own independent international program. The issue of international programming would figure significantly in the formation of MCC Canada years later.

The Board and MCRC leaders were also unhappy with MCC's repeated attempts to establish another relief office in western Canada through the 1940s and 1950s. They tolerated the short-lived Winnipeg office, staffed by David Schroeder, which attended to voluntary service matters between 1948 and 1952, but they rebuffed repeated requests from Kitchener and Akron for the establishment of a western MCC office. They felt that another MCC relief office was redundant; didn't they already have a relief office in Saskatoon, the headquarters of the Board and the MCRC? They were also worried that MCC was beginning to interfere in matters that should be attended to by Canadians.

In 1949, both Thiessen and Janz were distressed that they were not consulted when MCC Aid director William Snyder and Kitchener MCC manager Rempel met with federal government officials to discuss immigration matters. They asked, shouldn't the Board, which had long attended to matters concerning Mennonite immigration to Canada, rightfully be the one to negotiate with the federal government? As Thiessen wrote to a friend,

> *Es ist empoerend, dass das MCC auch in Ottawa aufdraengt, wenn es sich um die Einwanderung nach Kanada handelt. Es ist uns nie engefallen nach Washington zu gehen, um die Einwanderung nach USA zu befuerworten.* [It is outrageous that MCC forces itself on Ottawa when it concerns the immigration to Canada. It would never occur to us to go to Washington to deal with immigration to the USA.][30]

Janz feared that the new MCC Peace Section would inevitably want to represent Mennonite interests in Canada as it did in the U.S. He stated,

> It would be the duty of the Peace Churches of Canada to present their case to the Government of Canada, not of the MCC. This was the way in the past and will be also for the future as the conditions in Canada differ widely from conditions in the USA. No foreigners should speak for Canadians.[31]

Thiessen's and Janz's concerns expressed emerging questions about the nature of the relationship between the Canadian organizations and MCC. Despite the continued desire to work with MCC, some Canadians wondered about the appropriateness of MCC staff in the U.S. organizing and directing MCC's work in Canada. They still saw MCC primarily as a U.S. organization. Even Harvey Taves, Voluntary Service Coordinator and later manager of the Kitchener office of MCC, struggled to clarify this ambiguous territory. Like C. J. Rempel before him, he "chafed under Akron's continued close scrutiny" of his work and questioned Akron's "lack of trust" in some of his new projects, particularly the Ailsa Craig Boys Farm, a rural treatment facility for troubled youth which he established in the mid-1950s.[32] In Taves' view, Canadians should be determining the program run out of the Kitchener office, not Americans in MCC's Akron office. While his Akron colleagues referred to the Kitchener office as MCC's "Canadian Branch," Taves preferred to call it the "Canadian Headquarters of MCC."[33] In 1955 MCC incorporated the Kitchener office under the name "MCC, Ontario," but the office continued to operate under the direction of MCC supervisors in Akron.

THE FORMATION OF MCC CANADA

Despite Canadian frustrations with what they increasingly identified as "Akron," some voices in western Canada began to call for an MCC-type organization for Canada. As early as 1951, A. A. Wiens, British Columbia representative on the MCRC, wrote to J. J. Thiessen to propose amalgamating all the relief organizations into something resembling MCC.[34] Nothing much resulted at that point. But in 1957 the *Canadian Mennonite*, an English-language inter-Mennonite newspaper based in Altona, Manitoba, took up the cause and began to editorialize on the need for a Canadian organization similar to MCC.[35]

It appears that the editorials encouraged Wiens to raise the issue once again. At a joint MCRC/Board meeting in early 1958 he again broached the subject, with more positive results. This set in motion the series of developments that merged the Board and MCRC into one organization, the Canadian Mennonite Relief and Immigration Council (CMRIC) in 1959. In reporting to the Conference of Mennonites in Canada and the Mennonite Brethren Conference, CMRIC chairperson J. J. Thiessen indicated this merger was a step toward the creation of a larger all-Canada relief organization that would eventually include the NRRO in Ontario and the CMRC in Manitoba.[36]

Merger proposals advanced a whole range of reasons in support of the amalgamation of the numerous Mennonite relief committees into a Canadian-style MCC. First, they noted the redundancy of diverse organizations doing similar things; this multiplicity created confusion and duplication. J. M. Klassen provides an example from his home town of Steinbach that exemplifies this confusion. Two women lived on the same street in Steinbach: Mrs. Klassen (his mother) and Mrs. Guenther. Mrs. Klassen, as a member of a Mennonite Brethren congregation (a *Russlaender* church), sewed her layette bundle and delivered it to the CMRIC depot in Winnipeg where it went on to British Columbia and finally to MCC. Mrs. Guenther, as a member of an Evangelical MB congregation (a *Kanadier* church), sewed her bundle and delivered it to the CMRC depot in Altona, where it went to Ontario and then on to MCC.[37] According to Klassen, this duplication of services confused supporters and made them reluctant to get involved. Streamlining and simplifying the organizational structures would contribute to greater efficiency and effectiveness in Canadian Mennonite relief efforts.[38]

A second reason favoring an amalgamation was a growing desire for inter-Mennonite cooperation and for structures that manifested such cooperation. Many Mennonites were still deeply embarrassed that they had not been able to present a "united front" to the government during World War II when they negotiated provisions for alternative service. When they eventually formed the Historic Peace Church Council of Canada in 1957, they finally achieved an organizational structure that could represent all Mennonites and Brethren in Christ on peace-related issues and could serve as their common point of contact with government. This was no small achievement given the diversity of the Mennonite constituency across the country. But now a growing chorus of voices argued for a similar unity in the area of relief work. Younger adults in particular did not care about the historic reasons for the division of relief efforts between *Russlaender* and *Kanadier* in Manitoba. It made little sense to them that Manitoba Mennonites should have two separate inter-Mennonite relief committees.[39] Aside from the issues of duplication and inefficiency of service, these individuals felt a divided relief effort offered a very poor Christian witness. They were eager to see greater cooperation among Mennonites and Brethren in Christ across the country, as well as unity in organizational structure.

A desire to better capture the support and imagination of a younger generation was a third reason certain voices called for an amalgamation of relief organizations. Even after the Board and MCRC merged into CMRIC in 1959, the leadership remained in the hands of the same elderly men (bishops and ministers) who had been at the helm in World War II. One Akron official is known to have referred to CMRIC as "a dead horse."[40] Younger people were not particularly inspired by an organization in which they had no place and which focused largely on past immigrations and Paraguay. Forming a Canadian-type MCC would be a way of capturing the imagination and loyalty of younger generations.

For at least a few people there was yet a fourth reason, articulated privately. Some feared that "Akron" would quickly assume control of various Canadian relief and other programs if Canadians themselves did not establish a central organization of their own. This concern appears to be related to MCC's persistent efforts through the 1950s to establish an office in western Canada. Within CMRIC circles, MCC's appeals appeared as a desire not to supplement but to supplant their own work. Very likely CMRIC worried that if MCC took over Canadian operations, the CMRIC's program of support for Mennonite colonies in Paraguay would quickly cease. If Canadians didn't act soon, A. A. Wiens wrote in a 1958 letter to J. J. Thiessen, *"Dann sehe ich 'die Roemer kommen u. uns land u. Leute nehmen'"* (then I see the Romans coming and taking our land and people).[41]

While Canadian Mennonites, at least in western Canada, had begun to consider the idea of a Canada-wide relief organization, a broader vision emerged on the pages of the *Canadian Mennonite* and elsewhere. Editor Frank Epp and others visualized an organization that would do all that MCC was capable of and more. It would coordinate program in the areas of relief, immigration, voluntary service, disaster service, peace education, contacts with government, and more. Epp felt that the merger of relief committees represented a step in the right direction, but he saw a new organization as having a much broader and more comprehensive mandate than simply relief. Essentially, he saw it as facilitating all those things which Mennonites wished to do together. He also saw it as a vehicle for a bolder and more unified witness to Canadian society. He suggested that the recently formed Historic Peace Church Council of Canada, as the most representative of all inter-Mennonite organizations, could as likely become the starting point for a Canadian MCC as the CMRIC.[42]

In articulating new directions for inter-Mennonite mission in Canada, the *Canadian Mennonite* expressed the views of a new generation of Mennonite leaders with a different perspective on "the world." Many young Canadian Mennonites, both men and women, had by the late 1950s participated in MCC voluntary service abroad and at home. Some had served in alternative service in mental institutions and hospitals during the war. Others had moved into cities and had encountered very real needs there. Indirectly, Canadians were also influenced by new theological winds, originating in the U.S., which called for a more active and engaged service and peace witness.[43]

Harvey Taves in Ontario was convinced that it was not enough for Mennonites to be conscientious objectors to war. Mennonite commitment to nonresistant love must be expressed in active service and witness in peace-time as well as war-time. Taves' passion drove his efforts to build the voluntary service program in Ontario and elsewhere.[44] Epp, Taves, and others of their generation no longer saw "the world" as an evil and threatening place from which to withdraw but "a wounded and suffering place in need of Christian love, care and service."[45] They believed that Canadian Mennonites and Brethren in Christ should be more boldly and intentionally addressing these needs.

For a variety of reasons, many Mennonites in Ontario did not share the emerging vision of a new Canada-wide organization, whether the more limited vision of a relief organization or the more expanded one of a "multi-purpose" organization. Lucille Marr attributes much of this resistance to Mennonites of Swiss-German descent, who had their roots and continued family and other connections in the U.S. Despite the presence of several Swiss-Mennonite congregations in western Canada, the Ontario Mennonites typically held a much stronger attachment to Pennsylvania, Ohio, and Indiana than to the Canadian prairies.[46] They lacked the sense of Canadian "nationalism" which appealed to westerners. Moreover, after having hosted an MCC office in their midst for fifteen years—an office and program which many considered "theirs"—they were not keen to shift loyalties to something new, particularly if it was based in the west.[47]

Harvey Taves, MCC manager in Waterloo, felt quite conflicted about it all. Although his roots were in Manitoba, he had married into the NRRO-CHPC community and, after many years, identified with it and its concerns. Moreover, despite his own irritations with "Akron," he felt a deep loyalty to the mission and vision of MCC and did not want a reorganization to be construed as *against* MCC.[48] Along with Epp and some other younger leaders, Taves shared the vision that Canadian Mennonites should be boldly engaging the broader society in new forms of service and peace witness, but unlike some others he did not feel a new Canada-wide structural arrangement was necessary.

In September 1959, the HPCCC called a special meeting in Winnipeg to deal with organizational issues related to the newly emerging Mennonite Disaster Service (MDS) programs in various provinces and to address the call, coming from a variety of quarters, to help the creation of an all-Canada organization. Representatives of the provincial MDS organizations, the four existing relief committees—Board, MCRC, CMRC, and NRRO (Board and MCRC had not yet formally merged into the CMRIC)—along with members of CHPC and HPCCC, attended the meeting. The assembled representatives passed a resolution recommending further study in relief and related programs "in the hope of establishing a more unified effort."

At least some representatives expected that the HPCCC would thereafter actively pursue the creation of the new Canadian MCC. But this did not happen, largely because the meeting roused all kinds of "political" sensitivities that needed to be assuaged. For example, older leaders such as J. J. Thiessen and B. B. Janz were upset that a fledgling organization like the HPCCC should be taking the initiative to effect a re-organization. Surely, they thought, the older respected organizations (Board and MCRC) should be charged with that task. Others at the meeting thought that the denominational conferences, rather than the HPCCC, should be taking the lead. Additionally, some representatives connected with CMRC and NRRO learned that the Board and MCRC were in the process of merging into CMRIC and that CMRC and NRRO would be invited to join. These delegates interpreted the HPCCC resolution as facilitating the CMRIC merger, and the prospect of CMRC and NRRO being swallowed up by an expanded CMRIC frightened them.[49]

Even within the HPCCC, members held differing views on the mandate of the organization and its role in helping to mid-wife a new Canada-wide inter-Mennonite body. Treasurer Elven Shantz, for example, felt that the HPCCC's role should be to work within its prescribed guidelines of coordinating inter-Mennonite peace activities.[50] Vice-chair David P. Neufeld, however, was eager for the HPCCC to branch out into new areas of peace witness such as activism regarding nuclear testing, alcoholism, and capital punishment, as well as to forge ahead with the formation of a Canadian MCC.[51]

Given the various sensitivities and lack of clarity around how to proceed, there were few new developments toward a Canadian MCC until around 1962. In that year the CMRIC decided to hire a fulltime executive director and to move its office from Saskatoon to Winnipeg. The CMRIC invited J. M. Klassen, a Steinbach, Manitoba, native who had served with MCC in South Korea and who was then working in the MCC Akron office, to the position. Before responding to the request, Klassen solicited the opinions of a variety of younger Canadian leaders, asking their opinion on the future of CMRIC and whether he should accept the invitation. Almost without exception the respondents indicated that the Canadian Mennonite organizations were poorly equipped to face the future; they insisted that CMRIC's future lay in helping to create a Canadian MCC.[52] Larry Kehler, another Manitoban serving in Akron at the time, pointed out that CMRIC's approach must not be to serve as the "mother organization" which others should join. Rather, CMRIC should take its place within the new organization.

With this kind of feedback, Klassen agreed to accept CMRIC's invitation, provided that he have the blessing of CMRIC: 1) to develop a closer relationship with MCC; 2) to shift CMRIC's overseas programming significantly to MCC (and away from independent operations in Paraguay); and 3) to promote a closer working relationship with CMRC and NRRO,

> with a view to working toward . . . an all-Canadian MCC which could carry on its own domestic program of immigration, perhaps mental hospitals and Mennonite church/government relations as concerns the matter of nonresistance and alternative service, and its foreign service in cooperation with and through the Mennonite Central Committee.[53]

Klassen took up his new post with CMRIC in Winnipeg in summer 1963.

Even before Klassen had begun his new assignment, however, there were additional developments favoring the creation of an MCC-style Canadian organization. In late November 1962 the HPCCC convened a regular meeting but with an added public event. David Schroeder, a professor at Canadian Mennonite Bible College, who staffed the MCC Winnipeg office during its four-year existence from 1948-52, gave an address on the topic, "The Historic Peace

Church Council Serves the Mennonite Constituency." His basic thesis was that the HPCCC, and indeed the entire plethora of inter-Mennonite organizations in Canada, were not adequately serving the needs of Canadian Mennonites and Brethren in Christ. All the organizations functioned within fairly narrowly defined areas of activity; moreover, in the area of relief, the organizations duplicated one another's efforts, resulting in inefficiency of service. Schroeder called for a new body that would bring together all the functions of relief, service, immigration, peace, and government contact, and that would have the mandate to pioneer in new fields.[54] Rather than calling for the expansion of the HPCCC, he advocated for the creation of a completely new body, with members nominated by the denominational conferences. In response to Schroeder's address,

> the HPCCC gathering passed a resolution requesting a representative meeting of all existing inter-Mennonite relief and service organizations and of representatives of all Mennonite and Brethren in Christ conferences or churches in Canada for the purpose of studying and exploring the establishment of an inter-Mennonite organization that would include and coordinate the work of all existing inter-Mennonite organizations and related functions.[55]

The November meeting and its outcome signaled new energy and momentum toward the organization of a Canadian MCC-type organization. The follow-up meeting took place, once again in Winnipeg in late April 1963. Twelve different Mennonite and Brethren in Christ groups—the denominational conferences and the existing inter-Mennonite organizations—sent representatives to the gathering. The major topic of discussion was no longer *whether* to create a new organization, but *how*, even though serious concerns remained. The NRRO delegates in particular voiced their deep desire that the new organization work through MCC in its international ministry, that it strengthen the fellowship with U.S. counterparts, and that activity at the provincial level continue.

At the close of the two-day meeting, a resolutions committee brought forward recommendations that would eventually define the new organization. To be called "Canadian Mennonite Council," the organization would be "the administrative agency for peace education, relief, voluntary service, government contact, immigration and any other matter that would normally be the responsibility of a national body for the Mennonite Brotherhood [sic] of Canada."[56] The Council would have strong and autonomous provincial counterparts, would pursue a vital relationship with MCC, and would carry out its international ministry through MCC. Delegates at the meeting accepted the recommendations by a vote of forty-four to eight.

In the weeks after the meeting, a committee of six individuals— three from the west and three from Ontario—drafted a constitution and by-laws. In the summer months they presented their work to the denominational conferences for ratification. J. M. Klassen, now on the job as new director of CMRIC in Winnipeg, keenly observed the unfolding drama. At the Mennonite Brethren conference, he noted displeasure with the name, "Canadian Mennonite Council." Delegates said the name smacked too much of a mega-conference or the World Council of Churches.[57] In Ontario he became aware of continuing concerns. Indeed, he learned that some Ontario Mennonites interpreted the CMRIC's recent move to Winnipeg as pre-determining the location of the new organization's office. He was equally aware that the construction of a brand-new MCC office building in Kitchener alarmed some folks in the west.

In any case, delegates named by the denominational conferences, as well as one representative of each of the inter-Mennonite organizations, gathered December 12-14, 1963, in order formally to create the new Canadian Mennonite Council. The three most contentious issues at the meeting were: the name of the organization; the issue of international programming; and the location of the new organization's office. Sensitive negotiating behind the scenes helped to bring resolution to these issues:

First, following the suggestion of J. M. Klassen and Harvey Taves, the delegates approved naming the new organization Mennonite Central Committee (Canada) [later, Mennonite Central Committee Canada], rather than Canadian Mennonite Council.[58]

Second, although D. P. Neufeld (who would become the first chair) dreamed of an MCC Canada carrying out at least some independent international programming, the group passed a resolution stating that all overseas work would be done through MCC.

Third, despite a plea from Ontario that the new office be established in Kitchener, the meeting voted for Winnipeg as the site for the MCC Canada office with only one dissenter.

The delegates then elected a seven-member executive, mandating the executive to appoint staff and begin operations by June 1964. They also approved an initial budget of $13,750 and established the framework by which the various existing organizations would dissolve and transfer their functions and assets over to MCCC or the appropriate new provincial MCC.[59]

Thus MCC Canada was born in 1963. Its formation marked a historic moment in that it created a structure that could represent all the Canadian Mennonites and Brethren in Christ in issues collectively affecting them as Canadian citizens and could coordinate all those activities which they wished to do jointly. To be sure, the difficulties were far from over. It would be months, indeed years, before the reorganization was completed, even longer before loyalties were transferred from old structures to the new. In Ontario especially, "wounds healed slowly."[60] Nevertheless, the events of December 1963 were truly significant. The *Canadian Mennonite*, which had long advocated for a Canada-wide body, called the emergence of MCCC the finest Christmas present that could have been conceived.[61] In response to the strong reaction of one Ontario letter to the editor, the newspaper later nuanced its enthusiasm.

At one level, the story of the formation of MCC Canada is about the evolution and amalgamation of a range of Canadian inter-Mennonite organizations into something more befitting new times and new needs. At another level, it is the story of a growing vision for inter-Mennonite cooperation across Canada and for a bolder and more prophetic Mennonite ministry in Canada and beyond. It is also the story of a search for an authentic partnership between Canadian Mennonites and their U.S. counterparts.

CONCLUSIONS AND OBSERVATIONS

Some conclusions and observations are in order, particularly as we consider MCC Canada's formation in light of the New Wine/New Wineskins process that is reshaping the entire MCC system.

First, it is clear that many of the important and difficult questions around MCC Canada's beginnings are questions that have endured to the present. Many of these issues related to the relationship of Canadians to MCC or, to use the common shorthand, "Akron." As noted, Canadian Mennonites differed amongst themselves in how they understood this relationship. Ontario Mennonites felt that they "owned" MCC because of the office in Kitchener and because their own organizations and projects were so enmeshed with the operations of the MCC Kitchener office. The historic Swiss-Mennonite connections across the U.S.-Canada border also figured prominently. Western Mennonites—particularly the *Russlaender*—deeply cherished the relationship with MCC, but they saw MCC primarily as an American institution, notwithstanding their representation on its board. They eagerly sought a more equal partnership with Akron; they wanted Canadians, rather than Americans, making decisions about program in Canada. Furthermore, some also wanted MCC Canada to have the capacity for its own international programming. To use contemporary language, they desired a less "colonial" relationship with Akron. These issues have persisted since 1963 until the present.

Second, the formation of MCC Canada was possible because Canadian Mennonites were prepared to dismantle older expressions of inter-Mennonite mission and service to create something befitting a fresh vision of their common ministry. They were willing to let certain treasured institutions die to birth something new. This process was painful for many, particularly some of the Ontario folk, and involved considerable risk. While some of the western Canadian organizations had seen better days and did not have much to lose in a re-organization, this was not the case in Ontario, where in the early 1960s, inter-Mennonite cooperation in relief, service, and peace witness was growing and thriving. Lucille Marr observes that "Ontario Mennonites were forced to watch their carefully nurtured inter-Mennonite relations and cherished structure become embodied in something new."[62] With the formation of MCC Canada, the Ontario Mennonites gave up their beloved CHPC, NRRO, and unique relationship with Akron, and they also saw their work relegated to provincial status, as that work became subsumed in the new MCC Ontario. But the westerners were also prepared to compromise to gain the support of Ontario, giving up the administration of their program in Paraguay, consenting to do all international work through MCC, and agreeing to the name Mennonite Central Committee Canada. In the end all parties made compromises for the greater good of a unified Canadian relief, service, and peace witness.

Finally, the formation of MCC Canada—the vision for it and the process of getting there—was largely the work of a group of younger male leaders who emerged in the late 1950s. Somewhat impatient with the older guard who had led inter-Mennonite efforts for relief, immigration, and alternative service during the 1930s and 1940s, these young men were educated, assertive, and eager to see a new organization move in new directions. But like the previous generation, these men used their influence and their connections with one another to effect change.[63]

Moreover, despite their desire for equality and mutuality with their U.S. counterparts, they did not consider the issue of equality and mutuality with the women working alongside them. Sadly, women were not invited into the process of deciding whether a Canadian MCC was a good idea, even though they were integrally involved at the grassroots level in fund-raising, material aid, and voluntary service. It is especially unfortunate that the Ontario Sewing Circle Committee executive was not party to the process of discernment and re-organization, given how directly the Sewing Circle was linked to the success of the MCC program in Ontario.[64] But the times were such that women's voices in these matters were not heard, let alone sought. It would be some years before women would take their place with men at the board table and at the senior staff level. Moreover, MCC Canada has in many ways only begun to identify impediments to the participation of Mennonites and Brethren in Christ who are not of European descent. A lesson to be drawn from 1963 is the need for continual self-reflection as to who is welcome in the circle that defines MCC.

In 2001 J. M. Klassen, MCC Canada's first executive director, reflected on the formation of MCC Canada in 1963. He used the image of new wine and new wineskins to express how a new vision for Canadian inter-Mennonite mission required new structures. In his words, "The world has changed, and the demise of CMRIC, CMRC, NRRO, CHPC, and HPCCC was the end of an era. New wine had to be put into new wineskins; old wineskins could not contain the new wine."[65]

As of this writing, the entire MCC system is entering a process of transformation as a result of the official New Wine/New Wineksins process. There is anxiety and uncertainty about the shifts taking place. There is grieving over what will be some inevitable losses. In this current context of transition, I believe the story of MCC Canada's formation can offer hope and encouragement, for it witnesses to several profound biblical truths. First, it demonstrates that there are important moments when new visions demand new vessels and new wine new wineskins (Matt. 9:17). Second, it reveals the wisdom that oftentimes something needs to die in order for new life to take root, grow, and flourish (John 12:24). Finally, it lifts up the prophetic challenge to God's people to enlarge their tent and to lengthen its cords and stakes, to embrace a wider peoplehood (Isa. 54:2). These truths offer reason for hope.

NOTES

1. For reasons of simplification, I will not refer to Brethren in Christ specifically each time I refer to membership in MCC Canada. The Brethren in Christ

churches have been active participants in MCC Canada since its founding. Prior to that they were also actively involved in the Non-Resistant Relief Organization and the Conference of Historic Peace Churches in Ontario.

2. The initial name was actually Mennonite Central Committee (Canada). The parentheses around the word Canada were removed in 1982.

3. The research for my thesis provides much of the material for this essay. Esther Epp, "The Origins of Mennonite Central Committee (Canada)" (unpublished M.A. thesis, University of Manitoba, 1980).

4. For a different perspective, see Lucille Marr, *The Transforming Power of a Century: Mennonite Central Committee and its Evolution in Ontario* (Kitchener, Ont.: Pandora Press, 2003).

5. Esther Epp, 24-25.

6. It is ironic that the CMRC chose this name, given that it was essentially Manitoba-based.

7. Mennonites were apprehensive about Civil Defence because they perceived it as having a close link to the Department of Defence. In 1959 a major portion of Civil Defence jurisdiction was transferred to the Federal Department of Defence. Esther Epp, 90.

8. The two organizations had shared the same leadership for many years, the leaders were elderly, and younger people lacked interest in their work. Additionally, the federal government had taken over the role of immigration and so the CMBC had very little work to do in this area, other than maintain older records.

9. John Coffman was this "commissioner."

10. Esther Epp, 60.

11. Marr, 99-100.

12. Marlene Epp, "Mennonite Women in Canadian History: Birth, Food and War," John and Margaret Friesen Lectures in Anabaptist-Mennonite Studies, Canadian Mennonite University, November 2009.

13. "Report of Joint Meeting of Executive of Mennonite Central Committee and Delegates of Organizations of Peace and Relief Organizations," NRRO, XV-11.2.2, File: 1917-48, Mennonite Archives of Ontario (hereafter MAO).

14. "Report of my Trip to Ottawa on the 7th of November," NRRO, XV-11.2.2, File 1917-48, MAO.

15. "Report of MCC Canada Branch Office Investigation to the MCC Executive Committee, Atlantic Hotel, Chicago, Illinois, May3, 1952," MCC, IX-5-1, Box 3, File: March-June 1952, Archives of the Mennonite Church (hereafter AMC).

16. There is actually some discrepancy as to whether Thiessen joined the MCC board as a representative of Mennonite Central Relief Committee in 1946 or the Canadian Mennonite Board of Colonization in 1948. See Esther Epp, 147, fn 14.

17. Esther Epp, 129.

18. C. J. Rempel, interview with the author, Kitchener, Ontario, 24 May 1979.

19. William Snyder to Wilfred Ulrich, 20 February 1963, HPCCC, XV-12.1, File: 1962 and 1963, MAO.

20. Marr, 82.

21. Marr, 88.

22. Marlene Epp, *Mennonite Women in Canada: A History* (Winnipeg: University of Manitoba Press, 2008), 166.

23. Esther Epp, 132.

24. C. J. Rempel to Orie O. Miller and J. N. Byler, 9 December 1947, MCC, IX-6-3, Correspondence 1948, File: 35: MCC Canadian Headquarters Dec.-Jan., AMC.

25. Quoted in Frank H. Epp, *Mennonite Exodus: The Rescue and Resettlement of the Russian Mennonites Since the Communist Revolution* (Altona, MB: D.W. Friesen & Sons, 1962), 428.

26. Orie O. Miller to B. B. Janz, 14 December 1948, CMBC, Vol. 1307, File 851, Mennonite Heritage Centre Archives (hereafter MHCA).

27. B. B. Janz alludes to MCC's concern about dependency in "Bericht des Zentralen Mennonitischen Hilfskomittee von West Canada fuer das Jahr 1950, vorgetragen auf der Sitzung in Saskatoon, Sask., am 2. Maerz 1951, CMBC, Vol. 1392, File 1545, MHCA.

28. C. J. Rempel to Orie O. Miller, 31 May 1948, MCC, IX 6 3, Corr 1948, File 35: MCC Can. Headquarters April to May, AMC. In this letter Rempel was advising Miller how to deal with the *Glaubensgenossen* question with the westerners.

29. B. B. Janz to Orie O. Miller, 27 March 1951, "Bericht des Zentralen Mennonitischen Hilfskomittee fuer West Kanada an die Jaehrliche Hilfsversammlung von West Kanada fuer das Jahr 1950 abzuhalten in Saskatoon am 2. Maerz 1951," CMBC, XXII-A-1, Vol. 1307, File 851, Mennonite Heritage Centre Archives (MHCA).

30. J. J. Thiessen to B. B. Janz, 10 September 1949, CMBC, XXII-A-1, Vol. 1307, File 851, MHCA.

31. B. B. Janz to J. J. Thiessen, 15 March 1955, CMBC, Vol. 1391, File 1543, MHCA.

32. Marr, 141.

33. Marr, 141.

34. A. A. Wiens to J. J. Thiessen, 30 January 1951, CMBC, XXII-A-1, Vol. 1395, File 209, MHCA

35. *Canadian Mennonite*, 15 November 1957, p. 2.

36. J. J. Thiessen to B. B. Janz, 5 June 1958, BB Janz Collection, Group II, File 22 (f), Centre for Mennonite Brethren Studies in Canada; "Reorganisierung unserer Hilfsorganisationinen," CMBC, XXII-A-1, Vol. 1395, File 1568, MHCA. .

37. J. M. Klassen, *Jacobs's Journey: From Zagradowka toward Zion: The Autobiography of J. M. Klassen* (Winnipeg, MB: self-published, 2001), 207.

38. T. E. Regehr, *Mennonites in Canada: A People Transformed* (Toronto: University of Toronto Press, 1996), 392.

39. Ted Friesen was the secretary of the Canadian Mennonite Relief Committee of the *Kanadier* churches. He shared the passion of his father, D. W. Friesen, for inter-Mennonite cooperation. He was eager that the CMRC and the Manitoba branch of the CMRIC overcome the divisions of the past. He promoted several joint meetings and wrote about them, "We found that most of the work that we did was the same. . . . We found much unity in our common aims and goals." See Ted Friesen, *Memoirs: A Personal Autobiography of*

Ted Friesen (Altona, MB: Friesens, 2003), 71.
40. Klassen, 207.
41. A. A. Wiens to B. B. Janz, 24 March 1958, BBJ, Group II, File 21 (e), Centre for Mennonite Brethren Studies in Canada (hereafter MBSC).
42. *Canadian Mennonite* (13 June 1958), 2.
43. See, for example, Leo Driedger and Donald B Kraybill, *Mennonite Peacemaking: From Quietism to Activitism* (Waterloo, ON and Scottdale, Pa.: Herald Press, 1994), especially chapter 4.
44. See Marr, 118.
45. T. E. Regehr, "The Influence of World War II on the Conference of Mennonites in Canada" (unpublished paper, CMC history conference, 1997).
46. Marr does not discuss how *Russlaender* Mennonites in Ontario, who supported both the NRRO *and* the CMRIC, felt about a possible re-organization; they would have had strong connections to their relatives and friends in western Canada.
47. Marr, 152ff.
48. Marr, 153-4.
49. See Esther Epp, 161-2.
50. Elven Shantz to J. B.Martin, 4 November 1961, HPCCC, XV-12.2, File 1959-63, MAO.
51. David P. Neufeld to J. B. Martin, David P. Neufeld Collection, XX-74, Vol. 1103, File 44: HPCCC, MHCA.
52. The replies to Klassen's letter are found in J. M. Klassen Collection, XX-34, Fol. 646, MHCA.
53. The entire list of 11 "caveats" under which J. M. Klassen accepted the position are listed in Klassen's autobiography, 202-3.
54. David Schroeder, "The Historic Peace Church Council of Canada Serves the Mennonite Constituency," HPCCC, SV-12.1, File: Stirling Avenue, MAO.
55. "Minutes of the Annual Meeting of the Historic Peace Church Council held at the Canadian Mennonite Bible College, Winnipeg, Manitoba, November 29th. to December 1st., 1962," CMBC, XXII-A-1, Vol. 1398, File 1588, MHCA.
56. The full resolutions committee report was published in *Canadian Mennonite*, 26 April 1962, 2.
57. Klassen, 209.
58. Klassen reports that the suggestion was another way to reinforce the idea that the new body would do all its international program through MCC. Evidently the group sent an overnight telegram to the MCC Executive Committee meeting in Chicago, asking permission to use the MCC name. When no response was forthcoming, Canadians interpreted this as approval. In reality, the telegram never reached the Executive Committee. Klassen, 210.
59. "Meeting, Portage Ave. MB Church, Winnipeg, Manitoba, December 12-14, 1963," CMBC, XXII-A-1, Vol. 1397, File 1577, MHCA.
60. Marr, 173.
61. *Canadian Mennonite* (17 December 1963), 6.
62. Marr, 179.
63. These group of men would include D. P. Neufeld, T. E. Friesen, David Schroeder, Henry Epp, Frank Epp, and several others. If space allowed, one

could track how this group of men worked behind the scene to advance the development of MCC Canada, but that goes beyond the scope of this essay.

64. Marr, 173-4.

65. Klassen, 212.

Chapter 3

Turning Points, Broken Ice, and *Glaubensgenossen*: What Happened at Prairie Street on July 27-28, 1920?

JAMES C. JUHNKE

With benefit of historical hindsight and interpretive audacity, we might propose today that the most momentous meeting in American Mennonite history took place at the Old Mennonite Church on Prairie Street in Elkhart, Indiana, on July 27-28, 1920. The meeting marked the birth moment of Mennonite Central Committee. At Prairie Street the two major ethnic-cultural streams of early twentieth-century Mennonitism—the Dutch-Prussian-Russians and the Old Mennonites of Swiss and South German background—agreed to cooperate in a common organization for mutual aid to suffering Mennonites in Russia.[1] MCC eventually became the largest Mennonite relief agency in the world and the major means for Russian Mennonites and Old Mennonites in the United States to overcome cultural barriers between their two groups from 1920 on. In 2010 the Old Mennonite version of MCC beginnings is ascendant in popular narrations of the story and on the official MCC website. On the other hand, some Russian Mennonite descendants say that the unified relief effort in 1920 was an initiative of the Russians, and that MCC was born in Hillsboro, Kansas.

In 1920 the social-cultural differences between American Mennonites based upon immigrant origins in Europe were greater than we can easily imagine ninety years later.[2] Harold S. Bender wrote in 1926 that "The Swiss-South German and the Dutch-North German-Russian types of Mennonites are two historical families of Mennonites who have had practically no historical affiliation with each other."[3] That was only a slight exaggeration. One event of crossing the ethnic-cultural boundary came in the 1870s and 1880s when some 15,000 to 18,000 Mennonites migrated from Eastern Europe to North America. The Old Mennonites provided significant aid to the Russian immigrants. Clarence Hiebert, descendant of those immigrants, celebrated that mutual aid in his centennial coffee table scrapbook, *Brothers in Need to Brothers Indeed*.[4]

However, in the decades following the immigration, these so-called "Brothers" found it impossible to share communion with each other, to accept each other's ordination, or to come together in a common denominational organization. Their religious-cultural differences were too great. So the Old Mennonites and the Dutch Russians went their separate ways. Harold Bender considered the failure of the two streams to come together in the late nineteenth century to be one of the greatest missed opportunities in American Mennonite history.[5]

We don't have photographs or other descriptions of the Prairie Street meeting to know what attendees were wearing, who sat with whom, who spoke the most, etc. But we can make some reasonable assumptions based on what we know about the participants and their times. The Russians and the Old Mennonites were separated by distinctive clothing. The Old Mennonites, perhaps with the exception of Slagel and Smucker, wore regulation plain coats as prescribed by Old Mennonite church discipline. None of the Russians even owned plain coats. They probably wore lapel coats or less formal wear. The two kinds of Mennonites probably sat together in their separate groups rather than intermixed.

The groups were also separated by language. Their formal deliberations probably were in English, though the Russians spoke with a stronger German accent. The mother tongue of the Russians—the language they had learned in house and barnyard—was the North German dialect known as Low German. For most (perhaps all) of the Old Mennonites, the mother tongue was Pennsylvania German. The Old Mennonites, having had more decades of acculturation to Amer-

ican ways and language, probably spoke English more fluently and
High German less fluently than the Russians. We can assume that one
key person present, A. A. Friesen, a visiting Russian delegate from
Halbstadt in the Molotschna Colony, could not speak English. When
Friesen reported about needs in Russia he must have spoken in High
German, both in the smaller committee meetings and in the larger
public meeting in the evening. Someone had to translate for Friesen,
both so he could understand what others said, and so non-German
speakers could understand him. During the meeting breaks the Russians, when they were speaking to each other, probably conversed in
Low German—especially if they did not want the Old Mennonites to
know what they were saying!

Who attended the Prairie Street meeting? The sources do not
agree completely. It may well be that some people attended unoffi-
cially and sat at the edges.[6]

Mennonites of Swiss and   **South German Background**
Dutch-Russian Backgrounds

Aaron Loucks, MRCWS[7] (pres.)   A. A. Friesen, *Studienkommission*
   Scottdale, Pa.   Halbstadt, Molotschna

Levi Mumaw, MRCWS (secy.)   P. C. Hiebert, ERCMNA[8] (chair)
   Scottdale, Pa.   Hillsboro, Kan.

G. L. Bender, MRCWS (treas.)   H. H. Regier, General Conference
   Elkhart, Ind.   Mountain Lake, Minn.

S. C. Yoder, Menn. Gen. Conf.   W. J. Ewert, General Conference
   (moderator)   Hillsboro, Kan.
   Iowa

D. H. Bender
   Hesston, Kan.

Vernon Smucker
   Scottdale, Pa.

Orie O. Miller
   Akron, Pa.

Arthur Slagel
   Flanagan, Ill.

Daniel D. Miller
   LaGrange Co., Ind.

Eli G. Reist
   Mt. Joy, Pa.

The Old Mennonites far outnumbered the Russians, a fact not surprising considering that the meeting was held on Old Mennonite territory. Moreover, the Russian Mennonites in January in Hillsboro, Kansas, had sufficiently overcome their internal differences to decide that they wanted a unified mutual aid effort. The question at Prairie Street was whether the Old Mennonites would agree to join. A substantial delegation of Old Mennonite leaders was helpful to make that decision. The minutes recorded four sessions, one of which was a public gathering addressed by the delegate from Russia, A. A. Friesen.

Two important people not present at the Prairie Street gathering are worth noting. One was Martin B. Fast from Reedley, California. Fast was a journalist/editor from the Krimmer Mennonite Brethren group. In 1919 he had made a remarkable five-month trip to Russia, by ship from Seattle to Vladivostok and by Trans-Siberian Railway to Omsk. Fast had delivered fifty-one chests of clothing and a significant amount of money to needy Mennonites east of the Ural Mountains. The Russians at the Prairie Street meeting, perhaps also some of the Old Mennonites, had surely read Fast's published 124-page account of his trip.[9] Like the other Russians, Fast urged that all Mennonites in North America cooperate in a common effort of mutual aid to suffering Mennonites in Russia.[10]

On the Old Mennonite side, the most prominent absent person was Daniel Kauffman, editor of the *Gospel Herald*, author and editor of the *Bible Doctrine* book that set forth the authoritative teachings that Old Mennonite leaders promoted among their people.[11] Kauffman was a strong conservative, with extensive power in the church. At one point he was a member of twenty-two church committees and boards.[12] In a front-page *Gospel Herald* editorial, just a week before the Elkhart meeting, Kauffman warned against unity that did not include "full obedience to all the commandments of Christ." "The essential element of Christian unity is a oneness in the faith and hope of the gospel," wrote Kauffman.

> This kind of unity will not admit of ignoring one jot or tittle of God's Word. It implies faith in our Lord Jesus Christ as the Son of God, faith in the entire Bible as the word of God, a faith which includes full obedience to all the commandments of Christ. It means a coming together in oneness on the solid Gospel platform and a prayerful effort to "teach all nations. . . . to observe all things whatsoever" Christ commanded us. . . . [Let us] earnestly oppose, as soul-destroying, any coming together on any other platform.[13]

For Kauffman and other conservative Old Mennonite leaders, the "all things" included wearing the regulation plain coat and obeying the other "ordinances and restrictions" as set forth in the *Bible Doctrine* book. In the context of the upcoming meeting at Prairie Street for a unified relief effort, Kaufman's editorial constituted a stark warning: Beware any ill-considered "coming together!" All the Old Mennonites at the July 27 meeting surely had read Kauffman's editorial and were looking over their shoulders toward Scottdale, whether or not Kauffman's name came up in the discussions. Had the dominant Old Mennonite patriarch necessarily ruled out "coming together" for relief work? Or had he left the door open?

In the evening session of July 27, and again in the morning of July 28, the men meeting in Elkhart considered "the advisability of calling a general conference of all the Mennonites in America."[14] That radical proposal, which probably came from the Russians and certainly would have been opposed by Daniel Kauffman, was set aside. Instead they created a provisional three-man committee (Hiebert, Regier, and Mumaw), chose the name "Mennonite Central Committee for Russian Relief" and planned to make the arrangement permanent some months later at a meeting in Chicago. The minutes of the first meeting also offered a provisional list of cooperating relief agencies (called "organizations on our list"), their representatives, and their official publications. That list would grow in subsequent months.

Agencies, Representatives, and Official Publications Cooperating in the Mennonite Central Committee For Russian Relief, July 1920

Mennonite Relief Comm. for War Sufferers	Levi Mumaw Scottdale, Pa.	*Gospel Herald* (Scottdale)
Emergency Relief Committee of the GC	John Lichti Deer Creek, Okla.	*Bundesbote* (Berne)
ERC of the Mennonites of North America	D. E. Harder, secy Hillsboro, Kan.	
Relief Comm. of the Central Conf. of Ill. Menn.	Val. Strubhar, secy Washington, Ill.	*Christian Evangel*
MB Church of North America	P. C. Hiebert, secy. Hillsboro, Kan.	*Zionsbote*
Krimmer Mennonite Brethren	D. M. Hofer Chicago	*Wahrheitsfreund*

The list of official periodicals confirms the language difference between the Russians and the Old Mennonites. All of the Russian group periodicals were in the German language. All of the Old Mennonite periodicals were in English. Missing from the list was *The Mennonite*, which was read by Eastern District Mennonites of the General Conference. Missing also were *Vorwärts* (Hillsboro) and *Der Herold* (Newton), Kansas Mennonite publications read widely among the Russians for news about the churches, the nation, and the world. The list of agencies was a mix of relief committees and denominational groups.

The differences among subgroups within both the Russians (MB, GC, KMB) and those of Swiss and South German background (Old, New, Old Order, Amish) were substantial. Moreover, the years following World War I were times of painful theological and organizational disputes. The Russians attending the Prairie Street meeting were keenly aware of differences, even hostilities, among the Mennonite Brethren, the Krimmer Mennonite Brethren, and the Church Mennonites (*Kirchliche*) going back to splits in Russia. The Old Mennonites were concerned, in addition to differences between more and less conservative districts and institutions, about an alarming generational dispute. Youthful volunteers working under American Friends Service Committee in France had held a "Youth Conference" that condemned the leaders of the Mennonite Relief Commission for War Sufferers and older church leaders generally as incompetent.

These angry and restless young people appointed three of their own number (J. R. Allgeyer, A. J. Miller, and A. E. Hiebert) to investigate the possibilities for relief work in Russia. Allgeyer and Miller both did visit Russia. Miller eventually spent more time in Russia than any other American Mennonite, working on agreements to begin the aid program and then to carry it out.[15] The Old Mennonites at Prairie Street needed to take action to stay a step ahead of the energetic youthful activists in Europe.

The urgency of the Russian Mennonite call for united relief work should be seen in the context of their decades-long heritage of providing mutual aid to their ethnic relatives in Russia after their settling on the North American western frontier. Initially they had sent help individually to family members in Russia who wanted to emigrate themselves or who had fallen on hard times. But soon there were opportunities for corporately organized mutual aid. In 1883-84 some Russian Mennonites who had sought refuge in Central Asia fell victim to poverty, thievery, and bad leadership on an inhospitable swamp-land frontier near Khiva. At first private individuals in

America sent money to their stranded relatives. Then leaders in Kansas and Nebraska organized separate committees in Kansas and Nebraska to meet the need. Eventually a "Board of Guardians," and an "Aid Committee for the Needy in Khiva," combined to form an "American Mennonite Aid Committee." This mutual aid project enabled twenty-three families (117 people) from the failed settlement of Lausan, on the Amu Darya river north of Khiva, to migrate to Nebraska and Kansas. Later aid from the "American Mennonite Aid Committee" helped some fifteen families (79 persons) from the Central Asian settlement in the Talas Valley near the city of Aulie Ata— some 800 miles east of Khiva—to emigrate to North America.[16]

In subsequent years, the editors of German-language Russian Mennonite newspapers publicized needs in Russia and organized mutual aid efforts. One such editor was Martin B. Fast, born in Tiegerweide in South Russia. Fast had emigrated to Nebraska in 1877 and became editor of the *Rundschau* from 1903 to 1910. Fast included a sketchy historical account of the Russian Mennonite tradition of mutual aid in his 1919 book about his trip to Siberia. Part of the title read *Geschichtlicher Bericht wie die Mennoniten Nordamerikas ihren armen Glaubensgenossen in Russland jetzt und früher geholfen haben (Historical Report how the Mennonites of North America have helped their Comrades in Faith in Russia Now and in the Past).*[17] Fast reported that in 1906 he sent his first gifts to his *Glaubensgenossen* (faith comrades or brothers in faith) in Russia in 1906. He visited Russia personally in 1908 and made arrangements with an elder Unruh of Muntau who helped him find trustworthy persons in the Terek, Orenburg, and Siberian settlements who could distribute the aid to truly needy people. Fast reported that from 1906 onward he had forwarded $110,000 USD to the poor and to mission stations.[18] It is likely that other Russian editors could tell stories of similar work, though that topic has not been researched.

With the coming of the Great European War in 1914, Russian Mennonite editors in America collected money for the German Red Cross and forwarded the funds to the German ambassador in Washington D.C. The editors of both *Der Herold* (Newton, Kan.) and *Vorwärts* (Hillsboro, Kan.) collected funds and published the names of contributors. The largest amounts came from church collections. By December 1914, *Vorwärts* announced that a total of more than a thousand dollars had been contributed.[19] Those gifts, of course, came to an end when the United States declared war on Germany in April 1917. During American involvement in the war, from April 1917 to November 1918, Russian Mennonites in America were preoccupied with anti-German pressures in local communities and with military conscription and the imprisonment of some Mennonite draftees. Mutual aid from America to Russia probably fell off during the war, although, again, that matter also needs historical investigation.

From the Russian-American point of view, the postwar effort to organize Mennonite mutual aid efforts to *Glaubensgenossen* in Russia was another stage in a decades-long tradition of mutual aid. On January 4, 1920, nearly seven months before the Prairie Street meeting, representatives of different Russian groups met in Hillsboro and formed a combined Emergency Relief Committee of the Mennonites of North America (ERCMNA), with Peter C. Hiebert (Mennonite Brethren, or MB) chair, D. J. Regier (General Conference, or GC) treasurer, D. E. Harder (Krimmer Mennonite Brethren, or KMB) recording secretary, and Martin B. Fast (KMB) general secretary. This new ERCMNA—a kind of preliminary MCC on the Dutch-Russian side— designated D. R. Hoeppner (MB) to be their representative in Europe, and determined to invite the Old Mennonites to join in a wider combined effort.

Russian Mennonites in America in 1920 had access to excellent reporting in their German-language Mennonite-published newspapers (*Vorwärts* and *Der Herold*) about national politics and international events. The most knowledgeable, well-written, and thorough political reporting and commentary came from the typewriter of Jacob G. Ewert in Hillsboro.[20] Ewert wrote an extensive weekly front page column for *Vorwärts* titled *"Gegenwärtige Aussichten"* ("Current View" or "Current Prospects"), sometimes taking up half of the front page, or fifty column inches. At the outset of 1920, Ewert wrote a personal note to his readers telling his desire to continue writing his column, "inwardly convinced of my responsibility before God," and "only out of love for our people . . . especially to serve the causes of peace and nonresistance as long as God gives me the strength to do so, and as long as I receive the necessary reports from Washington, New York, and Europe." "Necessary strength" was an issue, because Ewert had long been a bedfast paraplegic, a man whose intelligence and astonishing productivity made him into a kind of Mennonite Stephen Hawking. Ewert was an outspoken Socialist who interpreted events in Russia after the Communist revolution of November 1917 with a distinct socialist bias.

Ewert's vigorous writing increased *Vorwärts'* popularity and circulation. But he also received severe criticism. Before the 1920 presidential election, Ewert denounced the Republican presidential candidate, Warren G. Harding, as a dangerous militarist and capitalist. In the October 29, 1920, issue, the *Vorwärts* editor, J. D. Fast, came to Ewert's defense. An English translation:

> Many criticize that we accept J. G. Ewert's articles, and see a great danger that our readers will be poisoned. Others go so far as to say that *Vorwärts* is a Socialist paper, because we publish so much of Ewert's work. The fact is that Ewert is diligent, while others who could set forth other views are silent. They make themselves comfortable and don't know anything better to do than to criticize and scold.
>
> Furthermore, we don't believe our readers are so naïve that they swallow hot broth without thinking. One knows that Ewert is an outspoken Socialist in the fullest sense of the word, and describes absolutely from one side. He himself does not believe that Bolshevism is good. However, because it has a socialist tendency and characteristics, he tends to sympathize with Bolshevism as something to be preferred over capitalism.
>
> *Vorwärts* attempts to present all points of view. . . .

Columnist Ewert and editor Fast promptly printed all the news they received about the suffering of Mennonites in Russia and about the attempts of American Mennonite relief committees to organize a response. With his many correspondents and up-to-date knowledge of current world events, Ewert interpreted (and occasionally corrected) Mennonite letters and reports in the light of current world events as he learned from the newspapers that he received from New York, Washington D. C., London, and Berlin. In its January 30 and February 6 issues, *Vorwärts* published reports and letters from J. R. Allgeyer, who had visited Odessa and who had formed an unofficial committee together with A. J. Miller and A. E. Hiebert to find ways to get aid into Russia. Such reports proliferated throughout 1919 and 1920. Ewert's reports and commentary made *Vorwärts* into the premier Mennonite newspaper for understanding the wider context behind the organization of Mennonite Central Committee. Among its other services, *Vorwärts* served as distributor for Martin B. Fast's book about his trip to Siberia.

In July 1920, the arrival in Hillsboro of the four-man delegation (*Studienkommission*) from Russia was a great event. No building could accommodate the crowds, so tents were set up for meetings on Saturday and Sunday, July 17 and 18. Editor Ewert reported that the delegates had already visited Scottdale (Pa.), Bluffton (Oh.), Berne (Ind.), Chicago (Ill.), Beatrice (Neb.), Henderson (Neb.), Newton (Kan.), and Goessel (Kan.). The delegates visited in Ewert's home, as he was bedfast and could not attend the public meetings. Their primary appeal was for American help for Russian Mennonite emigration, rather than for material aid.[21] On July 27-28, at the same time that J. J. Friesen of the delegation was attending the meeting in Elkhart, Indiana, the other three delegates addressed meetings at Mennonite churches near Pretty Prairie, Kansas, and in Deer Creek, Oklahoma.

The kind of vigorous political engagement in *Vorwärts* represented one dimension of the Dutch-Russian ethnic subculture in America. To understand what happened at Prairie Street in September 1920 it is helpful to imagine that the Russian members at the meeting were at least occasional readers, if not subscribers, to *Vorwärts*. The Old Mennonites did not have a comparable newspaper. They did not receive their secular national and world news through a Mennonite ethnic German filter.

In late December 1917, with war raging in Europe, the Old Mennonites had organized a Mennonite Relief Commission for War Sufferers (MRCWS).[22] They did not begin their own relief work but in early 1918 moved to work with the American Friends Service Committee for reconstruction work in France and with the American Committee for Armenian and Syrian Relief (later "Near East Relief") with headquarters in Constantinople. By the end of 1919, the MRCWS had sent about sixty Mennonites, mostly from the Old Mennonite branch, especially from Ohio, to work under AFSC. But the MRCWS was apparently controversial and provisional. In August 1919 the executive committee resolved to disband as soon as their mission of postwar relief was fulfilled. They expected this could be done by spring 1920.[23]

The young volunteers in France were often impatient with the Old Mennonite leadership, including the MRCWS leadership which they viewed as incompetent, authoritarian, and lacking in progressive vision. At their "Young People's Conference" in Clermont, France, June 1919, these volunteers set forth an extensive vision for church reform and progressive action. Daniel Kauffman and other Old Mennonite conservatives were offended by the leaders of this brash and outspoken "conference movement." One of the "Young People's Conference" resolutions called for action to investigate possibilities for relief work in Russia.[24] Ohio Bishop Samuel E. Allgyer was present at the conference and gave his blessing to the creation of the committee of young volunteers to work on Russian relief. One member of the committee, A. E. Hiebert, was chosen to represent the Dutch-Russian Mennonites.

The first MRCWS workers to go out under Near East Relief sailed on January 25, 1919. One member of the group, Orie Miller of Akron, Pennsylvania, proved to be an exceptionally capable administrator. Miller became convinced that Mennonites should establish their own independent relief work agency, and that it should focus on material aid to the suffering Mennonites in the Ukraine. In spring 1920, Miller returned home by way of Western Europe. In Basel, on March 29, Miller met the four-man delegation from Russia (the *Studienkommission*), made up of A. A. Friesen, B. H. Unruh, K. H. Warkentin, and John Esau. From these men Miller heard of the awful conditions in Russia, the desire of the Mennonites in the Ukraine to emigrate, and their appeal for food and material aid. Eventually Miller formed a plan to return to Europe for another term and to open the way for aid to Mennonites in Russia. He hoped to do it under an independent agency representing both Old Mennonites and Russian Mennonites in America.

Thus at the September 27-28, 1920, meeting in Elkhart the time was ripe for cooperative action. On one side were the Russians with their decades-long heritage of mutual aid to their *Glaubensgenossen*, an urgent concern to aid their ethnic relatives, and the conviction that all Mennonites in North America should cooperate in this effort. They had had one successful relief expedition, by way of Vladivostok. But now that door was closed. On the other side were the Old Mennonites whose work in French Reconstruction and with Near East Relief had put them ahead of the Russians in program organization and in number of overseas volunteers. But the Old Mennonites were hampered by factionalism between youth and adults and by conservatives who resisted being unequally yoked with Christians who did not follow the Bible in "all things." Both the Russians and the Old Mennonites told their constituencies that the recommendation of the *Studienkommission* was a primary reason for the unprecedented cooperation.

The only surviving account we have that tells something of the dynamic of the meeting in Elkhart comes from Orie Miller, as told to his biographer, Paul Erb.[25]

> Orie listened as they talked. They were unable to structure anything. They had never worked together and did not know how to get started now.
>
> The group turned to Orie. "You have had experience," they cried.
>
> "But how can I do without a committee to send me? There are five committees represented here. It's hard enough to work under one, let alone five," he answered.

Feelings were getting tense. Aaron Loucks said he could do it if he wanted to. By noon Orie had one of his "bawling spells," as he calls them. That broke the ice, and they thought they might get together in one sending agency. Orie said if they would do that, and would find two others to go with him, he would go.

There are problems with Erb's Miller-centered account. There were, effectively, two committees present at Prairie Street (MRCWS and ERCMNA), not five. The Russians since January 1920 had had a common agency, but limited programming. The Old Mennonites were poised for expansion of their already impressive work in Western Europe and the Near East with non-Mennonite agencies. The desire for a unified Mennonite-directed relief effort was not Orie's vision alone. The Russians had come to Elkhart for just that purpose. If Orie's "bawling spell" served to change any minds, it was among the Old Mennonites present, not among the Russians. In the context of relationships between Russians and Old Mennonites, Paul Erb's story is a partisan account, told from a point of view that represents one group. Orie Miller was breaking Old Mennonite ice.

Historical accounts of the origin of MCC tend to tell the story from either the Russian or the Old Mennonite point of view. For the fiftieth anniversary celebration of MCC in 1970, Guy F. Hershberger wrote an excellent essay that included fresh evidence he had gathered from the archives of the American Friends Service Committee and the MRCWS archives in Goshen. Hershberger attempted to sketch the history of both the Russian and the Old Mennonite relief efforts in a balanced fashion. But all his quoted sources were in the English language. He mentioned Martin B. Fast's 1919 expedition to Russia. But he failed to make reference to Fast's book of 1919 and its story of aid sent from America to Russia "now and in the past." He did not consult *Vorwärts, Der Herold,* or other Russian Mennonite ethnic newspapers. In Hershberger's telling, the "turning point" of the story came when Orie Miller met the Russian delegation in Basel.[26] Hershberger included Paul Erb's account of the Prairie Street gathering in a footnote. While Hershberger's 1970 article is a competent and careful historical account, it is shaped from the viewpoint of his own Old Mennonites.

The earlier (1929) account by P. C. Hiebert in *Feeding the Hungry* told the story from the Russian point of view. Like Hershberger, Hiebert aimed for nonpartisan balance. Orie Miller was listed as co-editor of the book. A key turning point for Hiebert (although he did not use that phrase) was the trip of Martin B. Fast to Siberia and its consequences. In Hiebert's celebrative words, "The reports and the

agitation of Bro. Fast led to the first general organization of Mennonites for relief purposes under the name, Emergency Relief Committee
of the Mennonites of North America."[27]

Hiebert's Russian viewpoint is also suggested in the special attention he gave to the work of Jacob G. Ewert in enabling Mennonites
in America to send aid to specific relatives and friends in Russia
through the food and clothing remittance program of the American
Relief Administration. The ARA food draft applications required
knowledge of English as well as German, along with the names and
addresses of the intended recipients in Russia. This program, tailored
for Americans who had specific personal targets for their aid, was
more appropriate for the Dutch-Russians than for the Old Mennonites. Together with assistants, Ewert filled out thousands of these applications amounting to $98,000. In March 1923, when he had filled
out the last forms, Ewert wrote, "I have written the last food draft application. MY WORK IS DONE." This herculean relief effort by the
bedfast Ewert weakened him severely. He became sick with in-
fluenza and died within a week. As Hiebert wrote: "We literally have
an example of a life worn out in the service of others. May the man,
who under an almost impossible handicap rose to the heights of hero-
ism, rest in peace."[28]

Today's popular accounts of the beginning of MCC, oral and
written, tell the story from the Old Mennonite point of view, focusing
particularly on Orie Miller and Clayton Kratz, their entry into the
Ukraine, and Kratz's disappearance and death. Today the very brief
"History of MCC" on the MCC web site says the following:

> Mennonite Central Committee (MCC) was formed when repre-
> sentatives of various Mennonite conferences met July 27-28,
> 1920, in Elkhart, Ind., and pledged to aid hungry people, in-
> cluding Mennonites, in Russia and Ukraine.
>   The first three MCC workers, Orie O. Miller, Clayton Kratz
> and Arthur Slagel, delivered aid in Russia, Ukraine and Turkey.
> Kratz disappeared and was believed killed. Miller and Slagel re-
> turned. Since then, more than 13,000 people have served one-,
> two-, three- and five-year assignments with MCC.[29]

This account refers to a momentous and dramatic time. But it is
not accurate to say that Miller and Kratz delivered aid to the Ukraine
(which was a province in Russia, not a separate country). They made
a preliminary investigation, hoping to set up arrangements. But they
did not actually deliver food or material goods. The Red army overwhelmed the counter-revolutionary White forces and refused to

allow the Mennonites or any other relief agencies into the country. Despite strenuous Mennonite efforts to create an avenue for independent mutual aid, MCC finally had to work under the umbrella of the American Relief Administration directed by Herbert Hoover and an agreement signed August 20, 1921 after "tedious negotiations" with Soviet government representatives.[30] The new Soviet Communist government was exceedingly sensitive to outside interference, especially in view of the United States' and allies' weak military attempts (via Murmansk and Archangel) at the end of the war to overthrow the Communist government.

The ARA presented itself as a private philanthropy, but it received an appropriation from the U.S. Congress ($18 million), surplus goods from the War Department, and "the name, the prestige, and a substantial amount of the power of the government agency it superseded."[31] Hoover remains the unsung hero of the first chapter of Mennonite Central Committee history, perhaps unacknowledged because Mennonites did not want to highlight their alliance with the United States government. All Mennonite aid to Russia came through ARA channels, from the north by way of Petrograd, rather than from the south by way of Constantinople. Orie Miller had not opened the door to Russia.

The popular dominance of the Old Mennonite narrative of MCC origins (leaving out Martin B. Fast, J. G. Ewert, Herbert Hoover, and the ARA) revealed itself when prominent Mennonites of Dutch-Russian background, such as Peter J. Dyck, repeatedly told the MCC origin story with Orie Miller and Clayton Kratz at the center, implying that MCC was Miller's idea and that Miller and Kratz opened the door for relief work in Russia.[32]

Despite the prominence of this narrative, today in Russian-Mennonite Canada one would find more popular awareness of the immigration story of the 1920s than of the MCC relief story.[33] Furthermore, at the Russian grassroots in Kansas there are stories emphasizing that MCC aid entailed helping ethnic Dutch-Russian *Glaubensgenossen*. One article written in 1995 by Wesley J. Prieb for MCC's seventy-fifth anniversary was in this tradition. Prieb told how the project to send Fordson tractors to Chortitza and Molotschna was the idea of a Kansas Mennonite farmer, how J. G. Ewert publicized the idea, and how MCC chairman P. C. Hiebert, "living in Hillsboro," took it to the MCC executive committee for approval and implementation.[34]

A recent unpublished autobiographical manuscript in Kansas even claims that MCC was born in Hillsboro (the brackets and parenthesis below are in the original):

In 1920 the Mennonite Central Committee was organized [in Hillsboro] to focus on humanitarian outreach. My grandfather, John Epp, Sr., contributed the initial $500 through the local Kansas church [Emmaus Mennonite Church, Whitewater, KS] to finance a tractor-plow unit to help relatives suffering through a devastating drought in southern Russia (present day Ukraine) where my grandfather spent his adolescence.[35]

It has been the genius of MCC that Mennonite folk at the grass-roots identify so personally and so strongly with its history and its ministries. Shall we insist that one or another of the origin narratives is correct and that others are wrong? What are the limits of interpretive audacity? Perhaps it would be better to accept a pattern of polygenesis, to let a hundred flowers bloom, or at least to allow the Old Mennonites and the Russians, not to mention the wide variety of other ethnic groups who have become part of the MCC story since 1920, to have their say regarding MCC's history and future direction.

NOTES

1. For shorthand, this paper refers to these two groups with the labels they most often used for each other in 1920: "Old Mennonites" and "Russians." On occasion in the text it will be necessary to use a more complex designation to distinguish the Mennonite "Russians" who immigrated to America in the 1870's and 1880's from the Mennonite "Russians" who lived in Russia in 1920. The stream of Swiss and South German Mennonites in America included, in addition to the Old Mennonites, other groups known as Amish Mennonites, Old Order Amish, Old Order Mennonites, and New Mennonites. I have benefitted from comments by Robert S. Kreider, John A. Lapp, and Miriam Nofsinger on a first draft of this article.

2. James C. Juhnke, "Mennonite History and Self Understanding: North American Mennonitism as a Bipolar Mosaic," in *Mennonite Identity: Historical and Contemporary Perspectives*, ed. Calvin Wall Redekop and Samuel J. Steiner (Lanham, Md.: University Press of America, 1988), 83-99. The cultural differences between Russian Mennonites and Old Mennonites is an organizing theme in my book in the Mennonite Experience in America series, *Vision, Doctrine, War: Mennonite Identity and Organization in America 1890-1930* (Scottdale, Pa.: Herald Press, 1989).

3. Harold S. Bender, review of book by J. E. Hartzler, *Education Among the Mennonites of America*, in *The Goshen College Record—Review Supplement* (May-June, 1926), 35.

4. Clarence Hiebert, *Brothers in Need to Brothers Indeed* (Newton, Kan.: Faith and Life Press, 1974).

5. I heard Bender's judgment in his history lecture to MCC PAX workers in Frankfurt, Germany, July 1958.

6. This list depends upon Guy F. Hershberger, "Historical Background to the Foundation of the Mennonite Central Committee," *The Mennonite Quar-*

terly Review 44/3 (July 1970): 213-23. Hershberger's list does not include Eli G. Reist. Another list by Aaron Loucks in *Gospel Herald* (Aug. 5, 1920) includes Reist, but omits G. L. Bender. See also Robert S. Kreider and Rachel Waltner Goossen, *Hungry, Thirsty, a Stranger: The MCC Experience* (Scottdale, Pa.: Herald Press, 1988), 22-23.

7. MRCWS was Mennonite Relief Commission for War Sufferers.

8. Hiebert was Mennonite Brethren; ERCMNA was Emergency Relief Commission of Mennonites of North America.

9. M. B. Fast, *Geschichtlicher Bericht wie die Mennoniten Nordamericas ihren armen Glaubensgenossen in Russland jetzt und früher geholfen haben. Meine Reise nach Sibirien und zurück nebst Anhang wann und warum die Mennoniten nach Amerika kamen und die Gliederzahl der verschiedenen Gemeinden* (Reedley, Calif.: Published by the author, 1919.)

10. Peter C. Hiebert in *Feeding the Hungry, Russia Famine 1919-1925* (Scottdale, Pa.: Mennonite Central Committee, 1929), 35, reports that "The reports and agitation of Bro. Fast led to the first general organization of Mennonites for relief purposes under the name, Emergency Relief Committee of the Mennonites of North America."

11. Daniel Kauffman, ed. *Bible Doctrine* (Scottdale, Pa.: Mennonite Publishing House, 1914). This book was an expansion of Kauffman's earlier book, *Manual of Bible Doctrines* (Elkhart, Ind.: Mennonite Publishing Co., 1898).

12. "Kauffman, Daniel, *The Mennonite Encyclopedia*, vol. 3 (Scottdale, Pa.: Herald Press, 1957), 156-157.

13. Daniel Kauffman, "Unity," *Gospel Herald* (July 22, 1920): 337.

14. "Report of the Mennonite Relief Committees, Elkhart, Ind., July 27, 1920," *Gospel Herald* (August 19, 1920): 413-15.

15. See A.J. Miller's extensive account, "The Door Opens for Relief Work in Russia," in Hiebert, *Feeding the Hungry*, 116-203.

16. Fred Richard Belk, *The Great Trek of the Russian Mennonites to Central Asia 1880-1884* (Scottdale, Pa.: Herald Press, 1976), 176-189. Walter R. Ratliff, *Pilgrims on the Silk Road: A Muslim-Christian Encounter in Khiva* (Eugene, Ore.: Wipf & Stock, 2010), 171-175.

17. M. B. Fast, *Geschichtlicher Bericht*, 5-9.

18. Fast's mutual aid efforts were acknowledged in Russia by Peter M. Friesen, in his massive work, *Die Alt-Evangelische Mennonitische Brüderschaft in Russland (1789-1910) im Rahmen der mennonitischen Gesamtgeschichte* (Halbstadt, Taurien: Verlagsgesellschaft Reduga, 1911), part 2, 69. Friesen called it *"Eine Ehre für die Amerikaner—Gott lohne es ihnen!—und eine traurige Reminiscenz für uns."* ("An honor for the Americans—God grant it to them—and a sad memory for us!") Apparently Friesen was embarrassed that the Mennonites in Russia, in relatively prosperous times, had to depend on aid from the outside.

19. James C. Juhnke, *A People of Two Kingdoms: The Political Acculturation of the Kansas Mennonites* (Newton, Kan.: Faith and Life Press, 1975), 88.

20. James C. Juhnke, "J. G. Ewert, Mennonite Socialist," *Mennonite Life* (January 1968): 12-15.

21. Jacob Gerhard Ewert, "Die Delegaten von der Ukraine," *Vorwärts* (July 23, 1920): 1. The delegation had also visited Orie Miller at his home, with Noah Mack, an Old Mennonite conservative, in Akron, Pa., a detail that

Ewert left out. See Paul Erb, *Orie O. Miller: The Story of a Man and an Era*
(Scottdale, Pa.: Herald Press, 1969), 141.

22. Guy F. Hershberger, "Historical Background to the Formation of the
Mennonite Central Committee," *The Mennonite Quarterly Review* 44/3 (July
1970): 213-244. In addition to this excellent article, Hershberger worked on a
book manuscript, which he did not complete, tentatively titled "The Mennonite Church and Foreign Relief 1898: A Twentieth Century Expression of
the Anabaptist Theology of Discipleship," in Archives of the MC USA,
Goshen, Ind.. Hershberger considered Old Mennonite "foreign relief" to be a
twentieth-century phenomenon, with an initial project in 1898 to aid famine
victims in India. Old Mennonite aid to Russian immigrants in the 1870s was
for their settlement in North America and not, strictly speaking, "foreign relief."

23. Minutes of the executive committee of the Mennonite Relief Commission for War Sufferers, August 8, 1919, Archives of MCUSA, VII-2-2. Box 4,
minute book. Cited in James C. Juhnke, "Mennonite Benevolence and Revitalization in the Wake of World War I," *The Mennonite Quarterly Review* 60/1
(January 1986): 22.

24. Hershberger, "Historical Background," 231-35. Jacob C. Meyer, "The
Young People's Conference Held in Clermont, France, June 20-22, 1919,"
Mennonite Historical Bulletin (July 1968): 5-7.

25. Erb, *Orie O. Miller*, 143. Miller was still living when the biography was
published, so we can assume that this story corresponded substantially to his
own telling. Guy F. Hershberger includes Erb's account in his article, "Historical Background," as an extended footnote, 242-43.

26. Hershberger,"Historical Background," 240. "It was the hearing of this
story, Miller's reflections upon it, and the subsequent visit of the *Studienkommission* to America, which proved to be the turning point in American Mennonite efforts for the opening of relief and reconstruction work in Russia."

27. Peter C. Hiebert and Orie O. Miller, *Feeding the Hungry, Russia Famine
1919-1925, American Mennonite Relief Operations Under the Auspices of Mennonite Central Committee* (Scottdale, Pa.: Mennonite Central Committee, 1929),
35.

28. Hiebert, *Feeding the Hungry*, 291-92. Peggy Goertzen, director of the
Center for Mennonite Brethren Studies in Hillsboro, notes that *Vorwärts*
printed the names of contributors and the amounts they contributed for the
food draft program. This personalized the aid program and subtly promoted
competition among the donors. The personal (gifts for family relatives) and
competitive dimensions were not present for Old Mennonite donors to MCC.
Conversation with the author, Newton, Kan., March 19, 2010.

29. http://mcc.org/about/history, accessed March 3, 2010.

30. Herbert Hoover, *The Memoirs of Herbert Hoover: The Cabinet and the Pres-
idency, 1920-1933* (New York: The Macmillan Company, 1952), 23.

31. Benjamin M. Weissman, *Herbert Hoover and Famine Relief to Soviet Russia: 1921-1923* (Stanford, Calif.: Hoover Institution Press, 1974), 35. Weissman
wrote: "And to millions of Europeans, the ARA continued to symbolize
America—the generous, successful giant who dispensed food to entire populations at the stroke of Herbert Hoover's pen."

32. John Roth, in a telephone conversation, March 2, 2010, noted that Peter

Dyck and others of Dutch-Russian background told of MCC origins with Orie Miller at the center.

33. See Frank H. Epp, *Mennonite Exodus: The Rescue and Resettlement of the Russian Mennonites Since the Communist Revolution* (Altona, Manitoba: D. W. Friesen & Sons, 1962). Epp pointed out that the U.S. government in May 1921 passed an immigration quota system that "ruined Russian Mennonite prospects for a mass resettlement to the United States" (70). The new U.S. quota system was itself a momentous turning point in American Mennonite history. If most of the Mennonite immigrants from Russia in the 1920s had gone to the United States rather than to Canada, it would have transformed inter-Mennonite relationships in the United States.

34. Wesley J. Prieb, "The Man behind the Tractors," *Mennonite Weekly Review* (August 24, 1995): 6.

35. Melvin D. Epp, unpublished autobiographical manuscript. n.d. n.p.

Chapter 4

Synergies in Mission:The MWC/MCC Relationship

RONALD J. R. MATHIES

[A]s the coming years give us opportunity, help us to help one another in all the good ministries of the gospel, of compassion and aid. . . .
—Harold S. Bender, Closing Prayer, MWC Assembly, Kitchener, Ontario, 1962.

The Mennonite and Brethren in Christ story must be seen within the wider context. The present size, geographical dispersion, and multicultural complexion of the groups that comprise MWC are a direct result of the modern missionary movement.
—Wilbert Shenk, "Highlights in Mennonite History 1945-1990," *MWC Handbook*, ed. Diether Goetz Lichdi (Carol Stream, Ill., 1990), 127-37.

MCC has long been committed to strengthening the ties among worldwide Mennonite and BIC conferences and congregations. MCC program has been designed to nurture a strong sense of mutuality and interdependence between the North American churches and Mennonite and BIC sisters and brothers in other continents.
—John A. Lapp, MCC Executive Committee minutes, Dec. 9-10, 1994.

The MCC/MWC friendship—incarnated in sharing counsel, resources,
people, and structures, is, we believe, both service to and blessings for the
global family of faith.
—Bedru Hussein and Larry Miller, MCC Executive Committee
minutes, March 30, 1998.

A recent Mennonite World Conference (MWC) press release announced the good news that the Vietnam Mennonite Church
(VMC) had received full legal status.[1] This development allows the
church to own real estate, establish a Bible Institute for training leaders, develop relationships with other denominations, and serve as an
official partner with Mennonite Central Committee (MCC) in relief
and development work. The government deputy director of the National Religious Affairs Committee noted the long-term involvement
of Mennonites in Vietnam, beginning with MCC (1954) and Eastern
Mennonite Mission (1957). MWC sent a *Koinonia* Delegation to Vietnam representing five continents to celebrate the church's formal
recognition by the government; in his words to the VMC, MWC General Secretary Larry Miller, noting the gathered witnesses from
around the globe, stressed: "These are the most important gifts we
bring to you, ourselves as an incarnation of communion with you in
the global body of Jesus Christ."

Given the turbulent history of Vietnam and the long struggle of
the VMC to gain public status, the government's recognition of the
church represented a momentous occasion. Mennonite Central Committee (MCC) had played its own role in the "incarnational gift" of
sharing with the Vietnamese church. MCC's incarnational gift included providing personnel to Vietnam during the "American War"
(with several workers remaining in the country after the collapse of
South Vietnam), being the first North American non-governmental
organization (NGO) invited back into the country after the end of the
war, and placing a total of 150 service workers in the country between
1954 and 2008.[2]

The case of Vietnam is but one illustration of an ongoing synergy
in mission between MWC and MCC. Indeed, it is my thesis that the
two organizations are made of the same cloth—the fabric of Anabaptist peoplehood—and have had an increasing impact on each other
and the mission of the church over the past decades.

The prayer delivered by H. S. Bender at the closing of the Kitchener, Ontario, MWC Assembly in 1962 was described by Bender's biographer Al Keim as "almost certainly the best remembered Mennonite prayer ever uttered." That prayer begins to lay the foundation

for the notion of "mission" as used in this paper.[3] To borrow a phrase from the late South African missiologist David Bosch, I contend that mission is not ours, but God's—the *missio Dei*. Mission consists of alerting the world to God's reign. Mission is not what we do but what God is doing through us. Mission thus requires that we bear witness both for and against: for salvation, healing, liberation, reconciliation, and justice; against unbelief, exploitation, discrimination, and violence.[4] Whenever, wherever, however we are involved in such witness, we are involved in mission.

As I explore the missiological relationship of MWC and MCC, I assume expansive definitions of both organizations. MWC, for example, refers not only to the specifically organized efforts of the assemblies, governance bodies, and staff of MWC, but also to the denominations and their congregations that together form this global faith family. MCC, meanwhile, certainly consists of programs and personnel (both paid staff and volunteers) but also includes the governance bodies, denominations, and congregations of its supporting North American constituency. The MWC-MCC "relationship" being charted here (past, present, future) suggests a continuum across counsel, coordination, cooperation, collaboration, and, potentially, consolidation.

Both MWC and MCC have been around for almost one-fifth of Anabaptism's five century history. What follows is a brief and limited outline of the MWC-MCC relationship, gathered from the minutes and other documents of the two organizations, related literature, and twenty-one interviews with governance and staff personnel of the two organizations.[5] Over the ensuing pages, I will outline three key components of the MWC-MCC relationship: 1) "relationship builders," i.e. factors which have contributed to strengthened interconnection between MCC and MWC; 2) "relationship complexities, criticisms, constraints, and concerns"; and finally 3) potential future relationship considerations.

RELATIONSHIP BUILDERS

Converging Purposes
Multiple elements have contributed to a movement toward closer connection between MCC and MWC over the decades. For example, the defined purposes of each organization, as articulated in their statements of identity, vision, and mission, have played key roles in the relationship between them. For example, MWC's identity,

vision, and mission statements have placed a strong emphasis on inter-Mennonite solidarity. The first gathering of the MWC in 1925, the four-hundredth anniversary of Mennonite beginnings, was "mainly concerned with celebration of the Anabaptist heritage, the life of Menno Simons, and relief."[6] From this initial inclusion of "relief" in the MWC's mandate, MWC participants have pushed for the conference to be more than a gathering (or Assembly, in current terminology). The 1967 MWC constitution spelled out three purposes: fellowship (bringing people together), communication (burdenbearing with other faith communities), and facilitation (promoting vision, mutuality, and theological reflection) to develop "faith and hope, and to stimulate and aid the church in its ministry to the world."[7] In 1985 Paul Kraybill asked the rhetorical question of MWC members: "What holds us together?" His answer: "A strong tradition of caring, community and mutual help; themes of peace, reconciliation, love and discipleship in daily life; our witness, not so much the words we believe, but the life of peace we live."[8] The current "communion/community" vision adopted in 2006 includes fellowship, worship, service, and witness as intertwined dimensions of building a community of faith, nurturing solidarity, and relating to other Christian communities. MWC's increasing sense of identity and self-confidence have played a "significant role in the impact in mission of [the Anabaptist] faith community."[9]

The 1937 MCC Articles of Incorporation, meanwhile, articulated how MCC had already functioned over the previous seventeen years, namely, "as a charitable organization in the relief of human suffering and distress and in aiding, rehabilitating and reestablishing Mennonite *and other* [emphasis added] refugees, and generally to support, conduct, maintain and administer relief and kindred charitable projects."[10] The 1976 "Principles that Guide Our Mission," subsequently updated every several years, spelled out the importance of embodying the "values and insights of this faith community," being in "continual consultation with constituent bodies . . . and Mennonite World Conference," learning "from the people with whom we work," and giving "priority to programs with Mennonite and Brethren in Christ churches and missions."[11] The current two-year global consultation process (New Wine, New Wineskins) with MCC partners asked anew how MCC's mission should be shaped and how best to organize for this purpose. From its inception, then, a key component of MCC's mission has been inter-Mennonite collaboration and assistance.

Programmatic Intersections

Orie Miller enunciated the twin foci of MCC's mission: first, MCC promotes mutual sharing within the Christian community (household of faith, Galatians 6:10); and second, through such sharing "light, life, and healing can flow to all of needy mankind."[12] Early observers of MCC's efforts acknowledged that "in all areas where Mennonite churches were located, especially in Europe, the MCC work led to close and fruitful interaction between North American and local Mennonites."[13] Mennonite unity came to be realized experientially through such interaction.[14] After World War II, the presence of service workers in Europe

> did more than provide emergency food and rehabilitation. They became the sinews for reconnecting churches that had been in opposing countries during the war. Through these workers the slow rebuilding of trust and mutual regard so necessary for the establishment of MWC took place.[15]

On the occasion of MCC's fiftieth anniversary, scholars noted the support MCC had given to various Mennonite church efforts globally, including the establishment of theological schools in Uruguay, Switzerland, and Indonesia, a variety of publishing efforts, exchanges for young people, and renewed inter-Mennonite interaction on issues of peace.[16] Moreover, for several decades of its early history (from the 1920 until the 1950s) MCC focused significant program resources and efforts on assisting the immigration of Mennonite refugees from the Soviet Union and Europe to North and South America.[17]

MCC's response to those both inside and outside the household of faith has helped to redefine Mennonites as a people who cooperatively pursue social justice around the world.[18] Of 497 MCC project partners in 2000, 67 were Mennonite or Brethren in Christ (MBIC) organizations.[19] The 2004 statistics indicate that in about half of the countries in which MCC operated one could find MBIC congregations. While serving as president of MWC, Million Belete thanked MCC for helping the faith community get to know one another regionally and worldwide.[20] For its 2008-2009 programs MCC partnered in 99 projects with the Anabaptist family, with financial resources totaling US$4.4 million.[21]

The MWC assemblies have provided fertile ground for a relationship with MCC. MCC jointly sponsored the Danzig 1930 gathering, together with Dutch and German Mennonite organizations, a gathering focused exclusively on the theme of relief efforts, past and present.[22] MWC requested that MCC take the initiative and invite the MWC to meet in the USA in 1948 and to accept the responsibility to organize, implement, and collect funds for the assembly. MCC organized all aspects of the assembly program, sent out invitations to international guests (and then toured them through the constituency afterwards), and oversaw all logistical details in Goshen, Indiana, and North Newton, Kansas, the two assembly venues.[23] The assembly examined the plight of refugees after the war during the Goshen part of its meetings and attempted to reconcile the choices made by Mennonites in different countries in the course of its North Newton gathering.[24] This two stage assembly represented the "largest single undertaking of the MCC in international Mennonite relations."[25]

MCC played significant roles in later MWC assemblies. For example, during the 1997 assembly in Calcutta, MCC India (MCCI) seconded Margaret Devadason, its administrator, to MWC already part-time in 1994, and later full time, while remaining on the MCC payroll. Most (national and expatriate) staff of MCCI actively participated in the assembly planning, with managers being given permission to spend up to ten percent of their time on the assembly.[26] Indeed, one of the original reasons for the MWC assembly being held in Calcutta was the presence of the MCCI office, which would later be the venue for the early preparation for the assembly.[27] Most recently, MCC's decades-old role in bringing Mennonite refugees to Paraguay in the 1930s into the 1950s, as well as the agriculture and road-building programs that followed, helped set the stage for the 2009 assembly in Asuncion.

THE ROLE OF INDIVIDUALS
IN NURTURING THE MWC-MCC BOND

Given the broad definition of MWC and MCC offered above, it should be clear that the MWC-MCC relationship consists of the people who make up the community of faith who nurture the relationship. But this broad, all-encompassing category, today numbering in the millions, can be broken down into three progressively narrower groupings. The first sub-group consists of the hundreds of thousands of governance board members, paid staffers, service workers, and informal volunteers who have participated in and shaped the activities of the two organizations. The second grouping consists of key people who have given leadership in both of the organizations: in MCC's first six decades, H. S. Bender, C. J. Dyck, Ray Schlichting, and Robert Krieder actively served in MWC alongside MCC; over the past two decades, Larry Miller, Reg Toews, Nancy Heisey, Kathryn Good, John A. Lapp, Paul Quiring, Tim Lind, Doris Dube, Liesa Unger, Herman Bontrager, Naomi Unger, Judy Zimmerman Herr, Paulus Widjaja, Cynthia Peacock, Bert Lobe, and Ray and Margaret Brubacher undertook projects for both organizations as well. At his retirement from the MWC treasurer position, longtime MCC leader Reg Toews quipped, "MWC is the hospital rehabilitation of MCCers."[28]

But one person, more than any other, personifies the MWC-MCC relationship. While Christian Neff is often viewed as the father of MWC, MWC's current organizational shape has arguably "been shaped more by Harold S. Bender than by any other person."[29] Bender rallied the community of faith behind his "Anabaptist Vision" as the theological vision for Mennonite organization in the twentieth century. During his initial doctoral study in theology at the University of Heidelberg, Bender spent much of his time in service to Mennonite refugees from Russia temporarily sheltered in Germany and organized part of the migration to South America, personally designating Paraguay as the country of choice.[30]

MCC had sent Bender to the 1930 Danzig assembly as its representative; Bender brought back a report that gathered support in North America for the refugees. He subsequently becameaAssistant secretary of MCC ("assistant" because at that time the staff leadership position was called "executive secretary") in 1931 until his death in 1962. Similarly, Bender served as secretary and then as president of the MCC Peace Committee from 1939 to 1962 and as president of the MWC from 1952 to 1962. Between 1945 to 1961 he spent thirteen summers (of the seventeen) in Europe working on MCC and MWC agendas; in 1947-8 he spent a whole year in Europe, encouraging MCC personnel, trying to deepen the spiritual life of churches, and promoting nonresistance.

MCC Support for MWC Program

MCC has provided significant financial support to MWC's programs over the past decades, beyond the funding of the 1948 assembly noted above. Beginning in 1952 MCC has assisted with travel funds for representatives from the Global South (initially for Indonesia, then Africa and South America). On occasion MCC has extended loans to MWC. MCC supported the International Mennonite Peace Committee, which later became the Peace Council of MWC, with a regular grant from 1972 until 2007. In 1995, to mark its seventy-fifth anniversary, MCC presented a $600,000 "jubilee" gift to MWC with no strings attached so that MWC could establish a Church Sharing

Fund to support denominational and congregational programs around the world.

Between 2001 and 2008 MCC designated just over US$1 million to a wide variety of MWC programs and initiatives, including MWC's General Fund, Travel Fund, the YAMEN! youth exchange program, Global Missions Fellowship, Global History Project, International Planning Commission, Zimbabwe Koinonia delegation, Service Consultation, Congo Forum, and the Global Youth Summit.[31] In addition to the financial support, MCC and MWC have collaborated on joint program development, including the Jerusalem Seminar in 1999 in which Mennonite leaders from Africa visited Holy Land sites and MCC projects in Palestine, a Service Consultation in 2006, and an internship program for young Mennonite leaders at the MCC United Nations Office in New York.

While MWC has deeply appreciated MCC support, this assistance has not been without its critics, with some within MWC worrying that the amount of MCC's assistance threatens to overwhelm MWC and render it dependent on MCC support, some concerned that increased levels of support to MWC could move MCC away from broader ecumenical and interfaith partnerships, and some distressed that projects implemented by MWC are often administered outside of MCC's program planning system for international programs and are thus not held to the same standards of accountability and scrutiny as other projects.

STEPS TOWARD CLOSER COLLABORATION

The program support and interaction outlined above, indeed the entire MWC-MCC relationship journey, has occurred in a context of intentional steps taken by both organizations to foster the relationship. Already in 1963 at the MWC General Council A. J. Metzler suggested that MCC should be represented at such meetings.[32] In 1964, MWC General Secretary C. J. Dyck, noting that H. S. Bender was no longer there to represent both bodies, wondered whether there could be an exchange of minutes and attendance at each other's important meetings.[33] At the Presidium meetings of 1972 the question was raised whether MCC (and other organizations) should be a member of MWC to increase mutual exchange.

The period between 1978 and 1990, a time of governance and staff leadership changes within both MCC and MWC, proved pivotal for intensifying the intentionality of the relationship. These years also witnessed probing challenges presented from and to different parts of the global faith family. At the Wichita Assembly (1978) the major speakers from the Global South raised hard questions about poverty and injustice in their settings, stressing how North Americans were complicit with unjust economic and political structures.[34] Mennonite leaders from the Global South called on MCC not only to continue its programming responses to economic injustice but also to highlight global economic and political issues to its constituency through MCC's annual meeting.

One particular MWC event also pushed MCC in the direction of more activist peacebuilding initiatives. At the MWC Strasbourg assembly in 1984, Ronald Sider issued his ringing challenge for Mennonites to engage in direct nonviolent intervention in areas of conflict. The speech energized North American denominations, their mission agencies, and educational institutions, with MCC standing at the forefront of a consultative process which eventually led to the formation of Christian Peacemaker Teams.

In 1990 four Mennonite mission boards and MCC jointly published the Mennonite International Study Project Final Report. The report, penned by Nancy Heisey and Paul Longacre following a two-year project of interviewing church leaders around the world, called for increased cooperation among overseas mission programs, stressed the need for consultation by North American Mennonite agencies with non-North American churches both in the design and implementation of these mission programs, and urged MWC to cooperate in implementing this process. MWC, they said, "had made it possible for small and struggling churches around the world to realize that they belong to something bigger than themselves. It has promoted significant discussion on mutuality in mission and the nature of the peace witness."[35]

MCC Executive Secretary John A. Lapp took the report seriously, in keeping with his earlier call for more effectively receiving counsel from the global MWC community and developing "functional structures for international work that emphasize the holism of the gospel mandate."[36] What was called for was bringing "Diakonia and Koinonia" together and dealing with the "credibility gap between being North American and functioning internationally."

Two study papers from 1993 had significant impact on the direction MCC and MWC would go in relationship to one another. MWC president Mesach Krisetya's paper "From Dependence to Interdependence in the Global Church," presented that year at the MWC General Council meeting in Bulawayo, Zimbabwe, called for changes in the way mission agencies operate and urged MWC to become "a center for international mission, a mediator or even 'glue' for church to church or conference to conference relations, and at the same time being an initiator for international mission."[37] The MCC Africa department had earlier that year held a consultation in Nairobi, Kenya, to seek counsel from African colleagues. Their report concluded that the primary focus for programs should be

> breaking down stereotypes [to] help . . . level the inter-people playing field . . . the old "fixing/saving/meeting human need" paradigm would be subsumed and transformed under a larger paradigm of building global community and particularly global church community.[38]

A statement of "Mutual Expectations," the first documented MWC-MCC agreement, was formulated by then-MCCer (and later MWCer) Ray Brubacher in 1995 and received its final approval at the MWC General Council in Calcutta in 1997. In this one-page, open-ended document, MCC offered to share its global infrastructure of staff, facilities, relationships, and institutional memory, while MWC offered its global accountability structure to which MCC could bring major questions for counsel. While MWC approved the document, the comments and questions raised by the MWC Executive Committee were instructive: Could MCC mobilize its constituency in the direction of closer collaboration with MWC? Should MCC be more accountable to the global church in how it conducts its programs and spends its money? If MCC and MWC were to have differing priorities as to how resources should be used, as would sometimes inevitably be the case, how would such differences be resolved? Should MCC internationalize its board? Could MCC help MWC raise its profile among Mennonites in Canada and the United States?[39]

These questions raised by the MWC Executive Committee in 1997 reflected issues with which MCC has been grappling over the past few decades, issues which can be grouped under the broad rubric of "internationalization." Brubacher had prepared a seminal paper on that topic, in which he outlined MCC's struggle in dealing with this issue. In that paper Brubacher concluded,

> While the presence of international persons in our midst can be very valuable, the primary focus should not be to bring international people into our structures, but to make our structures more open to direction by local groupings in places where we work. Our task is to acknowledge our "North Americanness" and with integrity relate to overseas partners as brothers and sisters who are one with us in Christ.[40]

The Global Anabaptist Mission Consultation (GAMCO) convened in Guatemala in conjunction with the MWC General Council
meeting in 2000 sought to tackle the "internationalization" agenda
facing MCC (as well as North American mission boards). An introductory comment suggested that this meeting is as important as the
early days of the radical reformation." Its concluding statement called
for MWC to establish a

> permanent, facilitated global mission council to provide forums
> for missiological discernment and training, to help the exchange
> of resources for use in new and ongoing mission efforts . . . and
> for existing mission agencies . . . of all MWC member churches
> to commit a fair share of their budgets for the implementation of
> the MWC mission council. . . .[41]

At the end, some participants from the Global South expressed frustration that churches and church agencies in the Global North were
still trying to control the mission agenda and forward progress was
inhibited by finely nuanced questions of structure and procedure.

A formal review of the MWC-MCC relationship in 2000, mandated by both organizations, issued multiple recommendations for
deepening and broadening the relationship. The recommendations
included the following: that MWC initiate an International Planning
Commission, supported financially by MCC, to project a five to ten
year vision for MWC; that MCC and MWC prepare a renewed Memorandum of Understanding and Cooperation (MOUC); that joint
projects between the two organizations be expanded; that MCC advocate for MWC, including especially within its Mennonite constituency in Canada and the United States; that the two organizations
continue to exchange participant observers at each other's meetings;
and that, "when the time is right," MCC invite four MWC continental
representatives to become part of MCC governance structures.[42]

The two organizations approved a new MOUC in 2002. Even
with the approval of the new MOUC, however, MWC concluded that
it was not appropriate to appoint MWC members to the MCC governance bodies: "to appoint our constituents to MCC programs is
healthy. To have MCC empower our constituents to work within our
own program is healthier."[43]

In 2004 MCC and MWC established a joint "Forum for Counsel
and Accountability" which mandated an annual meeting of three
senior staff and governance representatives from each organization.
Two years later, MWC and MCC convened a joint "Service Consultation" in conjunction with MWC's General Council with the purpose

of exploring the biblical foundation for service, documenting what programmatic cooperation the two organizations had already undertaken, and formulating future steps of collaboration. The Service Consultation concluded by calling for: sharing gifts both within and outside of the family of faith; a holistic understanding of *diakonia*; an increase in MCC's relationships with Anabaptist churches globally; and steps for greater involvement by global Anabaptist partners in MCC's decision-making processes.[44]

These calls surfaced again in 2008 when the MWC Executive Committee hosted and participated in MCC's global summit in Manila for the MCC New Wine/New Wineskins appreciative inquiry process. Continued discernment about how MCC cooperates with MWC member churches and global Anabaptist service agencies has been a key element of the New Wine/New Wineskins process and figures to remain a high priority agenda item as MCC undergoes a process of structural transformation over the coming years.

RELATIONSHIP COMPLEXITIES, CRITICISM, CONSTRAINTS, AND CONCERNS

While the relationship builders outlined above have increased and intensified the relationship between the two organizations, this joint journey has been complex and constrained, with early and continued criticism and concerns about the relationship expressed at denominational, governance, and staff levels.

Denominational

From MCC's and MWC's earliest days some Mennonites have harbored suspicions of inter-Mennonite efforts. In some cases fears of "modernizing" dimensions of ecumenism fueled these suspicions. Other persons, meanwhile, questioned whether inter-Mennonite efforts were sufficiently "spiritual." At the 1948 MWC assembly, for example, MCC leaders Orie Miller and Harold Bender attended not as members of their denomination (the "Old" Mennonite Church, which had reservations about the type of ecumenical movement which MWC represented) but instead only as members of MCC.[45]

Today, meanwhile, some MWC governance people question whether MCC's constituents in Canada and the United States are prepared to take the relationship with MWC seriously. At the same time, however, various Mennonite denominations have voiced concerns about MCC potentially overstepping its mandate with respect to Mennonite denominations in Canada and the United States in furthering the MWC-MCC relationship. Accordingly, North American Mennonite leaders have expressed considerable caution about the potential blurring of the organizational identities of the two organizations: this concern was voiced at the 1964 MWC Executive Committee meeting as the worry that North American Mennonite churches would not approve of "mingling the spiritual dimensions of MWC and the material work of MCC."[46] Thus, for the past several decades, the default position has been to approve joint collaboration on particular projects but not structural mixing.[47]

Governance

Some MWC and MCC governance voices have also cautioned against blurring organizational identities. One executive member of MCC summarized this concern: "There needs to be a clear recognition that we are two different bodies that work with a different mandate. MCC's mandate comes from a North American constituency, most of which does not understand the relationship."[48] Some would say that putting international voices on the governance bodies would be inefficient, counterproductive, and representative of a problematic tokenism.[49]

MWC, for its part, has raised concerns about MCC's program priorities. Does MCC work enough with the church, in particular Mennonite churches? Why does MCC hire non-Christians?[50] Why is MCC helping Muslims, when "our countries are struggling with Islam?"[51] At the same time, however, some in MWC have questioned whether MWC member churches really want to become involved in the ownership of MCC.[52]

Program

Many MCC staff members have voiced concerns about a closer relationship with MWC. Would such a closer partnership restrict ecumenical and interfaith programming? Would programs become too narrowly focused or fall outside the areas of MCC priority? Might MCC overwhelm MWC and make it dependent upon MCC?[53] Is MWC too much invested in the outcome of the Wineskins process?

To be sure, working at program collaboratively or jointly is complex. During the 1980s, MCC and MWC struggled with the question of which agency should take the lead in programming in the then-USSR, Paraguay, and Indonesia.[54] Joint initiatives such as the International Peace Committee in earlier years and more recently the YAMEN! young adult exchange and the internship program at the MCC United Nations Office in New York are not easy to administer when the goals of the two organizations are not congruent. The MCC planning mode, meanwhile, is experienced by some within MWC to short-change relationships, while some in MCC question whether many MWC member churches are committed to the rigorous program planning done by other MCC partner organizations and thus question whether it is a responsible use of MCC's resources to increase the amount and scope of partnerships with MWC member churches and church-related organizations.

FUTURE DIRECTIONS

The relationship between MWC and MCC once more stands at a pivotal point. Both organizations are engaged in direction-setting processes which will significantly shape their relationship. MWC is implementing the "Communion/Community" model that came out of the International Planning Commission. MCC is amid structural reorganization emerging from the New Wine/New Wineskins appreciative inquiry process. Given the flux within the two bodies, the MOUC governing their relationship which was due for review in 2009 has been pushed back to 2010.

Most, but not all, of the MCC and MWC workers whom I interviewed projected a move to a deeper level for the relationship, even as interviewees recognized that when structures are discussed, the conversations become more problematic. Many interviewees called for each organization to emphasize the importance of the other and called for both organizations to embrace structural change to enhance the mission of the church. Several indicated that MWC, for reasons of accountability, needed to be part of the MCC picture.

In Ethiopia in summer 2010, MWC convened a consultation of Anabaptist-Mennonite service agencies to discern possibilities for collaboration and joint action in the future. MCC agreed with the other agencies to work together to build a space for collaboration and information sharing under MWC auspices. As MWC and MCC change, they will need one another. Interviewees suggested that MWC's future depends on MCC's creativity in assisting MWC to change into a more dynamic and responsive body, while other interviewees claim that MCC needs MWC to move beyond an artificial separation of service and evangelism which sometimes characterizes MCC.

Interviewees raised many questions about how the MCC-MWC relationship will evolve. Questions for MCC included these: Is MWC a stakeholder, partner, a part-owner, or the owner of MCC? Will

MCC's future programmatic emphasis be on delivering more effective program or on making its agenda more credible to the global
community? Will MCC try to become a more effective NGO or will it
serve the church? Should the locus of MCC's program priority be the
"household of faith" or the wider ecumenical, and even inter-faith,
community? Or must these two dimensions of work stand in opposition to one another?

For MWC key questions include these: Will MWC's "Commu-
nion/Community" model be relational or programmatic in character? Will MWC member churches be able to develop organizational
capacity in order faithfully and effectively to carry out diaconal ministries, be it through partnership with MCC or by other means? And
for both organizations, the broad question remains open: Which constituency will decide these questions and by what mechanism?[55]

The relationship options for MCC appear to range across a spectrum that would at one extreme minimize the relationship to MWC
and at the other would maximize it. Within this spectrum, MCC
could in the future a) become a parachurch organization (a decidedly
regressive step in the relationship)[56]; b) become a Participant Member of MWC (a course of action approved by the MCC board in 2007,
but now under review); c) sit alongside other Anabaptist-Mennonite
service agencies at an MWC-convened "Round Table" to share information and strategize together (perhaps using MWC's Diaconal and
Mission Commissions now being formed as an institutional home for
such strategizing and information-sharing); or d) become the service
arm of the MWC mission. Where MCC ends up on this spectrum remains to be seen.

This sketch of the history of the MWC-MCC relationship has
identified several key factors which have nurtured as well as constrained the relationship. Two foundational issues underpin this
analysis of the MWC-MCC relationship. The first is identity.
MCC was founded as, is currently, and should remain an arm of the
church. While this is presently most visible (to its supporting constituency) in North America, it has always been thus internationally.
While there are occasional exceptions (e.g. North Korea, in some
ways in Iran, and sometimes as articulated and lived by individual workers), these do not obviate the rule.

If MCC is to continue to be an arm of the church, it is critical that
MCC's relationship with and accountability to the global church
(meaning, in the first instance, that part of the church that identifies
most directly with the Anabaptist communion, and then secondarily
but importantly, the wider church) be strengthened. Absent this clear

vision and identity, MCC would quickly move toward a parachurch institution at best and beg the question as to its very existence.

The second foundational issue is that of accountability or mandate. MCC has been clear over the years that its accountability in the first instance is to the supporting faith community. Over time this accountability has been increasingly shared with the people in the countries in which MCC does programming: MCC is not only accountable to constituents who give of their money, material goods, and time, but is also accountable to the organizations worldwide with which MCC works and to the program participants[57] in whose interest MCC and its partners operate. Often, as already noted, this more globalized form of accountability has been, and appropriately so, with and through the local expression of the Christian faith.

What form MCC accountability to Anabaptist-Mennonite churches worldwide can and should take requires careful thought and negotiation. An iterative or contingent process, i.e. a process in which a final blueprint need not be devised, only continued steps taken in the right direction, is perhaps a positive way to proceed. Requiring that all MCC country programs establish local Advisory Committees was an important step along the way toward this inter-Mennonite accountability. But there are further steps to be taken if the welfare of the global church and the efficacy and validity of MCC are to increase.

MCC has played a vital role in MWC from its origins. MCC has often provided the infrastructure for MWC's operational reality. But MCC also gains symbolically and in purpose, increasingly, from MWC's global churchly mandate. Thus it would be totally counterproductive, if even possible, to stop or even reverse this growing relationship. The current effectiveness of MCC would be diminished and the opportunity cost would be immense if the relationship did not stay on course. The immediate future steps forward in this decades-long relationship may not be clear. Yet the overall direction should be evident, one of moving toward new forms of partnership between MCC and MWC member churches and church-related agencies. The process will be incremental and risky, but the benefits are worth the risk and the potential cost of disengagement seems certainly immense.[58]

NOTES

1. "Religious Affairs Committee in Hanoi Legalizes Vietnam Mennonite Church," November 24, 2008.

2. For the story of one MCC service worker who remained in Vietnam after the fall of the south, see Earl S. Martin, *Reaching the Other Side* (New York: Crown, 1978).

3. Albert N. Keim, *Harold S. Bender, 1987-1962* (Scottdale, Pa.: Herald Press, 1988), 518.

4. See, for example, Bosch's *Witness to The World* (Atlanta: John Knox, 1980), *Transforming Mission* (Maryknoll, N.Y.: Orbis, 1991), and *Believing in the Future* (Valley Forge, Pa.: Trinity Press International, 1995).

5. Of the 21 interviewees, 16 had staff or governance experience with MCC, 15 with MWC. The interviewees included: Herman Bontrager (1,2), Ray Brubacher (1,2), C.J. Dyck (1,2), Peter Dyck (1), Ron Flaming (1), Kathryn Good (1,2), Karen Klassen Harder (1), Nancy Heisey (1,2), Arli Klassen (1), J.M. Klassen (1), Robert Kreider (1,2), Mesach Krisetya (2), John A. Lapp (1,2), Albert Lobe (1,2), Larry Miller (1,2), Danisa Ndlovu (2), Paul Quiring (1,2), Walter Sawatsky (1), Reg Toews (1,2), Pakisa Tshimika (2), David Wiebe (2). 1 indicates MCC staff and / or service in MCC governance structures; 2 denotes MWC staff and / or service in MWC governance structures.

6. Paul N. Kraybill, "MWC—A Growing Vision." Presented to the International Mennonite Peace Committee, Hyderabad, December 1985. (MCC Library, Akron, Pa. Hereafter MCCLPA) See also C. J. Dyck, "The History of the MWC," *MWC Handbook* (1978), 1-9.

7. MWC Presidium, July 1967. 36-44. (MCCLPA).

8. Kraybill (1985).

9. R. Mathies to MCC Annual Meeting. June 2005. (MCCLPA).

10. A creative tension, from the beginning of MCC to the present, has been what balance of assistance should be given to the "household of faith" and how much to the "other."

11. Last updated 1999.

12. Orie O. Miller, "Basic Principles Underlying he Services of the MCC and the Future of the Committee's Activities," proceedings of the 1948 MWC. (MCCLPA)

13. *Mennonite Encyclopedia*, vol. 3 (Scottdale, Pa.: Herald Press, 1957), 606.

14. Walter Sawatsky. AMBS course notes for forthcoming publication, "Mennonite History in Global Perspective."

15. John A.Lapp and Ed van Straten, "Mennonite World Conference 1925-2000: From Euro-American Conference to Worldwide Communion," *The Mennonite Quarterly Review* 77/1 (January 2003): 19.

16. "Mennonite Central Committee 1920-1970," *The Mennonite Quarterly Review* 44/3 (July 1970). See especially the articles by Robert Kreider, John A. Lapp, and Larry Kehler.

17. Robert S. Kreider and Rachel Waltner Goosen, *Hungry, Thirsty, A Stranger: The MCC Experience* (Scottdale, Pa.: Herald Press, 1988).

18. Donald B. Kraybill, "From Enclave to Engagement: MCC and the Transformation of Mennonite Identity," in *Unity Amidst Diversity: MCC at 75*, ed. Robert S. Kreider and Ronald J. R. Mathies (Akron, Pa.: MCC, 1996), 26-28.

19. Edgar Metzler, "Partnerships and Secondments: a Preliminary Survey and Some Policy Issues" (March, 2000). (MCCLPA).

20. Million Belete, MWC Presidium (1976). (MWC Office, Kitchener, Ont. Hereafter MWCKON).

21. Arli Klassen to MWC Executive Committee (July 2008). (MCCLPA).
22. MCC Executive Committee Minutes (August 1930). (Hereafter MCC ExCom) (MCCLPA).
23. MCC Executive Committee (June1948). (MCCLPA).
24. Nancy R. Heisey, "Pilgrimage, Place and People: A History of the Locations of Mennonite World Conference Assemblies, 1925-2003," *The American Society of Church History* (December 2006), 863.
25. John D.Unruh, *In the Name of Christ* (Scottdale, Pa.: Herald, 1952), 354.
26. MWC Officers Minutes (1994). (MWCKON).
27. MWC Officers Minutes (1992). (MWCKON).
28. MWC Executive Committee (1998). (MWCKON).
29. Erland Waltner, "The Ecumenical Mennonite," *The Mennonite Quarterly Review* 38/2 (April 1964): 71.
30. Much of this paragraph comes from J.C. Wenger, "Harold S. Bender: A Brief Biography," *The Mennonite Quarterly Review* 38/2 (April 1964): 39-46. See also Keim, 256.
31. "MCC Grants to MWC," (2008). (MCCLPA)
32. MWC General Council (November 1963). (MWCKON)
33. MWC Executive Committee (December 1964). (MWCKON)
34. MCC Workbook (1978). (MCCLPA).
35. Nancy Heisey and Paul Longacre, *Mennonite International Study Project: Final Report* (Elkhart, Ind.: Mennonite Board of Missions, 1990), 13.
36. Executive Secretary Report to MCC Excom. June 1988. (MCCLPA).
37. Mesach Kristeya, "From Dependence to Interdepence in the Global Church" (July, 1993). (MCCLPA).
38. Africa Department MCC, "Towards a Vision of Global Belonging: MCC and Africa" (December 1993). (MCCPLA).
39. MWC Executive Committee, (1997). (MWCKON).
40. Ray Brubacher,"Internationalization: Toward a Globalization of Accountability" (March 1997). (MCCLPA).
41. GAMCO Vision Discernment Team statement (2000). (MCCLPA).
42. Ray Brubacher and Pakisa Tshimika, "Review of the Relationship Between MWC and MCC" (April, 2000). (MCCLPA).
43. R. Mathies "Report on MWC to MCC Executive Committee," August 23, 2002 (MCCLPA).
44. "Listening Group Report and Recommendations" (March 2006). (MCCLPA).
45. Keim, 389-9. Lapp and van Straten, 19-20.
46. MWC Executive Committee (December 1964). (MWCKON).
47. MWC General Council (2000). (MWCKON).
48. MWC Executive Committee (June 2005). (MWCKON).
49. MCC Executive Committee (April 1997). (MCCLPA).
50. MWC Executive Committee (1999). (MWCKON).
51. Ibid.
52. MWC Executive Committee (1997). (MWCKON).
53. Brubacher and Tshimika (2000).
54. Kraybill, MWC Executive Committee (1982, 1986, 1988). (MCCLPA).
55. See also Will Braun, "A Priesthood of MCC Believers," *Canadian Mennonite* (November 10, 2008): 9.

56. MCC Executive Committee (June 2008), stated that this was not the direction to go.

57. Often the word *beneficiaries* is used.

58. R. Mathies to Inter-MCC Round Table (1998). (Privately held).

Part II

Imagining Mennonite Peoplehood in Canada and the United States: The Role of MCC

Chapter 5

The Mystery of Broad-Based Commitment: MCC in the Eyes of Mennonites and Brethren in Christ in the United States

Donald B. Kraybill

The survival of voluntary organizations depends on the goodwill and financial support of their stakeholders. Unlike businesses that manufacture or sell products, voluntary organizations such as MCC rely solely on the enthusiasm and economic benevolence of their constituents. Such support not only depends on the "facts" about an organization's activities and efficient use of stakeholder resources (facts typically provided by the organization itself), but perhaps just as importantly, if not more so, on stakeholder perceptions—whether accurate or not—of the organization. Perceptions may be shaped by the facts about an organization's behavior as well as a myriad of other sources of information.

This essay is about perceptions—regardless of their basis in fact—of how MCC *appears* in the eyes of some of its constituents. The information about the perceptions comes from survey evidence from two MCC-supporting denominations—Mennonite Church USA

(MC USA) and the Brethren in Christ Church (BIC). The sizeable number of respondents in the studies provides data to explore some of the social and religious factors associated with these perceptions. The connections that emerge in the survey data do not establish that any socio-religious factors *cause* the perceptions, but they do show *associations* with them. The associations that these data disclose show strong support for MCC across many social subgroups but leave us with a mystery—how to explain or unravel the reasons for constituent enthusiasm.

The Church Member Profile 2006 (hereafter CMP2006), conceived and conducted by the Young Center of Elizabethtown College, included three denominations: Mennonite Church USA, the Brethren in Christ, and the Church of the Brethren.[1] The project's instruments and methods were developed over several years and the survey was conducted in spring 2006.[2]

Two previous similar studies were conducted in 1972 and 1989. The earlier profiles (Church Member Profile I and Church Member Profile II) were directed by J. Howard Kauffman, Leland Harder, and Leo Driedger.[3] Those studies surveyed the members in five Anabaptist denominations (Brethren in Christ Church, Evangelical Mennonite Church, General Conference Mennonite Church, Mennonite Brethren Church, and Mennonite Church) living in Canada and the United States. CMP2006, in contrast, only sampled and studied members of three denominations in the United States.

The Mennonite Member Profile involved members of 124 MC USA congregations that were randomly selected from the denominational database of 965 congregations in 2005. A two-stage scientific selection process insured that members of these congregations would be representative of all members of MC USA. Using membership directories from the sample of congregations, the second stage of the process randomly selected members (18 years of age and older) from each sample congregation. This process yielded a representative sample of 3,080 MC USA members.

A 20-page questionnaire was mailed to the sample of members on February 14, 2006. Several rounds of follow-up contacts with nonrespondents through mid-May that year eventually resulted in useable questionnaires (2,216) from 76% of the MC USA sample.[4] The 76% response rate was superb because typical church survey response rates, according to Gallup, are 20% to 30% at best.[5]

The Brethren in Christ Member Profile used the same methods as the Mennonite survey. Thirty-six congregations were randomly selected from all BIC congregations in the United States.[6] The BIC re-

sponse rate from a sample of 1,001 members in the selected congregations was 73%, or 733 members.

Many core questions were used in all three denominational questionnaires. Other questions were customized for specific denominational interests and issues. Some questions, in identical or slightly revised form, were repeated from the 1972 and 1989 Church Member
Profiles. Still other questions were designed to match items in national surveys such as Gallup, the General Social Survey, and the
Roper Survey.

Three key questions in the Mennonite and BIC instruments in
2006 focused on MCC. The findings in this paper summarize the response of Mennonite and BIC respondents to these questions: 1) Do
you support the mission of MCC? 2) Are you satisfied with MCC's
programs and emphases? and 3) Do you support MCC offices in
Washington, D.C., and New York?

The second and third questions were asked in 1972 and 1989 and
thus enable trend analysis. The first question, measuring support for
MCC's mission, was new in 2006. The analysis throughout this paper
shows the broad response of MC USA and BIC members to these
questions and also explores in depth how issues such as sex, age, political views, among other factors, influence constituent perceptions
of MCC's mission and programs.

The historical comparisons in this report combine the responses
of Mennonite Church and General Conference Mennonites in the
1972 and 1989 studies to make equivalent comparisons with MC USA
members in 2006. Canadians were removed from the previous studies for historical trend analysis to make comparable comparisons
with CMP2006 respondents, all of whom lived in the United States.[7]

Many nationwide polls (based on random selection of respondents) in the United States use a sample of 700 to 1,000 respondents to
generalize to the entire nation with a 3% margin of error. Because the
Mennonite Member Profile has more that 2,000 respondents, the margin of error is likely less than 3%. The number of BIC respondents
(733) is somewhat lower, so the margin of error for that denomination
may, on some questions, be slightly higher than 3%.[8] The large number of MC USA respondents affords a high level of confidence in the
Mennonite results.[9]

SUPPORT FOR MCC'S MISSION

Respondents were queried in 2006 about the strength of their
support for the mission of MCC as defined in this question:

How much do you support the mission of Mennonite Central Committee (MCC) to "demonstrate God's love by working among people suffering from poverty, conflict, oppression, and natural disaster?"

Table 1-a. Support for MCC's Mission by Denomination in Percent

	MC USA	BIC
Strongly Support	66	58
Support	30	34
Not Sure	4	7
Oppose	0	1
Strongly Oppose	1	1
Total	100	100

In some tables the percentages total 99 or 101 because of rounding to the nearest whole number.

**Table 1-b. Support for MCC's Mission by Age,
Sex, Region, and Denomination in Percent**

		MC USA	BIC
Age			
	18-25	96*	70
	26-35	95	68
	36-45	95	69
	46-55	96	63
	56-65	96	61
	66 +	96	64
Sex			
	Male	96	64
	Female	95	66
Region			
	East	97	65
	West	96	79
	Midwest	94	56
	South	99	58

* Read: "96% of 18- to 25-year-old Mennonites 'support or strongly support' MCC's mission."

The findings in Table 1-a show remarkable support for MCC's mission: 96% (MC USA) and 92% (BIC). Two-thirds of Mennonites report strong support; only 1% express opposition. Moreover, as shown in Table 1-b, age, among Mennonites, exerts no influence on support. Members age 18 to 25 show identical levels of support (96%) as those over 65.[10] Among BICs younger people (70%) are slightly more likely to support MCC than the elderly (64%).

Table 1-c. Support for MCC's Mission
by Contextual and Background Factors in Percent

		MC USA	BIC
Previous Non-Menno or Non-BIC Membership			
	Yes	95	65*
	No	96	64
Active in Congregation			
	Active member	96	66
	Inactive member	93	60
Residence			
	Farm	97	52
	Small city	96	66
	Large city	90	76
Lived Outside the U.S.			
	Yes	98	70
	No	95	64
Occupation			
	Managers and professionals	98	62
	Service workers	95	74
	Operators and laborers	91	66
Educational Attainment			
	Some high school or less	92	70
	Tech school or some college	94	65
	Masters or Doctoral degree	99	75
Past Service			
	Voluntary service for over 3 months	96	72
	Overseas assignment for over 3 months	98	100
	Served with MCC for a year or more	97	92

*Read: "65% of BICs who at one time were members of a Non-BIC church 'support or strongly support' MCC's mission."

Sex makes virtually no difference in level of support, nor, for the most part, does region. MC USA level of support dips slightly among

**Table 1-d. Support for MCC's
Mission by Faith and Identity Factors in Percent**

		MCUSA	BIC
Church Attendance			
	Weekly or more	97*	66
	Rarely attend	82	53
Importance of Religious Beliefs			
	Very important	96	65
	Fairly important	93	53
Uniqueness of Jesus			
	He is the only way to God	95	64
	He is one of many ways to God	93	77
A Close Personal Relationship with Christ			
	It's the centerpiece of my faith story	96	66
	It's not part of my faith story	97	80
Salvation			
	It depends more on what one believes	96	65
	It depends more on how one lives	95	77
Religious Identity**			
	Fundamentalist	97	67
	Anabaptist	98	72
	Evangelical	97	65
	Mennonite or BIC	97	65
Portion of Income Given to Church and Charities			
	Less than 1%	93	67
	More than 20%	97	67

Read: "97% of Mennonites who attend church every week or more 'support or strongly support' MCC's mission." **Respondents could choose multiple descriptions.

Midwest constituents, but is still 94% there. Support levels are higher in all other regions of the country. The BICs show the largest regional differences in support with a gap of 23% between the Midwest (56%) and the West (79%). On every category of age, sex, and region, Mennonites express substantially higher support (ranging from 17%-41%) for MCC's mission than the BICs. The widest gap (41%) is in the Midwest, where Mennonite support is 94% but BIC support dips to 56%. Mennonite and BIC members are most alike in the West, with only a 17% gap (96%–79%).

Mennonites show astonishing high levels of mission support—94% or higher in every category of age, sex, and region—suggesting that these factors exert very little influence on members' enthusiasm for MCC's mission. The BICs consistently show less enthusiasm and are more influenced by age, sex, and region than the Mennonites.

Table 1–c displays the association between seven contextual factors and constituent enthusiasm for MCC's mission. The contextual factors are past membership in a non-Mennonite or non-BIC church, active status in a local congregation, residence, living outside the U.S., occupation, educational attainment, and service with MCC or another organization.[11] Mennonites show consistently high levels of support—90% or greater—across all categories of these seven variables. A 7% difference among Mennonites appears to be related to residence, occupation, and education. Members residing on farms show 7% more support than large-city dwellers, professionals more (7%) than equipment operators and laborers, and graduate degree holders more (7%) than those without high school diplomas. Despite these minor differences, the seven contextual factors account for little variation in shaping Mennonite levels of support for MCC's mission.

With one exception, BICs are consistently lower than Mennonites—as much as 45% among farmers—in supporting MCC's mission. The MC USA-BIC gap shrinks to 5% (97%–92%) among those who served with MCC for a year or more. And in a reversal, BICs who served in an overseas assignment for at least three months with any service agency top the Mennonites by 2% (100%–98%). Those with three months of overseas experience show 100% support for MCC, whereas only 52% of BICs living on farms express support. This 48% gap is the largest internal difference among BICs on these seven factors. Clearly, for both denominations, a service experience—especially one overseas—is highly associated with support for MCC's mission.

Table 1-d displays the association between constituent support for MCC's mission and variations within seven faith and identity factors: frequency of church attendance, the portion of income given to charity, self-identified theological designations, and differing understandings of Christology, soteriology, the salience of religious belief, and the importance of a close, personal relationship with Christ. Mennonite support for MCC's mission is 93% or higher across all cat-

**Table 1-e. Support for MCC's Mission
by Peace and Justice Factors in Percent**

		MC USA	BIC
Importance of Peacemaking/Nonviolence			
	Very important	96*	74
	Not very important	93	48
Complete Nonviolent Living is Important to Me			
	Completely disagree	88	62
	Completely agree	98	74
Ever Served in Armed Forces/National Guard			
	Yes	94	55
	No	96	66
Response to Military Draft			
	Military service	90	56
	Conscientious objector	98	73
Promoting Social Justice			
	Very important	98	69
	Not very important	96	53
Efforts to Stop Racism			
	Strongly support	96	83
	Strongly oppose	91	67
View of Immigration			
	Very good thing	98	80
	Very bad thing	87	53

*Read: "96% of Mennonites who believe that peacemaking and nonviolence are crucial 'support or strongly support' MCC's mission."

egories of the seven factors except one. Among those who rarely attend church, mission support drops to 82%—but even then, four out of five absentees on Sunday morning support MCC. The differences between categories of the other six variables are minuscule, suggesting their impotence to enhance or erode Mennonite commitment to MCC's mission.[11]

Comparing Mennonites with BICs in Table 1-d, the previous patterns persist, with BICs showing typically about 30% less enthusiasm than Mennonites and 40% less among respondents who describe their religious beliefs as only "fairly important." An interesting pattern emerges among BICs who, on three measures of religious faith, are less orthodox/conservative than other BICs. Those who view Jesus as one of *many* ways to God, who say, "a close personal relationship with Christ is *not* the centerpiece of my faith story," and who say, "salvation depends more on *how* one lives," are all at least 12% more likely to support MCC than more conservative-leaning BICs. However, on the issue of theological identity, regardless of the BIC respondents' primary identity, support for MCC only fluctuates by 7% at the most. Support for MCC is highest among those who identify themselves as Anabaptist (72%), but only slightly lower for those who identify as Fundamentalist (67%), Evangelical (65%), and BIC (65%).

Even more striking, theological identity among Mennonites makes no difference in support for the MCC mission. These data show that commitment to MCC transcends respondents' self-reported theological identity.

Finally, respondents—both Mennonite and BIC—indicate that their support for MCC is not tied to their giving to the church and other charities. Those who give less than 1% and those who give more than 20% of their incomes to charity report similar levels of MCC support.

The relationship between respondents' views on peace and justice issues and their embrace of the MCC mission is presented in Table 1-e. Mennonite support for MCC stands at 87% or higher across all categories of the seven variables. Mennonites who view immigration as "a very bad thing" support MCC at the 87% level. In eight other categories, Mennonite support is 96% or higher. Contrasting views of immigration drive the largest wedge between Mennonite constituents (98%–87%). Even nine out of ten Mennonites who say they would enter military service, if drafted, proclaim support for MCC.

BIC respondents consistently show less enthusiasm for MCC than Mennonites. However, inside the BIC fold, the intensity of support for MCC fluctuates with how respondents view peace and justice. Those who differ on the importance of peacemaking/nonviolence and on their view of immigration also show gaps (26% and 27%, respectively) in their support for MCC.

Table 1-f. Support for MCC's Mission by Political Factors in Percent

		MC USA	BIC
Conflict Between My Beliefs and Larger Society			
	Much conflict	98	74*
	No conflict	90	69
Political Views			
	Very conservative	96	70
	Conservative	96	62
	Liberal	98	63
	Very liberal	94	67
Political Affiliation			
	Republican	95	65
	Democrat	95	57
	Independent	97	77
Presidential Vote in 2004			
	George W. Bush	96	64
	John Kerry	97	76
Political Participation is Important			
	Mostly disagree	97	71
	Completely agree	95	69

*Read: "74% of BICs who report much conflict between their own beliefs and those of the larger society 'support or strongly support' MCC's mission."

When it comes to their view of the importance of a complete nonviolent way of living, the gap shrinks to 12% (74%–62%) among the BIC respondents. Respondent views of church-society relations and of political issues were cross-tabulated with support for MCC as shown in Table 1-f. Mennonite commitment to the MCC mission is 90% or higher across all categories of the five factors. Modest differences emerge between members on their views of the relationship of the church to the larger society. Those who see "much conflict" between their beliefs and those of the larger society are more likely to support MCC than fellow Mennonites who feel less tension with the larger world. What is most remarkable, however, in the findings presented in Table 1-f, is that the political views, affiliation, voting, and political participation of Mennonites are completely independent of their support for MCC. Republicans and Democrats, the very conservative and the very liberal, those who voted for Bush and those who voted for Kerry in 2004—all consistently report high levels, 94% or more, of support for MCC. Political views and behavior show no

**Table 1-g. Support for MCC's
Mission by God-and-Country Factors in Percent**

		MC USA	BIC
The U.S. is a Christian Nation			
	Completely disagree	96*	73
	Completely agree	94	70
God's Blessing on Nations			
	God blesses all nations	95	64
	God especially blesses America	96	65
The U.S. Has a Special Role in God's Plan			
	Completely disagree	98	77
	Completely agree	92	73
It's OK to Pledge Allegiance to the Flag			
	Completely disagree	99	100
	Completely agree	92	63
It's OK to Display the Flag Inside a Church Building			
	Completely disagree	98	88
	Completely agree	89	62

Read: "96% of Mennonites who completely reject the belief that the United States is a Christian nation 'support or strongly support' MCC's mission."

traces of association with members' endorsement of the MCC mission.

In general, the same pattern emerges in the BIC responses as well, though not quite as vividly. Those who experience conflict between their beliefs and those of the larger society do show more (5%) support for MCC than those who do not. In terms of political affiliation, Independents are 20% more likely than Democrats to support MCC. However, when it comes to actual voting, BIC Democrats were 12% more likely than BIC Republicans (76%–64%) to applaud the MCC mission. These results suggest that political views among BICs are more likely to be tied to MCC support than they are among Mennonites.

Politics may not shape Mennonite views of MCC, but flags do, at least a bit, as shown in Table 1-g. Mennonites may disagree sharply on their view of the United States as a "Christian nation," on which nations receive "God's blessing," and on whether "the United States has a special role in God's plan for the world," but, despite such cleavages, members endorse MCC's mission at 92% levels or higher.

Mennonite views of flags, however, do drive small wedges into their support for MCC, but even then, only small ones. Those who object to pledging allegiance to the flag are 7% (99%–92%) more likely to support MCC than those who find flag pledging acceptable. Likewise, those who want flags barred from church buildings show 9% (98%–89%) greater affection for MCC than those who welcome flags in such buildings.

Views of flags show sharper breaches among BICs, where flag pledgers are 37% less likely (63%–100%) to support MCC than the non-pledgers. Placing flags in church buildings produces a 26% difference (88%–62%) with only 62% of flag enthusiasts showing support for MCC's mission. Differences in BIC views of God and country in the first three issues in Table 1-g are not tied to their endorsement of the MCC mission.

SATISFACTION WITH MCC'S PROGRAM

Human societies and social organizations often show breaches between their ideals and social realities. Thus, it is not surprising to discover a gap between the level of support for MCC's mission and constituent satisfaction with MCC's actual performance. This section explores stakeholder satisfaction with the programs and emphases of MCC's operations. A later section of the chapter examines the mission-satisfaction gap.

How satisfied or dissatisfied are you, in general, with the program and emphases of Mennonite Central Committee?

Table 2-a. Satisfaction with MCC's Program and Emphases by Denomination in Percent

	MC USA	BIC
Very Satisfied	34	23
Satisfied	45	45
Partly Satisfied	7	6
Dissatisfied	1	1
Very Dissatisfied	1	1
Not Sure	12	25
Total	100	100

About 4 of 5 Mennonites report that they are satisfied with the programs and emphases of MCC, as seen in Table 2-a. In fact, only 2% reported outright dissatisfaction, while 12% reported they were "not sure." In other words, 79% are satisfied and 19% waver (partly satisfied or not sure) in their satisfaction but only 2% declare dissat-

Table 2-b. Satisfaction with MCC's Program by Age, Sex, Region, and Denomination in Percent

		MC USA	BIC
Age			
	18-25	68*	42
	26-35	69	53
	36-45	75	59
	46-55	80	74
	56-65	83	72
	66 +	85	78
Sex			
	Male	79	70
	Female	79	67
Region			
	East	81	72
	West	79	68
	Midwest	76	51
	South	83	67

Read: "68% of Mennonite 18- to 25-year-olds are 'satisfied or very satisfied' with MCC's program."

isfaction.[12] Although two-thirds of BICs (68%) report satisfaction, one fourth of that constituency is ambivalent about MCC—not sure

**Table 2-c. Satisfaction with MCC's Program
by Contextual and Background Factors in Percent**

		MC USA	BIC
Previous Non-Menno or Non-BIC Membership			
	Yes	72	66
	No	84*	70
Active in Cong.			
	Active member	82	75
	Inactive member	65	59
Residence			
	Farm	83	79
	Small city	80	66
	Large city	70	70
Lived Outside the U.S.			
	Yes	83	70
	No	78	68
Occupation			
	Managers and professionals	80	71
	Service workers	79	64
	Operators and laborers	84	64
Educational Attainment			
	Some high school or less	83	71
	Tech school or some college	77	57
	Masters or doctoral degree	85	86
Past Service			
	Voluntary service for over 3 months	84	59
	Overseas assignment for over 3 months	88	83
	Served with MCC for a year or more	92	92

Read: "84% of Mennonites who never held membership in a non-Mennonite church are 'satisfied or very satisfied' with MCC's program."

if they are satisfied or not. The 2% of BICs who are unhappy with MCC's program exactly matches the level of Mennonite discontent.

The relationships of age, sex, and region with satisfaction appear in Table 2-b. Among Mennonites, satisfaction with what MCC does rises slightly with age. Those over 45 years of age are 10% to 17% more likely to show satisfaction than younger people. Sex loses all of its explanatory power in these results; women and men alike report a 79% level of satisfaction.

Region of residence causes slight variation, with Midwesterners showing a 76% and Southerners an 83% vote of satisfaction.

More differences emerge among BICs, where those under 26 years of age are 36% less likely to approve of MCC's program than those 66 years of age and older. BIC men feel 3% more satisfaction than women and in the Midwest BIC satisfaction dips to 51%. As shown in Table 2-b, BIC satisfaction is lower than Mennonite in all the categories with the sharpest differences among youth (26%) and Midwestern residents (25%).

Table 2-c reveals the relationships between member satisfaction with MCC's program and seven contextual factors. Satisfaction among Mennonites ranges from 70% to 92% and among BICs from 57% to 92% across all the contextual factors. Those who have never held membership outside a Mennonite or BIC church are 12% and 4%, respectively, more likely to be satisfied with MCC's work than those who at some time were members of other churches.

Among Mennonites, engagement in local congregations exerts a 17% impact on satisfaction, which dips to 65% among the inactive compared with 82% among the active members. In terms of residence, the lowest satisfaction score comes from those living in large cities—10% lower than small-city dwellers (80%) and 13% lower than those who live on farms (83%). Both Mennonites and BICs living in big cities report a 70% level of satisfaction. Mennonites who lived outside the United States, machine operators and laborers, and those with graduate degrees are slightly more likely (5%–8%) than their counterparts to be content with MCC's performance. In terms of service experience, 92% of both Mennonites and BICs who have served with MCC say they are satisfied with MCC's program and emphases. BIC members with technical school training or some college report the lowest level of satisfaction—57%.

The connections between satisfaction with MCC's programs and religious faith and identity are shown in Table 2-d. Satisfaction among Mennonites ranges from a low of 51% to a high of 87%, with church attendance and giving to charities showing a hefty influence.

Table 2-d. Satisfaction with MCC's Program
by Faith and Identity Factors in Percent

		MC USA	BIC
Church Attendance			
	Every week or more	81*	73
	Rarely attend	51	42
Importance of Religious Beliefs			
	Very important	80	69
	Fairly important	65	47
Uniqueness of Jesus			
	He is the only way to God	78	69
	He is one of many ways to God	79	50
A Close Relationship with Christ?			
	It's the centerpiece of my faith story	79	70
	It's not part of my faith story	83	33
Salvation			
	It depends more on what one believes	74	67
	It depends more on how one lives	84	71
Religious Identity**			
	Fundamentalist	70	79
	Anabaptist	85	87
	Evangelical	79	77
	Mennonite/BIC	84	72
Portion of Income Given to Church and Charities			
	Less than 1%	61	29
	More than 20%	87	45

*Read: "81% of Mennonites who attend church once a week or more are 'satisfied or very satisfied' with MCC's program." **Respondents could choose multiple descriptions.

**Table 2-e. Satisfaction with MCC's Program
by Peace and Justice Factors in Percent**

		MC USA	BIC
Importance of Peacemaking/ Nonviolence			
	Very important	85	68*
	Not very important	55	70
Complete Nonviolent Living is Important to Me			
	Completely disagree	53	62
	Completely agree	87	74
Ever Served in Armed Forces/National Guard			
	Yes	62	64
	No	80	69
Response to a Military Draft			
	Military service	55	60
	Conscientious objector	85	84
Promoting Social Justice			
	Very important	85	70
	Not very important	71	65
Efforts to Stop Racism			
	Strongly support	80	65
	Strongly oppose	63	41
View of Immigration			
	A very good thing	82	71
	A very bad thing	65	63

Read: "68 percent of BICs who consider peacemaking and nonviolence crucial are 'satisfied or very satisfied' with MCC's program."

Weekly church attendees are 30% more likely (81%–51%) to be happy with MCC's program than those who rarely attend. Likewise, members who give more than 20% or their income to church and charity are 26% more likely (87%–61%) to be pleased with MCC than donors who give less than 1% of their income. Variations among Mennonites regarding three religious beliefs show little association with satisfaction: the uniqueness of Jesus (1%), a stress on a close relationship to Christ (4%), and views of salvation (10%).

Two other faith variables—importance of religious belief and theological identity—exert a 15% shift in perception of satisfaction. Those who say their religious beliefs are "crucial" are 15% more likely (80%–65%) to be satisfied with MCC than members whose beliefs are only "fairly important." Those who identify as Anabaptist show 15% (85%–70%) more satisfaction with MCC than members who think of themselves as Fundamentalists. Nevertheless, 70% of self defined Fundamentalists are satisfied with MCC.

Among BICs, the range of satisfaction with MCC stretches from a low of 29% (those who give less than 1%) to a high of 87% (those who identify as Anabaptist.) Six of the factors (church attendance, importance of religious belief, uniqueness of Jesus, close relationship with Christ, theological identity, and giving to charity) exert influences ranging from 15% to 37%. Interestingly, among the BICs, views of salvation have a smaller impact (4% and 8%, respectively) than they do among Mennonites.

Table 2-e shows the linkage between constituents' satisfaction with MCC's work and their views on seven peace and justice issues. The influence of six of these issues on Mennonite satisfaction with MCC ranges from 17% to 34%. The importance that respondents attach to social justice has little (6%) impact on satisfaction. Even 71% of those who say that social justice is "not crucial" report they are satisfied with MCC. Views of the importance of complete nonviolent living separate respondents on their satisfaction with MCC more than any of the other variables in Table 2-e. Mennonites who completely embrace nonviolent living are 34% more likely (87%–53%) to be satisfied with MCC than those who reject complete nonviolence. How Mennonite respondents say they would respond to a military draft shows a 30% effect (85%–55%) on their level of satisfaction with MCC. However, 62% of respondents who have served in the Armed Forces in the past say they are satisfied with MCC. Those who strongly support efforts to stop racism and those who see immigration as a good thing are 17% more likely to be satisfied with MCC than respondents who do not support those issues.

Among BICs, the spread on satisfaction in Table 2-e ranges from 41% (those who oppose efforts to stop racism) to 84% (those who would enter alternative service under a military draft).

Table 2-f. Satisfaction with
MCC's Program by Political Views in Percent

		MC USA	BIC
Conflict Between My Beliefs and Larger Society			
	Much conflict	81	71
	No conflict	74	47
Political Views			
	Very Conservative	75	78*
	Conservative	80	70
	Liberal	85	53
	Very Liberal	74	NA
Political Affiliation			
	Republican	78	72
	Democrat	82	51
	Independent	79	74
Presidential Vote in 2004			
	George W. Bush	77	72
	John Kerry	84	58
Political Participation Is Important			
	Completely disagree	83	86
	Completely agree	74	61

Read: "78% of BICs whose political views are very conservative are 'satisfied or very satisfied' with MCC's program."

The connections between political views and satisfaction with MCC's program appear in Table 2-f. What is remarkable among Mennonite respondents is the relatively small influence political factors exert in shaping constituent satisfaction with MCC. Whether respondents are Republican or Democrat makes only a 4% difference, and who they voted for in 2004 (Bush or Kerry) only a 7% difference in satisfaction. In fact, the biggest gap (11%) among Mennonites on all the issues in Table 2-f is between those who say their political views are "liberal" and "very liberal," with only 74% of the latter reporting satisfaction versus 85% for the liberals.

Among BICs, satisfaction across all these factors is lower than Mennonite satisfaction, with a few exceptions. BICs who say that

Table 2-g. Satisfaction with MCC's Program by God and Country Factors in Percent

		MC USA	BIC
The U.S. is a Christian Nation			
	Completely disagree	86	67
	Completely agree	80*	55
God's Blessing on Nations			
	God blesses all nations	79	62
	God especially blesses America	76	74
The U.S. Has a Special Role in God's Plan			
	Completely disagree	86	61
	Completely agree	73	68
It's OK to Pledge Allegiance to the Flag			
	Completely disagree	89	75
	Completely agree	70	66
It's OK to Display the Flag Inside a Church Building			
	Completely disagree	89	78
	Completely agree	64	60

Read: "80% of Mennonites who completely agree that the United States is a Christian nation are 'satisfied or very satisfied' with MCC's program."

their political views are "very conservative" are slightly more satisfied (78%–75%) than Mennonites of the same political persuasion.

Table 2-g presents the relationships between satisfaction with MCC's program and five God-and-country factors. Levels of satisfaction among Mennonites range from 64% to 89%. Beliefs about the United States as a Christian nation and about God blessing nations have little influence on satisfaction. However, those who think the United States has a special role in God's plan are 13% less satisfied (86%–73%) compared with those who think God blesses *all* nations. Different views of the flag generate the sharpest divisions among Mennonites: those who disapprove of pledging are 19% (89%–70%) more satisfied than the pledgers. An even sharper difference emerges when the flag moves into church buildings. Those who want flags banned from churches are 25% (89%–64%) more satisfied with MCC than those who welcome the stars and stripes at church.

Among BICs, satisfaction ratings range from 55% to 78% across the five God-and-country variables. As with Mennonites, flags in the church show the largest (18%) impact on satisfaction with MCC. Views of the United States as a Christian nation and of God blessing nations both exert a 12% impact on BIC satisfaction.

How satisfied or dissatisfied are you, in general, with the program and emphases of Mennonite Central Committee (MCC)?

Table 2-h. 1972-2006 Trend by Denomination in Percent

	Mennonites		BICs	
	Satisfied	Dissatisfied	Satisfied	Dissatisfied
1972	73	2	69	1
1989	65*	3	63	1
2006	79	2	68	2

*Read: "65% of Mennonites were 'satisfied or very satisfied' with the program of MCC in 1989."

The questions about satisfaction with MCC's "program and emphases" had identical wording in the 1972, 1989, and 2006 Church Member Profiles. This enables tracking of satisfaction trends over a 35-year period in both Mennonite and BIC churches.[13]

In 1972, 73% of Mennonites reported satisfaction, but it dipped to 65% in 1989 and then rose to 79% in 2006. BIC levels of satisfaction in the three studies moved from 69% to 63%, and back up to 68% by 2006. Apart from slight dips in 1989, a solid two-thirds of members in both groups say they are "satisfied" or "very satisfied" with MCC's work. BIC satisfaction is lower than that of Mennonites in all three snapshots, but the gap widens from 2% in 1989 to 11% in 2006. Although some members are unsure what to think about MCC's programs, only a consistently small portion (the most was 3% among Mennonites in 1989) express dissatisfaction with MCC.

SUPPORT FOR MCC'S WITNESS TO GOVERNMENT

The attitudinal support of Mennonites and BICs for MCC's witness to government through its offices in Washington, D.C., and New York City are shown in Table 3-a. Mennonite support for these offices in 2006 was rather robust—82% supported or strongly supported them.

Mennonite Central Committee (MCC) maintains offices in Washington, D.C., and New York City to witness to the United States government and the United Nations on war, peace, poverty, and social justice. How much do you support this form of Christian witness? (2006 Question)

Table 3-a. Support for Witness to Government in 2006 by Denomination in Percent

	MC USA	BIC
Strongly Support	40	24
Support	42	51
Not Sure	13	22
Oppose	3	2
Strongly Oppose	1	1
Total	100	100

Some 13% were uncertain and 4% opposed such witness to government. Although slightly lower, a full three-fourths of BIC members supported these MCC initiatives; 3% opposed them; and 1 in 5 respondents were uncertain about them. Thus, a sizeable majority in both denominations (82% and 75%) support these modes of MCC government witness.

Cross-tabulations of age, sex, and region with support for government witness are shown in Table 3-b. Those under 25 years of age are 7% more likely (87%–80%) to support government witness than those over 65; that said, one cannot find a consistent pattern of support related to age. The sex of respondents shows no influence on witness and the impact of region is very slight, with Midwesterners being a bit below residents of other regions. All age groups of BICs show 65% support or higher for government witness, but the support fluctuates slightly by category. Males are 3% more likely to show support than women and, unlike Mennonites, BICs in the Midwest are most likely (89%) to support government witness. Midwestern BICs are, in fact, 20% more supportive of government witness than their counterparts in the West or South.

Table 3-b. Support for Government Witness in 2006 by Age, Sex, Region, and Denomination in Percent

		MC USA	BIC
Age			
	18-25	87*	65
	26-35	81	75
	36-45	81	72
	46-55	84	81
	56-65	85	73
	66 +	80	75
Sex			
	Male	82	77
	Female	83	74
Region			
	East	83	75
	West	84	69
	Midwest	81	89
	South	86	68

Read: "87% of 18- to 25-year-old Mennonites 'support or strongly support' MCC's government witness."

Similar questions with slightly different wording were used in the 1972, 1989, and 2006 surveys. The response options were also somewhat different. Nevertheless, the wording and options of the three surveys are comparable enough to track general trends over time.

Opinions vary on whether the Mennonite Central Committee should maintain an office in Washington, D.C., and in Ottawa, Canada, to be in close contact with government officials to keep aware of matters that affect our church's life and witness and to present the concerns of our churches on matters of war and peace, the draft, and various social issues. Do you tend to favor or disfavor this type of contact with the national government? (1972 Question)

**Table 3-c. Support for Government
Contact in 1972 by Denomination in Percent**

	Mennonites	BICs
I tend to favor	57	56
I am neutral on this	17	19
I tend to disfavor it	12	8
I have no opinion	14	18
Total	100	100

In 1972, the question probed favorability of MCC *contact* with national government. The response scheme permitted a "neutral" response as well as a "no opinion" response, which are difficult to distinguish conceptually. They can arguably be combined into a "not sure" response. Table 3-c shows the Mennonite response frequency for 1972, with 57% favoring, 12% opposing, and 31% not sure. The BICs, with 56% favoring government contact, were virtually identical to the Mennonites; however, 37% of BICs were unsure about the issue.

The Mennonite Central Committee (MCC) maintains offices in Washington, D.C., and in Ottawa, Canada, to present the concerns of our churches on matters of war and peace, the draft, and various social issues. Do you tend to favor or disfavor this type of contact with the national government? (1989 Question)

**Table 3-d. Support for Government
Contact in 1989 by Denomination in Percent**

	MC USA	BIC
I tend to favor	72	69
I am neutral on this	24	27
I tend to disfavor it	5	4
Total	100	100

In 1989, the wording of the question "favor contact" was identical to 1972, but the response of "no opinion" was eliminated and "neutral" was the only option for uncertain respondents. As seen in Table 3-d, 72% of Mennonites favored contact with national government, 5% opposed it, leaving one quarter (24%) uncertain, all of which represented a significant gain in support of government contact among Mennonites. BICs likewise showed an increase in support (69%) and a decline in opposition and uncertainty.

**Table 3-e. Trend in Support for Government
Witness by Year and Denomination in Percent**

	Mennonites			BICs		
	Support	Neutral	Oppose	Support	Neutral	Oppose
1972	57*	31	12	56	37	8
1989	72	24	5	69	27	4
2006	82	13	4	75	22	3

Read: "57% of Mennonites 'support or strongly support' MCC's witness to government in 1972."

As noted before, in 2006 the wording *"witness* to the United States government and the United Nations" and "how much do you support this form of Christian *witness?"* was used in the survey, which arguably may have shifted the meaning from the more innocuous *"contact* with the national government" wording in 1972 and 1989. Nevertheless, the meanings are similar enough to merit comparison over this 35-year period, as shown in Table 3-e. The evidence clearly shows increasing support for government "contact" and "witness" by both Mennonites and BICs from 1972 to 2006 and a decline in opposition and uncertainty. The percentage of Mennonite support for MCC's witness to government increased from 57% to 82% between 1972 and 2006. Similarly, BIC support over the 35-year period grew from 56% to 75%. Thus, by 2006, four out of five Mennonites and three out of four BICs were solidly in support of MCC's Christian witness to the United States government and the United Nations through its offices in Washington, D.C., and New York.

GAP BETWEEN SUPPORT FOR MISSION AND SATISFACTION WITH PROGRAM

Table 3-f. Difference between Support for Mission and Program Satisfaction in 2006 by Denomination in Percent

	MC USA	BIC
Support of Mission	96	92
Support of Gov't Witness	82	75
Satisfaction with Program	79	68
Mission/Program Gap	**17**	**24**

The gap between support for MCC's mission and satisfaction with MCC's program is 17% for Mennonites and 24% for BICs, as shown in Table 3-f. Support for MCC's mission is remarkably high regardless of the influence of social variables such as age, occupation, residence, theological views, political affiliation, and so forth. However, satisfaction with MCC's program and emphases is somewhat influenced by numerous other variables. In other words, Mennonite respondents express high support for MCC's mission, regardless of their social position or cultural values, but how happy they are about what MCC actually does is associated with some cultural factors. For example, as shown in Table 1-f, regardless of whether they voted for Bush or Kerry in the 2004 presidential election, 96-97% of Mennonites supported the mission of MCC.

However, whom they voted for was associated with their support for MCC's government witness through the Washington, D.C., and New York offices. In 2006, 79% of Bush voters supported government witness versus 93% of Kerry voters. Nevertheless, regardless of how they voted, 4 out of 5 Mennonites support these urban bases of witness.

It is not surprising to find a gap between mission support and program satisfaction, for that is typical of the human experience. Human ideals rarely match social reality and incongruities abound between aspirations and actual behavior. There are no magic benchmarks to determine acceptable breaches between hope and performance. In some ways, a 17% slippage among Mennonites seems acceptable. The comparative 24% mismatch among BICs suggests cause for greater concern. Even so, a solid two-thirds (68%) of that denomination show satisfaction with MCC's performance.

THE MYSTERY OF
BROAD-BASED COMMITMENT TO MCC

MCC enjoys very high levels of support for its mission and program satisfaction from Mennonites and slightly lower levels from Brethren in Christ members. Mennonite support for MCC's mission, support of government witness, and program satisfaction are higher than that of BICs. This pattern holds for virtually all the variables and cross-tabulations throughout the study.

The Church Member Profile results are helpful reminders that support for MCC's mission and program satisfaction vary considerably by constituent groups. Moreover and importantly, the Church Member Profile findings only represent two of MCC's constituent groups whose members live in the United States. The voices and votes of Canadians, Amish, Mennonite Brethren, independent Mennonite churches, and many other MCC constituents are missing from this analysis. One may draw robust conclusions about MC USA and BIC perceptions of MCC from this study, but it is risky and unwise to generalize the findings beyond these two denominations.

In much social science research, factors like sex, age, education, and political affiliation are closely associated with religious beliefs, behavior, and commitments to causes and crusades. The commitment of MC USA and BIC members to MCC's mission transcends many of the typical demographic variables that are closely aligned with political participation, views of ethical issues, national movements, and engagement with organizations. Such demographic factors are not aligned with and do not appear to shape commitment to MCC's mission. Mennonite support for MCC, for example, is 96% among youth and elderly. Males and females are only 1% apart and region matters 5% or less (Table 1-b). The views of newcomers and old-timers in the church are virtually identical, and a difference of only 7% separates those who live on farms from urbanites, managers from laborers, and those without high school diplomas and graduate degree holders (Table 1-c).

Even theological identity and differing views of salvation and of Jesus (Table 1-d) cannot drive a wedge into support for MCC's mission, which is 95% or higher across all the categories of these factors. Strikingly, service in the military, political affiliation, and vote in the 2004 presidential election at best muster only a 2% difference among members in their enthusiasm for MCC's mission (Tables 1-e, 1-d).

What is it about the power of the MCC mission that can mobilize such strong and uniform commitment? These remarkably positive stakeholder perceptions suggest that, at least among Mennonites, commitment to MCC's mission is a deep and enduring one that stands independent from typical sources of social influence that are frequently associated with worldviews and perceptions. Although some of the cross-tabulations suggest some leads, the big, unsolved question is why and how MCC came to enjoy such widespread support, especially among Mennonites.

The survey data confirm strong levels of general satisfaction and program support with little variation between subgroups or constituent segments with different ideological orientations. To excavate the nexus of meanings and explanations beneath the surface of these results would require face-to-face interviews or more complex survey instruments. Survey research is always limited by the questions posed and the findings of this study hinge on two broad questions that may invite strong levels of support.

The first question, the one that taps satisfaction, is expansive and somewhat vague when it asks respondents if they are satisfied *"in general* with the program and emphases of MCC." Someone who dislikes a particular activity may nonetheless be content with the larger mix and intent of MCC's programs in general. Similarly, while not happy with a specific venture, one might be satisfied with MCC's general attempt to help others in the name of Christ. In addition, many respondents may not know much about particular programs but may have a warm emotional response to the broad scope of work, which this question probes.

The second question may be hard to reject without some pangs of guilt. Would anyone be comfortable categorically opposing a virtuous mission of "demonstrating God's love by working among people suffering from poverty, conflict, oppression, and natural disaster"? Support for such a socially desirable statement may indicate more about what people think they should affirm that what they actually do.

MCC's broad menu of programs—relief sales, material aid, international development, peace education, gender issues, refugee assistance, and so on—provides points of affinity for various interest groups. Some constituents may hone in on a particular program that reflects their vested interest and not attend to others that they might find distasteful. It is also possible that respondents hold deep convictions about the importance of service "in the name of Christ," convictions so salient and compelling that they transcend the socio-contextual identities of gender, age, political affiliation, residence, and theological orientation that often trump such convictions. Finally, people may project their expectations on MCC and imagine that it reflects their values and sensitivities more perfectly than it actually does, especially those who have little firsthand knowledge of MCC's actual operations. For example, different subgroups may project onto MCC what they want to see by focusing on the programs that resonate the most with them and filter out the rest.

These speculative scenarios that might explain the mystery of constituent support should not distract us from one overwhelming fact: support for MCC, at least among MC USA and BIC members is rather strong.

NOTES

1. The Senior Project Director for the three-denominational study was Donald B. Kraybill (Elizabethtown College, Pa.). Denominational directors were Conrad L. Kanagy (Mennonite Church USA; Elizabethtown College, Pa.), Carl D. Bowman (Church of the Brethren; Bridgewater College, Va.), and Ron Burwell (Brethren in Christ; Messiah College, Pa.). The CMP2006 label refers to the overall project, whereas the results of the two denominations (MC USA and BIC) reported in this paper are referenced as a Mennonite Member Profile and Brethren in Christ Member Profile (BCMP2006), respectively.

2. In general, the CMP2006 methodology followed the template of Don A. Dillman's *Mail and Internet Surveys*, 2nd. ed. (New York: John Wiley and Sons, Inc., 2000). Several enhancements were added to bolster the response rate.

3. The findings of the first Church Member Profile were reported in J. Howard Kauffman and Leland Harder, *Anabaptists Four Centuries Later: A Profile of Five Mennonite and Brethren in Christ Denominations* (Scottdale, Pa.: Herald Press, 1975). J. Howard Kauffman and Leo Driedger, *The Mennonite Mosaic* (Scottdale, Pa.: Herald Press, 1991), summarized the findings of the second study in 1989. In addition, Leland Harder, in *Doors to Lock and to Open: The Discerning People of God* (Scottdale, Pa.: Herald Press, 1993), prepared a congregational guide for discussion related to the 1989 survey.

4. The initial mailing was followed by two reminder postcards, an additional questionnaire (to non-respondents), an email reminder to pastors, and a phone call to non-respondents (with listed telephone numbers) in late April. The cut-off for receiving questionnaires was May 10. A short two-minute interview was conducted with a random sample of non-respondents to determine any non-response bias patterns.

5. George Gallup Jr. and D. Michael Lindsay, *The Gallup Guide: Reality Check of 21st Century Churches* (Princeton: The Gallup Organization, 2002). Although 2,216 Mennonites and 733 BICs returned useable questionnaires, not all respondents answered every question. Thus, the number of respondents in some of the tables in this paper may be less than 2,216 (Mennonites) or 733 (BICs) if some people did not answer one of the questions related to MCC.

6. Canadian BIC congregations were not included, nor were Spanish-speaking congregations in the Miami, Florida, area. Ron Burwell (Messiah College) did a later survey of the Canadian congregations using similar questions.

7. The 2006 results have been statistically weighted for sex and congregational response rate so that respondent answers reflect the distribution of these factors in the original sample.

8. A 3% margin of error means that if we discover that 80% of respondents "support MCC," the actual percentage may range 3% above or below 80%. In other words, the true response may range between 77% and 83% due to sampling and measurement errors.

9. See Conrad L. Kanagy, *Road Signs for the Journey: A Profile of Mennonite Church USA* (Scottdale, Pa.: Herald Press, 2007), for an overview of the survey findings for MC USA. Carl Desportes Bowman, *Portrait of a People: The Church of the Brethren at 300* (Elgin, Ill.: Brethren Press, 2008), summarizes the results of the Church of the Brethren survey.

10. Throughout the analysis and narrative of this report, respondents who "strongly support" and just "support" MCC's mission were combined into a single category of "support." The primary form of analysis throughout this article involves percentage differences *within* MC USA and BIC respondents and *between* MC USA and BIC respondents. Differences between vertical percentages under the MC USA column in the tables show the relative strength of association of factors, such as age or sex, on Mennonite attitudes toward MCC. Horizontal comparisons of percentages between MC USA and BIC columns show the difference that denomination makes on attitudes toward MCC among respondents who are alike in age or sex. Any differences of 5% or less may be miniscule due to measurement or sampling errors.

11. The tables that show associations between one of the three primary MCC questions and various social and political variables typically focus on two or three categories of some variables rather than all the answer options. This selective use of extreme categories was done to simplify tables and make a more efficient and parsimonious analysis.

12. The narrative analysis related to the tables that involve satisfaction with MCC's program combines "very satisfied" with "satisfied" for an overall "satisfied" category but does not include "partly satisfied." The latter response is considered more ambivalent and similar to "not sure."

13. Mennonite respondents in 1972 and 1989 consist of members of the Mennonite Church and the General Conference Mennonite Church who were 18 years of age or older and who lived in the United States. The combined number of such respondents was N=1,382 in 1972 and N=1,110 in 1989. The number of respondents of MC USA in 2006 was N=2,216. The number of BIC respondents (18 years of age and older and living in the United States) for the respective surveys was N=198 (1972), N=255 (1989), and N=685 (2006).

Chapter 6

MCC's Relationship with "Plain" Anabaptists in Historical Perspective

STEVEN M. NOLT

Mennonite Central Committee's origins in 1920 were remarkably inter-Mennonite, drawing into common cause groups representing different geographic centers, ethnic streams, immigration cohorts, and theological perspectives. During the nine decades that followed, MCC has continued to work across a strikingly broad Anabaptist spectrum—and, in fact, has often engendered a sense of Anabaptist identity that transcends constituent groups.[1] At the same time, the diversity of and among Mennonite and Mennonite-related groups in North America has grown since 1920, making the task of Mennonite ecumenics more complex. This increase in variety has coincided with shifts in the relative size of constituencies, with, for example, the so-called "plain groups"—old order and culturally traditional Amish and Mennonites—swelling in absolute number and in their share of the North American Anabaptist pie.[2]

Among MCC's constituent relationships, the ties with so-called plain churches[3] have been distinctive in several respects, including the old orders' inherent skepticism of institutions, some plain groups' resistance to members traveling overseas, and conservative churches' bias for supporting practical relief measures over more complex development strategies. Moreover, old order and plain church identities have not been static, and their reformulation during the course of the twentieth century has had significant implications for these groups' relationships with other Anabaptists. And, of course, MCC's ministry and structure has evolved over time, adding another layer to the history of this relationship.[4]

Behind all of these potential complexities is the notion of *constituency*, of groups constituting something else. In many ways the MCC canopy covers an imagined Anabaptist world—and who imagines whom in relationship to what is always in flux.[5] For example, mainline Mennonite[6] assumptions in 1955 about who constituted close spiritual kin were not the same as they had been in 1900—or are today. For example, in the mid-twentieth century few mainline Mennonites believed they had much in common with old order Anabaptists, or that old orders would even survive the advance of time.[7] Today, however, many mainline Mennonites are apt to claim some connection to the Old Order Amish, often by interpreting old order practices through one of several modern lenses, such as First Amendment religious rights or concern for the environment. Of course, old orders may understand themselves quite differently and imagine their connection to mainline Mennonites on other grounds, if at all.

In practical terms, MCC constituency relationships might be read historically in two related but distinct ways. First, MCC sometimes *represented constituent values* to others (often to state authority). Second, MCC *recognized constituent resources*, cultivating and connecting them to programs and building local relationships. Both efforts suggest something of the limitations and success of Anabaptist ecumenics. During the 1950s to the 1970s, an unusual dynamism in plain-group identity produced a new set of distinctly "plain" institutions that sometimes displaced MCC. Meanwhile, changes within MCC, particularly U.S. regionalization after 1980, resulted in a renewed recognition of resources within plain communities that in turn has fostered constituency.

SUCCESSES AND LIMITATIONS IN THE REPRESENTATION OF OLD ORDER VALUES

MCC's relationship with self-consciously traditionalist constituents began about 1940, when MCC was resurrected as an inter-Mennonite umbrella organization to coordinate Mennonite responses to World War II conscription.[8] In the United States MCC oversaw a system of Civilian Public Service camps where conscientious objectors (COs) worked in lieu of military assignments.[9] MCC administered 89 camps, involving some 5,000 COs, almost all of whom were Mennonites, Amish, or Brethren in Christ. Given its new mission and domestic agenda during these years, MCC's board expanded, assigning new seats to major parties participating in CPS: Church of God in Christ "Holdeman" Mennonites and Brethren in Christ in 1940, Conservative Amish Mennonite Conference in 1941, and Old Order Amish in 1942.[10]

The Old Order Amish representative to MCC was Shipshewana, Indiana, Bishop Eli J. Bontrager (1868-1958), who served on the board from 1942-1953. Bontrager tried to visit each CPS camp with Amish participants, once traveling more than 16,000 miles in a five-month period. He also donated some of his own books to CPS camp libraries.[11]

Amish participation in CPS was strong—much stronger, in fact, than that of most other MCC constituencies. Some 97 percent of drafted Old Order Amish men chose alternative service and almost exclusively worked in MCC camps.[12] Old Order churches supported CPS financially, the Amish giving more than $345,000 (the third largest amount provided by any group, and 12 percent of all donations to MCC-CPS) and Old Order Mennonites donating $43,137.[13] Amish CPS participants often forged friendships with fellow Mennonite campers, still evident in oral interviews decades later. Such men continued to connect MCC with their positive CPS memories (sometimes treating MCC and CPS as interchangeable), attended CPS reunions, and seemed to have been socialized into an imagined Anabaptist world defined by CPS participation.[14]

During the 1950s, MCC remained the structure for managing alternative service, which after 1952 participants commonly called the "I-W program," owing to the government classification code associated with such work. The I-W program differed significantly from the older CPS system, and mainline Mennonites, including MCC Peace Section staff, had invested a good deal of energy in negotiating the new rules. By the end of World War II mainline Mennonites had come to see CPS as problematic because COs received no pay, often worked in isolated rural locations, and lived in community units with a good deal of paternalistic oversight and little discretionary time. In contrast, the new I-W arrangement allowed COs to earn prevailing wages in nonprofit service agencies—typically as orderlies or custodians in urban hospitals—while living independently and managing their off-hours.[15] Yet these features were precisely the things that made I-W problematic for old orders and some culturally traditional Anabaptist groups, such as the Beachy Amish, all of whom were troubled by the program's lack of community and accountability, not to mention the system's frank encouragement of individual urban lifestyle.[16] The decentralized nature of the I-W system also meant that Amish alternative service experience during these years was not closely linked to MCC or to a broader sense of Anabaptist community.[17]

The Vietnam War's upward pressure on draft boards to increase conscription numbers only compounded old order anxieties and a sense that MCC was not actively representing conservatives' concerns to the government.[18] In 1966 Amish leaders from several states meeting in Indiana confirmed that "practically all church leaders . . . agreed that the present I-W system of so many of our boys going to the hospital [urban employment] is proving very unsatisfactory and harmful to our Amish Churches."[19]

A delegation went to Washington, D.C., to meet with J. Harold Sherk, MCC Peace Section staffer seconded to the National Service Board for Religious Objectors, to express their concerns. Minutes of that meeting are thin, but that evening, meeting alone in their hotel, the Amish decided they would need to form their own standing committee to act as a liaison to government and no longer rely on MCC, noting "the feeling . . . that the Old Order Amish are following too closely in the steps of the Mennonites, which is undermining our Amish way of life."[20] At a final meeting with Sherk in January 1967, the Amish announced they wanted to ask for Selective Service farm deferments, but Sherk was "rather reluctant" to represent such a cause, even though the "it was explained [to him] that more [Amish] churches are seriously considering taking the jail rather than going to the hospitals."[21] In the end—perhaps to the surprise of mainline Mennonites—Selective Service accepted the old order proposal and Amish participation in I-W work ended.

Meanwhile, this new Amish coordinating committee was feeling its way into uncharted organizational waters—including finding a name. Here the ambiguity of relationship with MCC was apparent. Midwestern leaders, who were among the key players (including the secretary and treasurer) in the new endeavor, argued for the name Amish Central Committee, suggesting that the group was replacing MCC. In the end, chairman Andrew Kinsinger (1920-1995), whose Lancaster County, Pennsylvania, residence placed him in geographic proximity to Washington, D.C., and made him the natural direct contact with federal officials, chose Amish Steering Committee.[22]

As the Old Order Amish took responsibility for representing themselves on matters of conscientious objection, they withdrew from the MCC board.[23] When board member Ammon Troyer died at the end of 1962, he was never replaced. The highly decentralized nature of old order church life no doubt contributed to the difficulty in identifying a replacement to fill such a position. But Amish unease with MCC as their mouthpiece seems to have been a factor; after all, Amish leaders were able to assemble their own modest organization within a few weeks in fall 1966 when they thought a committee would be useful.[24] In contrast, MCC—at least the binational organization—seems to have become less useful for old orders. Their relationship with MCC had formed after 1940 around pressing common concerns of conscription. As mainline Mennonite and old order conscientious objection ideals diverged in the Vietnam era, so did the connection between Amish and MCC. Members of the CPS generation retained warm memories of MCC, but those were not memories of the next generation.

RETOOLING THE
REPRESENTATIONAL RELATIONSHIP

Even as the formal relationship between MCC and old orders around military matters was coming to an end, two new patterns of relationships emerged, both of which pointed to future possibilities. The first example was in Ontario, where the provincial MCC (reorganized in 1962) saw its mission as supporting Ontario Mennonites and Amish in almost all facets of their witness. In other words, MCC Ontario would not simply be a regional conduit to Akron, Pennsylvania, but would develop its own domestic agenda growing out of locally identified needs.[25] Old order representatives had been members of one of MCC Ontario's predecessors, a war-era committee of Historic Peace Churches. But there was no Cold War draft in Canada and no parting of the ways over how to seek conscientious objection as had occurred south of the border: old order voices remained present in the new MCC Ontario. As a result, MCC Ontario worked with old order and other plain groups not so much by channeling those groups' energies toward grander MCC goals but rather by supporting tradionalists in the causes those groups chose—even though that meant that MCC Ontario sometimes pursued divergent ends.

MCC Ontario staff and financial resources backed Amish immigration to Canada, fought for old order exemption from the Canadian Pension Plan (a drawn-out battle during 1966-1974), and negotiated alternatives to jury duty, Social Insurance Numbers, compulsory school laws, and certain milk marketing regulations.[26] This contextually responsive orientation on the part of MCC Ontario won the respect of provincial plain groups, who have continued to see MCC as a resource and trusted spokesperson. For MCC Ontario, such work has become, in the words of Lucille Marr, "part of the postmodern framework" in which "the particularity of each situation" trumps otherwise overarching commitments to equality.[27]

A different pattern emerged in the United States. There, about 1970 MCC Peace Section began supporting third-party litigation on behalf of old orders—initially a high-profile case involving Amish parents who refused to send their children to public high schools. John A. Lapp, an academic and the Peace Section's director from 1969-1972, aligned MCC with the Amish cause via the interfaith National Committee for Amish Religious Freedom, a panel headed by a Lutheran pastor that took the lead in litigating on behalf of the Amish.[28] The key case, *Wisconsin v. Yoder*, eventually landed in the U.S. Supreme Court, which ruled in favor of the Amish in 1972. Lapp transported Pennsylvania Amish to hear the arguments in Washington and established a precedent of MCC financing Amish legal causes through third parties. Lapp was sympathetic to Amish convictions—unlike many mainline Mennonites who dismissed or derided Amish objections to high school—but he framed MCC support for Amish values with progressive notions of religious liberty that were consistent with liberal ideals.[29]

Following Lapp's precedent, the MCC Peace Section (later folded into MCC U.S.) has continued to fund and provide some logistical support for first amendment litigation coordinated by the National Committee for Religious Freedom.[30] For a number of reasons, however, by the late twentieth century such court cases almost exclusively involved the most sectarian of old orders whose intransigence versus the state is part-and-parcel of a highly separatist worldview that also makes them the least likely people to be involved with MCC work or to acknowledge progressive Mennonites as spiritual kin![31] In some ways, then, MCC U.S. advocacy in this instance is less a case of representing a constituency (as in Ontario) as much as it is a parallel to MCC justice work on behalf of, say, a marginalized non-Anabaptist group in Asia.

MCC AS CONDUIT FOR AMISH CHARITY

Alongside representation of constituent interests, MCC also serves as a resource for expressing constituent vales, particularly charitable giving. During and immediately following World War II,

MCC's work expanded into European refugee relief of various kinds, but most dramatically aiding Mennonites fleeing the Soviet Union. MCC's assistance to these Russian Mennonites proved a dramatic chapter of escape from the Soviet-occupied zone of Germany and re-settlement amid hardship in Paraguay.

In 1947 MCC workers Peter and Elfrieda Dyck, who worked closely with this effort, intinerated across North America raising funds for this aspect of MCC work. Indeed, the Dycks soon became the face of MCC and their story remained the definition of MCC's mission for more than a generation.[32] Because the Dycks showed a home movie about the refugees, few old orders attend their presenta-tions, but MCC executive Orie O. Miller arranged for Peter Dyck to speak to a Lancaster, Pennsylvania, Amish group. As Dyck later re-called this "first encounter with the plain people," the house was packed with adults, and his story of the hapless Russian Mennonites brought tears of compassion to the audience. Afterward, the group took an impromptu collection and handed Dyck a large amount of cash—uncounted and without any interest in receiving receipts or ac-knowledgement.[33]

Charitable giving has long been a practice among old orders,[34] but one that is difficult to track with any precision, given traditional-ists' concern to give anonymously—although children growing up in Amish families certainly got the message. One sixty-five-year-old Old Order Amish writer, recently reflecting on the spiritually forma-tive influences of his youth, cited his mother's feeding traveling hobos and "how Dad would always give generously to solicitors (fire companies, MCC drives, etc)."[35] To the degree that old orders consid-ered giving an obligation, fulfilling a command of Christ, charity was an end in itself. It was not a means to some other end, such as funding evangelism or development work—causes that animated Anabap-tists who operated with more rational worldviews. As a result, giving to "relief"—which characterized much of MCC's work in the 1940s and 1950s—matched Amish aims.[36]

At the same time, the specific nature of MCC relief work was doubly appealing to traditionalists because it allowed conservative Anabaptists to aid "suffering people of their own Anabaptist faith."[37] The themes of suffering—and especially of suffering under atheistic communism— made MCC's relief work with Russian Mennonites appealing to old orders closely attuned to an identity steeped in the *Martyrs Mirror*. The story of Russian Mennonite suffering resonated with traditionalists, serving as a latter-day recapitulation of six-teenth-century suffering.

But Peter Dyck's 1947 encounter, by his own account, also illustrated the way in which the Amish stood on the periphery for MCC. Old orders were difficult to contact, had no centralized organization, and resisted the new media, such as home movies, which MCC used to arrange otherwise effective and efficient itineration. As well, it seems safe to imagine that MCC staff shared the common mid-century mainline Mennonite assumption that old orders were a fading group who did not figure in North America's Anabaptist future.[38] Nevertheless, some old orders did become involved in the various grassroots MCC fundraising efforts launched by more progressive neighbors, such as the (Old) Mennonite-organized Gap (Pa.) Relief sale. That biennial auction begun in 1948 drew on neighborly contributions and labor from Old Order and Beachy Amish women and men, following a wartime-pattern of cooperative support for CPS camp needs.[39] And nationally, many old order and conservative Anabaptists participated in Mennonite Disaster Service from its earlier years.[40]

MCC as a channel for quiet, unobtrusive giving to relieve wartime and refugee suffering, particularly as it related to Russian refugees, but also to practical refugee causes generally, continued—and in many ways persists. Nevertheless, events in the 1950s-1970s realigned the values that defined plain people and with whom they imagined they shared much in common. To the degree that giving is about establishing and maintaining relationships, these dynamics were bound to reshape constituency.

CHANGING DYNAMICS OF PLAIN GROUP IDENTITY, 1950s-1970s

Although plain Anabaptists have never been frozen in time, the roughly quarter century from the late 1940s through the early 1970s was a particularly dynamic time in the reformulation of identity and were marked by two major developments. The first was a wide-ranging and controversial "mission movement" that emerged in most Old Order Amish settlements during the decade and a half following World War II. A significant number of Amish, especially young adults, promoted a sort of activism that sought both to reform old order social life and witness to outsiders in formal ways. Promoters sought to curb deviant youth behavior and encourage a more introspective devotional life. They also held mission conferences, distributed mission literature to thousands of Amish homes, and funded Old Order mission workers in Arkansas, Mississippi, and Ontario.

Several dozen attended college to obtain the formal credentials they believed such efforts entailed—and they did these all as old order church members.[41]

By the early to mid-1960s a clear reaction had set in, apparently ending for good the possibility of old order churches blessing formal mission work, proselytism, or higher education. Mission movement advocates moved out of the old order orbit, taking their commitments to assertive, reformist, and organizationally oriented ways into various Beachy Amish and conservative Mennonite churches, and thereby often reshaping those fellowships. For example, the Beachy Amish were suddenly infused with mission-minded members and the church adopted the movement's Mission Interests Committee. Evangelism, not car ownership, now became a leading marker of what it meant to be Beachy Amish. When Beachy Amish leaders organized Amish Mennonite Aid in 1955 to work with refugees in Europe, they assumed that evangelistic witness would accompany relief.[42] Meanwhile, in 1966 in Ohio a group that came to be known as the New Order Amish emerged, seeking a moderate mission path. New Orders encouraged indirect support for missions rather than establishing their own board or missionaries.[43]

The second major development that reshaped the plain world was a proliferation of culturally and theologically conservative Swiss Mennonite groups that swarmed from more progressive Mennonite conferences during the 1960s and 1970s.[44] These groups had never been old order but were heirs of a mainline Mennonite organizational renaissance of the early twentieth century, fully embracing verbal mission work, publication efforts, and the utility of boards and committees (but often suspicious of colleges). At the same time, they stressed plain dress, limiting interaction with mass media, and traditional gender roles.[45] Indeed, these groups typically were not merely attempting to "stop the clock" of cultural change, but actually became "plainer" and erected more marks of social separation from the world after splitting with Mennonite moderates.[46] Such groups, including the Eastern Pennsylvania Mennonite Church, Southeastern Conference, Nationwide Fellowship, Midwest Fellowship, and others, added a new cast of plain characters to the Anabaptist drama. On the one hand they could be quite critical of old order reticence to evangelize, yet they were often highly suspicious of mainline Mennonite organizations, which they viewed as compromised.[47] Some of these new plain Mennonites were influenced theologically by popular evangelical authors and radio speakers, but others, rejecting radios, were not.[48]

Taken together, these developments made for a more complex Anabaptist world by the mid-1970s, a world that included groups many observers lumped together as "plain people"—and who did share some commonalities but whose dispositions were often different. Old Order Amish and Mennonites were generally suspicious of formalized mission work, evangelical religious language, and heavy involvement with bureaucratic organizations.[49] For the Beachy Amish and the new plain evangelicals, however, traditional mores were now a mode of engagement with the world, often for evangelistic ends, and not a sign of withdrawal. Their distancing themselves from mainline Mennonite projects was a prelude to finding alternatives. Finally, some old order car-driving groups, such as Wisler, Markham, and Weaverland Mennonites, were somewhere in the middle, though by the 1990s many were moving toward the plain evangelicals.

These developments in the plain sphere of Anabaptist life coincided with important organizational and philosophical changes at MCC, including a shift in policy toward economic development and professionalized staff and projects. Some of these changes emerged directly from educated Mennonites' request for assignments that would use their college training (Teachers Abroad Program, for example), others emerged from communities and organizations with which MCC worked outside North America requesting workers with specialized training, and others were driven by educated Mennonites whose theologies linked peace with justice and who increasingly addressed complex problems with long-term perspectives. Moreover, much of MCC's highest profile work no longer involved other Mennonites and in fact often involved non-Christians. If in the 1940s old orders saw MCC as a congenial vehicle for feeding the hungry, by the late 1970s the widening array of plain groups and the evolving nature of MCC's mission meant that no such single or simple relationship was likely.

A NEW WORLD OF PLAIN INSTITUTIONS AND RELATIONSHIPS

As the plain world percolated during the 1970s, new ideas and initiatives combined with traditional impulses, and, in the hands of innovative leaders, produced new institutions and relationships.[50] One notable figure was David A. Bontrager (1915-1989), a Beachy Amish bishop near Goshen, Indiana, who melded mission movement ideals with a time-honored Anabaptist preferential option for the suffering church.[51] For Bontrager, and, it turned out, many old order and tradition-minded Anabaptists, the contemporary Christians whose experience most called to mind their sixteenth-century forebears were those in Soviet-dominated Eastern Europe.

In 1976 Bontrager launched "Jesus to the Iron Curtain Newsletter," seeking to raise awareness of religious persecution and soliciting money for Bible smuggling.[52] Bontrager's influence was greatest in Beachy Amish circles, but his message appealed to some other plain people, notably New Order Amish. In May 1978 New Orders from Holmes County, Ohio, started Iron Curtain Ministries to raise money for Bontrager's efforts and, starting in April 1980, appealed directly to Amish readers through a biweekly column in *The Budget* entitled "Our Suffering Brethren."[53]

The use of the term *brethren* was not a claim that the Protestants in Eastern Europe were Anabaptists; rather, the claim was akin to that made in van Braught's *Martyrs Mirror*, that a suffering church is a faithful and true church.[54] Indeed, sympathy for churches suffering under Soviet domination had been part of the message conveyed by Peter Dyck and through other MCC literature in the 1940s and 1950s—though that MCC story had typically been told in terms of suffering *Mennonites*.

By the 1970s, MCC work with Mennonite refugees had largely ended, and in fact MCC had come to downplay overt criticism of the Soviet Union so as to allow the possibility of engagement with Soviet Baptists.[55] While there is little evidence that plain groups directly rejected MCC's new approach, they clearly were attracted to messages such as Bontrager's for the same reasons they had found MCC's work appealing in the 1940s.

One of the New Order Amish men who was deeply impressed with Bontrager's activism was David N. Troyer.[56] Troyer's uncommon energy and vision eventually produced Christian Aid Ministries, the leading plain Anabaptist parachurch ministry of the twenty-first century. Engaged as he was with Iron Curtain Ministries, Troyer realized that "we were kind of limited to informing people about conditions . . . and I wanted to do more than inform." Troyer worked at a lumber company where he was accustomed to making contacts and shipping goods globally. As well, he was on the mailing lists of "all kinds of [mission] organizations." In 1981 he organized a New Order effort to ship gift packages through Berlin to eastern European Christians. It was a legal, but expensive and inefficient, enterprise; nevertheless, it was a concrete way to express solidarity with the suffering church, and plain people's faith was nothing if not oriented toward the tangible. Interest in shipping goods and literature grew as word of the possibility spread.[57]

In 1983 Troyer's small organization moved to an entirely new level as he negotiated to ship large amounts of food and Christian literature directly to Romania, Eastern Europe's maverick state desperate for food and unusually eager to curry favor in the West. At a pivotal 1983 meeting in the World Trade Center, Troyer negotiated transport to Romania via an Israeli shipping company.[58] Food would arrive by rail and Protestant Romanian partners would deliver it to warehouses in trucks that Troyer's group, now known as Christian Aid to Romania, would supply. Romanians would then go to the warehouses, taking a card they received from a partnering Protestant church that authorized them to pick up a food parcel. During the meeting a Romanian official surreptitiously told Troyer, "We know who you are and what you are doing, and we want to help you do it."[59]

For the next four year Christian Aid to Romania expanded its circle of supports in North America and its contacts within Romania. When Bucharest abruptly halted shipments in late 1987, Christian Aid shifted gears and by April 1988 was sending aid to Nicaragua and Haiti (building somewhat on established Beachy Amish work there; Troyer had by this time left the New Order Amish for the Beachy Amish), and soon also in Liberia, all under the new name Christian Aid Ministries.[60] The end of the Cold War allowed CAM to return to Romania but also shifted the locus of the suffering church. Although a commitment to Eastern Europe (Romania, Moldova, and Ukraine) has remained, by 2008-2009 much of CAM's new work was taking place in Muslim countries along with some clandestine programs in China.[61]

During these years CAM mushroomed, becoming a major mediator and shaper of plain Mennonite and Amish life. In 2008 CAM operated in 35 countries—seven of which hosted permanent office facilities, schools, or orphanages, with the rest receiving shipments of material aid or aid and Christian literature. In an additional 54 countries CAM only distributed Christian literature. In all, CAM estimated that its work touched more than six million people that year, which was a highpoint in the volume of goods—a volume that included, among other things, $150 million worth of medical and nutritional supplies, more than 75,000 food parcels, more than 3.7 million Bibles and doctrinal books, almost 30,000 pair of new shoes, and some 24,700 comforters.

In 2008 CAM received $24.8 million in cash donations.[62] (MCC received about $36.6 million in cash and relief sale proceeds for roughly the same year.[63]) Most of CAM's income, however, is in the form of gift-in-kind contributions, which accounted for 86 percent of CAM's contributions in 2008.[64] A small staff and hundreds of volunteers process donations at a network of warehouse and shipping facilities that CAM established in the 1990s in Illinois, Indiana, Iowa, Ohio, Ontario, and Pennsylvania, the last of which also housed a stationary meat canning operation not unlike MCC's.[65]

CAM's shape and growth reflect several of the evolving features of North America's plain Anabaptists, including their new liquid wealth. A shift away from farming, in which wealth was often tied up in commodities, to small businesses and self-employment means that liquidity and cash donations are now commonplace.[66]

But CAM's approach and the people it brings together are also novel. Throughout *its* history MCC often understood itself as bringing Mennonites together without the burden of extensive theologizing. After all, since the initial partners in MCC already had active mission boards in 1920, MCC could cede questions of evangelism and church polity to those entities. But for old order and other plain groups that did not (and perhaps still do not) have formal structures for evangelism, or who withdrew their support from the established Mennonite mission agencies during the 1960s and 1970s, an entity such as CAM, which mixes evangelism with material aid and disaster relief, is appealing. Such an entity is viewed as offering a "holistic" approach aligned with their values.[67] CAM has thus been able to attract various plain people who find added value in CAM's relief work as well as conservatives alienated from mainline Mennonite institutions and, often by extension, from MCC.[68]

Measured in terms of its formal organization, CAM is a largely Beachy Amish organization, since members of that church dominate CAM's board, and CAM's Statement of Faith closely mirrors one published by that church's *Calvary Messenger*.[69] Yet the national board and regional support committees have also included members of the Conservative Mennonite Conference, Conservative Mennonite Church of Ontario, Wisler Mennonites, Weaverland Conference Mennonites, New and Old Order Amish, and various independent Mennonites. Moreover, CAM's range of volunteers and donors is even larger and more varied that its formal organization.[70] The about 60,000 volunteer hours logged annually in the various North American clothing centers and warehouses vary somewhat from region to region. For example, Old Order Amish are conspicuously involved in Kalona, Iowa, and Shipshewana, Indiana; Wisler Mennonites are especially active in Shipshewana, as well, and

Weaverland Mennonites play a prominent role at Ephrata, Pennsylvania.[71]

The genius of CAM is the way it manages such a broad coalition, allowing participants to regard it as a friendly environment for acting on diverse plain agendas.[72] For CAM's core supporters—Beachy Amish, New Order Amish, and traditionalist Mennonites such as the Mid-Atlantic Fellowship—CAM effectively mixes traditional, practical material relief aid to impoverished or disaster-struck areas around the world with verbal evangelism in the form of Bible distribution, and more recently, billboard evangelism in North America.[73] And since these groups are fairly congregational in polity, they have few large denominational institutions that might compete with CAM.

Meanwhile, Old Order Mennonites and Amish, who are suspicious of verbal mission work, can engage CAM's practical, hands-on material aid packaging or donate cash for seeds or assemble school kits, much as they would (and often simultaneously do) support similar MCC projects. At the same time, CAM also provides a congenial venue for old orders who discreetly sympathize with an evangelical agenda privately to support orphan sponsorships or Bible distribution.

Managing a diverse constituency has its challenges, and CAM sometimes walks a fine line when discussing its evangelistic work. "We're not a church planting agency," David Troyer stressed in 2008, but churches have grown out of CAM work, and "that's ultimately what we're after."[74] Indeed, a bulletin board in CAM's board room announced, "The main reason for CAM to be involved in International Crisis projects is the opportunities these tragedies bring to be a Christian witness and to distribute Christian literature, sometimes in very dark places of the world."[75] The problem with church planting is not only that some old orders are cool to evangelism, but that CAM's diverse supporters who do support mission work each have different expectations of the disciplined Christian life. Overseas expatriate staff are expected to uphold their respective church standards, but it could be problematic for CAM to align with any one of them.

In many ways CAM's low-key, but direct promotional approach fosters diverse constituent interests. Its promotional literature repeatedly emphasizes that donors can choose the type of projects they wish to support—in effect, implying that CAM does not determine a particular agenda so much as makes available an array of possibilities from which donors can choose.[76] CAM has no web site, issues no press releases, and conducts no real advertising apart from direct mailing and a photo wall calendar. "We keep it simple, get to the point, and supporters appreciate that," David Troyer explained in 2008.

In the end, what unifies this constituency is a sense that CAM's "primary purpose is to provide a trustworthy, efficient channel for Amish, Mennonite, and other conservative Anabaptist groups and individuals to minister to physical and spiritual needs around the world."[77] Trust derives from a sense of working with "our people"— visually distinct from the world—and efficiency suggests practical, commonsensical relief in contrast to more complex or abstract notions of development. CAM's motive is explicitly Christian, although promotional materials leave the question of proselytism ambiguous. The audience and activities are reinforcing. Because many CAM supporters will volunteer time in North America but not live or travel oversees, CAM projects are light on expatriate staff and heavy on distribution of material aid or disaster relief. In turn, such work attracts Anabaptists who value such work and may be loath to leave home.

Although CAM is the most significant new institutional expression of plain values and cooperation, it is not alone.[78] In 1992, following Hurricane Andrew, a coalition of plain Mennonites organized volunteers to help with cleanup, thus birthing Disaster Response Services, an organization much like Mennonite Disaster Service.[79] DRS often works alongside MDS and hesitates to criticize MDS, but, as one CAM staffer admitted, "some of our people just feel less comfortable in some MDS situations. They find themselves working on a roof next to women in very revealing clothing and they are not sure that it a consistent witness." Indeed, DRS work typically combines physical reconstruction efforts with witnessing in the form of Sunday street evangelism meetings.[80] Weaverland Conference Mennonites have started a similar program known as Weaverland Disaster Service. In 2005 in the wake of Hurricane Katrina, an alliance of Old Order and Spring Garden Amish from Lancaster, Pennsylvania, formed CARE because it was too hard to find MDS placements that fit their work schedules. Said one, "There is enough work for all of us, so I don't see [us] and MDS as competing."[81]

In 2005 churches closely associated with CAM launched the Conservative Anabaptist Service Program, also under CAM auspices, "to provide a Selective Service System-approved place of employment for conscientious objectors to serve their required time should a draft be activated by the US government." CASP is piloting voluntary service units that have a "minimal code of conduct" for leisure time and discipline, while allowing churches freedom "to administer their own program" and "responsibility to control their own work projects and [COs'] associations and influences."[82]

RECOGNIZING RESOURCES: PLAIN MENNONITES AS AN MCC CONSTITUENCY (AGAIN)

In 1980, about the same time that CAM was getting off the ground, MCC in the United States began a significant restructuring process, creating four regional MCCs (e.g., MCC East Coast), each with a mandate to connect with supporting churches. This structure encouraged assisting constituents in carrying out MCC's mission in localized ways, which meant that MCC, broadly speaking, would be involved in more domestic projects and roles, much as MCC Canada had been doing. Regionalization also meant that MCC's local programming and constituent base would vary from region to region.

MCC East Coast, which included the largest numbers of plain church members of any MCC region, began to recognize—in a real sense, for the first time—these groups' resources and helped connect them with projects that appealed to them and were consistent with MCC's mission.[83] Observers credit Lowell Detweiler, who began serving as East Coast executive in 1980, and Lynn Roth, who assumed the role in 1989, for this shift, which became publicly apparent during the 1990s.[84] Detweiler knew plain group leaders through MDS and assumed they should be full partners in MCC work, while Roth diplomatically worked to include old order voices in decision making. MCC East Coast added board representation for Weaverland Conference Mennonites, Groffdale Conference (Old Order) Mennonites, and Old Order Amish in 1980, 1986, and 1990.[85]

MCC East Coast also created staff positions dedicated to connecting with plain groups, adding liaison work to Ken Sensenig's portfolio in 1996 and later hiring a Beachy Amish staff member. MCC's investment in a new mobile meat canner in 1993 hinged on a decision to make hands-on service opportunities available close to home for people committed to traditional forms of relief ministry. Today, plain Mennonites and Amish provide most of the canner's labor.[86] Old Order Amish men and women have also taken primary responsibility for the Gap Relief Sale, which has grown under their leadership, and which, for a time, included an innovative "Houses Against Hunger" component.[87]

Old Order Amish in Pennsylvania, who for various reasons have been less connected to CAM than are Amish in the Midwest, remain "the single largest identifiable cohort at the [MCC] Material Resource Center," in Ephrata, Pennsylvania, according to Sensenig. "We would not be doing what we're doing here—quilting, assembling health kits, and inspecting goods before shipping—without the Amish."[88] Amish have also started their own centers, loosely but clearly linked to MCC. In 1991 Gap Relief Sale committee members opened an MCC thrift store in White Horse, Pennsylvania. More recently, the Buena Vista (Pa.) Sewing Room, located in a converted tobacco barn, has been "a prime example of Amish ownership in MCC," according to Sensenig. Begun by women who wanted a social location to work on quilts, newborn kits, and the like, the center's work is done by women, but men help with packing and church districts organize young adult evenings.[89]

MCC's recognizing plain groups as resources was apparent in another way when Roth helped arranged a special motor coach learning tour to Mexico (since old orders will not fly). While exploring MCC work with Low German Mennonites, MCC staff sensed that those Mexican Mennonites might welcome economic and educational development work if it was advised by old order people whom the Low Germans trusted to understand their cultural taboos. From these contacts grew a cattle project and a school teacher training network, both directed by Old Order Amish and Mennonites from Indiana, Pennsylvania, and Ohio, with logistical and other support from MCC. Today the teacher training program operates rather independently from MCC, although a staff person often attends the coordinating committee meetings and the group's minutes credit MCC's initiative.[90]

The MCC Great Lakes region also includes sizable numbers of plain Anabaptists but for various reasons has been less successful in drawing old order and traditionalist Mennonites and Amish into its programming—a situation not unrelated to the stronger appeal of CAM in that region.[91] In recent years more intentional efforts to connect with plain groups included Great Lakes staff writing occasional pieces for *The Budget* (a plain communities correspondence newspaper), and MCC presentations in northern Indiana Amish schools during 2007, 2008, and 2009—schools that have, in turn, contributed more than 300 school kits per year to MCC.[92] Within the past year, Amish entrepreneurs in Ohio have helped design the new Millersburg MCC thrift shop.[93]

Forging relationships with and among various plain groups is not without its challenges, of course. Some plain groups—especially if they are informed by popular evangelical media—object to MCC's

work in the Middle East or its commitment to gender equality.[94]
Amish participation in the Peoria, Illinois, relief sale dropped dramatically when old orders felt that the sale's mainline Mennonite organizers simply wanted to use the Amish to attract media coverage
for the sale.[95] And even well-meaning MCC staff may not always understand the fault lines within plain communities, as for example,
when Beachy and Old Order Amish participate side-by-side in meat
canning in Lancaster, but in Romulus, New York, would not.[96] Of
course, CAM faces similar challenges. For example, its staff readily
admits that by forbidding smoking they offend certain tradition-
minded old orders. Old German Baptist Brethren, meanwhile, withdrew from CAM after it funded the start of a handful of Beachy
Amish churches overseas. All of these relationships, in fact, point to
the problem and promise of Anabaptist ecumenics.

REFLECTIONS ON NORTH
AMERICAN ANABAPTIST ECUMENICS

Giving and receiving, no less than formal representation, are
about relationships. MCC's relationships with constituents have
been built on shared history and shared theological priorities, princi-
pally the value of service "in the name of Christ." Yet, the past half
century of North American Anabaptist history has been marked by
strong divergences. An alliance such as MCC "works" to the degree
that participants imagine their commonality as more compelling
than their experiences of difference.

In the relationships reviewed above, who do we imagine ourselves—and others—to be? North American popular culture has
raised the profile of old order and other plain Anabaptist groups, le-
gitimizing them (occasionally valorizing them) and laying to rest the
notion that they are the last gasp of a soon-to-be-extinct way of life.
Mainline Mennonites have become more comfortable acknowledging their plain cousins, although mainliners rarely grasp the values
and complexity of the plain world. Few mainline Mennonites know
much about CAM or CASP or Weaverland Disaster Service, even
though the U.S. government recognizes the latter two, treating them
on par with MDS, and CAM attracts attention from *Forbes*, *Christianity Today*, and *Journal of Philanthropy*—much more attention than it receives from *Mennonite Weekly Review*.[97]

The growth and vigor of plain Anabaptists also afford them a
new measure of collective self-confidence, not least because their
numbers and resources have given rise to a range of schools and

other institutions that provide cohesion, sufficiency, and a concrete sense of "our people," clearly illustrated by sophisticated entities such as the plain brokerage Anabaptist Financial, which "assist[s] the brotherhood in channeling material resources . . . [and] provide[s] . . . financial counsel consistent with conservative Anabaptist beliefs and values."[98] Likewise, one could note the phenomenon of Haiti Relief Auctions, the network of benefit auctions held annually in plain communities and which parallel MCC relief sales (and rival them in size). The Haiti auctions emerged in an early 1980s context in which plain groups who had not often been involved in the leadership or control of MCC sales decided to organize their own sales to support ministries of conservative groups in the Caribbean.[99] In northern Indiana, Old Order Amish and plain Mennonite participation in the Haiti auctions is far stronger than in the Michiana Relief Sale, which is dominated by a board of mainline Mennonites.[100]

The relative success of MCC East Coast in relating to plain constituents, perhaps made easier by the historic proximity of the Akron office and the Ephrata Material Resource Center to Lancaster's old order and plain communities, stems from a commitment to approaching plain groups with the expectation that they possess distinct cultural resources and interests of value in themselves: imagining them as a constituency, as a people constituting MCC.[101] Such a posture more easily becomes interactive, as for example in 1998-1999 and 2004-2005 when MCC provided mediation and mediation training for various Old Order Amish households in the Lancaster settlement who were entrenched in conflict, or in 2006 when MCC became a liaison between outside observers and an Amish community grieving the high-profile killing of five school girls.[102] Relationships beget relationships, turning imagined connections into face-to-face trusting partnerships.

In the entire scope of MCC's ninety-year experience and work around the world, its connections with old order and plain Anabaptist groups are not necessarily more significant than its other constituent connections. But these relationships are historically deep and culturally complex. As MCC embarks on a journey of new priorities,[103] with a new structure, offering the possibility of rethinking the meaning of constituency and imagining both new and old relationships, the possibilities and limits of MCC's connections with plain people may be—quietly, unobtrusively, and humbly—instructive.[104]

NOTES

1. The seven groups represented at the July 1920 gathering in Elkhart, Indiana, were Central Conference of Mennonites, General Conference Mennonite Church, Krimmer Mennonite Brethren, Lancaster Mennonite Conference, Mennonite Brethren, (Old) Mennonite Church's Board of Missions and Charitable Homes, and Pacific Branch of the Relief Committee for the Suffering Mennonites of Russia.

2. Steve Nolt, "The Mennonite Eclipse," *Festival Quarterly* 19 (Summer 1992), 8-12.

3. Terminology is problematic and imprecise. Old Order Mennonite and Amish groups emerged in the mid-1800s with a concern to maintain established patterns of church life and ritual; very often they also sought to maintain cultural and social habits, many of which had implications for their interaction with technology, higher education, and the state. The term *plain churches* typically includes not only old orders but also a wider circle of Mennonite and Amish groups who emphasize nonconformity in highly visible ways, either through their dress or social conduct or both. Not all plain churches are old order, but old orders are plain groups. The general utility of the "plain" category is open to debate, but seems useful in this essay because of the way plain Anabaptists recognize a degree of commonality—commonality that shapes their self-understanding and their inter-Mennonite relationships. This essay deals only with MCC's plain constituents of so-called Swiss Mennonite background. It does not include plain groups such as Kleine Gemeinde, Chortitzer, or Old Colony Mennonites with roots in the Russian Mennonite tradition. These latter groups' relations with MCC may bear similarities to those explored here, but the differences are large enough to exclude them from this limited study. For some discussion of MCC and culturally-traditional Russian Mennonite groups, see several articles in the 2004 volume of *Journal of Mennonite Studies.*

4. This essay will focus disproportionately on plain groups' dynamism. MCC's own dynamic identity is certainly a critical factor, but the emphasis here will be on the historical development of constituent groups. Moreover, MCC is not one thing, but twelve distinct board and dozens of autonomous relief sales, thrift stores, and activity centers; as well, most constituents consider the historically related entities Mennonite Disaster Service and Ten Thousand Villages part of MCC. The context below aims to make clear what aspect of MCC is meant in each situation.

5. I allude to Benedict Anderson, *Imagined Communities: Reflections on the Origin and Spread of Nationalism* (London: Verso, 1991), though obviously there are differences between imagining Anabaptist ecumenicity and imagining the foundations of nationalism.

6. Again, terminology is problematic, but I use the term *mainline Mennonites* to refer to the culturally acclimated (Old) Mennonite, General Conference Mennonite, Mennonite Brethren, and Brethren in Christ mainstream that has dominated MCC's leadership and program development—recognizing that there have been and remain differences within and among these groups, and that through the 1970s a notable minority of (Old) Mennonites in the eastern United States and Canada appeared, by some measures, to be "plain."

7. Albert N. Keim, *Harold S. Bender, 1897-1962* (Scottdale, Pa.: Herald Press,

1998), 438; Rachel Waltner, "From Anabaptism to Mennonitism: *The Mennonite Encyclopedia* as a Historical Document," *Mennonite Life* 37 (December 1982): 13-19. Surveying the contents of academic writing in the 1950s, for example, one has the sense that a typical General Conference Mennonite leader of the time would have more quickly included the United Missionary Church (Mennonite Brethren in Christ) than the Old Order Amish when listing members of the Mennonite family. On mainline Mennonite appraisals of the Amish during 1950-1975, see chapter 4 in David Weaver-Zercher, *The Amish in the American Imagination* (Baltimore: Johns Hopkins University Press, 2001).

8. MCC initially operated—successfully, but briefly—during the 1920s as a vehicle for assisting war-ravaged Mennonite populations in the Soviet Union. Dormant for a decade, MCC reemerged in 1939 as a legal structure to handle North American Mennonites' ad hoc efforts to assist Russian Mennonite refugees settling in Paraguay. In neither case is there evidence of old order participation in MCC planning, funding, or programming—although there may have been incidental contributions, since some old orders at the time subscribed to (Old) Mennonite periodicals and may have read reports about MCC.

9. The administration was complex; MCC had joined Quaker and Brethren agencies in October 1940 to found the National Service Board for Religious Objectors, the entity recognized by the U.S. government, but in fact individual agencies, such as MCC, did the day-to-day administration of specific camps for their own members. See Albert N. Keim, *The CPS Story: An Illustrated History of Civilian Public Service* (Intercourse, Pa.: Good Books, 1991).

10. *Mennonite Encyclopedia*, vol. 3 (Scottdale, Pa.: Herald Press, 1957), 605; John D. Unruh, *In the Name of Christ: A History of the Mennonite Central Committee and its Service, 1920-1951* (Scottdale, Pa.: Herald Press, 1952), 371-72.

11. Eli J. Bontrager, *My Life Story* (Goshen, Ind.: Manasseh E. Bontreger,1982), 23-25, 30-33. Many of Bontrager's papers are now housed at the Northern Indiana Amish Library, rural LaGrange, Indiana, and a number of his books are inscribed with a phrase such as "loaned to the boys at camp ___." Bontrager implied that Harold S. Bender, then MCC secretary, asked him to join the board as an Amish representative, and Bontrager reluctantly agreed, stressing that Amish congregational polity meant that he was not authorized to speak for anyone other than his own church district (a situation that still characterizes old order participation on today's MCC boards and committees); see Bontrager's introduction in David Wagler and Roman Raber, *The Story of the Amish in Civilian Public Service, with Directory* (North Newton, Kan.: Bethel Press, 1986 [reprint of 1945 edition with expanded directory]), 5-6.

12. Unruh, *In the Name of Christ*, 285-86. There was one small CPS unit composed entirely of Amish men, but they accounted for very few of all Amish CPSers—see Boonsboro, Md., experimental farm in John M. Hostetter, *CPS Camp #24, 1942-1946* (Hagerstown, Md.: John M. Hostetter, 1999), 43-50, 80-81, 84.

13. Figures from Unruh, p. 476 ("Old" Mennonites provided 47% and General Conference Mennonites 18% of all donations to MCC-CPS). It is possible that the Old Order Amish numbers may be under-reported. Without a denominational bureaucracy to channel funds, local leaders collected and sent

money independently. Receipts in the Valentine Yoder (1880-1956) collection (unprocessed), Mennonite Church USA Archives-Goshen, Ind., show that Yoder, who was an Old Order Amish bishop in the Nappanee, Indiana, settlement, channeled his churches' CPS donations through the (Old) Mennonites' Elkhart, Ind.-based Mennonite Board of Missions—meaning the money may well have been credited to that group.

14. Various author interviews, e.g., with Harvey L. Stutzman (1916-2002), Bremen, Ind., 1 Dec. 1999. See also Amish memories of CPS as reported in Wagler and Raber, *Story of the Amish in Civilian Public Service*, 11-79; William and Malinda Beechy, comps., *Experiences of C.O.'s in C.P.S. Camps, in I-W Service in Hospitals, and During World War I* (LaGrange, Ind.: William and Malinda Beechy, 1990), 9-115; and Mose A. Schlabach and John A. Erb, comps., *Memories of CPS Camp Days, 1941-1947 and World War I, 1917-1919* (Berlin, Oh.: Hiland Printing, 1992), 2-93.

15. Albert N. Keim and Grant M. Stoltzfus, *The Politics of Conscience: Historic Peace Churches and America at War, 1917-1955* (Scottdale, Pa.: Herald Press, 1988), 139-49; Perry Bush, *Two Kingdoms, Two Loyalties: Mennonite Pacifism in Modern America* (Baltimore: Johns Hopkins University Press, 1998), 171-78. The "Mennonite Central Committee" entry in the 1957 *yclopedia* lists management of the I-W program as MCC's most recent "new field" of work (3:607).

16. Between 1955 and 1960 a few old order draftees simply refused the I-W option and went to prison; see, e.g., AP story in *Lancaster Intelligencer Journal*, 28 June 1957 and *New York Times*, 19 March 1960, A-9. Beachy Amish churches also disliked urban I-W employment, but most of their draftees were able to work in one of five retirement homes the Beachy Amish established during the 1960s, allowing them to remain in a "plain" context; see Albert N. Keim, "Military Service and Conscription," in *The Amish and the State*, 2nd. ed., ed. Donald B. Kraybill (Baltimore: Johns Hopkins University Press, 2003), 59.

17. Various interviews by the author, and I-W memoirs such as Beechy and Beechy, comps., *Experiences . . . in I-W Service in Hospitals*, 119-44. One Amish historian has told the author that if he were to write a history of the Amish and I-W it would be titled "Never Again." A I-W-approved program that *was* clearly linked to MCC was MCC's overseas PAX program, but at the time most old order churches discouraged members from traveling overseas.

18. Eventually major Mennonite groups also became disenchanted with the I-W program—the General Conference in 1967 and the Mennonite Church in 1971 both withdrew formal support from the I-W wage-earning program—but such disenchantment stemmed from a heightened sense of the Vietnam War and the meaning of "service" when soldiers were dying, not from unease with the I-W structure itself. In that sense, the Amish and Beachy Amish rejection of I-W was quite different from the mainline Mennonite rejection several years later.

19. *Minutes of Old Order Amish Steering Committee, from Oct. 20, 1966 to Oct. 25, 1972. First Volume* (Gordonville, Pa.: Gordonville Print Shop, [1972]), 1.

20. Ibid., 3, 5. The meeting was November 16, 1966.

21. Ibid., 8.

22. Interview with Freeman L. Yoder (1923-2003), Middlebury, Ind., 7 and 19 October 1999; Steering Committee minutes, p. 12, for February 15, 1967

meeting in Clark, Missouri, obliquely refers to "a debate" over the name.

23. Following Bontrager's retirement in 1953, Abe Troyer of Hartville, Ohio, served on the MCC board from 1953-1960. For two years the Amish seat was listed as "member undesignated," and then in 1962 Ammon Troyer of Sugarcreek, Ohio accepted the role; he died unexpectedly the same year. MCC Annual Workbooks, and information (provided by MCC) appearing in various issues of the *Mennonite Yearbook*.

24. Marc A. Olshan, "Homespun Bureaucracy: A Case Study in Organizational Evolution," 199-213, in *The Amish Struggle with Modernity*, ed. by Donald B. Kraybill and Marc A. Olshan (Hanover, N.H.: University Press of New England, 1994).

25. Lucille Marr, *The Transforming Power of a Century: Mennonite Central Committee and its Evolution in Ontario* (Kitchener, Ont.: Pandora Press, 2003), 25-97, 145-51, 183-229.

26. Marr, *Transforming Power of a Century*, 137, 144, 176-77, 192, 196-97, 243-44. Marr notes that initially it was difficult for MCC Ontario staff to take old order concerns seriously or understand old order values. See also Dennis L. Thomson, "Canadian Government Relations," 235-48 in *The Amish and the State*, ed. by Donald B. Kraybill (Baltimore: Johns Hopkins University Press, 1993); T. D. Regehr, *Mennonites in Canada, 1939-1970: A People Transformed* (Toronto: University of Toronto Press, 1996), 133-34, 226-27, 384-85, 399; and William Janzen, *Limits on Liberty: The Experience of Mennonite, Hutterite, and Doukhobor Communities in Canada* (Toronto: University of Toronto Press, 1990), 245-71.

27. Marr, *Transforming Power*, 244. MCC Ontario continues to represent old order concerns to provincial and federal governments; see file of correspondence related to various issues from the 1990s and 2000s, Heritage Historical Library, Aylmer, Ont.

28. William C. Lindholm, "The National Committee for Amish Religious Freedom," 109-23, in *The Amish and the State*, 2nd. ed.; Albert N. Keim, ed., *Compulsory Education and the Amish: The Right Not to be Modern* (Boston: Beacon Press, 1975).

29. National Committee for Amish Religious Freedom, 12.3 Official files, 1969-1976, Mennonite Central Committee IX-7 (Peace Section), Mennonite Church USA Archives-Goshen, Ind.

30. Telephone interview with Ken Sensenig, 2 June 2009. MCC U.S. provides up to $10,000 per year for such litigation, and Sensenig provides some transportation for defendants and has offered MCC mediation.

31. For a summary of recent legal conflicts involving U.S. old orders and the state, see Herman D. Bontrager, "Encounters with the State, 1990-2002," 235-50, in *The Amish and the State*, 2nd. ed. The National Amish Steering Committee quickly broadened its purview beyond conscription issues, and remains the old order liaison to government on most matters that can be amiably negotiated.

32. Peter Dyck remains a recognized figure among many Old Order Amish, who frequently report having read Peter and Elfrieda Dyck, *Up from the Rubble* (Scottdale, Pa.: Herald Press, 1991), or, more likely, a serialized version that appeared in a widely-read Amish monthly, *The Diary* (serialization began May 1998, 68-74, and ran through July 2003, 74-75). Younger genera-

tions have also heard Dyck speak. MCC East Coast staff arranged for him to tell stories in Amish schools in Lancaster County, Pa.; Great Lakes staff arranged for a similar itineration in northern Indiana Amish schools is 2007, but Dyck was unable to do so because of ill health. In May 2001 the author attended an evening gathering in a LaGrange County, Ind., chicken house where some 300 Amish adults and children listened in rapt attention for nearly two hours as Dyck told the story of the 1946 escape and resettlement of the Russian Mennonites. The event had been hastily arranged when an Amish businessperson learned that Dyck would be in the area to attend his grandson's college graduation. Word spread, and some Amish arrived from 130 miles away to hear Dyck. Other examples of Dyck's speaking to plain groups include MCC Annual Workbook (1980), 180; (1981), 176; and (1987), 198.

33. Dyck and Dyck, *Up from the Rubble*, 247-50. Financial tables in Unruh, *In the Name of Christ*, 377-83, illustrate Old Order Amish giving to MCC—beyond support for CPS—through 1950: $156,029 for relief (3.7% of total receipts to 1950), $2557 for MCC Peace Section (4% of total receipts to 1950); $105,672 for Mennonite Aid (6.4% of total receipts to 1950); and small amounts for mental health work and in support of voluntary service units in 1950 (only).

34. See, e.g., Amish women's contributions to aid war sufferers during the American Civil War, *Lewistown Gazette*, 8 October 1862; *Lancaster Daily Evening Express*, 15 January 1863.

35. Sam S. Stoltzfus, "Pequea Valley Memories," *The Connection*, August 2009, 55.

36. See, e.g., Erma Kauffman, *Shared Blessings: Origins and History of the Gap Relief Sale, 1929-1998* (S.l., n.d.), 6; noted Markham, Ontario, Old Order Mennonite preacher Thomas Reesor (1867-1954) was a supporter of MCC's "relief projects in providing food, clothing, and shelter"—*Whether by Word or Epistle: Letters of Frank W. Hurst and Other Weaverland Conference Mennonites of Pennsylvania to Thomas Reesor of Ontario, 1920-1948* (Ephrata, Pa.: Muddy Creek Farm Library, 2006), xxx-xxxii.

37. Dyck and Dyck, *Up from the Rubble*, 249. See comments regarding Russian Mennonite suffering and the good work of MCC in Donald Martin, *Old Order Mennonites of Ontario: Gelassenheit, Discipleship, Brotherhood* (Kitchener, Ont.: Pandora Press, 2003), 141-42. Martin is a member of the Markham, Ontario, Mennonite Conference, an old order group.

38. One way to read assumptions is to note the absence of references to old order groups in Unruh, *In the Name of Christ*, except for three CPS-related references (see index entries for "Amish, Old Order"), despite the fact that Unruh's financial appendices show Old Order Amish contributions to MCC work beyond CPS.

39. Kauffman, *Shared Blessings*, 7-8. After about 1991 responsibility for the sale shifted to an almost entirely old order board; until then, members of the Ohio and Eastern (later Atlantic Coast) Mennonite Conference were the organizers.

40. See scattered references and photos in Lowell Detweiler, *The Hammer Rings Hope: Photos and Stories from Fifty Years of Mennonite Disaster Service* (Scottdale, Pa.: Herald Press 2000). Pages 19-27 briefly describe MDS origins

(MDS became an MCC-led organization in 1955, and legally separated from MCC in 1993). MDS organizational representatives, 1955-2000, are listed on p. 178: Beachy Amish representation began in 1973, and representation of old order groups in 1994. Church of God in Christ (Holdeman) Mennonites had a representative beginning in 1967, but withdrew in the 1990s as they focused on their own Christian Disaster Aid programs.

41. Steven M. Nolt, "The Amish 'Mission Movement' and the Reformulation of Amish Identity in the Twentieth Century," *The Mennonite Quarterly Review* 75 (January 2001): 7-36.

42. Elmer S. Yoder, *The Beachy Amish Mennonite Churches* (Hartville, Ohio: Diakonia Ministries, 1987), 216-47 [Amish Mennonite Aid] and 247-53 [Mission Interests Committee]; see especially the section "Amish Mennonite Aid and Mennonite Central Committee," 234-36, which outlines the relationship between the two organizations from a Beachy Amish perspective. Interestingly, Beachy Amish representation on the MCC board began in 1956 when, at the invitation of MCC's executive secretary, an AMA board member began attending MCC meetings so that the two groups might avoid duplication in their European relief work. Nevertheless, Beachy Amish leaders emphasized that AMA was independent of MCC and that Beachy Amish participation on the MCC board did not imply approval of MCC's approach.

43. G. C. Waldrep, "The New Order Amish and Para-Amish Groups: Spiritual Renewal within a Tradition," *The Mennonite Quarterly Review* 83 (July 2008): 395-426; Edward A. Kline and Monroe L. Beachy, "History and Dynamics of the New Order Amish in Holmes County, Ohio," *Old Order Notes* 18 (Fall-Winter 1998): 7-19.

44. Stephen E. Scott, *An Introduction to Old Order and Conservative Mennonite Groups* (Intercourse, Pa.: Good Books, 1996), 159-232. For current listings of these groups, see two directories, *Mennonite Church Directory, 2009* (Harrisonburg, Va.: Christian Light Publications, 2009), and *Anabaptist (Mennonite) Directory, 2009* (Harrisonburg, Va.: The Sword and Trumpet, 2009). The two books have different content, but some churches in the latter compendium are not "plain" churches as I am using the term in this essay.

45. Scott, *An Introduction*, 137-58.

46. E.g., Eastern Pennsylvania Mennonite Church (begun 1969) soon banned radios, which many members would have already had for fifteen years; likewise, most EPMC adult members in 1969 were high school graduates, but the church soon effectively discouraged parents from allowing children to complete high school.

47. A striking example is the book G. Richard Culp, *The Minority Report: A Behind-the-Scenes Story of Civilian Public Service* (Halsey, Ore.: Richard Culp, 1999), in which Culp uses his own experience in CPS to sharply criticize MCC and mainline Mennonite groups, warning fellow conservatives to avoid the corrupting influence of the apostatizing Mennonites and their institutions, particularly MCC. Culp is a member of the Western Conservative Mennonite Fellowship, which formed in 1973.

48. E.g., the monthly magazine *Sword and Trumpet*, published by traditionalist Mennonites, includes regular references to popular evangelical authors, while a doctrinal publication of another plain group, *Decrees for to Keep for the Pilgrim Mennonite Conference of the Church of Jesus Christ* (s.l., 1995), does not—

see, e.g., statement on politics (p. 33) that does not in any way resemble that of the "religious right."

49. Isaac R. Horst, *A Separate People* (Waterloo, Ont.: Herald Press, 2000), 190-93. Horst is an Ontario Old Order Mennonite, but he represents old order opinion on these matters generally.

50. The decentralized nature of the plain Mennonite and Amish world makes it difficult to inventory all the institutions, mission, and service entities that operate within these circles. One list, including nursing homes, mutual aid groups, mission boards, publishers, Bible schools, and so on, established appears on pp. 190-94 in *Mennonite Church Directory 2009*. Other organizations, operated entrepreneurially by plain Mennonites, serve wider constituents, such as Golden Rule Travel, Hutchinson, Kan. (www.goldenrule-travel.com).

51. At one point in the 1970s Bontrager had visited Romania and preached in a Romanian Baptist church (see *The Budget*, January 14, 1981, 2), likely through connections made by Romanian exile-activist Richard Wurmbrand (1909-2001), whom Bontrager knew.

52. "Jesus to the Iron Curtain," was published from 2 January 1976 until 1 April 1986, once a month or less frequently. In 1986 it merged with Richard Wurmbrand's newsletter "Jesus to the Communist World," becoming "Christian Missions to the Communist World." That publication, in turn, changed its name in 1991 to "Christian Mission Charities," and in 2001 folded into Christian Aid Ministries. During 1952-1953 expatriate Russian Baptist activist Basil Malof hooked Old Order Amish minister Erlis A. Kemp (1897-1978), Nappanee, Indiana, into a plan to smuggle Bibles into the Soviet Union. Kemp's letters in *The Budget* in support of this plan were controversial in Amish circles, not because of the goal but because of Kemp's tactics and his printing the booklet *Atomic Bibles for Russians* under his own name. See David Luthy, "Erlis Kemp and 'Atomic Bibles' for Russia," *Family Life*, August/September 1990, 17-20.

53. *The Budget*, April 2, 1980, 10: "Iron Curtain Ministries was established to create a greater awareness among the plain people of the trials and sufferings of our fellow believers in countries under Communism. Also to alert us to our Biblical responsibilities as stated in Matt. 25:34-46 Romans 12:13, 15, etc. and to provide a trustworthy channel to anyone interested in helping our Brethren." This first entry also mentioned the itinerate speaking of Russian Baptist dissident Georgi Vins (1928-1998), who had arrived in the United States in 1979 and settled in Elkhart, Ind., near sizable Amish populations. "Our Suffering Brethren" still appears very occasionally in *The Budget* (e.g., 22 Apr. 2009) highlighting stories of persecuted Christians.

54. This theme is prevalent throughout these entries, although sometimes the writers did draw theological connections, as in Oct. 1, 1980, 8, where unregistered Baptists in the Soviet Union are said to practice adult baptism, priesthood of all believers, and separation of church and state; and April 16, 1980, 19, where Christian conscientious objectors are being forced into the Soviet army to fight in Afghanistan. Some letters do mention a Baptist dissident named Rudolph Klassen, who is said to have had Mennonite grandparents.

55. MCC hosted Soviet Baptists in 1964 and 1972—see Beulah Stauffer Hostetler, *American Mennonites and Protestant Movements: A Community Para-*

digm (Scottdale, Pa.: Herald Press, 1987), 319-20.
56. Interview with David N. Troyer, Berlin, Ohio, June 5, 2008. He joined the Beachy Amish Church in 1982.
57. Troyer continued working fulltime at Holmes Lumber for 2-3 years after launching the ministry; CAM operated out of his house until 1985.
58. Romania was the only East Bloc nation that had diplomatic relations with Israel.
59. Interview with Troyer. Troyer recounted CAM's origins in less detail in CAM's 2007 Annual Report, 4, "Dear Supporter Friends."
60. Early work in Nicaragua is recounted in Pablo Yoder, *Angels over Waslala* (Flemingsburg, Ky.: Harbor Lights, 1998).
61. Interview with Troyer; CAM Annual Reports, 2007 and 2008.
62. CAM Annual Reports 2007 and 2008. These full-color, 40 page publications include financial statements and descriptions of CAM's range of activity, including child sponsorships, International Crisis Projects (Afghanistan, Myanmar, Iraq, North Korea, Indonesia, etc.), publishing, Christian-Martyrs-Fund, clothes bundling, a micro-loan program, and more.
63. MCC Annual Report 2009. Note that reporting years are not parallel; CAM fiscal year is January to December and MCC's is April to March.
64. CAM Annual Report 2008, 27, valued gifts-in-kind at $160,116,119. (In comparison, in 1999 CAM took in about $11 million in cash and $67 million worth of gifts-in-kind.) MCC's 2009 Annual Report listed gifts-in-kind of $4 million. Accounting methods for gifts-in-kind vary greatly between the two organizations.
65. CAM Annual Report 2009, 39. The 55,000-square-feet distribution center and meat canning facility in Ephrata is very near MCC's Material Resource Center.
66. Donald B. Kraybill and Steven M. Nolt, *Amish Enterprise: From Plows to Profits*, rev. ed. (Baltimore: Johns Hopkins University Press, 2004); and Steven M. Nolt, "Mennonite Identity and the Writing on the 'New Giving' since 1945," *Journal of Mennonite Studies* 23 (2005): 59-76. According to the Non-profit Ministry Organization Survey, January 2009 (as reported in John W. Kennedy, "The Nor-for-Profit Surge," *Christianity Today*, May 2009, 22-27) the average annual gift to CAM is $850—meaning CAM "finished far and away as having the highest average giving amount from individual donors" of any Christian charity. CAM itself reported that the average annual contribution for 2008 was $1255, but CAM also expected income to be down 10-15% in 2009 since "many Christian Aid contributors are employed in construction and furniture making, two hard-hit industries during the current recession." See John W. Kennedy, "A Simple Old-Fashioned Fashioned Fundraiser: How Does an Anabaptist Charity Get Donors to Give $1,200 a Year?" *Christianity Today*, May 2009, 26.
67. The combination is obvious in CAM publications and promotional materials, e.g., Disaster Response Services/International Crisis Projects, *Labors of Love: A Tribute to Our Volunteers. An Amish-Mennonite Witness for Christ 2002-2006* (Berlin, Ohio: TGS International, 2009), 22. Interview with L. M., Shipshewana, Ind., 25 Feb. 2000. In deference to old order desire for anonymity, I use only initials to identify living interviewees.
68. E.g., between 1980 and 1995 the theologically conservative Mennonite

periodical *Sword and Trumpet* frequently published both appreciative pieces on MCC relief work and sharp editorial critiques of MCC's peace and justice work (e.g., May 1984, 3; February 1986, 11; June 1989, 20-22; September 1995, 40). At the end of 1995 *Sword and Trumpet* abruptly ceased publishing MCC news, perhaps because Linden M. Wenger (1912-2005), who had residual good will for MCC, stopped editing the news section. Criticism of MCC for not combining verbal evangelism with material aid is central to Culp, *Minority Report*, and the supporting endorsements from plain Mennonites on the cover.

69. Interview with Troyer. "Statement of Faith" appears on p. 2 of each Annual Report and as a separate flier. Interestingly, *Mennonite Church Directory*, published by Christian Light Publications, directly identifies CAM as a Beachy Amish ministry (see p. 191 in the directory's 2009 edition). Beachy Amish minister, writer, and sometime-MCC board member, David L. Miller, has occasionally written about the relative loyalty Beachy Amish donors feel to CAM versus Amish Mennonite Aid or MCC; see his essays in *Calvary Messenger*, April 1993, 15-16; and June 1998, 21.

70. In June 2008 a staff member at CAM's Millersburg office suggested that CAM had a thousand regular contributors who had no Mennonite or Amish connections; "we never target those people," he emphasized. "Most heard about us from an Amish or Mennonite neighbor. That's how all our donations come in—word of mouth." The large quantities of medical supplies contributed to CAM (a sizable portion of the value of each year's gifts-in-kind on the CAM balance sheet) come from pharmaceutical firms with no Anabaptist connections.

71. Interview with Troyer; interview with F. B., 5 Sept. 2006, Goshen, Ind. [F. B. is an Arthur, Ill. resident]; interview with L. M.; Interview with B. R., Aug. 28, 2009, Elizabethtown, Pa.

72. One way to gauge constituency is to consider the sources from which CAM editors draw material for the monthly periodical *The Seed of Truth: A Christian Magazine*, which functions as a kind of reader's digest of plain publications. The editors, who in 2009 were members of Beachy Amish and Weaverland Conference Mennonite churches, typically reprint with permission articles from periodicals associated with Nationwide Fellowship, Beachy Amish, Eastern Pennsylvania Mennonite, Midwest Fellowship, Conservative Mennonite Church of Ontario, and Old Order Amish.

73. "Gifts and Projects Catalog, 2007-2008," 10; Annual Report 2008, 33.

74. Interview with Troyer. CAM helped begin churches in countries where they have permanent staff (Haiti in 1997; Romania, 1996; Liberia, 2000), and some CAM funds subsidize those church planting efforts—see Annual Report 2008, 14.

75. Observed June 5, 2008. CAM partners with various Christians overseas. Since CAM typically insists that evangelical literature must accompany material aid, evangelical Protestants have been most willing to partner with CAM, but CAM has also worked with Assyrian Orthodox in certain Middle Eastern settings.

76. E.g., "Gifts and Projects Catalog, 2007-2008" (24-page booklet). This was also the message of a slide program shown at the Millersburg office in June 2008, in which the narration stressed that donors choose who, where,

and what they wish to support.

77. Language used in various CAM publications.

78. TGS International, a for-profit subsidiary of CAM (all TGS profits go into CAM) which does shipping and other services, also operates Good Samaritan Travel and Tours, a tour company specializing in trips to Europe, Israel, and CAM work sites in eastern Europe. CAM's spawning organizations from disaster relief to a travel agency is not unlike MCC—including its spinning off a travel and tour agency (Menno Travel Service); see Calvin W. Redekop, "The Organizational Children of MCC," *Mennonite Historical Bulletin*, 56 (January 1995): 1-8.

79. See the coffee table book *Rebuilding Hope: Disaster Response Services* (Millersburg, Ohio: Christian Aid Ministries, 2002). Similarities and differences in style and ethos between MDS and DRS may be read through a comparison of this book and the strikingly similar MDS book *The Hammer Rings Hope* (Scottdale, Pa.: Herald Press, 2000). DRS's more recent book, *Labors of Love*, documents DRS work in fifteen domestic disaster sites in ten states, between 2002 and 2006, and lists 23 domestic activity sites, 1992-2001. International Crisis Projects is an arm of CAM sending rebuilding teams outside North America, and the book describes that work in Pakistan and Indonesia, 2005-2007. ICP grew out of a 2001-2002 DRS project in El Salvador following an earthquake.

80. Disaster Response Services/International Crisis Projects, *Labors of Love*, 82-83.

81. Interview with B. R. The Old Order-Spring Garden relationship was not without tension; if MDS and DRS would have enough placements for volunteers, the future of C.A.R.E. might be in doubt. A group of Old Order (Stauffer) Mennonites from Tunas, Missouri, had trouble finding volunteer placement after Katrina—both MDS and DRS were full—so the old orders joined a disaster relief group from First Baptist Church of Lebanon, Missouri; see J. Stauffer, "Giant Broom of Destruction," *Family Life*, January 2006, 15-19; "By Giving, We Receive," *Family Life*, February 2007, 22-23.

82. Six-panel brochure "Conservative Anabaptist Service Program (CASP). A Draft Preparation Service Program. A Division of Christian Aid Ministries." The initial board included Beachy Amish, Midwest Fellowship, Mennonite Christian Fellowship, Amish Mennonite, and Tampico Amish Mennonite churches.

83. See details in Kenneth Sensenig, "Old Order Amish: MCC's Invisible Partner, 1990-2010." Much of the description in the section that follows comes from Sensenig's paper, and from a review of MCC Annual Workbooks since 1980.

84. During the 1980s MCC East Coast board chair Norman Shenk was also instrumental, as was the vision and energy of the old order and conservative board members. On MCC East Coast highlighting its inclusion of plain groups, see *Mennonite Weekly Review*, 17 March 2003, 1.

85. See also MCC Annual Workbook (1990), 181; (1994), 137-38. Since the idea of representative board service is largely foreign to old order culture, the representatives initially served as "listeners" charged with conveying information (about a grain drive, for example) back to their various church contacts, but they gradually "grew into board members," participating fully and

sharing their ideas and opinions—telephone interview with Lynn Roth, 31 August 2009. The broadening of board representation during these years was part of a general broadening of the vision of MCC East Coast and the addition of Latino and African-American board members from New York City, Philadelphia, and Brethren in Christ from south Florida—interview with Roth: "The board became the one place, at least on the east coast, where all these groups could talk about what is our common ministry and what gifts do we bring to that ministry?" In a parallel development, MDS added formal Old Order and New Order Amish and Old Order (Groffdale) Mennonite board representation in 1994.

86. Interview with Sensenig; interview with Les Gustafson-Zook, Goshen, Ind., 30 July 2009; email correspondence with Marlin Yoder, Kidron, Ohio, 9 September 2009; Interview with F. B.

87. Interviews with Sensenig; Kauffman, *Shared Blessings*. MCC food canning began in 1943 and was directed at feeding CPS camps; after World War II canning began for postwar relief. Unruh, *Service for Peace*, 255-56.

88. Interview with Sensenig. Key personal relationships through the years, as well as the fact that MCC is headquartered in their backyard while CAM's office is in Ohio, are two things that help explain the greater Lancaster loyalty to MCC. In 2007 when authors of the book *Amish Grace: How Forgiveness Transcended Tragedy*, asked Amish leaders in the Lancaster settlement if the book's royalties should go to MCC or CAM or both, one bishop indicated that he preferred MCC because he knew and trusted the staff, whereas he was unfamiliar with CAM's leadership, adding with concern, "I hear there's charismatics in that group."

89. Interview with Sensenig; interview with Roth. See also Annual Workbook (1994), 137-38; (1995), 155; (1999), 144; (2002), 151.

90. Interview with Roth; correspondence with Yoder; interview with S. Y., Goshen, Ind., 12 May 2009; back issues of *Old Colony Mennonite Support Newsletter* (2000-); "History Report, Old Colony Mennonites in Mexico [1995-2008]," 11-page mimeograph, author's files; and Rachel Miller, *A Vision for the Journey* (Sugarcreek, Ohio: Carlisle Press, 2008). See also *Mennonite Weekly Review*, 24 April 1997, 2 and 10 April 2006, 3; MCC Annual Workbook (1995), 156; (1996), 151; (1999), 144.

91. Correspondence with Yoder. Proximity played a role for locally-oriented old orders; those living in Wayne County, Ohio, volunteer more readily with MCC because the material resource center is in Kidron, while those living in Holmes County, Ohio, work more with CAM because their center is in Millersburg. Nonetheless, there are striking differences between MCC East Coast and MCC Great Lakes reporting in MCC Annual Workbooks during the 1990s. The EC report always mentions Mennonite, Amish, and Brethren in Christ constituencies, while the GL report consistently omits the "Amish" (e.g., 1992, pp. 149 and 151). As well, EC reports discuss the Amish learning tours to Mexico, while the GL reports do not, even though a good number of the tour participants were from the GL region. Prior to 2005, GL reports made only two references to programming with plain groups, Annual Workbook (1998) 149; (2002), 153.

92. See, e.g., "Are you the Girl Living with Dora?" *The Budget*, 27 August 2008, 26, which introduces MCC's International Visitor Exchange Program,

and describes a Laotian IVEPer who lived with an Ohio Amish family. The *Budget* essays are written by Marlin Yoder or Sara King. (CAM also provides reports in *The Budget*, e.g., 20 May 2009, 1); correspondence with Yoder; interview with Gustafson-Zook. One Indiana Amish school also collected 35,960 aluminum cans for scrap, giving the proceeds to MCC.

93. Correspondence with Yoder. Amish volunteers had long worked in the former thrift store.

94. Interview with Gustafson-Zook and correspondence with Yoder.

95. Interview with F. B. [F. B. is an Arthur, Ill. resident]. Old Order Amish in Arthur continue to support MCC meat canning and will donate items to the Peoria Relief Sale, but were angered when, in the 1990s, they saw mainline Mennonite sale organizers arrange for local TV crews to film Amish sale goers and volunteers specifically. According to F.B., Amish attempts to raise this concern with sale organizers the next year went nowhere, so the Amish decided to stop attending. This story (and I have never tried to ask organizers for their "side") illustrates the difficulty of discussing MCC *in general*. Each relief sale is autonomous and managed by local volunteers, almost always a group of mainline Mennonites rather than a board representing a spectrum of groups, who may approach such matters very differently from, say, the approach of MCC Great Lakes staff.

96. Interview with Sensenig.

97. CAM is recognized as a major charity, see, e.g., *Forbes'* annual list of "America's 200 Largest Charities" [based on IRS Form 990, annual reports], includes CAM, but not MCC. See William P. Barrett, 11.21.07, http://www.forbes.com/2007/11/21/largest-american-charities-pf-philo-07charities-cz_wb_1121charities_land.html. On federal recognition of plain groups, see reference to Weaverland Disaster Service and CAM, alongside Mennonite Disaster Service, in *Selective Service 2006 Fiscal Year Annual Report to Congress*, p. 29. See also Michael S. Hamilton, "More Money, More Ministry: The Financing of American Evangelicalism Since 1945," 131, in *More Money, More Ministry: Money and Evangelicals in Recent North American History*, ed. Larry Eskridge and Mark A. Noll (Grand Rapids, Mich.: W. B. Eerdmans, 2000), which lists CAM as "one of the seven largest parachurch mission agencies" in America, along side World Vision and Compassion International. During the past decade *Mennonite Weekly Review* has run several feature articles on CAM—28 January 1999, 1-2; 28 Apr. 2003, 1; 7 March 2007, 2—and, indeed, the difference in space given to the two organization is not necessarily an editorial shortcoming on the part of MWR. Since CAM does not issue press releases, each story MWR publishes on CAM is an original feature story intentionally researched by MWR staff, whereas MWR can cover MCC by printing MCC press releases. The fact remains that few mainline Mennonites know much about CAM.

98. The board is "drawn from different sectors of our conservative Anabaptist community." See also Biblical Stewardship Services (a subsidiary of CAM for financial and estate planning).

99. Interview with L. M.; interview with F. B.; correspondence from Yoder; various brochures and fliers for Haiti Benefit auctions in author's files. The first Haiti Benefit Auction was in northern Indiana, and initiated by Alvin E. Miller, pastor of Milford Chapel, to support work of the Mennonite Gospel

Mission. Four years later a parallel auction began in Ohio, and later others started in Arthur, Illinois; Sarasota, Florida; Holmes County, Ohio; and Lancaster, Pennsylvania. Soon the auctions were raising more money than the Mennonite Gospel Mission needed, so the loosely-structured board of fourteen Beachy Amish, Old Order Amish, Wisler and other plain Mennonites who coordinated the auctions began sending funds to a variety of medical and educational development projects in Haiti. The Ohio Haiti Auction gives a portion of its proceeds to Christian Aid Ministries, but that is the only indirect connection between the two entities.

100. Author observations. Most of the auctioneers, support staff, and a large portion of the crowd are Old Order Amish, and the rest are Beachy Amish, Wisler Mennonites, and other plain Mennonites.

101. See clear examples in MCC Annual Workbook (1995), 155; (1996), 151.

102. Interview with Sensenig; email correspondence from Carolyn Schrock-Shenk, 15 Sept. 2009; MCC Annual Workbook (2002), 151. The mediation in 1999 successfully resolved painful issues within an extended family system, while the mediation in 2005 resolved a protracted dispute that facilitated an excommunicated Amish man's return to church membership shortly before he died, to the great joy of his family. This latter, 30-year conflict had been quite public, which had added to Amish anxiety, and joy in its resolution; see Lancaster *Intelligencer Journal*, 3 May 2001, 1, 4, and 29 March 2002, B1-2. On MCC's role in the wake of the school shooting, see Annual Workbook (2006-2007), 113.

103. Doubtless many aspects of MCC's New Wineskins process build on mainline Mennonite assumptions about decision-making, but the process also attempted to include "plain" Anabaptists, e.g., a New Order Amish man from the Conneautville, Pa., settlement attended a New Wineskins consultation in Winnipeg, Manitoba—see *The Budget*, 12 November 2008, 26.

104. Special thanks to Anna R. Showalter, who assisted with research, and to a grant from MCC that assisted with travel.

Chapter 7

Shaped by Travel: MCC and Mennonite Mobility

NANCY R. HEISEY

"What we call holy in the world—a person, a place, a set of words or pictures—is so because it is a transitional place, a borderland, where the completely foreign is brought together with the familiar. . . . Pilgrimage is always going toward that 'world's end' that is still somehow within the world, to the place where . . . God has decided to make his name dwell."[1]

"If I were to choose the life of a vagabond, I would choose it in France this time of year."[2]

MCC WORKER AS PILGRIM/TOURIST: ELSIE C. BECHTEL'S DIARY

When Elsie Bechtel sailed from New York for Le Havre in September 1945, she was joining an ancient family of travelers whose journeying had been shaped by a religious sense. While equally complex and multi-faceted, religious travel sets itself off from human travel for commerce or for warfare by its orientation to the other/Other met in travel and by its interest in the places sojourned in or traversed en route. It differs from the travel of the refugee/immigrant by being founded on choice. Elsie's travel would bring her into contact with refugees. However, her voyage to France, and the many trips, short and long, made during her Mennonite Central

Committee assignment at the Colonie d'Enfants at Lavercantière, as recorded in her diaries and letters, offer bare hints of her religious orientation. Instead, these writings reflect the sensitivities of a particularly observant and reflective wanderer.

Beginning with Elsie Bechtel's reflections, this chapter considers the role travel has played in the shaping of MCC's identity and task. It draws on reflections from the sociological/anthropological literature on pilgrimage and tourism, arguing for an understanding that allows these identities to exist together rather than one that sharply distinguishes them. It then notes that formal study of MCC's history throughout its ninety years has largely ignored the impact of travel, and considers, through a case study of reports from MCC and its workers, the diminishing recognition of the place of travel in MCC's work. Finally, it suggests that conscious acceptance of the pilgrim/tourist identity for MCC will be useful to its future mission.

Before her travels began, Elsie gave a public rendering of her motivation for going to France as part of MCC's post-World War II relief effort: "Relief Service gives us a chance to test and put into practice one of the important Christian beliefs. We have been saying very loudly that love is the greatest thing in the world. I doubt if many of us have realized this other than as theory." [3] Elsie's diary also opens with notes of reflections on a chapel service at the MCC headquarters in Akron, Pennsylvania, linking the work she was anticipating with the contemporary postwar situation she expected to meet:

> Can the world recover from broken hearts, lives, and the wounds inflicted on the soul and mind through war and desolation? In the cross of Christ is found the power to renew and revitalize our souls and minds. Christ's death heals the broken hearted, makes the blind see. Let us be cross bearers![4]

However, not intended for public view, the diary does not dwell on religious reflection or motivation. Indeed, readers might find it hard to imagine how this writing could be pressed into use for the missionary biographical or autobiographical narrative with which Elsie would have been familiar. In her own Brethren in Christ community, the writings of early twentieth-century missionary H. Frances Davidson would have been available to her.[5] The pages of the Brethren in Christ periodical *Evangelical Visitor* had also been full of missionary reports for decades when Elsie began her MCC assignment.[6] Yet for most Mennonites and Brethren in Christ, personal accounts of mission and service work and travel would only begin to be published later.[7]

That Elsie understood her work as "relief service," and felt a need to solicit support for it, might point to a differentiation in her mind, or in the minds of her proposed audience, between the work she anticipated in France and what she understood as missionary work. Yet Elsie appears to have thought through the boundaries, to whatever extent she was aware of them, in describing her activities. "There is plenty of chance for missionary work," she wrote after a conversation with a colony child who said there was no good God,[8] and when an MCC car arrived at the chateau in Lavercantière with clothes for the children, she emoted, "I was proud of being a Mennonite for the first time in my life. That's true religion!"[9] (The question of the relationship between mission and service has endured for decades into the present, as evidenced, for example, by Samuel Escobar's sermon on Luke 10:17-20 on the occasion of MCC's seventy-fifth anniversary.)[10]

Elsie's diary is full of travel references, as the epigraph makes visible. From the days when she waited impatiently for clearance to sail from New York, through the ocean voyage to France, to the multiple trips to and from Lavercantière, to the extended vacation she took to Italy with fellow service workers, her first MCC experience shaped her not only through her tasks and relationships but also through the comings and goings that organized her days. Travel, even at its simplest and most mundane, evoked for her a sense of something remarkable. One day in February 1946, for example, she noted that "in the afternoon borrowed a bicycle and rode off into no where." The countryside, she observed, was "the most beautiful I've ever seen . . . [filled with] perfect harmony and music."[11]

ANTHROPOLOGISTS AND SOCIOLOGISTS ON RELIGIOUS TRAVEL

Elsie's observations interface in interesting ways with the burgeoning anthropological and sociological literature on pilgrimage and tourism. The categories of pilgrimage and tourism themselves, however, require careful analysis. In the ancient Christian context, pilgrimage "is not a sacrament, has no doctrine, and unlike . . . the Qur'an, the New Testament does not make it obligatory."[12] In early usage, the Greek, Latin, and Syriac terms which are frequently translated as having to do with pilgrimage represent concepts of foreignness and wandering.[13] And while recent accounts have explored the travel of ancient Roman pagans as "tourists,"[14] the use of that term only becomes active in the eighteenth century.[15]

Scholarly considerations of early religious travel warn against simplistic use of terms such as pilgrimage and underline the "fuzziness" of named categories.[16] Religiously motivated travel to attend festivals, seek healing, or consult an oracle was taking place outside the Jewish Christian framework and before the emergence of particular accounts of Christian travel.[17] Second-century records include reports of Christians traveling to gather at the tombs of martyrs.[18] Scholars have referred to Melito of Sardis as the "first Christian pilgrim" because of his travel to "the place where these things were preached and done" (that is, Jerusalem), although his stated reason was to get an accurate list of books of the Old Testament. In the third century, Origen wrote that he traveled to Rome because he wanted "to see the most ancient church of the Romans."[19]

In their classic twentieth-century study on pilgrimage, Turner and Turner analyze the anthropological particulars of ancient, medieval, "syncretistic," and modern forms of religious travel, concluding famously that "a tourist is half a pilgrim, if a pilgrim is half a tourist."[20] Since that formulation, challenges have been posed to the simplicity and singularity of the Turners' reading. Eade and Sallnow question "earlier, structuralist modes of interpretation" of religious travel advanced by both Durkheim and the Turners; they call instead for study of pilgrimage as "a realm of competing discourses."[21] Some contemporary tourism studies have reflected on the disjunctions between pilgrimage and tourism. For Cohen, tourism is more "anarchical" than pilgrimage, and less "obligatory." Preston asserts that "modern tourism" weakens the impact of pilgrimage because it is too comfortable.[22] Swatos seeks examples of modern pilgrimage that do not have tourism trappings about them.[23]

On the other hand, Frey, drawing on Adler's work on travel as performative art, proposes that "the categories pilgrimage and tourism are more efficiently understood as similar forms of human mobility, rather than binary oppositions."[24] Further, Tomasi, in a collection of studies on pilgrimage and religious tourism, traced the path of "*homo viator*," comparing this creature's common search throughout the centuries for "what was the *supernatural* in the past and is now the *cultural-exotic*, but also the *sacred*."[25] Adler pushes the linkage between tourism and pilgrimage into antiquity, insisting that "focusing our gaze upon (the) holy men of antiquity helps free us" from the illusions that the study of tourism must begin with modernism and that "recreational" travel can be "neatly distinguished from the history of religious travel, itself identified with overly narrow conceptions of pilgrimage."[26] Badone and Roseman underline that "the observation that pilgrims may have mixed motivations is neither rare nor particularly recent" and conclude that even in modern tourism religious behaviors can be witnessed at "ostensibly secular sites" such as Graceland or Ground Zero.[27]

In the early Christian period, itinerant religious travel was an important aspect of early Christian women's participation in a community that in other ways continually sought to regulate and limit women's "official" roles. No ancient Christian sources suggest that this kind of female engagement in such "deep religious expression" was unacceptable.[28] The diary of the fifth-century Spanish pilgrim Egeria and the account of the sixth-century Roman ascetic Melania the Younger both reflect the likelihood that their choices and actions were seen as positive religious models for other Christian women.[29] The preservation of both records confirms Adler's suggestion that aspects of gender within travel performance, while minimally studied, tend to focus on admiration for women travelers.[30] Indeed, the *Life* of Melania repeatedly emphasizes Melania's gender, albeit by insisting on her "manly" distinctiveness from traditional ideas about womanly behavior.[31]

Among scholars who locate pilgrimage and tourism in a common conceptual field, Adler's analysis of both travel forms as performance art provides a framework for readings of religious travel. Adler views travel performance as shaped by the quest for knowledge, the desire to preserve travel's "fleeting experiences" by marking both the places visited and the place of return, an awareness of an audience, and "an allegorical miniature of earthly life" or "a search for a vantage point from which to grasp and understand life 'as it really is.'"[32]

Given Elsie Bechtel's own reflections on the theological underpinning of her assignment as an MCC worker, the issue of travel for mission also calls for attention. Scholarly observations on the importance of travel to missionary effort can be found, although not in balance with the size of the western-northern missionary enterprise over the centuries. Sixteenth-century Jesuit missionaries paved the way: "Not only did Jesuits gain their knowledge of the natural world while traveling in the service of their order, but the knowledge thus gained helped their traveling by enabling the Society to operate with increased effectiveness in remote corners of the world. . . ."[33] Diaries of nineteenth-century missionary graduates of Princeton Seminary comment on "spiritual lessons" evoked during travel by sea.[34] Twentieth-century observers issued cautions about the "time, energy, and money expended" on ecumenical travel and expressed fears about the ease with which areas of the world known as mission locations became playgrounds for people looking for mission-related tourism.[35] The centrality of global mobility to twenty-first-century Pentecostal-Charismatic communities has been noted.[36] Yet for the most part, the significance of travel remains underthematized within scholarly assessments of Christian missions.

MENNONITE RESEARCH AND COMMENT ON TRAVEL

Mennonite immigrant experiences have spawned scholarly studies, literary reflection, and numerous published personal accounts.[37] Likewise, MCC's important and ongoing program focus on the needs of refugees and internally displaced people is visible in historical records—from the days when the first Mennonites fled the Russian Revolution, to the needs of Palestinian refugees in the Middle East after World War II, to the devastation wreaked by the U.S. war in Vietnam.[38] Interestingly, MCC's involvement in the resettlement of refugees in Canada and the U.S. has received relatively scant attention, although at its seventy-fifth anniversary the global movement of people is identified as a twenty-first-century trend of significance for organizations like MCC.[39]

The difficulties of travel, especially in war zones or areas of less economic development, are also standard in MCC research. MCC's first program efforts in Russia and Ukraine were carried out amid the extreme difficulties of MCC workers traveling by sled during a severe blizzard and the lack of adequate transportation capacities to move relief supplies or of a maintained road system.[40] Irvin Horst's report of the 1939-1949 period noted realities also apparent in Bechtel's diary, namely, the difficulty of traveling in postwar Europe and the way in which providing transport itself became a focus of MCC programming.[41] The account of the dangerous 1947 sea voyage of a group of Mennonite refugees to Paraguay is recounted in a biography of Elfrieda Dyck, the worker who accompanied them.[42]

In contrast, mission and service travel, despite the dramatic increase in numbers of people traveling and miles traveled in the period after World War II, has not been carefully observed. By its fiftieth anniversary, the MCC history and institutional weight had become a focus of particular research. Articles in the 1970 anniversary issue of *Mennonite Quarterly Review* offered historical background, consideration of MCC's overall impact on Mennonites in the U.S. and Canada, and discussion of theological issues raised through MCC's experi-

ences, including MCC's "peace mission." The list of proposed research topics included only one travel-related subject: "The Menno
Travel Service Tours as Educational Agencies."[43] That educational
theme was also sounded elsewhere in the volume, as was the relationship of the travel and service experience to the (re)shaping of
identity among U.S. and Canadian Mennonites.[44] Yet in reflecting on
the self-understanding of MCC workers at the fifty-year mark, Peter
Dyck offered this lament: "Although we have left the isolation of our
farms, flock to colleges and universities, and jet around the world, we
are still in a ghetto."[45]

A series of conferences on "Mennonite educational and cultural
problems," sponsored by Mennonite and Brethren in Christ colleges
in the U.S. and Canada, reported on studies of the relationship between travel for service, education, and Mennonite identity. Held between 1942 and 1967, some of the research presented at these gatherings drew on MCC programs or the experiences of MCC workers. A
1959 survey reported on the experiences of Europeans who came to
study in the U.S. and Canada in a program where MCC served "as
the agent of Mennonite colleges." "Only one (of the 83 respondents)
indicated that he had not done additional travel while in America,"
both to visit "college friends" and for "sightseeing."[46]

Later conference observations pushed deeper into the inter-
woven experiences of higher education, mission, and travel. In 1963
Atlee Beechy noted the influence of "Mennonite college graduates
now scattered throughout the world" and recommended that the colleges "should provide education for life in a rapidly changing world
. . . [stressing] principles of and approaches to change, flexibility and
mobility."[47] Arthur Climenhaga contrasted the complex experiences
of those whose educational travel was part of their preparation for
mission to that of a tourist, who "passing quickly through a country
and almost completely encapsulated in his hotel, the airport, and
other protective devices . . . feels this intellectual, esthetic, and moral
nausea very little."[48] And Robert Kreider identified "mobility" and
"traveling light" as motifs of Christian vocation to be nurtured
among college students rather than "academic professionalism."[49]

The 1967 conference heard several papers which represented surveys of Mennonites who had participated in international travel.
Only four percent of Mennonite service workers (the paper unfortunately does not specify the time frame of the survey) stated that the
opportunity to "leave home, see the world, travel overseas" was their
"most important reason for entering service."[50] But, referencing Marshall McLuhan's metaphor of the global village, conference partici-

pants were urged to take note of the increasing travel among Mennonites and challenged to become "aware of the people from their congregations who are going overseas on business, for study, or government assignments [to challenge] them to be active representatives of the Christian faith. . . ."[51]

In 1995, at MCC's seventy-fifth anniversary, two conferences were held whose papers and responses were later published. As with the official scholarly musings in 1970, travel for service was barely noted in these materials. Nevertheless, the issues of identity and educational travel appeared in the discussion. Donald Kraybill underlined that the "mobility of modern society" had an impact on Mennonites and referred to the role of "historical tours" in connecting Mennonites to their past.[52] Ronald Mathies reported that his students, through participation in service programs, had their eyes opened to "third world tourism." Reflecting on the reality of which the Bechtel diary and letters are a striking example, he further noted that "testimonials" of such service experience "are part of a long tradition of 'sojourner stories' that have always fascinated the home audiences of returning travelers."[53] Only a brief note in response to Vinay Samuel's paper on "The Church and the Pain of the World" acknowledged the power conferred by access to travel: "MCC has placed a high priority on 'presence,' on being there, yet in most cases we are not really there because we have an escape route—we can leave, at least physically."[54]

A CASE STUDY OF MENNONITE THOUGHTS ON RELIGIOUS TRAVEL: *THE MENNONITE* 1930-2005

Formal studies and historical documentation, however, are not the only means by which we can gain a better understanding of how Elsie Bechtel's travels and reflections on those travels in diary and letters relate to broader MCC experience. Here we turn to a survey of reports, articles, and advertisements from and about MCC as they appeared in one Mennonite periodical over a seventy-five-year period. *The Mennonite*, now the official church periodical of Mennonite Church USA, offers a fascinating and changing understanding of MCC-related travel.[55] As we will see, these efforts by MCC to communicate with its supporting churches move from a time and context where travel is meaningful to a reality where, although extensive travel is obviously part of the effort, it goes virtually unnoticed.

Elsie Bechtel's fall 1945 sea voyage aboard the U.S.S. Argentina and her arrival in France were both reported to readers of *The Men-*

nonite.[56] Such detailed keeping track of the movement of MCC workers is for decades a striking feature of this periodical's content. In the
years before World War II, such travel was infrequent while noteworthy. In 1930, for example, H. S. Bender reported "a very pleasant voyage home" after two and a half months in Germany working on the
needs of Mennonite refugees.[57] By 1940, with war engulfing Europe,
a series of voyages by "commissioners" accompanied the plotting
out of MCC responses to the disaster.[58]

In the immediate aftermath, again the travel of relief workers
was a central concern. Here *The Mennonite* allowed its readers
glimpses of the struggles workers faced (also revealed in Elsie's reflections about her impatience in waiting for clearance to sail).[59] In
January 1945, for four women planning to travel to the Middle East,
"passage to points beyond Lisbon was still a prayer concern."[60] In
February, seven of ninety-one workers assigned were en route, while
eight were "awaiting sailing arrangements."[61] In March and April,
workers awaited clearance for travel both to Europe and to "the Orient." S. F. Pannabecker and P. P. Balzer were "placed on 'alert,' being
ready to leave for India on an hour to hour basis. . . ."[62] Travel notes
also followed the progress of these service journeys, noting the "vali-
dation" of Pannabecker's and Balzer's passports in India and their
eventual arrival in China.[63]

Detailed and regular reporting of worker travel continued into
the 1950s, but by 1960 the number of MCC workers had increased
and the pattern of their assignment changed enough that *The Mennonite* instead carried the news releases listing the number of workers
oriented in a particular group. By 1965, photos of MCC as well as
other assigned mission and service workers were included in *The
Mennonite*, primarily those from the General Conference Mennonite
denomination. This pattern persisted for decades, but by the year
2000 worker photos were no longer included, and most information
about assigned workers had to do with pastoral transitions within
the denomination in the U.S. rather than of service workers. Perhaps
not unrelatedly, a 2000 MCC news release also reported a study revealing that MCC workers did not feel connected to their home congregations.[64]

In addition to commenting on the movement of MCC workers,
during this period remarks on the means of travel shifted from the experiences of people to the ways that commodities were transported
around the world. Travel itself had been interesting to Mennonite
readers, as evidenced in a series of stories in 1930 about the trip across
the United States of long-term General Conference leader H. J. Kre-

hbiel, the only American Mennonite to attend the 1925 Mennonite World Conference assembly in Switzerland, and from a Christian Endeavor Friendship Tour to Europe.[65] But for MCC, in 1930 the "work of moving Mennonites from Germany" was central. "Relief Notes" from MCC Executive Secretary Levi Mumaw noted regular movement of "transports" of Mennonite refugees to South America.[66]

The problem of indebtedness was raised with a call for offerings to help repay Canadian Pacific Railway the "over $1,000,000" owed for earlier movement of Mennonite refugees to that country.[67] A letter from Fernheim Colony in Paraguay reported the arrival of a group of refugees who "reported a pleasant voyage from Hamburg to Buenos Aires on the German steamer 'Villgarcia' [sic] and from there on the river steamer 'Mexico.'"[68] After World War II, notices of travel means turned to the search for ways to travel, given the scarcity of resources. Because even bicycles were "precious and scarce," a proposal was floated that young people in Canada and the U.S. send bicycles to relief workers in Europe.[69] The Pannabecker and Balzer voyage to China would take place by "any available means."[70] Security issues on the high seas were recorded when four women traveled to the Middle East "via neutral ship."[71] Occasionally a new opportunity for travel was mentioned, as when "Waldo Hiebert with Mrs. Hiebert left for Paraguay by plane."[72]

Sometimes means of travel were named in ways that emphasized the frustration, extent, or difference from what Mennonite audiences were familiar with. A Dutch Mennonite leader wrote, "This week a ship is sailing to America and I wish to . . . send word of our welfare."[73] R. C. Kauffman wrote from India about his "first Indian train ride," where passengers "hang out on all sides like turnips." He added that he had access to a 1938 Plymouth for his work, but that he was "not particularly anxious to use it until I get used to traffic conditions here."[74] Arthur Jahnke "traveled on the back of an open truck down to the heel of the Italian peninsula" to help refugees returning to Italy.[75] Executive Secretary Orie Miller was "detained in England due to the extreme difficulty in securing passage to the states [sic.]"[76]

Finding ways to move needed supplies was central in the postwar programming. Elsie Bechtel's colleague Mary Miller described cleaning the building selected for the MCC headquarters in Châlon, southern France: "Ellen Harder and Henry Buller made a trip of twenty miles and at the end of the day came back with the waited rags which we still guard zealously."[77] Young men with farm backgrounds were called to accompany dairy herds to be shipped to "relief areas in Europe."[78] Eventually, travel means ceased to be noted when workers themselves traveled, except, as we will see, when they were reporting on "exotic" experiences in assignment settings. Moving relief supplies around the world, however, continued to attract occasional interest. During the 1960 upheavals that displaced large numbers of Congolese people, Archie Graber reported: "I expect to fly to Luluabourg to buy a load of salt and some milk. . . ."[79] A 1975 photo caption explained the air-freighting of "fifty pregnant heifers" to Jordan.[80] A 1980 corn shipment to Somalia was described in language reminiscent of the 1940s: "The Mormacsaga steamed out of Baltimore . . . carrying with it 1,000 tons of corn destined for the critically undernourished refugees in Somalia. . . . Fifty trucks hauled the bags to the pier at Baltimore. . . ."[81] Twice in recent years, MCC ads featured the tractors shipped to the Ukraine, in 1920, one of the earliest major MCC relief/development efforts. "We're not sitting on the job," proclaimed the one, including in its list of MCC acitivites not only "tractors to Chortitza," but "olive trees to Hebron," and "seed corn to Bulawayo."[82]

Elsie Bechtel's engagement with Spanish refugee children, one of the major populations in the children's colony in Lavercantière, put a striking personal face on work that would continue to be at the forefront of MCC effort—and a continuing reminder that refugees, in contrast to MCC workers, were mostly forced to travel in ways they would not have wished. Following the reports of the transports of Mennonite refugees in the 1930s, post-World War II accounts repeatedly underlined the needs of refugees. M. C. Lehman compared efforts to flee war to "the stampede of cattle before an advancing prairie fire." Uprooted people, Lehman noted, included "war fugitives," "evacuees," and "prisoners of war," with numbers in Europe at around 30 million.

Lehman further described the serious psychological problems that resulted from such forced movement, a reality which called for relief workers possessing a "rudimentary knowledge of psychotherapy and a cheerful Christian disposition."[83] This disposition, revealed throughout Bechtel's diary, also appeared in *The Mennonite*. Grace Augsburger, who as Elsie was waiting to sail for France was escorting refugees from the Middle East home to Yugoslavia, described a particularly difficult "flight"—an eight-day boat journey with 1300 people, including several with tuberculosis and other chronically ill passengers.[84]

Throughout the years, refugees continued to play central roles in MCC reporting. The needs of refugees in Europe occupied programs for decades. In the 1960s and 1970s refugees and displaced people from Vietnam took center stage in MCC programming.[85] The 1980 MCC annual meeting passed a resolution adopting a special focus on refugees for a three-year period.[86] In the 1990s stories turned readers' attention to the needs of immigrants and refugees to the United States and Canada.[87]

Within the broad story of refugee travel were specific stories of pain and success in which MCC worker travel and the movement of refugees intersected. Accounts of the difficulty of getting to the Paraguayan Chaco were standard from the early days of Mennonite settlement there. The commitment to keep those immigrants connected to both their Paraguayan and the Mennonite worlds reverberates in *The Mennonite* for decades. The first effort, in 1945, was to build a road "to prevent the Chaco from reclaiming its own," stretching from Fernheim Colony to the railroad 60 miles away.[88] In 1955 five PAX workers were sent from Peru to Paraguay to "help with the construction of Mennonite colony roads."[89] Later that year, a high Paraguayan official visited the MCC headquarters, calling on Mennonites to provide personnel and management for building a road to Bolivia if the Paraguayan government could obtain a loan to fund the project.[90]

By July 1960, the Trans-Chaco highway, built with MCC manpower, had reached Kilometer 117 from the south end. "In November 1959," the report added, "construction was at Kilometer 89."[91] And in 1965, Willard Smith, who had worked in Paraguay twenty years earlier as MCC director, noted the completion of this highway. He also described "the modern Asunción airport which handles large jets" but pointed out that the Trans-Chaco was not yet an all-weather road, leading to long delays during rainy season.[92]

A more tragic travel account was the death at sea of MCC worker Marie Fast. On May 15, 1945, a headline declared "Marie Fast is Reported Missing," based on a cable to her brother, H. A. Fast, MCC's vice chair from 1943 to 1960. A week later a paragraph offered "the very faintest hope that she may still be alive" and described the explosion on the ship on which she was traveling, accompanying refugees returning from Egypt to Yugoslavia. One more week was all that was needed to receive the heartbreaking account of the incident from fellow traveler and MCC worker Richard Yoder. After the explosion in the middle of the night, Yoder had been directed into a lifeboat. Reaching shore after seven hours, he learned from a United Nations official that the lifeboat in which Fast was being lowered broke loose, throwing her and a British naval officer into the sea. That week's editorial shaped the meaning of Fast's death through her "voyage undertaken for the welfare of [people who were not of her own nation or tongue]" and named it "a glimpse of what peacemakers can be like and often are."[93]

Although MCC's early years were marked by the frequency of reports on MCC worker travel and the travel means they used, and despite the centrality of the refugee motif to the image of MCC, occasional notes of reflection on themselves as travelers allowed a different perspective on MCC travel. As in much tourist writing, stories of travel troubles were frequent in the early years observed in this case study. As already noted, in the years surrounding World War II, MCC workers frequently mentioned travel delays in their writing, such as being "already at Akron headquarters awaiting sailing notice."[94]

Reprinted letters to family of workers who were familiar to early *Mennonite* readers were sometimes sources of such travel stories. Sam Goering described his voyage to England in early 1945 as "long and hard," then added "it could have been worse.... Now that it is all over I recall with pleasure, even the cockroaches that befriended me on the way...."[95] Pannabecker, whose long journey to China was noted above, wrote from Calcutta: "I have traveled for monotonous days over endless seas."[96] Reporting on his visits to Mennonite refugees in Germany and Denmark, C. F. Klassen noted: "The nights are cold and rain makes traveling unpleasant, but I don't mind as long as I can bring some comfort to these, my suffering brethren."[97]

Difficult travel conditions caused by war eventually gave way to problems in places where poor travel infrastructure was part of overall economic conditions. A worker in Paraguay described riding in a truck from the port to the Mennonite colony where he worked: "The road had been dusty and by the time we got settled we were pretty dirty."[98] But such stories were rare; one may guess that they continued to be told in letters and e-mails to friends and family, but they were not included in the more formal news releases that became central to MCC communication with the Mennonite press.

The idea that these stories interested readers, however, did not disappear. In 1995 an account by nurse Margaret De Jong described delivering triplets by the roadside after failing to reach the Haitian hospital in time because of "rough dirt roads."[99] Six months later De Jong's adventure was profiled in an MCC ad, which shared a synopsis of her story and the headline: "Is God Calling You to Offer Your Skills on New Roads?"[100]

Travel troubles because of political and military situations continued to reflect MCC experience through the decades. Richard Blackburn, working with MCC and UNRRA (United Nations Relief and Rehabilitation Administration), was part of a planeload of American relief workers repatriating refuges whose plane was forced down over Yugoslavia and who were interned for thirteen days in 1946.[101] In 1965 MCC doctor Arnold Nickel reported fleeing the Baptist mission station where he was working during rebel activity in the Congo. Twenty-one adults and seven children were "packed like sardines into a slow overloaded (river) boat" provided by the Catholic mission, an experience that, after they reached safety, Nickel pronounced an "adventure."[102] During the civil war in El Salvador in the 1980s, Nathan and Elaine Zook Barge were "caught in the middle of an army-guerrilla confrontation while traveling from the capital to their village by bus."[103] Such travel experiences were deadly serious, a sober reality further exemplified by reports noting the shooting deaths of Lebanese and Guatemalan MCC employees during the 1980s and by the 2010 shooting death of MCC worker Glenn Lapp in Afghanistan along with other aid workers.[104]

It is perhaps noteworthy that this case study found no reference to problems related to air travel, despite the fact that air transport means had become the most common means of reaching assignments by the 1960s. Mention of the numbers of miles traveled was also rare, and after the war reporting, so was the question of time spent on travel—and the fact that some MCC workers continued through the decades to experience long delays in going to assignments while waiting for visas was also absent from the reporting.

However, the sense that distances traveled and the time spent traveling mattered occasionally surfaced: intriguingly, such mention of travel distances and times often occurred in descriptions of administrative travel. In 1945 MCC Executive Secretary Orie Miller reported that he "traveled about 27,000 miles in 114 days . . . visiting needy areas in Europe, the Near East, and Africa. . . ."[105] In 1960 Robert Miller, director of Foreign Relief and Services, returned from "a seven-week trip to South America."[106] A 1985 meeting of the Council of International Ministries, an inter-Mennonite body including MCC, was profiled as a gathering of "globe-trotting executives": "Thirty-two of the best-traveled Mennonites in the world gathered . . . allowing themselves no vanities except long coffee breaks and frequent references to their most recent administrative jaunts. . . ."[107]

Further, MCC in the years covered by this case study made almost no effort to include the costs of travel in its analysis of program. In 1930 MCC reported that, to maintain contact with Mennonite immigrants to Paraguay, they would ask missionary T. K. Hershey, working in Argentina, to visit. Hershey was ideal for the assignment,

Levi Mumaw commented, because he could speak Spanish and was nearby, making the travel less expensive. MCC would pay Hershey's expenses, Mumaw was quick to add.[108]

The Mennonite did attempt to bring mission-related travel costs to the attention of its readers in 1965: "Missionary travel during the summer months will cost . . . between $30,000 and $40,000. . . . Special contributions are solicited."[109] However, MCC statistics, listed in annual reports inserted into The Mennonite in the 1980s and 1990s, counted dollars, workers, and the value of material resources shipped but not miles traveled. As the articulation of MCC's effort to work for justice grew, the link to travel was not made. A 1980 article calling for "simple personal lifestyles" as a response to hunger called for systemic change in "patterns of living, investments, and purchases."[110]

A sense that travel costs have now entered the MCC reporting arena is finally found in a recent issue of the MCC periodical A Common Place, when interim executive director Bert Lobe quoted what is known as the "travelers psalm" (Ps. 121), and then discussed the environmental costs of travel: "At MCC we are exploring ways to reduce our negative impacts on the environment, such as reducing air travel . . . embracing a policy of carbon offsets for air travel and promoting energy efficiency."[111]

As travel became more frequent and widespread among Mennonites, the value placed on roving the world for education and exchange became visible. MCC-related travel agents played a role. MCC's report of its 1950 annual meeting mentioned that Menno Travel Service, the travel desk founded in 1947 by MCC to coordinate MCC worker travel which later became an independent business, had served 371 individuals, including MCC workers, the year before: the report hastened to add that MTS was "self supporting financially."[112] Also that year, the same report that mentioned 88 Mennonite refugees sailing from Italy for Brazil and Paraguay also noted that 45 students left the United States for a study tour to Europe, "the M.C.C. Voluntary Service office assisting."[113] By 1960, MTS was offering its own "spring Europe and Holy Land" tours.[114] MCC itself became directly involved, in a way whose dimensions are surely not adequately noted in this case study: a tour of 42 Japanese young people to the United States in 1965, a Peace Section tour to the Middle East in 1970, and a Nigerian women's choir to Canada and the U.S. in 1995.[115]

The most reflective comments on the travel of MCC workers illustrate that, like Elsie Bechtel, other MCC workers acknowledged their identities as pilgrim-tourists (or at least they grappled with the

question of to what extent they were tourists), even as they also identified themselves as relief and service workers. The long journey of
Pannabecker and Balzer to China in 1945 was broken by ten days in
Palestine, which Pannabecker named a "high point." In true pilgrim
fashion, he described how they "trudged, day after day, through the
city of Jerusalem, with its many memories."[116]

Another worker's reactions to the exotic realities of Java led to
the raising of a question that would be echoed in later such reflections: what exactly are MCC travelers? Are they tourists? If so, are
they something more? Meryl Grasse, in prose evoking the colonial
gaze, wrote that as his plane, the "Flying Dutchman, "swooped
down on Batavia [now Djakarta]," he observed rice paddies, water
buffalo, and "coolies," "lithe, strong-muscled little brown men."
"One might say," he added, "that these are merely impressions of a
tourist or a traveler, but," he quickly added, "I have come 'in the
name of Christ'. . . ."[117]

Following the same process, Austria MCC director Norman
Wingert's travel narrative similarly began with a descending flight,
this one from London into "Vienna the tragic." "Why should we not
endeavor to see deeply?" he asked. "Mennonite Central Committee
workers are not classified in the category of the tourist." Wingert,
however, went even further, attempting to draw the reader into this
blended traveler identity: "Will you, too, though busy with your own
concerns with a lively and sympathetic imagination, span the water
that lies between, and join us as we walk and work among these people?"[118]

The intersection of service, tourism, and pilgrimage seemed especially apt for the young men assigned to the PAX program. For several years, MCC Paxmen assigned in Europe were invited to travel as
a group to Palestine, extensively described in the "Youth" section of
The Mennonite. "We were pilgrims," asserted James Juhnke. "The specific purpose of the pilgrimage was to visit places of biblical significance." One evaluation declared: "Everyone seemed to agree that the
PAX Pilgrimage to Palestine was more than a vacation—it was a spiritual experience." Photos of the 1960 group included one of Elsie
Bechtel, holding her own camera, back in Europe with MCC for a
later assignment as a "Pax matron."[119] Ten years later, the director of
the United Mission to Nepal offered his description of the PAX workers there: "a little shy," "eager to learn Nepali," and "in moments of
leisure cycle[ing] through the narrow streets of the capital . . . intrigued by the friendly people and the bewildering differences of
types and dress."[120]

The metaphor of mobility was heard occasionally even as specific comments about travel became less frequent in the Mennonite press. On the occasion of MCC's fiftieth anniversary in 1970, *The Mennonite* editor Maynard Shelly reflected on the organization as "God's miracle among us," with the prayer: "May there continue being rather than becoming, mobility rather than arrival. . . ."[121]

MCC's own reporting, meanwhile, became more insistent in its efforts to break any link between MCC's traveling workers and tourism, even as MCC reporting reflected a profound ambivalence about the travel so integral to the organization's work. In 1960, carefully worded articles reporting on a delegation visit to the Soviet Union had acknowledged the tourist status of its members yet included enough details that readers would understand that status as a necessary evil to allow visits to Mennonites behind the Iron Curtain: "Despite previously confirmed reservations, the four Mennonites currently visiting the Soviet Union have had their traveling route changed by Intourist, the official tourist agency. . . . [These changes] will undoubtedly decrease the number of Mennonites they will be able to see."

Upon their return, the visitors to the USSR offered details on distances traveled ("about four thousand miles") and descriptions of the kinds amenities they found in "deluxe" hotels. Adding that "most of the Bibles and other Christian literature carried . . . were impounded at the border," they regretted that they "did not have the opportunity to . . . deliver greetings" in the churches they visited.[122] If the MCC visitors to the Soviet Union in 1960 grudgingly accepted their tourist status, a 1970 article adapted from one of MCC's fiftieth anniversary publications sought to differentiate MCC workers from tourists in stark terms: "The Christian volunteer . . . is not on an extended safari to exotic-land, nor on a slow-paced tourist's joyride, nor a long weekend into the urban jungle, any from which he can emerge again at whim, unscathed and unmoved." [123]

MCC workers occasionally evinced an awareness of the power represented by access to travel. As one worker wrote in 1975: "We are rich. . . . We have a radio and a camera. We travel in airplanes." An MCC news article acknowledged the privilege the ability to travel conferred, noting that workers "can choose to stay [in their assignment] or board an airplane and begin a new life or pick up their old one. . . ."[124] Yet even as MCC workers and news articles recognized the power embodied in MCC worker mobility, MCC news releases also took pains to disentangle MCC workers from tourists. An MCC news release from Nepal, for example, began by evoking that coun-

184 A Table of Sharing

try's tourist vistas—"stunning snow-capped mountains and the promise of adventure (for backpackers)"—only to contrast the travel of the tourist with MCC worker travel, describing an MCC nurse driving and hiking for hours to provide medical assistance to remote villages. This nurse, Ruth McCaslin, the article insisted, "is not a tourist. She is a Mennonite Central Committee nurse."[125]

The decline in direct references to MCC travel in MCC news releases and in Mennonite press depictions of MCC work, together with the repeated insistence, bordering on a mantra, that MCC workers are not tourists, calls for critical reflection. Clearly the travel so essential to MCC's work in the twenty-first century must be taken more seriously in light of the reality that the gap between those who can travel and those who cannot travel, or between those who travel for work or pleasure and those upon whom travel is forced by war, natural disaster, or the dynamics of a globalized economy, has not lessened. Further, increasing costs of travel, heightened security risks, and knowledge of the environmental impact of fossil-fuel-based journeys all ought to enter into a self-critical analysis of MCC travel.

Acknowledging the foundational human orientation to travel might be a first step toward such a self-critical appraisal of MCC travel, one which does not all-too-hastily (and defensively) seek to cordon off MCC travel from other forms of travel, like tourism. As John Daniel put it,

> All of us are descended from peoples whose way was to roam with the seasons, following game herds and the succession of edible plants.... Along the way, lately, we have lost much of the sensory acuity our saga evoked in us, our ability to smell danger or read a landscape or notice nuances of weather, but the old knowing still stirs an alertness, an air of anticipation, when we set out on our various journeys.[126]

Such "alertness" of anticipated journeys, an alertness markedly evident in the writings of Elsie Bechtel, must be taken into account in future theological musings about the call to service. Elsie's tourist-like pleasure in a bicycle ride through the countryside around Lavercantière cannot be divorced from her deeply embodied love for the refugee children for whom she cared. Through her words, we can see her MCC assignment at the chateau of Lavercantière as a pilgrimage to a holy borderland "where the completely foreign is brought together with the familiar...."

So too, we may argue, are all MCC workers pilgrims. Although theologian William Cavanaugh seeks in the context of globalization to distinguish the tourist from the pilgrim, his reflections offer otherwise helpful reflections on the kind of mobility that can sustain the Christian community for its contemporary witness:

> To embrace the identity of the pilgrim now is first of all to embrace a certain type of mobility in the context of globalization. The church has been unmoored and should joyfully take leave of the settledness of Contantinian social arrangements that gave it privilege and power. . . . A church that desires to be a pilgrim does not claim the power to treat every location as interchangeable and impose global solutions on the world.[127]

Learning how to be more than numb through airports and on jets, how to live within those realities with a recognition of their rooting in privilege and power, and how to build on what they make possible on behalf of "the universal Christ (as) found in the one lonely migrant who knocks at the door"[128]—this is certainly enough of a challenge moving into MCC's second century.

NOTES

1. Rowan Williams, *Ponder These Things: Praying with Icons of the Virgin* (Norwich, England: The Canterbury Press, 2002), xiv.

2. Elsie C. Bechtel, Diary, October 16, 1946, in possession of M. J. Heisey, State University of New York Potsdam (hereafter ECB diary).

3. Bechtel, "Why We Should Support Relief Services," *Evangelical Visitor*, July 16, 1945, p. 5.

4. ECB diary, July 25, 1945.

5. H. Frances Davidson, *South and South Central Africa: A Record of Fifteen Years' Labors Among Primitive Peoples* (Elgin, Ill.: Brethren Publishing House, 1915).

6. Nancy R. Heisey, "Of Two Minds: Ambivalence in the Language of Brethren in Christ Missionaries," *Brethren in Christ History and Life* 11 (April-August 1988): 10-43, 95-132.

7. See, for example, T. K. Hershey, *I'd Do It Again* (Elkhart, Ind.: Mennonite Board of Missions and Charities, 1961); Allen Buckwalter, *Out of the Cobra's Clutches* (Nappanee, Ind.: Evangel Press, 1987); Susan Yoder Ackerman, *Copper Moons* (Scottdale, Pa.: Herald Press, 1990); Sally Schroeder Isaak, *Some Seed Fell on Good Ground* (Winnipeg, MB: Henderson Books, 1994); Joseph C. Shenk, *Silver Threads: The Ups and Downs of a Mennonite Family in Mission, 1895-1995* (Intercourse, Pa.: Good Books, 1996); Jolene Kaufman Pauls, *All Things Working for Good: Letters of a Young Man's African Journey* (Hutchinson, Kan.: Pauls Publishing, 2004); Roy Kreider, *Land of Revelation: A Reconciling Presence in Israel* (Scottdale, Pa.: Herald Press, 2004); Lynda Hollinger Janzen, *A New Day in Mission: Irene Weaver Reflects on Her Century of Ministry* (Elkhart, Ind.: Mennonite Mission Network, 2005).

8. ECB diary, March 10, 1946.

9. ECB diary, May 23, 1046.

10. Samuel Escobar, "Mission as Service for the 21st. Century," *Unity amid Diversity: Mennonite Central Committee at 75* (Akron, Pa.: Mennonite Central Committee, 1996), 143-149.

11. ECB diary, February 13, 1946.

12. Wendy Pullan, "'Intermingled Until the End of Time': Ambiguity as a Central Condition of Early Christian Pilgrimage," in *Pilgrimage in Graeco-Roman & Early Christian Antiquity: Seeing the Gods*, ed. Jaœ Elsner and Ian Rutherford (Oxford: Oxford University Press, 2005), 388.

13. Susanna Elm, *"Virgins of God:" The Making of Asceticism in Late Antiquity* (Oxford: Clarendon Press, 1994), 279; Maribel Dietz, *Wandering Monks, Virgins, and Pilgrims: Ascetic Travel in the Mediterranean World, A.D. 300-800* (State College, Pa.: Pennsylvania State University Press, 2005), 150.

14. Tony Perrottet, *Pagan Holiday: On the Trail of Ancient Roman Tourists* (New York: Random House, 2003).

15. "Tourist," Oxford English Dictionary, http://dictionary.oed.com /cgi/entry/50255230?query_type=word&queryword=tourist&first=1&ma x_to_show=10&sort_type=alpha&result_place=1&search_id=DcXb-ojiVP5-11345&hilite=50255230, accessed 7 May 2009

16. Elizabeth Weiss Ozorak, "The View From the Edge: Pilgrimage and Transformation," in *On the Road to Being There: Studies in Pilgrimage and Tourism in Late Modernity*, ed. William H. Swatos Jr. (Leiden: Brill, 2006), 67; Dietz, 35.

17. Elsner and Rutherford, "Introduction," 31. See also specific articles in the Elsner and Rutherford collection on Classical, Hellenistic, and Roman pilgrimage.

18. Robert L. Wilkin, *The Spirit of Early Christian Thought: Seeking the Face of God* (New Haven, Conn.: Yale University Press, 2003), 238.

19. Eusebius, *Ecclesiastical History* 4.26, 6.14; Dietz, 35.

20. Victor Turner and Edith Turner, *Image and Pilgrimage in Christian Culture: Anthropological Perspectives* (New York: Columbia University Press, 1978), 17-18, 20.

21. John Eade and Michael J. Sallnow, *Contesting the Sacred: The Anthropology of Christian Pilgrimage* (London and New York: Routledge, 1991), 3, 5.

22. Erik Cohen, "Pilgrimage and Tourism: Convergence and Divergence," in Alan Morinis, *Sacred Journeys: The Anthropology of Pilgrimage* (Westport, Conn.: Greenwood Press, 1992), 56-58; James J. Preston, "Spiritual Magnetism: An Organizing Principle for the Study of Pilgrimage," in Morinis, 36.

23. William H. Swatos, Jr., "For Charles and for England: Pilgrimage Without Tourism," in *On the Road to Being There: Studies in Pilgrimage and Tourism in Late Modernity* , ed. Swatos (Leiden: Brill, 2006), 1-31.

24. Nancy L. Frey, "Stories of the Return: Pilgrimage and its Aftermaths," in Ellen Badone and Sharon R. Roseman, *Intersecting Journeys: The Anthropology of Pilgrimage and Tourism* (Urbana, Ill.: University of Illinois, 2004), 89.

25. Luigi Tomasi, "*Homo Viator*: From Pilgrimage to Religious Tourism via the Journey," in Swatos and Tomasi, *From Medieval Pilgrimage to Religious Tourism: The Social and Cultural Economics of Piety* (Westport, Conn.: Praeger, 2002), 1.

26. Judith Adler, "The Holy Man as Traveler and Travel Attraction: Early

Christian Asceticism and the Moral Problematic of Modernity," in Swatos and Tomasi, 25.

27. Ellen Badone and Sharon R. Roseman. "Approaches to the Anthropology of Pilgrimage and Tourism," in Badone and Roseman, *Intersecting Journeys: The Anthropology of Pilgrimage and Tourism*, 2, 6.

28. Dietz, 220.

29. George, E. Gingras, ed. and trans., *Diary of a Pilgrimage* by Egeria (New York: Newman Press, 1970); Elizabeth A. Clark, trans. and comp., *The Life of Melania the Younger* by Gerontius (New York: The Edwin Mellen Press, 1984).

30. Judith Adler, "Travel as Performed Art," in *American Journal of Sociology* 94 (May 1989): 1380.

31. *Life of Melania* Prologue, 39.

32. Adler (1989), 1370, 1375, 1378, 1382.

33. Steven J. Harris, "Mapping Jesuit Science: The Role of Travel in the Geography of Knowledge," in *The Jesuits: Cultures, Sciences, and the Arts, 1540-1773*, ed. John W. O'Malley (Toronto: University of Toronto Press, 1999), 233.

34. David Calhoun, "Of Ships and Books: The Travel Journals of the Early Princeton Seminary Missionaries," *Presbyterion* 12/1 (Spring 1986): 34.

35. R. K. Orchard, "The Significance of Ecumenical Travel," *Journal of Ecumenical Studies* 15/3 (Summer 1978): 477-502; Annette Brown, "Tourism and Mission," *Caribbean Journal of Religious Studies* 8 (1987): 35-44.

36. Murray W. Dempster, Byron D. Klaus, and Douglas Peterson, *The Globalization of Pentecostalism: A Religion Made to Travel* (Irvine, Calif.: Regnum, 1999); Simon Coleman, "Moving Toward the Millennium?" *Journal of Ritual Studies* 14/2 (2000): 16-27.

37. Representative scholarly works in English include: Frank H. Epp, *Mennonite Exodus: The Rescue and Resettlement of the Russian Mennonites Since the Communist Revolution* (Altona, MB: D. W. Friesen for the Canadian Mennonite Relief and Immigration Council, 1962); John B. Toews, *Lost Fatherland: The Story of Mennonite Emigration from Soviet Russia, 1921-1927* (Scottdale, Pa.: Herald Press, 1967); Jiwu Wang, *The People on the Move: The Relationship Between Migration and Faith: An Aspect of Mennonite Life and Faithfulness from the Sixteenth Century to the Present*, unpublished M.A. thesis (Winnipeg, MB: University of Manitoba, 1994; Richard Warren Davis, *Emigrants, Refugees and Prisoners: An Aid to Mennonite Family Research* (Provo, Utah: R. W. Davis, c. 1995); Lynda Reynolds Klassen, *The Aftermath of Trauma and Immigration: Detections of Multigenerational Effects on Mennonites Who Emigrated from Russia to Canada in the 1920s*, unpublished Psy.D. thesis (Fresno, Calif.: California School of Professional Psychology, 1997); Marlene Epp, *Women Without Men: Mennonite Immigration to Canada and Paraguay after the Second World War* (Toronto: University of Toronto Press, 2000). Examples of personal narratives in English include: Jacob Klaassen, *Grandfather's Description of the Trip to Central Asia, 1880: Asienreise* (H. T. Klaassen, 1964; in Menno Simons Historical Library); Anna Reimer Dyck, *Anna, From the Caucasus to Canada* (Hillsboro, Kan.: Mennonite Brethren Publishing House, 1979); Cornelius C. Funk, *Escape to Freedom* (Hillsboro, Kan.: Mennonite Brethren Publishing House, 1982); Franz Bartsch, *Our Trek to Central Asia* (Winnipeg, MB: CMBC Publications, 1993); Wilmer A. Harms, *The Odyssey of Escapes from Russia: The Saga of Anna K* (Hillsboro, Kan.: Hearth Publishing, 1998); John B. Toews, *Journeys:*

Mennonite Stories of Faith and Survival in Stalin's Russia (Winnipeg, MB: Kindred Press, 1998). See also John D. Roth and Ervin Beck, eds., *Migrant Muses: Mennonite/s Writing in the U.S.* (Goshen, Ind.: Mennonite Historical Society, 1998).

38. See Readings 13, 18, 33 in *From the Files of MCC*, MCC history vol. 1, ed. Cornelius J. Dyck (Scottdale, Pa. and Kitchener, Ont.: Herald Press, 1980); Readings 24, 27, 53 in *Responding to Worldwide Needs*, MCC history vol. 2, ed. Cornelius J. Dyck (Scottdale, Pa.: Herald Press, 1980); Chapter 3 in *Hungry, Thirsty, a Stranger: The MCC Experience*, MCC history vol. 5, by Robert S. Kreider and Rachel Waltner Goosen (Scottdale, Pa.: Herald Press, 1988).

39. Bryant L. Myers, "The Global Context of Christian Relief and Development," *The Conrad Grebel Review* (Fall 1995): 397-398.

40. P.C. Hiebert and Orie O. Miller, *Feeding the Hungry: Russia Famine, 1919-1925* (Scottdale, Pa.: Mennonite Central Committee, 1929), 188-9, 212, 248.

41. Irvin B. Horst, *A Ministry of Goodwill: A Short Account of Mennonite Relief, 1939-1949* (Akron, Pa.: Mennonite Central Committee, 1950), 29, 65.

42. Marian Keeney Preheim, "Elfrieda Dyck," *Something Beautiful for God*, MCC history vol. 4, Cornelius J. Dyck, ed. (Scottdale, Pa.: Herald Press, 1981), 244-255.

43. Melvin Gingerich, "Research Notes; Research Topics on the Mennonite Central Committee," *The Mennonite Quarterly Review* 44/3 (July 1970): 330-334.

44. "Many in the withdrawal experience of living apart from their home communities, discovered for the first time their Mennonite identity," wrote Robert Kreider in "The Impact of MCC Service on American Mennonites," *The Mennonite Quarterly* Review 44/3 (July 1970),:249.

45. Peter J. Dyck, "A Theology of Service," *The Mennonite Quarterly Review* 44/3 (July 1970): 269.

46. Paul Bender, "Evaluation Study of the Mennonite College European Student Program," *Proceedings of the Twelfth Conference on Mennonite Educational and Cultural Problems* (Goshen, Ind.: Council of Mennonite and Affiliated Colleges, 1959), 11.

47. Attlee Beechy, "The Role of the Mennonite College in Education for World Mission," *Proceedings* (1963), 20, 31.

48. Arthur Climenhaga, "The Role of Foreign Service and Foreign Study in Education for World Mission," *Proceedings* (1963), 37.

49. Robert S. Kreider, "Christian Vocation in the Light of World Needs," *Proceedings* (1963), 59-60.

50. Wilfred J. Unruh, "An Evaluation of Mennonite Service Programs," *Proceedings* (1967), 152.

51. Larry Kehler, "A Profile of Mennonite Personnel Involved in International Experience," *Proceedings* (1967), 35, 38.

52. Donald Kraybill, "From Enclave to Engagement; MCC and the Transformation of Mennonite Identity," *Unity Amidst Diversity: Mennonite Central Committee at 75*, ed. Robert Kreider and Ronald J. R. Mathies (Akron, Pa.: Mennonite Central Committee, 1996), 21-22.

53. Ronald J. R. Mathies, "Service as (Trans)formation: MCC as Educational Institution," in Kreider and Mathies, 74-75.

54. Judith Dueck, "Response," *The Conrad Grebel Review* (Fall 1995): 246.

55. *The Mennonite* was the official periodical for the General Conference Mennonite Church, a bi-national (U.S. and Canada) denomination until 1998, when it became the periodical of the newly formed Mennonite Church USA.

56. "Relief Notes," *The Mennonite* (hereafter TM) Oct. 2, 1945, 12; Oct 9, 1945, 11.

57. "Relief Notes," TM Oct 2, 1930, 3.

58. "Relief Notes," TM Feb 27, 1940, 6; Apr 23, 1940, 7; May 14 1940, 4; Sept 3, 1940, 13; Oct 1, 1940, 7.

59. ECB diary, Aug. 29, 1945.

60. "Relief Notes," TM Jan 2, 1945, 12.

61. "Relief Notes," TM Feb 6, 1945, 15.

62. "Relief Notes," TM Mar 27, 1945, 13; Apr 3, 1945, 21-22

63. "Relief Notes," TM Sep 18, 1945, 13; Oct 16, 1945, 10.

64. Pearl Sensenig, "Study: MCC workers lack church support," TM Jan 4, 2000, 9.

65. H. J. Krehbiel, "Second Installment of Auto Trip Across the Continent," TM Aug 14, 1930, 12; "Installment No. 8 of Trip Across the Continent," TM Aug 28, 1930, 7; "Conclusion of Trip Across the Continent," TM Sep 25, 1930, 5-6. Emma Ruth, "The Christian Endeavor Friendship Tour," TM Aug 21, 1930, 11-12; "On to Berlin," Sep 4, 1930, 12; "The Personnel of the C.E. Tour," TM Sep 18, 1930, 9-10. Krehbiel in particular paid attention to travel details, noting the layout of Albuquerque, New Mexico, as for "the time when every citizen of the U.S. will own two autos," and listing the number of miles he traveled and the highest and lowest prices he paid for gasoline. See also "Krehbiel, Henry J. (1865-1940)." *Global Anabaptist Mennonite Encyclopedia Online.* 1957. Global Anabaptist Mennonite Encyclopedia Online. Retrieved 07 August 2009 , http://www.gameo.org/encyclopedia/contents/krehbiel_henry_j._1865_1940

66. "Relief Notes," TM Jul 24, 1903, 4; Jul 31, 1930, 4.

67. David Toews, "The Danzig Mennonite Relief World Conference," TM Oct 30, 1930, 3-4.

68. "Relief Notes," quoting letter from G. G. Hiebert, TM Nov 13, 1930, 4.

69. "Bicycles for Europe," TM Dec 11, 1945, 10.

70. "Relief Notes," TM Mar 27, 1945, 13

71. "Relief," TM Jan 2, 1945, 12.

72. "Relief," TM Feb 6, 1945, 11.

73. "Dutch Mennonite Leader Appeals for Help," TM Jul 17, 1945, 4

74. "R.C. Kauffman Writes From Calcutta, India," TM Jan 16, 1945, 10.

75. "Relief," TM Nov 13, 1945, 13.

76. "Relief," TM Oct 9, 1945, 12.

77. "Relief," TM Nov 20, 1945, 7.

78. "Relief," TM Aug 21, 1945, 12.

79. TM, Dec 6, 1960, 788.

80. TM Jan 28, 1975, 57.

81. "Massive corn shipment en route to refugees in Somalia," TM Dec 9, 1980, 716.

82. TM Jun 10, 1980, 378; TM Apr 11, 1995, 12.

83. M. C. Lehman, "Needs and Conditions in Europe: Uprooted People," TM Jul 10, 1945, 7-8.

84. "Relief," TM Aug 14, 1945, 14.

85. Willard Krabill, "Vietnam's Challenge," TM Aug 2, 1960, 429; Murray and Linda Hiebert, "Future Dim on Refugee Road," TM May 6, 1975, 288.

86. "MCC to Expand Ministry to Refugees," TM Feb 19, 1980, 118.

87. "West Coast MCC Asks Compassion for Immigrants," TM Jan 24, 1995, 13-15; Gladys Terichow, "Winnipeg Church Makes Difference in Refugee Lives," TM Sept 26, 1995, 15.

88. "Relief," TM Sept 11, 1945, 11.

89. "MCC News Notes," TM Jan 4, 1955, 14.

90. "A Trans-Chaco Roadway in Prospect for Paraguay," TM July 19, 1955, 440.

91. "MCC News," TM July 12, 1960, 448.

92. Willard Smith, "Changes in Paraguay," TM Nov 30, 1965, 744-6.

93. "Marie Fast is Reported Missing," TM May 15, 1945, 7; "Marie Fast Evidently Lost at Sea," TM May 22, 1945; "Report of Sea Incident in Which Marie Fast was Lost," "Editorial," TM May 29, 1945, 2-3, 8.

94. "Relief," TM, Jan 9, 1945, 13.

95. "Sam Goering Writes From England," TM Apr 24, 1945, 10.

96. S. F. Pannabecker, "The Mennonite Central Committee in the Far East," TM Aug 7, 1945, 2, 6-7.

97. "Relief," TM Nov 20, 1945, 7.

98. "We Visit and Work in Volendam Colony, Paraguay," TM Feb 21, 1950, 124.

99. Margaret De Jong, "MCC Worker Writes of Three-In-One Miracle," TM May 23, 1995, 17.

100. MCC full-page ad, TM Dec 26, 1995, 21.

101. "Relief," TM Sept 10, 1946, 13.

102. "Canadian Doctor Flees Attacks; Catholic Boat Used in Congo," TM Apr 13, 1965, 249-50.

103. TM Jul 23, 1985, 368.

104. For 1980s deaths see TM, Apr 9, 1985, 157; Apr 23, 1985, 179. For Glen Lapp see TM Sep 1, 2010, 38.

105. "Jottings," TM Nov 20, 1945, 15.

106. TM Nov 8, 1960, 726.

107. Glenn M. Lehman, "CIM Faces Dilemmas of Modern Missions," TM Jun 25, 1985, 322.

108. "Relief Notes," TM Dec 11, 1930, 3.

109. "Words and Deeds," TM Jul 20, 1965, 468.

110. Paul Longacre, "Hunger: Simple personal lifestyles are important now as models of the kingdom and as a call to systemic change," TM Jun 10, 1980, 412-3.

111. A. C. Lobe, "Caring for Creation," *A Common Place*, (May/June 2007), inside front cover.

112. "Mennonites Contribute Two Million Plus for 'the Healing of the Nations,'" TM Apr 4, 1950, 221.

113. TM Jun 27, 1950, 449.

114. TM Dec 20, 1960, 817.

115. TM Sep 21, 1965, 590; TM Feb 10, 1970, 93; "Nigerian Choir Builds Bridges," TM Apr 25, 1995, 13.

116. S. F. Pannabecker, "Our Mennonite Relief Work in the Middle East," TM May 15, 1945, 9-10.

117. Meryl Grasse, "Java Its Sights and Sounds," TM Nov 28, 1950, 788-9.

118. Norman Wingert, "In Old Vienna," TM Dec 5, 1950, 800-1.

119. Charles Yoder, "Pax Pilgrimage to Palestine," TM Jul 12, 1955, 458; James Juhnke, "Pax Pilgrimage 1960," TM Jun 7, 1960, 381.

120. Samuel R. Burgoyne, TM Feb 3, 1970, 80.

121. Editorial, TM Mar 10, 1970, 176.

122. TM Feb 23, 1960, 125; Jun 28, 1960, 432; Aug 2, 1960, 488-9.

123. "MCC Got Its Start in a Revolution," TM Jul 28, 1970, 476-8.

124. "Volunteers are rich on a shoestring," TM Nov 4, 1975, 625.

125. Pearl Sensenig, "In remote Nepali mountain villages, MCC nurse helps create medical miracles," TM Jan 25, 2000, 9.

126. John Daniel, "A Word in Favor of Rootlessness," in *The Future of Nature: Writing on a Human Ecology from* Orion *Magazine*, sel. and ed. Barry Lopez (Minneapolis, Minn.: Milkweed Editions, 2007), 165.

127. William T. Cavanaugh, "Migrant, Tourist, Pilgrim, Monk: Mobility and Identity in a Global Age," *Theological Studies* 69 (2008), 351.

128. Cavanaugh, 356.

Chapter 8

The Missiology of MCC: A Framework for Assessing Multiple Voices Within the MCC Family

STANLEY W. GREEN AND JAMES R. KRABILL

How would I describe MCC's "missiology"? Ha! That is one of MCC's biggest problems. It doesn't have one!
—Longtime MCC worker, 2007

Not being expected to plant churches is, in some ways, liberating. It allows us to have a reduced "agenda," to approach people more willing to listen, to work easily with a wide variety of local church partners and to move into areas where church planting is actually forbidden. But just because we do not have a mandate to plant churches does not mean that we should not have a missiology. We need a missiology as much as mission boards do.
—Ray Brubacher[1]

The real question may . . . not be whether Mennonites have a theology of service . . . but whether our philosophy of service, being rooted in Scripture, is in fact a theology of service under another name.
—Peter Dyck[2]

The preaching of the gospel and the service of [human need] are equally authentic and essential parts of the Church's responsibility. But neither is a substitute for the other. No amount of service, however expert and however generous, is a substitute for the explicit testimony to Jesus Christ. . . . But equally, the preaching of that Name will be empty, if he who speaks it is not willing to deal honestly and realistically with the issues that his hearers have to face.
—Leslie Newbigin[3]

Our charge in this chapter is to explore the missiology that has guided the development and delivery of MCC programs and interventions during the past nine decades. The charge presupposes, of course, that MCC *has* had an operative missiology by which its work has been shaped. This presumption is not, however, universally shared. The first anecdote provided above suggests that the notion of an MCC "missiology" is not even assumed by some of MCC's key stakeholders. This raises the question: Does MCC *have* a missiology? To answer that question it may be helpful, first, to understand what is meant by the term.

WHAT IS MISSIOLOGY?

Missiology as a discipline had its beginnings in the post-Enlightenment era. This temporal point of origin, no doubt, led to the common practice in the earlier part of the twentieth century of referring to missiology as the "science" of missions.

Some have described the discipline of missiology from the perspective of human engagement, thus emphasizing strategy and a grappling with insights of the social sciences like anthropology and the fields of communication and culture in the interest of helping mission to be more effective and appropriate.[4] The primary interest in this case is to answer the "how" questions of the church's engagement with a world that is other than Christian.

Others have focused on the "why" questions, the questions of divine purpose. Orlando Costas, for example, describes missiology as

the critical reflection that takes place in the practice of mission. . . . [It occurs] in the concrete missionary situation, as part of the church's missionary obedience to and participation in God's mission, and is itself actualized in that situation. . . . Missiology arises as part of a witnessing engagement to the gospel in the multiple situations of life.[5]

Following in this vein of defining missiology against the larger canvas of God's purpose and the human response it evokes, or *should* evoke, Johannes Verkuyl frames the undertaking of missiology in trinitarian terms that address the kingdom of God as the embodiment of those purposes. For him, missiology is first and foremost

> the study of the salvation activities of the Father, Son, and Holy Spirit throughout the world geared toward bringing the kingdom of God into existence; [and secondly, it is] the study of the worldwide church's divine mandate to be ready to serve this God who is aiming his saving acts toward this world.[6]

Based on the various descriptions encountered here, we would offer the following statement as our understanding of what constitutes missiology as a *formal* discipline: It is the deliberate, purposeful exploration of the nature of our engagement with the world in light of our understanding of God and God's intended outcome for the world.

While missiology as a discipline has received greater acceptance in the academy, we would hasten to add that it is not the sole preserve of scholars and academics. We note that, mostly in informal ways, the discipleship considerations which preoccupy all believers serve to generate contemplations regarding the Christian's role and calling in response to God's purposes in the world. Most followers of Jesus, thus, have an *informal* "missiology," even if it is indeterminate and imprecise.

Formal missiology is, by contrast, the reflective, critical, and systematic activity that seeks to discern how God's purposes in creation, along with the redemptive acts embodied in the life, death, and resurrection of Jesus Christ and through the recreative work of the Spirit, shape the church's witness and discipleship. As a result, missiology's goal is to locate, through careful biblical-theological study, the people of God within the frame of God's purposes in creation and redemption and to identify and inspire those responses which advance the divine purposes in the world today.

DOES MCC HAVE A MISSIOLOGY?

MCC documents are peppered with biblical references. Position papers, reports, promotional pieces, and transcripts of addresses are permeated with texts from Scripture. Usually these references are offered in support of particular programmatic activities or approaches. The frequent use of biblical references does not, however, guarantee the missiological integrity of a particular thought, posture, or action. We are all too familiar with the resort to textual references in a reflexive attempt to justify particular positions. Ray Brubacher noted this potential pitfall for MCC when he wrote,

> We need a missiology to avoid a superficial use of Scripture. I sense sometimes that we draw up plans using social science theories and then paste a Bible verse at the end to make it feel religious. Our favorite verses deal with justice, peace and aid to the poor. These are good verses, but I fear we sometimes run the risk of proof-texting.[7]

Just as having a theology is not the outcome of academic learning, so, too, is missiology not the product of formal training. As we have suggested above, we all have a "missiology" in the same way that we all have a "theology." Often, however, it is a missiology that is assumed rather than articulated, reflexively embraced rather than emerging out of critical engagement with God's purposes and the world's needs. The question, thus, is not *whether* MCC has a missiology, but rather, *what is the nature* of MCC's missiology?

Adopting the challenge in this way presents us with a dilemma. Indeed, we are faced with more than just *one* dilemma. The first dilemma is this: Who is MCC? Does MCC consist of its board(s)? Is MCC to be located in its staff and administrators, or is it the volunteers, the constituents, or the partners? So when the question is posed, "Does MCC have a missiology?" we are forced to ask who or which MCC is being investigated.

An even more complex dilemma is the question, "Who speaks for MCC?" Is there a single voice that can be identified as representing the agency? Where are we to look or listen for an authoritative articulation of MCC's identity and convictions? Across the years and around the globe, a variety of voices have sought to situate MCC. Some have been bold in translating anecdotes into declarations which pronounce that *this* is what defines the agency. Others have interpreted programmatic initiatives as expressions of the essence of MCC.

For most of its ninety years MCC has been blessed with dynamic storytellers, exceptional executives and administrators, dedicated volunteers and partners, and a few erudite researchers and scholars, along with persons who have provided leadership through governance. Many of these have been ardent spokespersons for particular conceptions of MCC's identity and distinctiveness. Whose voice should be heard as the definitive voice?

In our grappling with this question we have listened to a variety of voices. As we paid attention to this wide diversity we came to discover a certain consistency of voice shared among people within different segments of the MCC family. This *consistency* of voice should not be mistaken, however, for a *uniformity* of voice. For while there emerges a consistency of expression that hints at a shared perception with regard to MCC's identity and distinctiveness among the many voices, the shared perception is by no means generalized. There is no uniform articulation of an MCC "missiology." There are, instead, widely differentiated understandings advanced by various spokespersons from within different segments of the MCC family.

In seeking to answer the question about MCC's missiology against the backdrop of these many differentiated understandings, we could attempt to undertake what we deem to be the impossible task of resolving which voice speaks authoritatively for MCC. That course seems doomed to failure. We propose, instead, to accept that there are a variety of MCC "missiologies," each shared among the people who comprise a particular segment of the MCC family.

Our objective therefore will be to identify the spectrum of missiologies which coexist within MCC and to report on the distinctive nature of each one. It will become clear from our account of what we discovered that one or another of these missiologies has been predominant at a particular time. At other times another missiological position has predominated. We will investigate each of these operative missiologies and make some assessments regarding our sense of which of these is most closely aligned with God's purposes. This alignment, we believe, represents missiological integrity or, more simply, faithfulness in our discipleship.

Missiological integrity—that is, mission thinking and practice which embrace the totality of God's purposes—must reflect those purposes as they are revealed to us in the life, death, and resurrection of Jesus Christ who is the embodiment of God's mission in the world. In the charter of Jesus' mission which he references in his first public address in a synagogue in Nazareth, Jesus speaks of preaching the gospel, healing the sick, liberating the oppressed and those in bondage, and responding with compassion to the hurting (Luke 4:18ff). When questions arise early in Jesus' ministry about whether he actually is the fulfillment of the messianic promises, Jesus sends back a message to John the Baptist via his disciples that they should report what they have seen: The sick are healed, the hungry are fed, those in bondage are set free, and the poor have the good news preached to them. These reports by Jesus about the way in which he is the fulfillment of God's mission in the world are the foundation of a bona fide missiology. Such a missiological position must include both evangelism and service as essential components of a faithful representation of God's purposes for humanity.

SIX "VOICES" WITHIN THE MCC FAMILY ON THE RELATIONSHIP OF SERVICE TO EVANGELISM

As we have listened to various voices in our research, we have heard at least six identifiable responses to the question of how service and evangelism relate in the formulation of what we are calling in this essay "the missiology of MCC." In each of the six cases, we have selected a term which in our view captures the essence of that relationship. These terms are *Preparatory—Complementary—Separate—Oppositional—Prioritized—Successor.*

Presenting them in this fashion, with movement from left to right, hints at the potential impact history has played in the emergence and development of the various voices articulated and approaches taken as MCC, now ninety years old, has acted and reacted to a constantly changing socio-political and religious environment throughout much of the twentieth century and into the twenty-first. But we should not too hastily limit ourselves to assumptions of chronology in this matter. For our research would also indicate that all six of these voices can and do exist simultaneously, though in varying degrees, at any given point in time within the MCC family— all of which only complicates the exercise we have undertaken to determine what, if any, has been the predominant missiology shaping MCC as an agency.

Here, then, are the six "voices" as we have heard them. After presenting each of them, we will attempt to offer some concluding observations in the form of questions for ongoing reflection and debate within the Anabaptist faith community and beyond.

Preparatory: service paves the way for evangelism

The earliest MCC programs were initiated in places where North American mission agencies had no work, such as Russia, Europe, and Paraguay. This pattern was repeated in many later instances as well when MCC responded to needs in an area and, after a period of time, invited mission groups to further nurture the emerging relationships by developing longer-term church-building programs—in Ethiopia,

Puerto Rico, Taiwan, Bolivia, Korea, Haiti, Hong Kong, Japan, the Middle East, and in various European locations.

Orie O. Miller, one of MCC's first relief workers and its executive secretary for over twenty years (1935-1957), referred to this preparatory function played by the agency as a "John the Baptist" forerunner role, where MCC lays the initial groundwork for "gospel outreach obedience" and then "phases out" as mission and global church partners develop the deeper relationships of longer duration.[8] This perspective informed Miller's approach already in his 1919 response to the pre-MCC crisis in Russia when he called for designing the relief effort in such a way that large numbers of short-term workers with little Russian language proficiency could be deployed "as agriculturalists, mechanics, orphanage workers and nurses" and whose work on the ground would be organized and monitored by permanent personnel, knowledgeable in Russian and engaged in "direct missionary work, administration and supervision."[9] MCC's capacity over the years to respond quickly in this way to short-term, urgent needs has made it possible, according to William Klassen, for the organization to "innovate more readily than a college or a mission board." And this is true, says Klassen, because "it is less tied to brick and mortar, has great staff turnover," and "is less inhibited by restrictive controls."[10]

The theological underpinning for this preparatory role of service in the mission of the church was well articulated by Peter Dyck:

> Just as Israel was to be a servant revealing the true nature and intent of God to the Gentiles, so the twentieth-century Christian is called through his service to point men to the sovereign God who is Lord of history. [. . .] To point men to God, whether by word or deed, is to serve.[11]

Complementary—service and evangelism work hand in hand

Mennonite church historian Guy Hershberger praised MCC at its fiftieth-year mark in 1970 for keeping focused on the vision for integrating evangelism and service: "Preaching the Word, comforting the afflicted, feeding the hungry was the way Menno Simons said and did it."[12] Citing Orie O. Miller, then secretary emeritus of MCC, Hershberger reaffirmed the conviction of Mennonite church leaders that preaching and ministering to human needs were "united" because "evangelism and service belong together."

This belief in the complementary character of service and evangelism has at various times and places over the years created a spirit of mutuality and reciprocity between MCC and mission agencies where invitations to join ministry efforts have been issued, as noted, by MCC to mission boards, but also by mission boards to MCC to help expand existing programs in countries such as Algeria, Honduras, Indonesia, Liberia, and in Japan with a peace ministry.[13]

For Christians, serving others in a seamless, comprehensive way is, according to Peter Dyck, simply "a part of our new nature":

> Such service does not distinguish between word and deed, between "kerygma" and "diakonia"; it is not fragmented but total, as total as man's need and God's love. In such service bread and bread of life are mingled together, blending into one even as body and soul are forged together as long as we live and Christ's own earthly ministry allowed for no dichotomy. Serving thus in word and deed is evidence that we are a "new creation" and an extension of the incarnation.[14]

Some field reports from service locations record exactly this kind of integrated approach to meeting the whole needs of individuals and communities. Such would be the case in this 1957 account of MCC's work with a mobile clinic in Taiwan:

> We visited 45 villages. We examined and treated 6,210 people for various conditions—eye, parasites, digestive trouble, tuberculosis, dermatitis, respiratory, rheumatism, anemia, vitamin deficiency, ear and nose, applying dressings, etc., when necessary; 2,426 more received dental care, extractions, fillings, etc. . . . Our team usually consists of a doctor, a dentist or dental assistant, nurse or nurse aide, preacher or evangelist, and a unit leader. The preacher usually is the interpreter, but helps also with giving out medicine. The leader helps wherever he can, medically and spiritually and is the driver and takes care of business.[15]

Separate—service and evangelism are parallel activities with little interconnectedness

MCC was in its origins "primarily a service agency dedicated to the alleviation of suffering."[16] But this desire to address physical needs was clearly understood as only one part of a broader, multifaceted response to the human condition. "We inherited a concern for the world in mission," wrote Orie O. Miller, "which logically spilled over into relief, for our heritage included both."[17]

Over the years various Mennonite organizations have been created to promote and administer differentiated tasks on behalf of the church. In this arrangement, mission agencies have stereotypically been charged with spiritual matters, preaching the gospel, "saving souls," and planting churches, whereas MCC has been assigned to ministries focusing more on meeting physical needs. In an article written forty years ago, Larry Kehler outlined "the many activities" of MCC taking place in its *work abroad* (e.g., agriculture, education, medical services, material aid, child sponsorship, and needlework and crafts sales), as well as *on the home front* (e.g., voluntary service, mental health services, Mennonite Disaster Service, Menno Travel Service, mutual aid societies, and reinsurance initiatives).[18]

Some twenty years later, Nancy Heisey identified MCC global involvements as a particular set of "gifts and responsibilities" carried out by the agency on behalf of its supporting constituency. These gifts and responsibilities included: 1) recognizing and lifting up community resources to meet community needs, together with listening to the communities' expression of outside resources they believe to be useful to them; 2) standing with and advocating for those suffering from injustice; 3) providing food and other kinds of material assistance to people facing the emergencies of war, natural and human-caused disaster; and 4) carrying out any task with the understanding that agency workers are servants rather than masters.[19]

Now, the differentiation of "gifts and responsibilities" between organizations can be and often is a very good thing. At its best it eliminates redundancy and creates centers of expertise for more effectively accomplishing kingdom goals. The institutional impulse, however, can lose sight of the larger kingdom vision in which both word and deed are present, focusing instead on only one part of the gospel mandate, elevating that part to a place where it is viewed as the *whole* gospel to be embodied or proclaimed. When this happens an agency's mission and identity can become all-encompassing, or *totalisant,* as the French call it. In such a case, the more limited mandate is transformed little by little into the *whole* mandate and becomes a world all of its own, severed and independent from the broader vision necessary for reciprocity, balance, and shared convictions with those well positioned to complement a single group's own best efforts.

Every human organization struggles with this tendency and MCC is no exception. As new recruits and older alumni gather around the agency's central mission, core values, and principal activities across the globe, an institutional identity is formed, nurtured, and passed along from one generation to the next. This helps to explain how several years ago, a speaker from a Mennonite mission organization was disinvited by a congregation when a member of the church's Peace and Service Committee caught wind of the invitation and questioned its appropriateness by asking, "Why are we having someone from a mission agency come to speak at our church? We are an *MCC* congregation!"

Oppositional—service and evangelism are in conflict

Viewing evangelism and service as separate, independent activities does not necessarily mean they must be understood as conflicting, though in some instances opposing camps have formed and mobilized precisely along such lines.

No sooner, in fact, had MCC been officially organized in fall 1920 than a serious crisis developed within the ranks of the (Old) Mennonite Church between college-oriented members and the denomination's central leadership. Framing the controversy in those days was the larger Fundamentalist-Modernist debate of the 1920s—the "era of the social gospel" whose exponents, according to historian Guy Hershberger, were "charged with the promotion of mere humanitarian reform to the neglect of the gospel of Christ." According to Hershberger,

> it was in the matter of relief and service . . . and in what might be called the issue of social responsibility, that the polarization between the college-oriented group and the general church leadership was most conspicuous. The former was eager for an aggressive program, but too enamored of the social gospel school of thought to appreciate its theological weakness; while the latter was too enamored of fundamentalist theology to appreciate its failure to understand the social implications of the gospel.
>
> Consequently, although recognizing a Christian duty to relieve suffering, the church leadership was handicapped by its fear of contamination by the social gospel, while the college-oriented group believed the leadership was lacking in vision, dragging its feet. Moreover, as each group grew more critical of the other distrust and suspicion increased, the collegiate group regarding the church leadership incompetent, and the leadership regarding the other as disloyal, until genuine cooperation within the brotherhood became very difficult to achieve.[20]

How much this rift shaped views of evangelism and service within the Mennonite community over the ensuing decades is difficult to discern. But one still finds it alive today whenever more serv-

ice-minded members of the church describe verbal witness as disre-
spectful, inappropriate, and ultimately unnecessary, and when more
evangelistically inclined folks express doubts about the ability of
compassionate action, no matter how sincere and well-intentioned,
to carry the full weight of the gospel mandate. This latter group finds
little comfort in reports like the following one, issued by an MCC volunteer from an international work location:

> As of yet, I have done no oral witnessing and don't have a
> definite plan to start this. . . . these students are not '"lost
> souls," neither do I feel they need any more white mission-
> aries to *tell* them *the* way. If the way I live is helpful to them,
> let them take of me—but please don't say I should *tell* them.
> They've had enough of this.[21]

*Prioritized—service is more important
than evangelism*

In an overly saturated world of mass media where words become
meaningless by their sheer ubiquity, there are plenty of good reasons
to emphasize acts of service in confronting human need. This pen-
chant toward action over words comes easily for most Mennonites of
European origin. Particularly instructive in this regard is an observation by Peter Dyck that in many Dutch Mennonite homes, a Delft blue
plate has traditionally graced the walls with this Mennonite motto:

> *Dopen wat mondig is,* Baptize those of age,
> *spreken dat bondig is,* Speak what is binding,
> *vrij in 't christelijk geloven,* Free in Christian faith,
> *daden gaan woorden te boven,* Deeds are above words.

This emphasis on deeds, noted Dyck, "in time led to an absence
of words to the point where in many Mennonite families . . . all
prayers were silent" and church members became increasingly "ill-
prepared to articulate [their] faith." Dyck pointed to an MCC film-
strip, "Sermons in Overalls," as another statement about the importance of deeds over words. In this theology, says Dyck, "the loudest,
clearest language God ever 'spoke' was when 'the Word became flesh
and dwelt among us.'"[22]

Robert Kreider refers to this preference of action over proclamation as the "cup of cold water approach" to ministry. He further notes
that this approach

has been congenial in MCC programming to the verbally inar-

ticulate, the young and immature, the Amish youth with theological hesitations about evangelizing, the theologically illiter-
ate, and those with a high view of words who are reluctant to
verbalize their faith for fear of mouthing clichés.

Yet, "again and again in MCC programs," continues Kreider,
"questions have arisen: Is relief enough? How can MCC work contribute to building the church?"[23]

Successor—service has
superseded evangelism and now replaces it
Lastly, there is yet another version of the service/evangelism dynamic that argues for a view in which evangelism, however valuable
(or destructive!) it may have been in the past, must now give way to a
less aggressive, more service-inspired modality of interacting with
people of other faiths and cultures. Donald Lloyd suggests this approach may find its origins already in the American colonies when religious sectarians, exhausted by bloody conflicts and constant harassment, "settled and mingled," and "found peace in common silence."
This stream of early settlers eventually gave birth to a group Lloyd
refers to as the "Quietmouth Americans"—people who may well be
friendly, helpful, and even chatty, but who never disclose what they
really think.[24]

Other reasons for replacing words with actions might be found in
the fatigue and embarrassment over loose-cannon preachers, tele-
vangelists, street vendors, and door-to-door peddlers of spiritual
wares who all too often use words to "hook," "deceive," "manipu-
late," and "tactically out-maneuver" unsuspecting and ill-prepared
victims by their verbal onslaughts.

All of this represents a broader malaise among some Mennonites
regarding how and whether to engage people of other faith traditions. One Mennonite writer no doubt speaks for others in asserting,

> I am a Christian because it is a part of the Western tradition of re-
> ligion, and I am also from that tradition. But the longer I live, the
> more convinced I am that different religions are the different
> socio-cultural manifestations of the same Creative Spirit at
> work. After all, why would a loving, all-powerful and jealous
> deity reveal itself only to a small group of wandering tribespeo-
> ple, expecting them to spread a rather imperialistic message
> around the world?
>
> And where is the justice in dooming persons to eternal tor-
> ment simply because they had the misfortune of being born in

an area not yet "penetrated" by this "good news?" Thus, the idea of "converting" to another religion has lost its importance for me. More important is "converting" to a deeper and more meaningful understanding of one's own religious heritage.[25]

Ray Brubacher recognized this challenge within the MCC family of program participants:

> I observe many MCC workers grasping for clarity about the uniqueness of Christ in a context of religious pluralism. MCC is good at being flexible and sensitive, nurturing wide ecumenical relationships and interfaith connections. These are virtues I embrace. But when do these virtues merge into a form of universalism?
>
> At times I sense unease about acknowledging Christ as the way to salvation. It is hard to perceive our many friends of other faith traditions as being outside the salvation of God. Many of us have learned valuable lessons and, in fact, been spiritually inspired by these friends. Nevertheless we need to come to terms with the uniqueness of Christ.[26]

QUESTIONS FOR ONGOING REFLECTION AND CONVERSATION

It will be no easy task navigating the many voices resounding within the MCC family as the agency approaches its second century of ministry. As outsiders looking in on the process, we can but suggest a few questions that MCC may wish to consider, should it choose to work at formulating a more focused, reflective, and systematic missiological stance for the years ahead.

Are "good ethics" good enough?
In an insightful essay delivered at the MCC seventy-fifth anniversary symposium, Ted Koontz hinted at some of the complications that arise from the commitments MCC has made in living out its little-contested identity as "a Christian resource for meeting human need." Koontz noted that MCC's theology "stresses the horizontal, rather than the vertical."[27] He alluded to the problem of the theology of MCC being focused primarily, if not entirely, on issues of right living, rather than on the generally accepted focus of theology on systematic thought about God. As such, MCC's theology is more akin to ethics than theology proper. MCC's preoccupation with ethical considerations is, no doubt, due to the widespread tendency among

many Mennonites to make discipleship and service or "servant-hood" the starting point from which we construct our response to God's purposes in the world.

One problem, however, with making servanthood or disciple-ship our starting point is not only that it "can lead to a focus on *our* work*," but it also can promote a certain kind of hubris, or worse still, the impoverishing limitation of reliance on *our* power. The danger of this focus on human need and human power, Koontz observes, is that it can cause us only "to see *ourselves* and other human beings, not first and foremost *God*."[28] Viewed from this perspective, the work of MCC is little distinguished from any other humanitarian enterprise that seeks to address human need.

One might additionally observe here that the overwhelming, al-most exclusive preoccupation with resolving material and physical needs by some in MCC stands in stark contrast even with many liber-ation theologians who studied Marx's dialectic materialism to make sense of their context of inordinate wealth amid grinding poverty in order that the gospel may indeed be good news to those on the un-derside of history. According to Gustavo Gutierrez, salvation "em-braces *every* aspect of humanity: body and spirit, individual and soci-ety, person and cosmos, time and eternity."[29]

Must "evangelism" and "service" be ranked in importance?

If we grant that our witness as Christians does, indeed, call us to more than responding to physical, material needs—that it requires, as well, verbal proclamation—does that make either of these re-sponses of lesser value? Some have suggested that giving bread to the hungry may be important but is of lesser priority than preaching the gospel. Others have even deigned to regard the sharing of bread as instrumental—of little value in and of itself, but helpful if it creates space for a verbal proclamation of the gospel. What, then, is the rela-tive value of efforts at relief, development, and advocacy on behalf of the poor and the oppressed vis-à-vis verbal proclamation?

Leanne Van Dyk makes the case for a positive missiological eval-uation of ministries of justice and compassion against the backdrop of the reality where many in the church can see only an instrumental value, or, at best, a limited usefulness to these ministries. Van Dyk counters that "it may be possible to contend that proclamation is an essential element of the church's witness and at the same time to de-fine proclamation as embodied in more than preaching in the church or evangelistic messages."[30]

From this perspective, proclamation includes other modes of participation in witness to God's purposes. Living an authentic Christian life before a watching world is one expression of proclamation. Furthermore, the intentional praxes embodied in service or servanthood are consistent with the purposes of God. Van Dyk embraces acts of service and compassion like hospitality, presence, listening, seeking justice and peace, taking up the cause of the widow and the orphan, and visiting the prisoner as important dimensions of proclamation, claiming that "proclamation both in verbal forms, typically understood to be the preaching of the gospel, and in service forms are at their best when *authentically integrated*" (emphasis ours).[31]

Does "the differentiation of tasks" ultimately distort and reduce the full impact of the gospel message?
A major challenge for MCC—and perhaps for Mennonites more generally—is that the full scope of Jesus' mission is reduced to little more than an incarnation into "servanthood." Jesus becomes limited to a mere segment of his witness. By contrast the biblical witness reveals Jesus as the one who not only proclaimed and incarnated the kingdom of God in his response to hurting and suffering humanity, but who also invited all people to experience the transforming grace of God through repentance and faith and who cultivated and sustained a vital relationship with God through prayer, obedience, and submission to God's purposes.

Does the singular focus on servanthood produce a truncated Christology and border on "heresy"?
Susan White suggests that certain Christian trends which reflect a limited preoccupation with Jesus and the abandonment of a "clear sense of intertrinitarian relations" approaches "heresy." She reminds us that the root meaning of the word *haeresis* is choice—choice among mutually exclusive options in thought, word, and action. She suggests that in the church we are facing the choice between two distinct theological options, and she cautions that when we make a choice it can have deleterious consequences. She suggests, for example, that when we abandon a rich trinitarian basis for our work and worship we

cannot help but set our work toward interfaith understanding many steps backward. This is particularly important for our relationships with those who share with us the worship of the God of Abraham, Isaac, and Jacob, that is, for relations with our Jewish and Muslim brothers and sisters. To replace a robustly trinitarian theocentrism with a narrowly conceived Jesus-centered theology will place a very serious obstacle in the path toward true interreligious dialogue.[32]

Does focusing on Jesus' servanthood ethic put MCC out of touch with the growing edges of the global church?

In grounding its engagement with the world in the "servant-hood" ethic of Jesus, large parts of MCC may be out of touch with much of the church of the twenty-first century, especially the new emergent churches populated by young adults who are looking for contemporary, more creative, and more faithfully missional expressions of the church. In the last few decades vast segments of the Christian church have embraced the *missio Dei* concept to extricate themselves from the limitations of a narrowly christological approach to the Christian calling in the world. According to the leading missiologist David Bosch:

> During the past half a century or so there has been a subtle but nevertheless decisive shift toward understanding mission as God's mission. During preceding centuries mission was understood in a variety of ways. Sometimes it was interpreted primarily in soteriological terms: as saving individuals from eternal damnation. Or it was understood in cultural terms: as introducing people from East and the South to the blessings and privileges of the Christian West. Often it was perceived in ecclesiastical categories: as the expansion of the church (or of a specific denomination). Sometimes it was defined salvation-historically: as the process by which the world—evolutionary or by means of a cataclysmic event—would be transformed into the kingdom of God. In all these instances, and in various, frequently conflicting ways, the intrinsic interrelationship between Christology, soteriology, and the doctrine of the Trinity, so important for the early church, was gradually displaced by one of several versions of the doctrine of grace.[33]

Bosch welcomes this movement to a trinitarian basis for mission as an innovation that advances the possibilities for greater missiological integrity:

> Mission was understood as being derived from the very nature of God. It was thus put in the context of the doctrine of the Trinity, not of ecclesiology or soteriology. The classical doctrine on the missio Dei as God the Father sending the Son, and God the

Father and the Son sending the Spirit was expanded to include
yet another "movement:" The Father, Son and the Holy Spirit
sending the church into the world. As far as missionary thinking was concerned, this linking with the doctrine of the Trinity
constituted an important innovation.[34]

*Has the time come for a fresh conversation and re-
newed relationship between MCC and the church's
mission agencies?*
An invitation to embrace a more comprehensive missiological
engagement may unnerve some in the MCC family who place a high
value on tolerance, sensitivity, and the protection of human dignity.
For many of these persons, verbal witness is sometimes associated
with the insensitive and dehumanizing impositions that were too-
frequent expressions of the colonial missionary enterprise.

In the same way, however, that it would be unreasonable to question whether MCC should be engaged in relief efforts because some
NGOs act in ways that demean and humiliate people, it is likewise
rash to infer that verbal witness is inherently oppressive or manipu-
lative. Many persons who care deeply about protecting the dignity
and advancing the cause of justice and liberation of others believe
that there is a way to bear witness to God's healing and hope in Jesus
Christ which is consistent with the life-giving and liberating purposes of God.[35]

Does this mean that MCC's new wineskins should necessarily be
stretched to include evangelistic programming? Of course not! But it
might well mean that a renewed embrace of God's cosmic purposes
embodied in the good news of the kingdom, inaugurated in Jesus
Christ, and sustained in the trinitarian grounding of our witness
could see MCC significantly reinforcing its efforts in the coming
years both to prepare and orient its program participants in new and
more proactive ways to support the work of the church, directly or indirectly, in every place where MCC goes.

It could also mean that MCC would become clearer and more intentional about identifying its particular calling and ministry limitations. In such a case, the agency would apply increased vigilance to
avoid positioning or promoting its ministries as the full representation of discipleship requirements for followers of Jesus Christ and
would move more readily to affirm and bless the work of co-partners
in God's purposes whose primary calling is in evangelism, church
planting, and the strengthening of faith communities around the
world.

In a compelling essay on Christian engagement with the world, Gerald W. Schlabach offers these words of encouragement and challenge to both MCC and the church's mission agencies alike as *together* we seek new ways of affirming and blessing each other and participating as joint members of Christ's body in God's purposes in and for the world:

An Abrahamic community is one that celebrates the calling and grace that has shaped its identity, yet knows instinctively that it cannot hoard this "blessing" for itself without losing that identity. . . . No Christian community can place itself faithfully within the company of Abraham unless *mission and service* are an integral part of its life together, not the special interest of a few. The Abrahamic paradigm should form and test programs associated with "word" and with "deed" ministries alike. Do they truly respect the integrity of other communities and peoples, seeking to serve their good? Are they prepared to die to their church's own ecclesiastical self-interests?[36]

In all the work that we do, whether as MCC or mission agency personnel, we must ask: Are we *fully* aligned with God's purposes for all of creation? That is the pressing question for MCC as it reflects on what missiology or missiologies will implicitly or explicitly guide its work at the end of its first century and into its second.

NOTES

1. Ray Brubacher, "A Missiology for MCC," *Intercom* (October 1991): 8.

2. Peter Dyck, "A Theology of Service," *The Mennonite Quarterly Review* 44/3 (July 1970): 263.

3. Cited in an editorial by Robert L. Niklaus in *Congo Mission News* (January-March 1969). Referenced in Dyck, 271.

4. Alan Neely in a dictionary entry describes it as "a conscious, intentional, ongoing reflection on the doing of missions." See Neely, "Missiology," in *Evangelical Dictionary of World Missions*, ed. Scott A. Moreau (Grand Rapids, Mich.: Baker, 2000).

5. Orlando E. Costas, *Theology of the Crossroads in Contemporary Latin America: Missiology in Mainline Protestantism, 1969-1974* (Amsterdam: Rodopi, 1976), 8.

6. Johannes Verkuyl, *Contemporary Missiology: An Introduction*, trans. and ed. Dale Cooper (Grand Rapids, Mich.: Wm. B. Eerdmans, 1978), 5.

7. Brubacher, 8.

8. Orie O. Miller, "The Mennonite Central Committee, God's Miracle among Us: The Past Fifty Years," *The Mennonite Quarterly Review* 44/3 (July 1970): 317.

9. O. O. Miller report, MRCWS Papers: Near East file, April 8, 1919. Cited

in Guy F. Hershberger, "Historical Background to the Formation of the Mennonite Central Committee," *The Mennonite Quarterly Review* 44/3 (July 1970): 238.

10. Cited in Robert Kreider, "The Impact of MCC Service on American Mennonites," *The Mennonite Quarterly Review* 44/3 (July 1970): 259.

11. Dyck, 263.

12. Miller, 244.

13. See Kreider, 247.

14. Dyck, 273.

15. Fourth Annual Report, Mennonite Christian Hospital, Milun-Hualien, Taiwan, 1957, 6. For other stories of this nature, see the November 1996 issue of MCC's *A Common Place* magazine dedicated in its entirety to the topic of the importance of keeping "word and deed" together in MCC ministries.

16. John A. Lapp, "The Peace Mission of the Mennonite Central Committee," *The Mennonite Quarterly Review* 44/3 (July 1970): 281.

17. Quoted in Paul Erb, *Orie O. Miller: The Story of a Man and an Era* (Scottdale, Pa.: Herald Press, 1969), 70.

18. Larry Kehler, "The Many Activities of the Mennonite Central Committee," *The Mennonite Quarterly Review* 44/3 (July 1970): 298-315.

19. Nancy Heisey, "MCC Missiology Statement," unpublished manuscript commissioned by Ray Brubacher in response to his October 1991 editorial in *Intercom*; available from MCC Archives, Akron, PA, 10 pp. See p. 8. The language of institutional "gifts" is also used by Alain Epp Weaver in his proposal of how various Mennonite-Anabaptist agencies might view their specific roles and callings in the Middle East—MCC as a "relief agency," CPT (Christian Peacemaker Teams) in "short-term, direct action types of ministries," and MBM (Mennonite Board of Missions) in presenting "a different face of Jesus to Jewish people in the region." See interview with Epp Weaver in "Peace in Palestine," *A Common Place* (November 1997), 17.

20. Hershberger, 226.

21. Letter from an overseas Mennonite worker, cited in Dyck 1970, 268.

22. Dyck, 266-269.

23. Kreider, 253.

24. Donald Lloyd, "The Quietmouth American," in *The Peace Corps Reader* (Washington, D.C.: Office of Public Affairs, 1968), 121.

25. Quoted in James R. Krabill, *Is It Insensitive to Share Your Faith? Hard Questions about Christian Mission in a Plural World* (Intercourse, Pa.: Good Books, 2005), 4-5.

26. Brubacher, 8.

27. Ted Koontz, "Commitments and Complications in Doing Good," in *Unity amidst Diversity: Mennonite Central Committee at 75* (Akron, Pa.: Mennonite Central Committee, 1996), 99.

28. Ibid., 100.

29. Gustavo Gutierrez, *A Theology of Liberation* (Maryknoll, N.Y.: Orbis Books, 1973), 151-152. More recently Leonardo and Clodovis Boff have also addressed this comprehensive sense of salvation which includes human transformation and the fullness of life in the physical realm. The Boff brothers draw on a distinction promulgated by the final document of the 1979 Latin American Episcopal Conference (CELAM) at Puebla, Mexico, between "par-

tial liberations" and "integral liberation." They argue that there is more to salvation than even a full and complete liberation, for the kingdom of God signifies not simply a reformation but a profound transformation of life, a radically new existence, such as is demonstrated in Jesus. Liberation, they argue, involves more than simply changing the forms of human life; it creates conditions in which human beings can flourish. But the creation of a new quality and community of life is never fully realized in any historic liberation movement. Historical liberations both express and anticipate the deep and total transformation of existence which is eschatological salvation. See Leonardo and Clodovis Boff, *Salvation and Liberation* (Maryknoll, N.Y.: Orbis Books, 1984), esp. chapter 2.

30. Leanne Van Dyk, "The Church's Proclamation as a Participation in God's Mission," in *Trinitarian Theology for the Church: Scripture, Community, Worship*, ed. Daniel J. Treier and David Lauber (Downers Grove, Ill.: InterVarsity Press, 2009), 232.

31. Ibid.

32. See: Susan J. White, "Whatever Happened to the Father? The Jesus Heresy in Modern Worship," available at http://gbod.org/worship/white.pdf

33. David J. Bosch, *Transforming Mission* (Maryknoll, N.Y.: Orbis Books, 1991), 389.

34. Ibid., 390. Jacques Matthey goes further than Bosch and suggests that this Trinitarian grounding of mission is *more* than a mere helpful innovation; it is, in fact, a much-needed protection against other pitfalls. In responding to the query about whether we can "continue to use the *missio Dei*, or do we need a different paradigm?" he reminds us that "If we were to lose the reference to *missio Dei*, we would again put the sole responsibility for mission on human shoulders and thereby risk, missiologically speaking, believing that salvation is gained by our own achievements." See Jacques Matthey, "God's Mission Today: Summary and Conclusions," in *International Review of Mission* 92/367 (October 2008): 582. In a similar vein Peter Dula and Alain Epp Weaver in a discourse about the character of MCC affirm the value of the *missio Dei*. They suggest that MCC is in fact, at its best, a hybrid, "a cross between a religious order and a professional humanitarian organization, a hybrid of the missionary and NGO worlds." In light of its Christian identity they offer that MCC "should be looking to participate in the *missio Dei*, in the movement of God's Spirit in the world, a mission that can't be captured exclusively by the discourse of humanitarianisms." See Peter Dula and Alain Epp Weaver, "MCC, Intervention, and 'Humanitarianism,'" *Mission Focus: Annual Review* 20/13 (2005): 68-81.

35. Wilhelm Richebächer, in investigating the contribution of the *missio Dei* concept to a more appropriate way of witness, suggests that "when Christians speak of the mission of the triune God, they are talking about something that they themselves cannot bring to people of other faiths, because he, as their creator and sustainer, is already at work in them. However, Christians continue to bear witness to him, in faith and for the sake of Jesus Christ, as the one whom they themselves can 'understand' as a merciful and forgiving God, over and against all their own assumptions about the where and how of his efforts. . . . Christians must realize that their convincing words and actions

in themselves are not the gospel for others; God's Holy Spirit has to create trust in both the Christian messenger and the person who does not yet believe in Christ, so that the message can occur of itself. . . . Christ's messenger cannot rouse a person to interest in the faith; that is the work of the Holy Spirit, wherever and whenever it may blow." See Wilhelm Richebächer, "Missio Dei: The Basis of Mission Theology or a Wrong Path?" *International Review of Mission* 92/367 (2003): 599.

36. Gerald W. Schlabach, "Beyond Two- versus One-Kingdom Theology: Abrahamic Community as a Mennonite Paradigm for Christian Engagement in Society," *Conrad Grebel Review* 11/3 (Fall 1993): 202, 208.

Part III
Race, Gender, and the Conflicted Expansion of MCC Identity

Chapter 9

Whitening Conflicts: White Racial Identity Formation Within Mennonite Central Committee, 1960-1985

TOBIN MILLER SHEARER

Mennonite Central Committee workers at one time felt welcomed in inner-city African-American neighborhoods. By 1967, however, they began to notice a shift. In urban communities in Atlanta and Cincinnati, those who had once greeted the workers with enthusiasm now "quietly tolerated them." Amid urban rebellions and Black Power agitation, MCC volunteers listened to "demands for 'whitey' to leave." Although administrators did not capitulate, the external critique sparked internal conflict. That conflict in turn prompted white Mennonites at MCC to evaluate their racial identity.

This essay explores the process of white racial formation within a single organization between 1960 and 1985. Bounded on one end by MCC's engagement with the Civil Rights Movement and on the other by increased representation of people of color on boards and in departments, this twenty-five year span provides a new perspective on whiteness studies. Rather than treating whiteness as a static identity, this study frames whiteness as a diachronic conflict process, one that unfolded over time with varying degrees of intensity and led to contradictory outcomes. Within MCC, those processes are best described as whitening conflicts.

As such, this essay confirms MCC Executive Committee board member Asrat Gebre's June 2008 observation that Mennonite Central Committee has been "a white, male-dominated organization," while suggesting that his follow-up question—one that echoed the 1967 demands for "whitey" to leave—is based on a false assumption. Gebre suggests that MCC has been white in the same way through its ninety-year history. Whiteness, according to the argument presented here, is a process defined by conflict and change rather than static continuity. Rather than ask as Gebre did, "So how do you change that?" the more appropriate question is, "So how has that—i.e. MCC's racial idenity—been changing?" Only by understanding the way whitening conflicts have unfolded can Gebre or any other board member hope to change the organization.[1]

Study of racial formation within any organization demands clarity about the idea of race. As numerous scholars have argued, race is a social construct grounded in European science.[2] Scholars articulated racial taxonomies in the seventeenth century when European military powers colonized and enslaved Africans. Those who promoted the idea of race found Africans, Pacific Islanders, and other indigenous peoples inferior to an idealized European phenotype. The social divisions and political inequality arising from racial categories in turn concretized the taxonomy. In sum, historical actors created race and maintained the inequities and ideas, like whiteness, that flowed from it. In an effort to counter that history, I use racial terms to explore social stratification and not biological differentiation.

The idea of whiteness also has a history. African-American historian and activist W. E. B. Du Bois observed that white workers sought "public and psychological wages" for separating from African Americans.[3] Labor historian David Roediger adds that European immigrant groups became white over time.[4] In short, white people also underwent racial formation. Expanding on the work of novelist James Baldwin, Roediger also argues that white identity is false, dangerous, void of cultural vibrancy, defined by power and privilege, and—simultaneously—a way to differentiate people of European descent from African-Americans.[5]

Some scholars have critiqued Roediger for imprecise and ahistorical analysis. In particular, labor historian Eric Arnesen claims that Roediger and his imitators write about whiteness as if it were "a blank screen onto which those who claim to analyze it can project their own meanings."[6] He faults Roediger for using few archival sources, ignoring differences within the white community, and applying contemporary racial concepts to historical subjects.[7] In the wake of Arnesen's critique, other historians have called for precise definitions of whiteness that foster regionally specific studies and incorporate the observations of multiple racial groups.[8]

Mennonite scholars have ignored whiteness studies. Except for normative comments discussed below, Mennonite scholars have seldom examined white racial identity. Although authors have explored racially specific histories of African-American and Latino communities, they have failed to examine how white Mennonites responded to racial changes within and without the church.[9] Bucking this trend, sociologist Jeff Gingerich has argued that white Mennonites in twentieth-century Philadelphia appealed to ethnic rather than racial identities to sidestep issues of power and privilege and avoid acknowledging their white identity.[10] Although he offers a historically nuanced study, Gingerich employs a static concept of whiteness that places the identity outside time.[11] By way of contrast, historians of Mennonite Central Committee have bypassed racial dynamics within the organization in their entirety, and, in the process, made both black and white racial experience invisible.[12]

This study attempts to answer Roediger's critics by offering a precise definition of whiteness grounded in the experience of a white Mennonite organization. As suggested above, I define whiteness as a highly conflictual historical process involving multiple racial communities that has led to one group achieving or maintaining social dominance. The position of dominance has been expressed through group members' relative ability to benefit from and control institutional resources. As such the process of whiteness has unfolded amid conflict. Moreover, rather than a static identity, the process of whiteness has been defined by diachronic flux. At times whiteness has been more or less active, influential, or visible to members of the dominant group. This historically mediated struggle for dominance has not, according to this definition, resulted in white identity. The struggle itself has been white identity.

The phrase *whitening conflict* may offer an alternative to that of whiteness. Rather than a noun form that suggests static, unchanging identity, the adjective *whitening* implies an ongoing, open-ended process. Likewise, the phrase echoes actual practice. Instead of interpreting unspoken intentions, I examine how MCC staff and constituents used the term *white*. Although political, social, and biological references appear, most often period authors indicated the latter. They, like most Americans at the time, associated race with biological rather than political or social divisions. Grassroots church members then felt justified in frequently stating that racial categories were divinely ordained.[13] I employ the neologism of whitening conflicts to tie the racial formation process active within the Mennonite community to those biological and theological assumptions and to highlight the fluid nature of racial formation itself.

RACIAL CONTEXT
OF THE MENNONITE COMMUNITY

In 1960, the time this study opens, African-American, Latino, Aboriginal/Native, and Asian people made up less than one percent of the about 225,000 adult Mennonites and Brethren in Christ in North America. Despite such low numbers, African-American and Latino churches were expanding rapidly. By the end of the study, Latino membership had increased from 185 members in 1955 to 2,450 in 1986 and African-American membership had risen from 150 members in 1950 to nearly three thousand by the mid 1980s.[14] Although Native and Asian congregations made fewer gains, racial demographics had begun to change.

African-American and Latino leaders let their presence be known. Members of these communities had been active in Mennonite congregations since the 1890s in Chicago and the first three decades of the twentieth century in Pennsylvania and Virginia. Through the 1950s, few African-American or Latino/a Mennonites critiqued Mennonite cultural standards or racial assumptions. Although African-American church planter and bishop James Lark had long challenged the church to support black Mennonite initiatives, his critique had not focused as directly on Mennonites' racial attitudes and privileged status.[15]

In 1959 the Woodlawn congregation in Chicago hosted a conference on race relations at which African-American associate pastor and future historian Vincent Harding enjoined those gathered to stop "slavishly and silently" conforming to "American attitudes on race and segregation."[16] During the same period, Latino pastor and missionary John Ventura began critiquing the leading Mennonite church mission agency for racial disparity in missionary pay scales and failing to support Latino church starts in Denver.[17] By the 1960s, Harding, Ventura, and their contemporaries had begun to call the white Mennonite community to look at themselves with a racial lens.

Such criticism from people of color emerged at the same time that a new kind of conflict prevailed among Mennonites. Beginning in the

1960s, local and national leaders found their power diluted, congregational members successfully challenged dress and leisure restrictions, and a central division emerged in the church between those focused on biblical authority, individual submission, and traditional morality and those promoting social justice, pacifism, and congregationally based mutual aid.[18] The latter conflict in particular affected MCC. The largest and wealthiest regional constituent body of MCC, Lancaster Conference, went through a difficult schism in 1969 over lifestyle issues that threatened a significant donor stream.[19] These external pressures minimized the impact of racial criticism within MCC. Administrators focused on financial stability ignored those who did not represent wealthy donors.

1960-1964: CIVIL RIGHTS INVOLVEMENT, CONFLICT REVEALED

The small but growing African-American and Latino communities had not been included in MCC. As 1960 opened, no people of color served on any MCC board or Akron office staff position.[20] In the 1950s MCC had placed Clarence Sakimura, a Japanese-American member of the Brethren in Christ Church, in Austria, but similar field placements of people of color rarely took place through the 1960s.[21] Although MCC field staff employed domestic workers overseas, the nationals' names did not appear in published personnel listings. When people of color inside the North American Mennonite Church read personnel listings and heard about activities of both domestic and international service workers, they did not see their names represented.

African-American Mennonite converts and activists like Rosemarie and Vincent Harding began to scrutinize MCC's homogeneity as they became involved in the Civil Rights Movement. From 1960 through 1964 in Atlanta, the Hardings fostered connections between an interracial group of volunteers and civil rights groups like the Southern Christian Leadership Conference. In addition, Vincent's high-profile arrest during SCLC's 1962 Albany campaign challenged Mennonites to reconsider their quietist withdrawal. During a speech at the Mennonite World Conference a few weeks after his arrest, Harding criticized Mennonites' involvement in the "mold" of the "white, western world."[22] Although MCC administrators had paid Harding's bail, they also advised him not to "cut off his water" by challenging white Mennonites so directly.[23] Criticism of Mennonites' racial profile proved more controversial than did breaking the law.

Although Harding named MCC's racial identity, few others followed. Between 1960 and 1964, only Mennonite Disaster Service director Wayne Clemens made a specific reference to MCCers' race in an MCC annual report. Clemens explained his decision to support local church building efforts in the South rather than bring in "white northerners."[24] One other administrator placed "white" in quotes when describing a group of MCC workers interacting with children of color and others coupled "white and Negro" to describe interracial groups in general.[25] Following passage of the 1964 Civil Rights Act, attention to white identity decreased.[26] In every case, MCC leaders referred to white people only when volunteers or church leaders worked alongside African Americans.

Despite MCC administrators' reticence to describe their personnel and constituency in racial terms, others in the church began to identify white Mennonites. At first, church leaders referred only to white people outside the denomination. In 1960 Goshen College professor Guy F. Hershberger enjoined Mennonites to witness to both "hardened segregationists" and "'good' whites" outside the church, the same group prayed for by Gulfport, Mississippi, service director Orlo Kauffman.[27]

Four years later, white racial labels appeared more frequently. In 1964, a "lady in a Mennonite community" complained that it was a "sin and a crime to be a white person."[28] That same year students at the MCC-sponsored Intercollegiate Peace Fellowship conference noted that a majority of the participants came from "all white" home congregations.[29] Across the generations, a new, if temporary, focus on white Mennonite identity emerged at a time when MCC administrators grew increasingly reluctant to identify themselves as white people.

1965-1969: WITHDRAWAL, TEMPORARY FOCUS, AND CONFLICT UNSETTLED

The foray into civil rights activism that prompted new reflection on white identity during the first half of the 1960s did not last through the decade. Despite efforts within the organization to renew attention to "white racism," MCC pulled back from direct racial engagement between 1965 and 1969.[30] Following Vincent and Rosemarie Harding's abrupt departure from their Atlanta position in 1965, MCCers withdrew from civil rights initiatives.[31] Rather than street-based agitation, Voluntary Service and Peace Section leaders supported interracial service initiatives. In particular, an assignment focused on "racial reconciliation" in rural Mississippi shifted attention to race problems in the South and outside the Mennonite church.[32]

Black Power advocates did not, however, let the organization turn away from their white identity. As noted above, by 1967 African-Americans only "tolerated [white MCC workers] as the specter of riots and Black Power demands" increased calls for "'whitey' to leave."[33] That same year, Vincent Harding kept attention on white Mennonites' racial identity by using an address at the Mennonite World Conference to excoriate "the power of Mennonite prestige, the power of middleclass respectability, the power of whiteness."[34] In response, some white Mennonites affirmed Harding for bringing the Mennonite community into "the deep sea of bearing our brother's burdens" while others criticized him for presenting "plain nonsense" that was "an expression of immaturity."[35] Amid such divided response, MCC administrators took little action to identify what the "power of whiteness" might look like in their organization.

One program under the MCC institutional umbrella did, however, attend to white Mennonite identity. In response to challenges posed by Harding and other African-American Mennonite pastors and activists, Mennonite Disaster Service personnel addressed "white racism within ourselves."[36] Following intensive study of urban race relations, MDS Executive Coordinator Delmar Stahly and his colleagues concluded in 1968 that "white racism of which we were part, and guilty" produced urban riots.[37] In response to such self-criticism, they ceded project authority to Black Nationalist groups in St. Louis and Pittsburgh.[38] Local leaders informed MDS staff that "whites were never to be trusted, churched or unchurched, and there was no point in taking chances now with some offbeat sectarian group called Mennonites."[39] This racialized experiment in giving local partners increased authority drew the attention of the church press and caused no small controversy within Mennonite Disaster Service.[40]

Such focused attention on white racial identity did not last long. By 1969, MDS personnel expressed regret that they had not "really mov[ed]" to the cities."[41] In place of "white racism," administrators opted for a less confrontational description of the "chasm" between the races.[42] Without additional explanation, MDS returned to traditional service projects that did not require discussion of white racial identity or shared power.

Unlike MDS administrators, church press editors focused on white Mennonites' racial identity through 1969. The somber mood evident in MDS extended to MCC, its constituency, and the nation in the aftermath of Martin Luther King Jr.'s assassination the previous spring. Dozens of white Mennonites reflected upon King's life.[43] Several developed themes of white identity. Paul Landis, a leader from Lancaster Conference and member of MCC's Peace Section, called on his fellow Mennonites to confess "attitudes of white supremacy."[44] Vern Miller, a white Mennonite pastor and conference leader from Cleveland, declared, "The next move now is Whitey's."[45] Others discussed the need of "white persons" to fight "white racism" in the "white community" and the harvest of racial strife planted by "we . . . white people."[46]

As vocal constituents highlighted the church's racial demographics, MCC administrators did little to diversify. By 1969, MCC's staff and boards remained exclusively white and male. Those boards approved new urban initiatives made possible by a four-year string of increased giving. Following the lead of other white Christian institutions, MCC entered urban communities of color through existing voluntary service programs as a way to relieve pressures emerging from the urban rebellions of 1968 and increased criticism by Black Nationalist groups.[47] Rather than change their racial profile, administrators shifted their programmatic placement.

1970-1978: INITIAL DIVERSITY, MINORITY MINISTRIES COUNCIL, AND CONFLICT AVOIDED

People of color and white women filled MCC board and headquarters positions for the first time from 1970 through 1978. Although few in number, those who joined challenged the racial identity of the organization. In the main, external pressure from new groups like the Minority Ministries Council prompted the appointments. Having achieved a modicum of diversity, administrators sought to avoid racial conflict. People of color within and without MCC, however, intensified internal debate by critiquing the organization. In short, MCC's whiteness became more visible as the institution became less white.

The financial strength of the nine-year period made race-specific programming possible. Each year topped the next by up to twenty-five percent of the previous year's contributions.[48] Such increases prompted new initiatives. In a foundational move, administrators placed domestic programming in one department, the newly formed U.S. Ministries. Continuing a trend fostered by Voluntary Service program leaders, U.S. Ministries staff decided in 1975 to focus on "social issues and areas of injustice."[49] Such domestic service relieved mounting pressure to attend to human need at home and abroad.

More than any other external critics, leaders from the Minority Ministries Council made MCC administrators uncomfortable. Already in 1969, African-American Mennonite minister John Powell and his colleagues from the Urban Racial Council had asked the Mennonite Church to fund programs by and for "minorities."[50] As the group expanded, hired personnel, and changed its name to the Minority Ministries Council, their influence also grew. Although they focused first on funding urban programs and critiquing the Mennonite Church, Minority Ministries staff also evaluated MCC.

The first person of color to serve on an MCC board, Lee Roy Berry, an African-American Mennonite convert from Florida and northern Indiana, was a founding member of Minority Ministries.[51] After Berry joined the MCC board in 1970, Minority Ministries Executive Director Powell took a tour through Europe and Africa.[52] White leaders in Akron and field administrators on both continents expressed nervousness about relating to Powell as a "black" man.[53] The contrast between a nearly all-white program team in Africa and a black, well educated, Mennonite pastor and church administrator put many service workers and administrators within MCC on edge. They hardly knew what to do with John Powell.

That uneasiness intensified when the associate director of MMC excoriated MCC's hiring practices. In mid-February 1973, Lupe De León asserted that requiring two years' voluntary service of all Akron-based administrators amounted to "institutional racism."[54] Such a prerequisite prohibited talented African-American young adults like Tony Brown from serving with MCC. In his view, the institution excluded "minorities from top positions in church administration" by demanding that they conform to an inflexible tradition, one that ignored alternate forms of service performed within domestic communities of color.*[55]

As 1973 came to a close, the pressure applied by De León, Powell, and other Minority Ministries Council personnel lessened. Following meetings in Sandia, Texas, Mennonite Church administrators dissolved the Council and redistributed staff.[56] Although officials said they wanted to integrate the Council into the larger church to avoid racial segregation, Minority Ministries leaders felt they had been censored.[57] The Council's restructuring meant that leaders of color within the church had less energy to attend to MCC's hiring practices. Without external pressure, internal efforts to increase diversity stalled. Once again, MCC leaders avoided conflict.

For the next five years, white MCC administrators like Executive Secretary William Snyder focused on race inside the organization only when prompted by external pressure. Furthermore, administrators and board chairs brought in people of color to forestall conflict rather than transform identity. Board appointments make the point. To be certain, the Peace Section Board had made the most significant changes. By 1978, they had appointed one woman of color, one man of color, and four white women to a twenty-two-member board. They far outpaced, however, all the remaining boards combined. The executive committees and boards of MCC binational and MCC Canada together included two men of color and twelve white women amid sixty-three white men. Although white women had made noticeable advances, men of color remained tokens, and only one woman of color served on an MCC board.

Despite these limited shifts in racial representation, former Minority Ministries members noticed the changes. In 1974, De León again contacted MCC leaders. This time he affirmed them for appointing Lawrence Hart, a Native American, and Lee Roy Brown, an African-American, to MCC's Executive Committee. At the same time he noted the absence of Latinos on the committee.[58] Former Council members also noted when Tony Brown joined MCC in 1976 as an assistant secretary in the personnel department. For the first time, a person of color worked for MCC in an administrative post. Brown's tenure was, however, short. By 1978, he had left the organization. De León and other Mennonite leaders of color noted his departure as well.

Outside the organization, Mennonites refocused attention on the church's whiteness. Most significantly, Hubert Brown, an African-American pastor, wrote *Black and Mennonite*. In his 1976 text, Brown argued that, contrary to the church's nonconformity doctrine, Mennonites had accommodated themselves to the dominant culture and become "white-oriented."[59] Before Brown, African-American church leader Lee Roy Berry chided "white Mennonites" who pursued worldly interests, white peace activist Peter Ediger lambasted "whitey['s]" silence in the face of racial inequity, and white Minority Ministries staffer Lynford Hershey condemned "white, Anglo, Mennonite immigrants" for holding "racist attitudes."[60] Following Brown, white author Katie Funk Wiebe reported that African-American Mennonites had discussed "the blindness of white Mennonites" during a 1978 symposium in Philadelphia.[61] By contrast, MCC administrators and staff remained uniformly silent about their organization's white identity.

1979-1985: MCC U.S.
RELIEVES AND SUSTAINS RACIAL CONFLICT

After nine years of avoiding conflicts over the organization's white identity, MCC leaders set a course during the next seven years that both relieved and sustained whitening conflicts. Between 1979 and 1985, Mennonite Central Committee U.S. came to carry the organization's racial agenda. Once defined in their role, the staff and board of MCC U.S. turned aside external pressure by initiating race-focused programs and hiring people of color. At the same time, by lodging racial agenda in MCC U.S., the rest of the institution had little reason to pay attention to ongoing concerns about white dominance. Subsequent internal conflicts through the 1990s can be traced back to this foundational separation. More than hiring people of color or increasing racial diversity on boards, shifting race relations to MCC U.S. produced the most significant change in the organization. An explanation of that shift follows.

A strongly worded memo initiated the change process. In June 1979, future MCC personnel director and Mennonite Church moderator Dwight McFadden wrote to MCC Executive Director William Snyder. McFadden was then serving as an associate general secretary for the Mennonite Church, a position created to integrate staff and agenda from the Minority Ministries Council into the denomination. In his widely copied memo, McFadden first noted that "white, German-Dutch" Mennonites of various denominational stripes dominated MCC. He then enumerated "racist" actions of white administrators and staff toward people of color: relationships avoided, insults proffered, hiring promises broken, and prohibitions placed on qualified African-American candidates for overseas positions.[62] McFadden emphasized that white MCCers fostered strong relationships with international partners but "could not relate to their black brothers in the U.S."[63] Furthermore, McFadden reported that Africans wanted white MCCers to stop trying "to relate to them" until they developed relationships with people of color in North America.[64] McFadden's blunt tone and specific detail arrested Snyder's attention.

In contrast to MCC, the Mennonite Church had aggressively recruited people of color for churchwide posts. In addition to McFadden and the second Associate General secretary, Lupe De León, numerous African-American and Latino Mennonites served on churchwide committees. Eleven years previously the Mennonite Church's Committee on Peace and Social Concerns had appointed "Black persons."[65] The process of appointing people of color to churchwide

posts then commenced in earnest as the Minority Ministries Council
drew national attention from 1969 forward.

By 1971, Minority Ministries staff had garnered church wide
posts for African-Americans like Hubert Brown and set agenda for
the church through organized conferences dominated by African-
American and Latino speakers.[66] Minority Ministries members like
Gerald Hughes served on mission boards and an international conference held in Africa in 1973 brought African-American and African
Mennonites together in face-to-face dialogue. White administrators
from MCC felt threatened and undermined by the exchanges.[67] By
1978, African-American, Latino, Native American, and white Mennonite Church leaders had struggled through a decade's worth of intense racial conflict. Unlike white MCC leaders, Mennonite Church
leaders had dealt with racial conflict rather than avoided it.

McFadden and his colleagues from the Mennonite Church's
Black Caucus thus brought experience, passion, and the backing of
MCC's largest constituent body when they met with MCC administrators in December 1979. Caucus members focused on the experience of African-Americans who had served with MCC in African
countries. According to a report offered by Rich Sider, MCC's personnel director, eight out of eighteen African Americans placed in Africa
between 1966 and 1979 did not complete their terms.[68] By comparison to this termination rate of forty-four percent, only seven percent
of all MCC workers had terminated their assignments early from
1975 through 1977.[69] McFadden and other Black Caucus members
Margaret Allen, Harold Davenport, Frances Jackson, Raymond Jackson, and Cynthia Peacock pressed administrators to hire more people
of color, require overseas country directors to examine "personal attitudes and prejudices" before they assumed leadership duties, and
follow through on past commitments to increase programming in
urban centers.[70] Although the meeting ended with a round of prayer
and plans to meet in the future, tension between Black Caucus members and MCC administrators remained high.

In the aftermath of the meeting, MCC administrators made two
critical decisions. They hired African-American administrator Pleas
Broaddus and shifted all urban and minority programming to MCC
U.S. Prompted in part by an MCC Executive Committee directive to
"prepare a concrete proposal on how to increase the involvement of
minorities in MCC," Reg Toews, MCC's Associate Executive Secretary for administration and resources, oversaw the hiring initiative.[71]
In June 1980 he reported to the Black Caucus's assembly that MCC
had enacted a modified affirmative action program in which four po-

sitions were "specifically identified for minority recruitment."[72] Since two of those positions had been filled when he wrote the report, six people of color held headquarters assignments and two more would soon join them. Toews did not, however, report on conflict over hiring Broaddus for a new position in MCC U.S. McFadden and his colleagues cried foul when MCC did not move to hire Broaddus for an executive position. Broaddus had raised concerns about salary and advancement that the personnel director at the time, Lowell Detweiler, had not answered to Broaddus's satisfaction.[73]

Two years later, however, Broaddus served as the director of the newly formed Office of Urban Ministries in MCC U.S.[74] In that capacity, Broaddus drew MCC U.S. personnel into relationships with African-American, Latino, Asian, and Native American young adults. He also initiated a vocational training process for minority college-age youth and expanded a summer service program that provided work for young adults in their home congregations and neighborhoods.[75] Both programs garnered strong interest. By 1982, college-age summer service workers testified to the love they offered children in their home community through their service at the Diamond Street Mennonite Church's summer day camp in Philadelphia. Due to efforts of the summer service workers, local children participated in recreational day trips, Bible study, drama, sports, and crafts.[76] Images of people of color serving with MCC rather than being served by MCC began to appear in the church press as a result of Broaddus' new initiatives.

As race-focused programming gained attention, so did staff and board member efforts to hire more people of color. In 1983, Latino church member Art Montoya joined MCC U.S. to work at Minority Peace Education.[77] Although administrators initially hired Montoya under a short-term contract, they indicated that token inclusion was no longer acceptable. By 1985, MCC U.S. administrators had approved hiring two more Latino Mennonites, Abel Aquino and Carlos Neuschwander, alongside Broaddus. The public listing of headquarters staff in the rest of MCC, however, remained entirely white.

The focused introduction of people of color into significant headquarters positions affected the rest of the institution. In 1984, MCC Peace Section staff published a newsletter on racism for the first time.[78] Broaddus maintained strong connections with Black and Latino Caucus members in the Mennonite Church and they in turn supported his efforts.[79]

These informal connections led to increased representation of people of color on MCC boards. Often, well-known caucus members

joined MCC's governing bodies. By 1985, African-American Men-
nonite leader Hubert Brown had sat on the MCC U.S. Executive Com-
mittee, African-American church leader Margaret Allen and Latino
Mennonite Sam Resendez on the MCC U.S. Peace Section board,
African-American administrator Joy Lovett on the international
Peace Section board, and African-American church leader Frances
Jackson on the MCC board. All had served as leaders in the Black or
Latino Caucuses. Although the MCC Binational Executive Committee, arguably the most powerful governing MCC body, had included
people of color from 1974 though 1978, none served on the committee
from 1979 through 1985. By contrast, the executive committee of
MCC U.S. included people of color from its inception in 1981 and
continued to do so for the next quarter century. MCC U.S. thus initiated MCC's shift from an exclusively white institution primarily by
changing itself.

Even while MCC U.S. changed the organization's racial profile,
robust funding undermined efforts to end white dominance at MCC.
By the end of 1985, MCC had recorded funding increases for six
straight years. In 1979 alone contributions increased by 15.1 percent
and many years saw increases of six to eight percent over the previous year. Such robust increases funded new personnel placements
and program initiatives like Broaddus's Urban Ministries. The new
programs in turn allowed other MCC headquarters personnel to ig-
nore racial concerns. MCC administrators seemed content to allow
one arm of the organization to address racial issues on behalf of the
whole. Other than in MCC U.S., white MCCers in Akron had little
reason to reflect on their racial identity. Although MCC workers serving in Mozambique, South Africa, Swaziland, and Zimbabwe referred to white people through 1985, no other overseas or administrative Akron-based personnel joined them.[80] With finances ample
enough to expand domestic programs without cutting international
outreach, personnel came to view discussion of white racial identity
as the work of MCC U.S. and those involved with international freedom struggles.

The whitening conflict inside MCC continued past 1985. In sum,
MCC U.S., rather than external groups like the Minority Ministries
Council, initiated internal changes. For example, Pleas Broaddus
prompted MCC to honor the Martin Luther King holiday in 1986.[81]
Again the impetus came from MCC U.S. to the rest of the organization. MCC U.S. also initiated a Racism Awareness Program that, by
1995, focused on the maintenance of "power and privilege for white
people."[82] Increasing the percentage of people of color at leadership

levels proved more difficult, but here again MCC U.S. continued to lead the rest of the organization.[83] Overall by 1994, fourteen African-Americans, eighteen Latinos, and seven "Asian or Pacific Islanders" served with MCC, accounting for about six percent of all MCCers in the U.S. and abroad.[84] Through to the present MCC administrators struggled to achieve staffing levels that reflected their rapidly expanding African-American and Latino constituencies.

FINDINGS: CONFLICT AT THE CORE

As noted in the opening anecdote, "whitey" did not leave the inner city or MCC. Rather, white people dominated program and personnel. The racial shifts chronicled in this paper offer insights into "whitey's" significance. As noted above, whiteness scholars have offered insufficiently detailed and imprecisely situated claims about white individuals' access to a set of privileges afforded them by virtue of their skin color. This study of MCC corrects those shortcomings by expanding the notion of whiteness to include conflict along with privilege. In southeastern Pennsylvania during the mid-1960s to mid-1980s, the white identity of Mennonites and Brethren in Christ also incorporated conflict. In addition to power and privilege, white identity encompassed clashes within and without the organization that forced otherwise quiescent racial identity into common view.

To push the point, whiteness was conflict. In the absence of conflict with people of color, Mennonites of European descent in MCC had no reason to notice their white identity. When whitening conflicts quieted, other social and theological dynamics took precedence. Debates about women's leadership, ecumenical involvement, witness to the state, and the primacy of service over evangelism became more prominent. Racial identity for white MCCers only became a conscious issue when conflicts with people of color forced them to look at themselves.

Linking whiteness with conflict should not suggest that white racial formation is an entirely conscious process. Scholars have offered convincing evidence that racial forces operate even when dominant group members remain unaware of them.[85] I argue instead that white identity took on existential—and thereby overtly historical—meaning for the actors in this study when they responded to the world around them as white people. Mennonites in this study became white, as it were, by being forced to think about it.[86]

The MCC experience also links racial consciousness with the definition of whiteness. To nuance the definition offered at the beginning of this essay, within MCC between 1960 and 1985, whiteness—what I have referred to as the whitening conflicts—was a series of historical struggles between members of a racially dominant group and members of subordinate racial groups that resulted in the dominant group becoming relatively more conscious of their position. My point is that when the actors were least aware of their racial identity, they were most likely to respond out of other social identities and interact with other social forces. When whitening conflicts were quiescent, white MCCers maintained their social dominance by ignoring racial dynamics that African-American, Latino/a, Native American, and Asian church members dealt with daily. The conflict between these two existential realities both prompted incremental changes in board and staff composition and prohibited more substantive change.

This definition suggests several additional findings central to the story of MCC's whiteness. First, whitening conflicts in MCC focused not only on power and privilege but also on service. During the breadth of this study, white MCCers responded to racial conflict by intensifying service to communities of color both domestically and overseas. Even during the tumultuous 1960s and early 1970s, MCC workers served communities embroiled in racial conflict and, in many cases, supported local partners with integrity.

The Atlanta Unit makes the point. After Vincent and Rosemarie Harding resigned in 1965 and connections with SCLC, SNCC, and other civil rights groups attenuated, MCCers sought new ways to support the African-American community.[87] They backed away from direct leadership during the ascendancy of the Black Power movement but remained in the city.

Service to communities of color in Atlanta and elsewhere did not, however, resolve whitening conflicts within MCC. In some ways, service actually intensified whitening conflicts. Black Caucus members, for example, raised the disparity in early termination rates between white and black workers to which MCC leaders responded by sending more white people into African-American and Latino communities. The disparity remained and, with it, a whitening conflict. Only in the last five years of this study did MCC personnel directors begin to invite African-Americans and Latinos to serve in their own communities. In effect, white MCCers attempted to resolve conflict about their racial identity through service and, in so doing, often initiated new rounds of racial struggle.

Second, MCC's story suggests whiteness scholars need to examine questions of sequence rather than of degree or kind. Asking whether MCC was whiter than other organizations or whether staffers displayed a different kind of white behavior, i.e. a different kind of whiteness, reveals little. These questions reify the idea of whiteness by treating it as a constant, unchanging, and ahistorical social reality. By examining the shifts and changes in white racial identity over time, however, scholars can delineate racial conflicts, note varying levels of racial consciousness, and trace the interplay of internal and external forces. Study of sequence also dispels the myth that European groups invariably become more conscious of their racial identity over time. In the case of Mennonite Disaster Service, personnel became less aware of racial issues after their intense focus on racism from 1968 through 1970.

To be certain, MCC's whitening conflicts were not the sole racial conflicts present in the Mennonite community during this period. African-American and Latino/a Minority Ministries Council members, for example, struggled among themselves for power and influence even as liberal and conservative leaders inside their organization disagreed over which programs would most effectively support Mennonites of color.[88] Other racial conflicts having little to do with white racial identity also flared up during this period. Those stories also need further exploration. MCC's experience with whiteness provides insight into only a small portion of the larger Mennonite race relations narrative.

Finally, this study demonstrates that MCC's whitening conflicts did not have predetermined outcomes. When Vincent Harding chided Mennonites for accepting the "power of whiteness" in 1967, no one knew that MDS directors would turn over local control to Black Nationalists in Pittsburgh two years later. When Hubert Brown criticized "white oriented" Mennonites in 1976, it was not apparent that MCC leaders would hire their first African-American administrators that same year. When Margaret Allen, Frances Jackson, Cynthia Peacock, and others called for immediate changes within MCC in 1979, no one knew whether administrators would be any more proactive than they had in the past. If the MCC experience is any indication of what has taken place in other organizations, then whitening conflicts have led to multiple outcomes.

The only certainty we can carry away from the MCC story is that racialized conflicts have taken place and will, for the foreseeable future, continue to erupt. If Asrat Gebre and other MCC leaders want to change the "white, male-dominated" nature of MCC, this history points particularly to one strategy: They will have to seek out racial conflict. Such focused struggle over white identity, and that alone, has been the engine of change within MCC.

NOTES

1. As a source for the first reference to "white" in these introductory paragraphs see *Mennonite Central Committee Workbook* (Akron, Pa.: Mennonite Central Committee, 1967), C-8; for the ongoing comments on white related to Asra Gebre's observations see Robert Rhodes, "Governance Issues, Ethnic Diversity Top MCC Annual Meeting," *Canadian Mennonite* 11/3 (2007).

2. Winthrop D. Jordan, *White over Black: American Attitudes Toward the Negro, 1550-1812* (Chapel Hill, N.C.: University of North Carolina Press, 1968); Audrey Smedley, *Race in North America: Origin and Evolution of a Worldview* (Boulder, Colo.: Westview Press, 1993); Elliott R. Barkan, "Race, Religion, and Nationality in American Society: A Model of Ethnicity—from Contact to Assimilation," *Journal of American Ethnic History* 14/2 (1995).

3. Scholars who have built on W. E. B. Dubois' observation include the following: Cheryl I. Harris, "Whiteness as Property," in *Critical Race Theory: The Key Writings That Formed the Movement*, ed. Kimberlé Crenshaw, et al. (New York: New Press, 1995); Ian F. Haney López, *White by Law: The Legal Construction of Race* (New York: New York University Press, 1996); Toni Morrison, *Playing in the Dark: Whiteness and the Literary Imagination, The William E. Massey, Sr. Lectures in the History of American Civilization* (Cambridge, Mass.: Harvard University Press, 1992); David R. Roediger, *The Wages of Whiteness: Race and the Making of the American Working Class* (New York: Verso, 1991), 137; David R. Roediger, *Towards the Abolition of Whiteness: Essays on Race, Politics, and Working Class History* (New York: Verso, 1994), 24.

4. Roediger, *Towards the Abolition of Whiteness*, 185-86. Other historians have offered parallel studies of the formation of white identity in the United States. See, for example: Matthew Frye Jacobson, *Whiteness of a Different Color: European Immigrants and the Alchemy of Race* (Cambridge, Mass.: Harvard University Press, 1998); Noel Ignatiev, *How the Irish Became White* (New York: Routledge, 1995); Kirk Savage, *Standing Soldiers, Kneeling Slaves: Race, War, and Monument in Nineteenth-Century America* (Princeton: Princeton University Press, 1997).

5. Roediger, *Towards the Abolition of Whiteness*, 12; Roediger, *The Wages of Whiteness*, 13; David R. Roediger, "Is There a Healthy White Personality?" *Counseling Psychologist* (March 1999): 239ff.

6. Eric Arnesen, "Whiteness and the Historians' Imagination," *International Labor and Working-Class History*, no. 60 (2001): 3.

7. Ibid.: 3, 21.

8. See, for example: Peter Kolchin, "Whiteness Studies: The New History of Race in America," *The Journal of American History* 89/1 (2002).

9. Le Roy Bechler, *The Black Mennonite Church in North America 1886-1986* (Scottdale, Pa.: Herald Press, 1986); Rafael Falcón, *The Hispanic Mennonite Church in North America, 1932-1982*, trans. Ronald Collins (Scottdale, Pa.: Herald Press, 1986); Hubert Brown, *Black and Mennonite: A Search for Identity* (Scottdale, Pa.: Herald Press, 1976).

10. Jeffery Phillip Gingerich, "Sharing the Faith: Racial and Ethnic Identity in an Urban Mennonite Community" (Dissertation, University of Pennsylvania, 2003), i-ii.

11. Ibid., 200-03.

12. Robert S. Kreider and Rachel Waltner Goossen, *Hungry, Thirsty, a*

Stranger (Scottdale, Pa.: Herald Press, 1988), 298; Lowell Detweiler, *The Hammer Rings Hope: Photos and Stories from Fifty Years of Mennonite Disaster Service* (Scottdale, Pa.: Herald Press, 2000); Guy F. Hershberger, "Historical Background to the Formation of the Mennonite Central Committee," *The Mennonite Quarterly Review* 44/3 (1970); John D. Unruh, *In the Name of Christ: A History of the Mennonite Central Committee and Its Service 1920-1951* (Scottdale, Pa.: Herald Press, 1952). The one exception to this race-exclusive trend is a short but insightful paper by Nancy Heisey that traces MCC's history of gender and race. Although she notes that her work was not meant to be comprehensive, she nonetheless identifies the turning point noted below in 1979 and suggests that racial issues would continue to challenge the church into the twenty-first century. Nancy R. Heisey, "Race, Ethnicity, and Gender in MCC Work," in *Unity amid Diversity: Mennonite Central Committee at 75*, ed. Robert S. Kreider and Ronald J. R. Mathies (Akron, Pa.: Mennonite Central Committee, 1996).

13. Lynford Hershey, "What Is the Mennonite Attitude on Race Relations?" *Gospel Herald*, March 23, 1971, 262-64.

14. Rafael Falcón, *Hispanic Mennonites* (Global Anabaptist Encyclopedia Online, 1989 [cited September 23 2008]); Bechler, *The Black Mennonite Church*, 174-77; James E. Horsch, ed., *Mennonite Yearbook and Directory*, vol. 71 (Scottdale, Pa.: Mennonite Publishing House, 1980); James F. Horsch, ed., *Mennonite Yearbook and Directory*, vol. 76 (Scottdale, Pa.: Mennonite Publishing House, 1985), 127.

15. Bechler, *The Black Mennonite Church*, 51-54.

16. Vincent Harding, "The Task of the Mennonite Church in Establishing Racial Unity," April 17-19 (Woodlawn Mennonite Church, 1959), 29, Archives of the Mennonite Church in Goshen, Indiana [hereafter cited as AMC], Hist. Mss. 1-48 Box 60, John H. Yoder (1927-1997) Collection Race/Urban issues, file 60/1.

17. Felipe Hinojosa, "Making Noise among the 'Quiet in the Land': Mexican American and Puerto Rican Ethno-Religious Identity in the Mennonite Church, 1932-1980" (Dissertation, University of Houston, 2009).

18. Fred Lamar Kniss, *Disquiet in the Land: Cultural Conflict in American Mennonite Communities* (New Brunswick, N.J.: Rutgers University Press, 1997), 6, 86-87.

19. Robert B. Graber, "An Amiable Mennonite Schism: The Origin of the Eastern Pennsylvania Mennonite Church," *Pennsylvania Mennonite Heritage* 7/4 (1984).

20. A set of complete statistical data on the racial composition of MCC's Akron staff and boards based on a compilation of publicly presented personnel listing in Mennonite Church yearbooks is available from the author. The Mennonite Church was then the largest of the MCC constituent conference bodies.

21. Heisey, "Race, Ethnicity, and Gender in MCC Work," 59.

22. Vincent Harding, "The Christian and the Race Question," August 6 (Mennonite World Conference, 1962), 4.

23. Edgar Stoesz, "Vince Harding Visit to Akron," August 14 (Mennonite Central Committee Voluntary Service, 1962), 1, AMC-MCC Correspondence, IX-6-3, "Inter-Office Peace Section", PS 1962; Edgar Metzler to Vincent Hard-

ing, July 26, 1962, Akron, Pa., AMC IX-6-3.100 MCC Correspondence 1962, Folder Atlanta Mennonite Service Unit 1962.

24. *Mennonite Central Committee Workbook* (Akron, Pa.: Mennonite Central Committee, 1963), E1-E2.

25. *Mennonite Central Committee Workbook* (Akron, Pa.: Mennonite Central Committee, 1960), C-4; *Mennonite Central Committee Workbook* (Akron, Pa.: Mennonite Central Committee, 1962), B-3-4.

26. The report on the Hardings' activity in Atlanta mentioned race in 1964 but the topic did not appear elsewhere. *Mennonite Central Committee Workbook* (Akron, Pa.: Mennonite Central Committee, 1964), B7-8.

27. Guy F. Hershberger, "Nonresistance, the Mennonite Church, and the Race Question," *Gospel Herald*, June 28, 1960, 577, 78, 81, 82.

28. Maynard Shelly, "Editorial," *The Mennonite*, November 10 1964, 708.

29. "Race News: Mennonite Students Discuss 'Northern Race Relations,'" *Youth's Christian Companion*, June 7, 1964, 13.

30. *Mennonite Central Committee Workbook* (Akron, Pa.: Mennonite Central Committee, 1968), E1-E2.

31. Edgar Metzler to Peace Section Members, April 6, 1965, Akron, Pa., AMC, CESR papers I-3-7, Box 7, Folder 12.

32. *Mennonite Central Committee Workbook* (Akron, Pa.: Mennonite Central Committee, 1965), B8-9.

33. *Mennonite Central Committee Workbook*, 1967, C-8.

34. Vincent Harding, "The Peace Witness and Revolutionary Movements," *Mennonite Life* 22/4 (1967): 164.

35. R. de Zeeuw et al., "Echoes from Amsterdam," Ibid.: 175-76.

36. *Mennonite Central Committee Workbook*, 1968, E1-2. Other African activists at the time included Curtis Burrell, Raymond Jackson, Mattie Cooper Nikiema, and John Powell.

37. Ibid.

38. Ibid., E1-E2.

39. Melvin L. Lehman, "Mennonites and Pittsburgh," *Christian Living*, March 1970, 2-7.

40. Clyde Jackson and James Burkholder, "Interacting Where Asked," Ibid., 7-9; Lehman, "Mennonites and Pittsburgh."

41. *Mennonite Central Committee Workbook* (Akron, Pa.: Mennonite Central Committee, 1969), E1-E2.

42. Ibid., E2.

43. "The Death of Martin Luther King, Jr.," *Sword and Trumpet*, June 1968, 1-2; "'Collective Guilt' in Dr. King's Death Called a 'Mischievous Myth'," *Sword and Trumpet*, July 1968, 19; "White Racism Blamed for City Riots," *The Mennonite*, April 2 1968, 237; "Who Was He?" *Gospel Herald*, May 21, 1968, 449; Sandra Froese, "The American Dream," *The Mennonite*, May 7, 1968, 329; James A. Goering, "Martin Luther King and the Gandhian Method of Nonviolent Resistance," *Sword and Trumpet*, October 1968, 1-5; Walton N. Hackman, "A Letter from an Atlanta Funeral," (Mennonite General Conference Committee on Peace and Social Concerns, 1968), Hackman 68; Daniel Hertzler, "On the Death of King," *Christian Living*, June 1968, 40; Martin Luther King, Jr., "'I Have a Dream . . .,'" *The Gulfbreeze*, January-April 1968, 1; Paul G. Landis, "Tribute Lauds King's Life, Work," *Gospel Herald*, April 23, 1968, 374; Paul

G. Landis, "Dr. King's Message Often Misunderstood," *Mennonite Weekly Review*, April 18, 1968; John A. Lapp, "The Greatness of Martin Luther King, Jr.," *Christian Living*, June 1968, 18-19; Frank H. Littell, "Martin Luther King, Jr.," *Mennonite Life*, July 1968, 99; Carol Loganbill, "One Night in Alabama," *The Mennonite*, November 19, 1968, 725; Vern Miller, "We Shall Overcome," *Gospel Herald*, May 14, 1968, 425; William Robert Miller, "The Misunderstanding of Martin Luther King," *The Mennonite*, November 19, 1968, 714-17; Harold Regier, "He Lives On," *The Mennonite*, May 7, 1968, 336; Marie J. Regier, "Bitter Harvest of Hate," *The Mennonite*, November 26, 1968, 732; John C. Rezmerski, "For Martin L. King Jr.," *Mennonite Life*, July 1968, 99; Edgar Stoesz, "A Mennonite Reflects on Martin Luther King," *Gospel Herald*, May 14, 1968, 437.

44. Landis, "Tribute Lauds King's Life, Work"; Landis, "Dr. King's Message Often Misunderstood."

45. Miller, "The Misunderstanding of Martin Luther King."

46. "Black Group Asks $500 Million in Reparations," *The Mennonite*, June 3 1969, 378; Don Bender, "Black and White Together; Days of Optimism Passed," *The Mennonite*, April 8, 1969, 239-40; Don Bender, "Whites in a Black Community," *Gospel Herald*, May 13, 1969, 428; Melvin Gingerich, "The Race Revolution in America," *Gospel Herald*, April 1, 1969, 292-93.

47. *Mennonite Central Committee Workbook*, 1969, C-14.

48. *Mennonite Central Committee Workbook* (Akron, Pa.: Mennonite Central Committee, 1975), 2.

49. Ibid., 109-10.

50. "Mennonite General Conference Urban-Racial Concerns," *Gospel Herald*, October 7, 1969, 871.

51. "Minutes of the Committee on Peace and Social Concerns," April 27-29 (Mennonite General Conference Committee on Peace and Social Concerns, 1969), 5, Lancaster Mennonite Historical Society Archives, Lancaster, Pennsylvania [hereafter cited as LMHS]-Paul G. Landis Coll., Mennonite General Conference Committee on Peace and Social Concerns, 1968-1971.

52. Vern Preheim to Treasurer's Office, July 18, 1972, Akron, Pa., AMC IX-6-3 Box 132 Mennonite Central Committee Correspondence 1972, Folder Powell, John 1972.

53. Peter J. Dyck, "John Powell Visit to Europe," January 31 (Mennonite Central Committee, 1972), AMC IX-6-3 Box 132 Mennonite Central Committee Correspondence 1972, Folder Powell, John 1972.

54. Lupe De León Jr. to Lavon Welty, February 14, 1973, Elkhart, Ind., AMC IX-6-3 Box 137 Mennonite Central Committee Correspondence 1974, Folder Minority Ministries Council 1974.

55. Ibid.

56. Mary Martin, "Minority Ministries Council Executive Committee," October 19-21 (1973), AMC IV-21-2 Box 1 Minority Ministries Council, 1969-74, File 1/1 MCM, Mionirty Ministries Council Minutes, 1968-1974 (General Board Set).

57. Mattie Cooper Nikiema, Raymond Jackson Jr., Lee Roy Berry, Gerald Hughes, Hubert Brown, and John Powell, interview with John Sharp, Lee Heights Fellowship, Cleveland, Ohio, July 17, 2004.

58. Lupe De León, Jr., "Señor Snyder," March 6 (Minority Ministries Council, 1974), AMC IX-6-3 Box 137 Mennonite Central Committee Correspon-

dence 1974, Folder Minority Ministries Council 1974.

59. Brown, *Black and Mennonite*, 28.

60. Lee Roy Berry Jr., "You May Be a Worldly Christian," *Christian Living*, January 1970, 16-17; Peter J. Ediger, "Psalm 95 and Voices from Black America," *The Mennonite*, November 17, 1970, 709; Lynford Hershey, "God's Altar and Race Relations," *Gospel Herald*, August 17, 1971, 682-83.

61. Katie Funk Wiebe, "Mennonites Like Me," *Gospel Herald*, August 22, 1978, 634.

62. Dwight McFadden, "Dear William," June 14 (Mennonite Church, 1979), 1-3, AMC I-6-7 African-American Mennonite Association, Records, 1969, 1976-91, Box 28 (Large), Folder Mennonite Central Committee 28/1.

63. Ibid., 1.

64. Ibid., 3.

65. "Committee on Peace and Social Concerns Executive Secretary's Recommendations," November 7-9 (Mennonite General Conference Committee on Peace and Social Concerns, 1968), LMHS-Paul G. Landis Coll., Mennonite General Conference Committee on Peace and Social Concerns, 1968-1971; Workbook Committee on Peace and Social Concerns, Washington, D.C., November 7-9, 1968.

66. "Minority Ministries Council Annual Assembly," October 15-16 (Minority Ministries Council, 1971), Eastern Mennonite Missions Record Room, Salunga, Pennsylvania [hereafter cited as EMM Record Room]-4th Cabinet of row on far left wall upon entering room, Second Drawer: Unmarked, Folder: MINORITY MINISTRY COUNCIL 1970-71; "Cross-Cultural Theological Consultation," April 26-29 (Minority Ministries Council, Mennonite Church General Board, 1973), LMHS-Landis Paul G., Papers: (SCCO minutes and report, 1966-71, Cross-Cultural Theological Consultation, 1973, Kitchener 71).

67. "Interracial Council Approved," *Gospel Herald*, July 23, 1968, 669; "AFRAM Report," (AFRAM, 1974), AMC—IV-21-4 Box 1, MBM, Minority Ministries Council, Data Files #1, A-K, Folder: AFRAM-John Powell 1972-74; Urie A. Bender, "Where Color Doesn't Matter," *Missionary Messenger*, February 1974, 8-9; Nikiema et al., interview with Sharp.

68. Rich Sider, "Summary: Minority Applications and In-Service Report," December 4 (Mennonite Central Committee, 1979), AMC I-6-7 African-American Mennonite Association, Records, 1969, 1976-91, Box 28 (Large), Folder Mennonite Central Committee 28/1.

69. Rich Sider, "Early Terminations-Totals Compared to Minorities," December 3 (Mennonite Central Committee, 1979), AMC I-6-7 African-American Mennonite Association, Records, 1969, 1976-91, Box 28 (Large), Folder Mennonite Central Committee 28/1.

70. Faith Hershberger, "MCC/Black Caucus Representative Meeting," December 4 (Mennonite Central Committee, 1979), AMC I-6-7 African-American Mennonite Association, Records, 1969, 1976-91, Box 28 (Large), Folder Mennonite Central Committee 28/1.

71. Heisey, "Race, Ethnicity, and Gender in MCC Work," 60.

72. Reg Toews, "Mennonite Central Committee Report to the Black Caucus Assembly," June 9 (Mennonite Central Committee, 1980), AMC I-6-7 African-American Mennonite Association, Records, 1969, 1976-91, Box 28 (Large), Folder Mennonite Central Committee 28/1.

73. Lowell Detweiler to Dwight McFadden, July 7 1980, Akron, Pa., AMC I-6-7 African-American Mennonite Association, Records, 1969, 1976-91, Box 28 (Large), Folder Mennonite Central Committee 28/1.

74. Gerald Handrich Schlabach, "Participation the Cornerstone to MCC U.S. Urban Ministries," March 19 (Mennonite Central Committee, 1982), AMC I-6-7 African-American Mennonite Association, Records, 1969, 1976-91, Box 28 (Large), Folder MCC Office of Urban Ministries Pleas Broaddus 28/26.

75. Ibid.

76. "Three Serve Summer Urban Program in Philadelphia," *Gospel Herald*, September 21, 1982, 643.

77. Art Montoya to Joy Lovett, et al., August 17, 1983, Akron, Pa., AMC I-6-7 African-American Mennonite Association, Records, 1969, 1976-91, Box 28 (Large), Folder Mennonite Central Committee 28/1.

78. *Mennonite Central Committee Workbook* (Akron, Pa.: Mennonite Central Committee, 1984).

79. Dwight McFadden, "Dear Henry," February 12 (Mennonite Church, 1982), AMC I-6-7 African-American Mennonite Association, Records, 1969, 1976-91, Box 28 (Large), Folder MCC Office of Urban Ministries Pleas Broaddus 28/26; Pleas H. Broaddus to Georgia Lovett, September 21 1982, Akron, Pa., AMC I-6-7 African-American Mennonite Association, Records, 1969, 1976-91, Box 28 (Large), Folder MCC Office of Urban Ministries Pleas Broaddus 28/26.

80. *Mennonite Central Committee Workbook* (Akron, Pa.: Mennonite Central Committee, 1985), 23-24, 41-43.

81. Pleas H. Broaddus to John Lapp, January 7, 1986, Akron, PA, AMC IX.6.3 Mennonite Central Committee Correspondence 1986, Reel #14 [I-2765]; Pleas H. Broaddus, "Dr. Martin Luther King Jr. First National Birthday Observance Monday, January 20, 1986," January 15 (Mennonite Central Committee, 1986), AMC IX-6-3 Mennonite Central Committee Correspondence 1986, Reel #14 [I-2765].

82. *Mennonite Central Committee Workbook* (Akron, Pa.: Mennonite Central Committee, 1995), 193-94. In interest of full disclosure, the author served as the first director of MCC U.S.'s Racism Awareness Program.

83. Ibid., 180.

84. Heisey, "Race, Ethnicity, and Gender in MCC Work," 61.

85. Morrison, *Playing in the Dark: Whiteness and the Literary Imagination* (Cambridge, Mass.: Harvard University Press, 1992); Benjamin DeMott, "Put on a Happy Face: Masking the Differences Between Blacks and Whites," *Harper's* 291, no. 1744 (1995); Elizabeth Ellsworth, "Double Binds of Whiteness," in *Off White: Readings on Race, Power and Society*, ed. Michelle Fine, et al. (New York: Routledge, 1997); Grace Elizabeth Hale, *Making Whiteness: The Culture of Segregation in the South, 1890-1940*, Vintage Books ed. (New York: Random House, 1998; reprint, June 1999); Monica Beatriz deMello Patterson, "America's Racial Unconscious: The Invisibility of Whiteness," in *White Reign: Deploying Whiteness in America*, ed. Joe L. Kincheloe, et al. (New York: St. Martin's Press, 1998).

86. Here I echo Robert Terry's foundational observation, "To be white in America is not to have to think about it." See: Robert W. Terry, "The Negative Impact on White Values," in *Impacts of Racism on White Americans*, ed. Ben-

jamin P. Bowser and Raymond G. Hunt (Beverly Hills, Calif.: Sage, 1981), 120.

87. *Mennonite Central Committee Workbook* (Akron, Pa.: Mennonite Central Committee, 1970); *Mennonite Central Committee Workbook* (Akron, Pa.: Mennonite Central Committee, 1976).

88. Mary Martin, "Minority Ministries Council Mass Assembly," October 19 (1973), AMC IV-21-2 Box 1 Minority Ministries Council, 1969-74, File 1/1 MCM, Minority Ministries Council Minutes, 1968-1974 (General Board Set).

Chapter 10

Writing Women
into MCC's History

BETH GRAYBILL

W riting women into history is a political act. As historian Laurel Thatcher Ulrich has famously written, "Well-behaved women seldom make history."[1] Those that do may be seen as controversial and contentious. Those that don't may be lost to memory and the historical record. Thus an essay on women over ninety years of MCC history faces particular challenges. By virtue of my own area of expertise, this essay will reflect more on MCC's U.S. Mennonite constituencies during the latter half of the twentieth century (although some of my claims, I expect, would also be relevant to MCC's Canadian Mennonite contexts). Rather than following a strictly chronological approach to the question of women's roles in MCC, I offer a five-part thematic framework in which I use the lens of gender as my primary viewfinder.[2] I end with suggestions for change.

Joan Wallach Scott has famously written in her influential 1986 book that gender is "a constitutive element of social relationships based on perceived differences between the sexes."[3] Thus gender provides a socially constructed set of assumptions, meanings, and normative concepts that are attributed to masculinity and femininity and employed in everyday action and discourse. The task of the historian is to examine how changing understandings of gender have been lived out at various times and places. Gender in religion has shaped women's understanding of their lives, their images of God, their understandings of family life, their work both at home and in the paid workforce, and their interpretations of suffering.[4] Moreover, as Scott argues, "gender has functioned as "a primary way of signifying relationships of power."[5] Thus it is fruitful to examine women within religious institutions like MCC. Finally, this definition of gender as fluid and constructed by experience holds out the promise of change.

I offer the following, five-part framework for looking at women in MCC through the years. First, I begin by noticing women's absence in history, including MCC's history. Next I discuss how often the stories we do have of women within Mennonite history and MCC's history are of notable (white) women. I proceed to note scholarly efforts to recover ordinary women's experience in the form of social history. After that, I describe and assess MCC efforts to compensate for women's lack of influence or participation within MCC, concluding with an examination of women's access or lack thereof to power and decision-making.

Step one in my interpretive framework comes from theologian Mary Malone, author of the comprehensive three-volume history, *Women and Christianity*, who notes in her series introduction that we begin by noticing the places were women are *not* mentioned, absences in the historical record that need to be addressed.[6] Research by Nancy Heisey has countered the absence of women within dominant MCC narratives of service, particularly in MCC's initial decades, narratives which highlight men in Civilian Public Service camps and the PAX and Teachers Abroad Program (TAP); Heisey documents women's active roles as overseas workers during World War II and in postwar reconstruction and resettlement. In fact, MCC personnel records show that about 1,250 women served in relief efforts from 1946 to 1960.[7]

Rachel Waltner Goossen's ground-breaking study, *Women Against the Good War*, looks at women's participation in the MCC-sponsored wartime Civilian Public Service program more generally.[8] As she has so ably documented, an estimated 2,000 women played direct roles in Civilian Public Service (CPS) camps as nurses or dieticians, as summer service volunteers, or as wives and girlfriends who lived in or near CPS camps.[9] After the war ended, MCC transformed the women's summer service CPS units into a coed voluntary service program that attracted hundreds of college students.[10]

My research of Mennonites at mid-century suggests the war years provided a significant watershed for women, with MCC trends mirroring trends among Mennonites in the U.S. more broadly. Before World War II, Mennonites had largely subscribed to a view of gender that primarily limited women to the home sphere: "the hand that rocks the cradle rules the world."[11] But ideas about gender roles changed during and after the war.

Since fewer Mennonite men were in school during the war, women were recruited to fill college classes at Bethel College in Kansas.[12] Women dramatically outnumbered men during the war years at Eastern Mennonite College.[13] At Goshen College the ratio of female to male students was three to one; the year 1945 (before CPS men returned to school) marked the largest fall term enrollment to date in the history of the college.[14] In 1951 Eastern Mennonite College began a major in home economics, and in 1953 Goshen College strengthened its home economics major to address the interests of women students.[15] Mennonite women who might not otherwise have attended college found encouragement to do so during this period.

By 1963, eighteen percent of Mennonite women were employed for pay outside the home, as compared to an estimated five percent in 1940.[16] Another indication that more women were entering professions during these years was the founding of the Mennonite Nurses Association in 1942 and the addition of nursing to Goshen College's curriculum, with the first class graduating in 1953.[17] Moreover, in the late 1940s Laurelville Mennonite camp instituted "Professional Girls' Week" for "teachers, nurses, and stenographers." In addition, the war also created new teaching opportunities for Mennonite women. As Mennonite parents became uncomfortable with patriotism and the military emphasis in public schools, church schools opened and enrollment in both elementary and secondary Mennonite schools shot up. From 1940 to 1949, thirty-nine Mennonite elementary schools opened their doors in several states, with a majority of teachers employed in these new schools being women.[18]

Historian Beulah Stauffer Hostetler has described the 1950s in the Mennonite Church as an Awakening, which she defines as "an adjustment of religious understandings to the cultural milieu."[19] Thus women who served with MCC through the 1950s exemplified widening gender roles within the larger Mennonite cultural milieu, with Mennonite women encouraged to use their gifts in new ways.

The second step in my interpretive framework encourages us to notice that often the stories we do have of Mennonite women's involvement in MCC are of notable, or exemplary, women, specifically notable *white* women. To the extent that we are familiar at all with

women who served MCC historically in its earlier decades, we may
have heard of Lois Gunden Clemens or Elfrieda Klassen Dyck, who
served during and after the Second World War; Edna Ruth Byler, who
founded the SELFHELP Crafts, later Ten Thousand Villages, enterprise; Doris Janzen Longacre, whose MCC service led to her write the
More-with-Less Cookbook in 1976; or Nancy Heisey, who served MCC
international programs in a variety of leadership capacities during
the 1980s.[20] Sadly many of us are less familiar with the names of
women of color who have devoted years of their lives to MCC,
women like Cynthia Peacock, a long-term MCC worker in India;
Doris Dube, a long-term MCC partner in Zimbabwe; Wilma Bailey,
who served on the MCC board during the 1990s; and Maria de Leon,
current chair of the MCC Central States board, who has served on
MCC boards since the 1990s.

In the case of those notable white women with whose names we
are familiar, some were the wives or daughters of prominent church-
men. Ironically, few of us today would know that Edna Ruth Byler
was the second wife of J. N. Byler, one-time professor of social science
at Hesston College (where the couple met and married), who undertook wartime relief work in Europe with MCC and later served in
Akron as director of Foreign Relief and Services, from 1945 to 1960.
Byler often traveled with her husband on his MCC administrative
trips. Just as early to-mid-twentieth-century Mennonite ministers'
wives often gained voice and status by extension of their husbands'
positions, so too MCC administrators' wives likely had easier access
to recognition and standing. Edna Ruth Byler is rightly recognized for
founding the entire fair trade movement. Yet like some other MCC
foremothers who made significant contributions in their own right,
she almost certainly found her way made easier, came to prominence,
found fuller acceptance, and has been remembered by history in part
because of family connections. Notable women of color in MCC history typically did not benefit from such social capital.

The situation for early women in MCC service was arguably similar to the reality faced by women described in *Women's Leadership in
Marginal Religions*, a study that suggests that the presence of active individual women leaders in a particular religious movement does not
necessarily guarantee wider roles for all women in that same movement. Exceptional women, often enabled by prominent male family
members, can exercise authority without challenging the larger patri-
archal structures that constrain most other women.[21]

Lucille Marr, in her account of MCC Ontario's history, notes that
wives of prominent Canadian Mennonite church leaders at mid-cen-

tury viewed their roles as supporters of their husbands' public work through motherhood, homemaking during their husbands' extended absences, and hosting and hospitality offered to visiting ministers in their homes. Through oral history interviews, Marr has documented the "joy of service" and the ways in which "[church] service was a family enterprise."[22]

The third step in my interpretive framework asks us to look not exclusively or even primarily at prominent families when analyzing women's participation in MCC but to recognize and reclaim ordinary women's daily experience, known as the work of social history. Catherine Brekus has noted that social historians are linked together by "their common belief that historical change does not only come from the top down, but also from the bottom up" and emphasizes the collective power of groups.[23]

Countless unnamed women serving the MCC cause in their local communities have knit bandages, made soap, or knotted comforters for overseas relief, collecting supplies and assembling relief kits. Lucille Marr reminds us that Mennonite women's mission and sewing circles, generating material aid products, most of which flow through MCC channels, have existed for at least 100 years, predating MCC itself.[24] Mennonite women's sewing circles reached the height of their flourishing between 1953 and 1969, according to Gloria Neufeld, writing from the Canadian context. While the number and frequency of sewing circle gatherings have declined since 1970 due to women pursuing education and/or joining the paid workforce, they are still active, providing quilts and comforters for relief.[25] Since 1948, thousands of Mennonite, Amish, and Brethren in Christ women each year stitch quilts and prepare food for sale at the thirty relief sales held annually across the country in the U.S. Thousands more sort goods and staff the fifty-two U.S. thrift stores, in most years the second largest source of MCC income after individual contributions.

Interestingly, these expressions of everyday women's labor, which form such an important contribution to MCC, illustrate the lack of women's representation and influence in the organization. As Agnes Hubert wrote in a 1997 gender audit of MCC Canada, entitled, "A Less Than Central Irritant":

> The women who work in the material aid program and the thrift shops are MCC's most direct and most sustained link to its supporting constituency. That these programs are important to the women participating in them is demonstrated by the tenacity of involvement and the concern about their future. Yet, despite their importance to MCC, the women involved in these

programs do not, by and large, have access to meaningful influence in the organization that benefits so greatly from their
work.[26]

Another frame for interpreting these everyday acts of service is
the concept of "lived religion," described by its best-known theorist,
Robert Orsi, as everyday religious practice and lived experience.
David Hall notes that lived religion emphasizes commonplace behavior by ordinary people in American society as expressions of belief.[27] As in the preceding examples, lived religion can be gendered.
Historian Steve Nolt extends the analysis of gender and lived religion to consumers of third-world handicrafts through Ten Thousand
Villages, a program of MCC through 2000, now an independent entity. He writes of the ways in which this program transformed
wardrobes and dinner tables,

> By the 1970s, for example, Pennsylvania women long taught to
> eschew jewelry as "plain people," but determined to help poor
> women around the world, tried their hand at marketing neck-
> laces and earrings made by women in the developing world.
> Bypassing Madison Avenue, they accepted fashion sense from
> a global Christian sisterhood.[28]

Nolt describes the many stores, "almost all in Mennonite-popu-
lated, rural small towns—locations professional marketers undoubtedly would never have chosen to sell world art in the 1970s and
1980s"—with product lines including "jewelry and various display
objects that often were highly decorative—even gaudy—by traditional Mennonite standards."[29] Women's participation in this fair
trade project is another example of lived religion on the part of ordinary women participating in this MCC project through everyday
channels.

The fourth step of my interpretive framework recognizes efforts
within MCC to compensate for women's lack of influence or participation. This is related to Gerda Lerner's "compensatory history" that
sought to write women back into history.[30] However, as I use compensatory history I am more concerned with identifying the ways in
which MCC power brokers have sought to make up for, counteract,
and offset women's marginalization in its history and workforce.
Here I note three sincere attempts related to personnel issues and
also discuss gender issues from the perspective of MCC's "international" programs (i.e. programs outside of Canada and the United
States).

In 1976, MCC's Human Resources department changed its filing practices. Formerly MCC women workers were filed under their husbands' last names, a particular problem in cases where women retained their maiden names upon marriage. Thus to look up Jane Doe one had to know or remember that she was married to Dan Jones. Beginning in 1976 and up until the present, married couples have been cross-filed under whichever last name comes first alphabetically.[31] This shift reflected a revised gender consciousness that saw women as individuals in their own right, not as subordinates or as extensions of their husbands.

A second sincere example of MCC attempting to bring its personnel policies in line with new gender expectations was the "Maternity Leave Policy Approved by Office Management, May 12, 1986," later codified as Human Resources policy #566, "Leave When Child Joins Family Through Birth/Adoption/Foster Care," and formally adopted in 1994. This generous policy allowed six weeks paid leave followed by six weeks unpaid leave and remained in effect until replaced by a U.S. family and medical leave policy (#564) and a short-term medical leave income protection policy (#588) in 2008. The original maternity leave policy recognized and seemed to validate a gendered notion that for women to remain in the work force during child-bearing years required special compensation to make that possible.

A third personnel situation ended less amicably. Former MCC U.S. Women's Concerns director Emily Will remembers discussion during the mid-1980s about the possibility of including an onsite daycare center in the architectural plans for a new MCC building. At the meeting, single women staffers and non-staff, stay-at-home wives of MCC male administrators united to oppose the proposal for onsite day care as an unfair and unnecessary concession to working women.[32] Fortunately, Diamond Street Early Childhood Center, located a few blocks away at nearby Akron Mennonite Church, was at that time expanding from a part-time day care to a full-time community resource for working mothers, which filled the need for MCC staff. While not onsite daycare, it was a crucial nearby resource for working mothers like myself, who benefited enormously from its close proximity to MCC headquarters.

Other initiatives designed to address or compensate for female marginalization relate to women, gender, and development from an international perspective. The first MCCer to address these concerns was Luann Habegger Martin, part-time service worker to the MCC Peace Section Task Force on Women in Church and Society, formed in

1973. (Incidentally, one could also observe the creation of this Task Force on Women as a step, in its own right, toward compensating for women's absence. The Committee for Women's Concerns, as the task force came to be called, at one time had paid national staff in the U.S. and in Canada. Today the U.S. Women's Desk is called Women's Advocacy desk of MCC U.S.)

In 1976, Habegger Martin published an MCC "Women & Development" monograph #3.[33] In it she argued that systematic inattention to women's involvement in development by national planners actually increased women's work. To improve the situation, development agencies should consider women-oriented projects in intermediate technology, formal and non-formal education, handicrafts, childcare, credit, family planning, and cooperatives. In 1979, MCC's overseas program implemented an internal field process to follow up on these issues, pushed to do so by the Committee on Women's Concerns and by colleague agencies in the field. But as Nancy Heisey noted already by 1984, this evaluation process had been discontinued.

It would be ten years before MCC returned to this issue in earnest, and twenty years after the publication of Habegger Martin's piece, until MCC published on women and development again. Ironically, according to staff I have interviewed, the impetus for paying attention to gender and development came from CIDA, the Canadian International Development Agency, a key MCC donor which required attention to gender and development for MCC to access its funds, a requirement some staff resented. Kathy Shantz didn't

> think real change happened until CIDA did a review of MCC Canada. In that review, MCC Canada was sharply criticized for the lack of women in leadership roles. This would not be the first or last time that government policy dictated the agenda for MCC Canada, but it was certainly one of the more ironic examples.[34]

In 1994, the MCC Peace Office drafted an overseas department statement on gender and began a project to explore the importance of gender issues in MCC's international development work. MCC staff visited El Salvador, Zambia, and India in the course of the study. Debra Simpson reported in-country findings from the study project in the MCC Occasional Paper published in 1998 entitled *The Call To a New World Yet To Be: MCC Gender and Development Project*.[35]

The focus on gender illustrated a movement within the wider nongovernmental and development community away from Women and Development (WAD) approaches that emphasized economic empowerment of women toward Gender and Development (GAD) approaches that emphasized gender relations and socio-cultural power. At the same time, MCC Peace Office published *Questions to Ask: A Gender Guide*, a booklet designed for MCC country programs and workers to think about their assignments, to guide program planning, and to "provide a focus for discussion and reflection within MCC and in our relationships with local partners and advisors."[36]

Reflecting on her work on the gender project, Gwen Groff observed that "we developed a tool to do gender analysis with MCC's partners overseas. In interviews in overseas program settings, we heard clear suggestions that if MCC was subjecting our partners to a gender analysis, we should also turn the spotlight on ourselves."[37] Thus in 2000, the MCC Binational Board adopted a gender statement, included in *A Gender Guide* as an appendix. The statement committed MCC to "take gender into account as it develops international program and relationships," encouraged workers to "become aware of the different roles of men and women" while they "seek to be respectful of differences in cultural assumptions," in turn "finding culturally appropriate ways to explore gender roles and realities." The statement sought to "ensure that workers and country programs understand a gender perspective and can apply this understanding to an analysis of their context and activity." It concluded by noting that MCC commits itself to "valuing all persons, women and men, as created in God's image."[38]

Note that the terminology calls essentially for consciousness-raising without commitment, understanding without accountability for action, and all is subject to the constraints of cultural sensitivity. The questions in *A Gender Guide*, if used, are thought-provoking and comprehensive. I know, because during my tenure at MCC, from 1999 to 2004, I led orientation sessions for new MCC international service workers in which we attempted to flesh out the gender guidelines. The problem, according to an evaluation done by Bruce Guenther in 2008, is that the guidelines were seldom used in-country and, as noted above, had little authority.

In fact, the nature of the question format itself may have served to undercut their influence. In a decisive chart comparing MCC and CIDA statements, Guenther noted that while both MCC and CIDA emphasized women's equal participation in decision-making and the distribution of resources, CIDA pointed to gender equality and women's rights as the goal, while MCC simply called for an "awareness" of gender roles and a hope for their "transformation."[39]

In other 2008 critiques, Guenther noted "little enforcement" of existing MCC gender policies by area directors and international pro-

grams, "the absence of mechanisms to evaluate how MCC's programs are specifically tackling structural causes of gender discrimination throughout the program planning process," a general lack of
implementation, and the absence of a commitment to advancing gender equity as a criteria for MCC partnerships, as specified in *A Gender
Guide*. His research, he stated, "raises significant questions about
overall compliance with MCC's own gender policies." Thus, while
attempting to address and compensate for women's marginalization,
MCC practice undercut the very values MCC was purportedly trying
to advance.

The final step in my interpretive framework calls us to examine
women's access or lack thereof to power and decision-making. Historian Joan Wallach Scott has written that important components of
gender analysis are contest, conflict, and power: how power is exer-
cised and by whom. Scott calls for employing a broader notion of politics that incorporates these elements and considers "all unequal relationships as somehow 'political' because involving unequal distribu-
tions of power."[40]

A primary way in which gender at MCC has been politicized and
in which the organization has spoken truth to power in relation to
gender has been through the MCC Women's Concerns work in the
U.S. and Canada on abuse response and prevention.[41] Already in
1978 and 1979, two issues of the newsletter, *Women's Concerns Report*,
were published on the theme of family violence.[42] The topic lan-
guished for six years until a task force on family violence was established and jointly funded from 1985 to 1991 by MCC Canada Victim
Offender Ministries and the U.S. Office of Criminal Justice. The Committee for Women's Concerns (CWC) published the "The Purple
Packet" on domestic violence in 1987 and "Broken Boundaries," the
packet on child sexual abuse, in 1989. Both were well-received, if controversial: 9,500 copies of the first and 7,000 copies of the second were
requested, according to CWC records.[43]

Peggy Unruh Regehr, Women's Concern staff in Canada during
this period describes her work with MCC as that of breaking through
silence and skepticism:

> There were always those who either did not want to believe this
> abuse was happening in our circles or just wanted it to go away.
> But I worked hard, and spoke about it in my presentations
> wherever I went in the constituency. Very slowly some of the
> skepticism vanished. And every time I spoke about it, women
> let me know about their own experience or that of their daugh-
> ter or mothers. It was heartbreaking to hear their stories.[44]

Throughout the 1990s, staff at the women's desk continued to develop and disseminate educational resources on abuse and prevention, advocated on behalf of sexual abuse victims (in one egregious case, forty women had been molested by a single ordained perpetrator), and worked with church conferences and denominational offices to develop guidelines for handling pastoral sexual misconduct that are in use today. A five-year evaluation in September 1995 to the MCC U.S. board mandated a continuation of this focus on abuse. Furthermore, the evaluation recognized that on this issue MCC should continue its role as "catalyst and resource" and recommended that "MCC and the church need to reaffirm this focus as integral to our peace witness."[45]

In a 2002 evaluation of the U.S. Women's Concerns Desk, ninety-three percent of respondents indicated "unequivocal affirmation" that its work as a voice to the wider church was essential, and "nearly all the respondents" perceived the need to "continue being a prophetic voice to the church at large."[46] Gender had become political and was affirmed as such.

In 2003, MCC Canada took the lead in developing a web site on these issues at http://abuse.mcc.org/. Resources are now available in German, French, and Spanish. Space does not permit a full discussion of this chapter of MCC gender history. Suffice it to say that significant change was effected because, to paraphrase Laurel Thatcher Ulrich, women reformers at MCC remained neither silent nor well-behaved. It is also worth noting, however, that while the first abuse conference organized with MCC sponsorship, "Shedding Light in the Darkness," was held in Upland, California, in January 1990, with conferences to follow in every MCC region, outreach to the Hispanic Mennonite community lagged behind. The first MCC-sponsored abuse conference for this constituency took place in May 2001, under the banner *"Trabajando Juntos Como una Iglesia Comprometida con la Paz y la Prevención de la Violencia Familiar"* (Working Together as a Church Committed to Peace and the Prevention of Family Violence).

Sexual harassment, still a live issue today, is another issue of gender and power that MCC staff have sought to address, first outside the organization and later, prompted by CIDA, from within.[47] In 1991 MCC Women's Concerns produced the packet *Crossing the Boundary: Sexual Abuse by Professionals*. Two years later, MCC adopted an internal policy against sexual abuse/harassment under the title, "Procedures to Prevent, Report and Resolve Harassment," Policy #133.

Ten years passed until sexual harassment became a point of discussion at MCC orientation sessions. Jennifer deGroot served MCC as a nine-month gender analysis consultant, funded by CIDA, through September 2000, visiting MCC international programs on three continents. Surprised that this major aspect of women's experiences overseas was not dealt with in MCC orientations, deGroot developed a sexual harassment training based her experiences. Recognizing that Western women can be particular targets of harassment in the field, deGroot's packet of training materials, role plays, and range of responses became part of MCC orientation sessions in 2001 and continue to this day.[48]

We need to examine women's access or lack thereof to power and decision-making authority within MCC leadership itself. As Gwen Groff, a former Women's Concerns director, has noted,

> working toward gender equality is hardest when working on equality issues within MCC. . . . Analysis makes the people being analyzed uncomfortable. They sense their good intentions are mistrusted. . . . Through the years, when Women's Concerns turned its attention outward on society, even on our constituent congregations, we had institutional support. But when the lens turned inward, when the Women's Concerns desk focused on the status of women within MCC as an institution, the struggle became more bitter.[49]

In MCC's first several decades, not surprisingly, few women served on MCC boards. Betty Epp of Henderson, Nebraska, listed in the board minutes as Mrs. Aaron Epp, became the first woman to serve on MCC's board.[50] In 1974, Dorothy Yoder Nyce, through her role on the women's task force of the MCC Peace Section, advocated for women's leadership through board presentations and a task force study paper on MCC employment policies and practices toward women.[51] The MCC Executive Committee authorized the formation of an advisory group and invited Nyce to address the January 1975 MCC Annual Meeting on these issues.[52]

To address the charge that there were no qualified women to serve on MCC boards, the Committee for Women's Concern published a *Resource Listing of Mennonite Women* in 1978, 1980, 1982, 1985, and 1988.[53] Women eventually began to assume some leadership positions on MCC boards. So, for example, the chairperson of the MCC U.S. board in the mid-1980s was Anna Juhnke of Newton, Kansas.[54] The MCC Binational Board, however, was not chaired by a woman until Karen Klassen Harder in 1999.[55] Laura Schmidt Roberts currently serves as MCC Binational vice chair, and MCC Binational has had a female executive director since 2008.

While women at MCC's Akron, Pennsylvania, offices have always predominated numerically, they have been concentrated in administrative support positions. As Linda Gehman Peachey's research
demonstrates (see text box below), women have moved from six to 30
percent of upper-level leadership roles and from 20 to 57 percent of
middle-level leadership roles at MCC since 1975, but most of that
percentage gain took place in the first decade. There has been little
statistical change in the last 25 years. This phenomenon is often characterized as "the higher, the fewer," that is, the higher up you go in an
organization, the fewer women you are likely to see in leadership.[56]

Linda Schmidt, who staffed the Women's Concerns desk in the
early 1980s, remembers being criticized for describing MCC as a
"benevolent patriarchy," because, at the time, men held *all* the top-
level administrative positions.[57] Since, according to U.S. Labor statistics, women have achieved near parity with men in the workforce
overall (women's share of U.S. employment reached a record high of
49.96 percent in October 2009, due in part to the recession and the dis-
proportionate number of male layoffs) we might expect them to hold
half of all positions of power.[58] But the MCC "glass ceiling" for
women mirrors national trends as well as Mennonite Church USA directions.[59]

**Statistical Overview and Analysis of Women
in MCC's Offices in Akron, Pennsylvania**
By Linda Gehman Peachey

MCC in Akron	Upper level Management		Mid-level Positions		Administrative Support	
	Men	Women	Men	Women	Men	Women
1975	94%	6%	80%	20%	13%	87%
1985	76%	24%	50%	50%	12%	88%
2001	77%	23%	46%	54%	28%	72%
2009	70%	30%	43%	57%	14%	86%

These are not exact figures, since it is difficult to know how positions were counted over the years. Also, since past figures primarily

reflected employment at the MCC offices in Akron, Pennsylvania (housing MCC Binational and MCC U.S.), these figures again formed the basis of the 2009 count. Unfortunately, the same kind of data was not available for MCC Canada. Further, this chart does not separate out the positions held by women and men of color in MCC. They would have had different experiences and faced different challenges than white women and men.

With these caveats, one can make several observations:

- There have been significant changes in gender roles since 1975, with women moving from 6% to 30% of leadership roles. In MCC U.S., this is even more pronounced. Of the eight top-level management positions in MCC US, five were held by men (62.5%) and three by women (37.5%). In MCC Binational, 11 of the 15 top-level positions (73%) were held by men and four by women (27%).
- The largest changes in leadership and mid-level positions happened between 1975 and 1985, with much less change happening over the past 25 years.
- There has been little change in the administrative support column. The figures from 2001 are different because they included some maintenance and housekeeping personnel whereas these were omitted in the other years. For 2009, if all administrative support, maintenance, printing, and housekeeping positions are included, the results would be 35% for men and 65% women, figures that are more in line with 2001. But this also reveals that women still predominate in administrative support positions.
- The most equitable distribution of positions between men and women is at the mid-level range. This grouping includes positions such as writers, graphic artists, peace and justice program coordinators, and personnel placement coordinators.

Historically, one painful period for many women employees at MCC involved the organizational adoption of the Hays classification system for jobs, an organizational model widely used in the corporate arena, which went into effect January 1, 1988. The system ranked jobs by pay and responsibilities. Women's Concerns staff at the time remember the system being adopted despite determined opposition from staff at many levels who saw it as biased toward gendered responsibilities more typically held by men in the organization. Emily Will noted: "MCC adopted the Hays classification system to organize its hierarchy. . . . I witnessed 'natural' abuses of power that come with a hierarchy, especially one dominated by white men with well-developed egos, high educational levels, and high visibility within a relatively small ethnic community."[60] Peggy Unruh Regehr remembers,

> I heard from female support staff within the office about their positions within MCC. They were often on Voluntary Service, and even when they had worked for a significant period, it was difficult for them to get on salary. When they did, their pay was low. As a result, when the Hays Commission salary grid was present to MCC for discussion, these women strongly opposed it, as it was a particularly male dominant structure with the supposed male dominant characteristics given higher value and higher salaries.[61]

During my own tenure at the Women's Concerns desk fifteen years later, I heard about "classification battles" from several women in the organization whose rank and pay were not increased, even when their job responsibilities were. In one particularly egregious case, a female employee's job was reclassified two levels higher only after she announced her resignation and MCC was recruiting for her (male) replacement.[62] MCC discontinued the Hays system in 2008, after contracting with compensation analysts to conduct surveys of like agencies and design a new classification system based on market trends and best practices.

Various MCC administrators have worked at encouraging MCC women's gifts. In 1995, Lynette Meck, then MCC U.S. Executive Director, led a discussion among MCC Executive Council members—staff directors in upper-level administrative positions—about why more men than women held leadership positions at MCC. In a memo sent to the MCC Executive Director she listed nineteen barriers to women's leadership, identified by the Executive Council, barriers later reprinted in a 2002 issue of *Women's Concerns Report*.[63] In the memo Meck noted the importance of Executive Council administrators being aware of the aspirations of "high-performing, high-potential women in low-to-mid-level positions in the organization" for mentoring and training to move up in MCC. She writes,

> We need to be aware of women's professional goals. We need to actively consider with them where their skills could be put to use in other MCC positions. There are many smart, capable and committed women in MCC. They may be doing exactly what they want to be doing. Or they may be doing what they are because their choices are limited. We won't know without asking.[64]

The memo was never formally acted on.

Seven years later, the May-June 2002 issue of *Women's Concerns Report* identified seven barriers to women's leadership, many of which remain salient today. These included traditional understandings of gender roles, work-family balance, and the ways in which work is structured according to white masculine norms that can marginalize women and people of color. Traditional ideas about gender, and gender role stereotypes, have limited women's advancement and blocked their initial hiring, at MCC and in larger U.S. society.[65] Sociologists like Barbara Reskin, who study women in the workplace, discuss the tendency in hiring of "like hires like," that is, most factors being equal, we will promote or hire the person who is most similar to us.[66] Given that the majority of MCC leaders have been white men (a 2002 graph of MCC leadership positions held since 1971 by race and gender shows that two women of color, three men of color, 15 white women and 56 white men have filled these top positions) the danger of perpetuating sameness is great.[67]

Stereotypes and cultural expectations not only affect hiring but can also influence staff evaluations affecting promotions. In a 1998 MCC study entitled, "Doing Our Best: An Informal Analysis of the Cultural Context of Mennonite Central Committee," Eloise Hiebert Meneses cited an MCC Germanic Mennonite "low-key emotional style" with a strong taboo on the overt expression of anger that is confusing and unwelcoming to "Newcomers."[68] In like manner, Iris de Leon-Hartshorn, Latina former director of MCC U.S. Peace and Justice Ministries, noted:

> Regarding communication styles, one of the things that I've gotten criticized for is expressing myself with full body language. . . . [It] is an issue that has been raised with me, and with other women of color. I get emotional, but I can't change that. It is part of who I am, part of my culture, and how I see life. This can become a threat to people that operate more passive aggressively and don't want to tell you what is going on.[69]

This style difference on the part of a woman of color with workplace cultural norms can be perceived as a disadvantage because of its contrast with white Germanic (masculine) norms.

Women may end up feeling pressured to overwork to prove ourselves within MCC's dominant (white, masculine) culture. In fact, overwork has been noted as a characteristic of MCC workplace culture. MCC Human Resources staff in the U.S. and Canada prepared a 2005 Culture Report, based on fifty-one interviews with current and former staff, which noted, "The work ethic at MCC is work hard, hard, hard; not only because people believe in what they are doing, but because other people might be watching. . . . Working overtime is expected, and many people work too long and too much, due to job descriptions that are too big."[70]

This can create a time bind for working women, who usually shoulder greater responsibilities than men for domestic work and childcare at home—what Arlie Russell Hothschild has called a "second shift."[71] Charmayne Denlinger Brubaker, MCC Human Resources director from 2000 to 2005, noted that few women applied for leadership positions at MCC during her tenure, even when directly encouraged to do so, and that nearly all cited family reasons for not wanting to apply.[72] Linda Shelly, former director of Latin America and Caribbean programs at MCC, said people always told her that it was good she didn't have children because of how much she needed to travel, yet no one made that observation about her male colleagues, who traveled just as much, all of whom were married with children.[73]

This may create special stress for women of color. As de Leon-Hartshorn has noted:

> Another issue for me as a woman of color in a leadership position is the sense that I always have to prove myself. That contributes to overwork. Not only do I have to do my job, but I have to work above and beyond my job. I think that women leaders in general, not just women of color, feel this pressure. But I think sometimes women of color feel more pressure."[74]

The clash between personal culture and workplace culture can affect staff retention. In 2009, Rick Derksen of the MCC Binational and MCC U.S. Anti-Racism desks analyzed statistics regarding early terminations in MCC U.S., examining 247 tenures since January 1, 1999. He found that within the organization, white men averaged 49.1 months in their jobs, men of color averaged 42.5 months, white women averaged 39 months; and women of color averaged 36.2 months. The interplay of both gender and race contributed to almost a full year shorter term of service.[75] As the authors of a 1999 Organizational Report Card pointed out in a section on retention, "Generally, organizations retain those members who conform to the organizational culture and reject those who don't."[76]

To keep good people, Conrado Grimolizzi-Jensen, management consultant and Binational board member from MCC Great Lakes, argues that ideals are not enough; workplace culture has to change. In fact, we have seen through our discussion of gender and international programs that having statements in place does not necessarily mean that they will be followed without measurable steps toward implementation and accountability. The question for MCC may be how to de-center a white masculine office culture as the norm, how to "live our way into a new way of thinking," rather than the reverse.[77]

By way of conclusion, and as a means of moving us toward new ways of living and thinking, I would like to offer a model for change borrowed from feminist studies. Latina theorist Maria Lugones first proposed the concept of "world-traveling" to describe the dislocation/creativity felt by women who by virtue of race, class, or orientation simultaneously inhabit more than one "world," or social reality, and are called to travel back and forth between those "worlds" on a fairly regular basis. Shifting from being in one world to another is "travel." Most people outside the North American mainstream are world-travelers as a means of survival, argues Lugones, and world-travelers have the experience of being different people in different worlds. Rather than seeing this as a detriment, Lugones offers it as a skillful, creative, enriching, and loving way of being and living.[78]

Writing from a law background, Isabel Gunning sought to extend Lugones' model in her efforts to understand and find a way to speak to a foreign culture practice (female circumcision) without the cultural imperialism that so often accompanies Northern Hemisphere spokeswomen addressing Southern Hemisphere issues. Gunning proposed a three-step model for multicultural dialogues: Seeing oneself in one's own historical perspective, seeing oneself as the other might see you, and seeing the other in her own cultural context. She argues that by "traveling" to someone else's world we can understand what it is to be them and to be ourselves in their eyes.[79] Thus we do not relinquish our right to offer critique, but we do so after looking at our own culture first.

It seems to me that many women in MCC history, especially but not only women of color, have had this experience of world-traveling. In fact, many MCCers who return from overseas service can identify with the dislocation of reentering U.S. culture. Some of us leave MCC, others of us remain and make from these experiences sites of creativity and enrichment. This model offers us a frame for examining our own culture while retaining the ability to speak in international settings and to various worlds in U.S. society, having first done the work of critical self-analysis.

In conclusion, renowned women's historian, Gerda Lerner, has written that the greatest challenge in writing history is that the outcome is known; there is no element of drama or surprise. But the great drama that is the MCC story is both historical and ongoing. Our history of ninety years is unfinished; much remains to be written, as we consider the interplay between gender and men's and women's contributions—paid and unpaid, recognized and unrecognized—in the overall MCC story. As Lerner has written, "The past becomes part of our present and thereby, part of our future. . . . Being human means reflecting on the past and visioning the future."[80] As "world-travelers," at home or abroad, may we bring these past reflections into new visions for MCC and its contributions to the wider Mennonite and non-Mennonite worlds.

NOTES

1. This iconic quotation first appeared in Laurel Thatcher Ulrich, "Virtuous Women Found: New England Ministerial Literature, 1668-1735," *American Quarterly* 28 (1976): 20. It later served as the title of a 2007 book by Ulrich (New York: Alfred A. Knopf, 2007) in which she examined various means of female "misbehavior" historically.

2. Catherine Brekus has pointed out that the language of gender may be an evasion: "studying 'gender' sounds more 'objective' and 'neutral' than studying 'women.'" See Brekus, ed., *The Religious History of American Women: Reimagining the Past* (Chapel Hill, N.C.: University of North Carolina Press, 2007), 11. I use the term *gender* not for this reason, but rather for its greater analytical potential.

3. Joan Wallach Scott, *Gender and the Politics of History* (New York: Columbia University Press, 1999, rev. ed.), 42.

4. See, for example, *Women's Concerns Report* No. 164 (Nov-Dec 2002), "An Anabaptist Theology Opposing Violence against Women." See also Linda Gehman Peachey, "Bearing the Cross: What did Jesus Mean by Urging Us to Take up Our Cross?" *The Mennonite* (April 4, 2006).

5. Scott, *Gender and the Politics of History*, 44.

6. Mary T. Malone, *Women and Christianity: From 1000 to the Reformation* (Maryknoll, N.Y.: Orbis Books, 2002).

7. Nancy R. Heisey, "Race, Ethnicity and Gender in MCC Work," prepared for the conference "Unity amidst Diversity," March 9-12, 1995, Fresno, California.

8. Rachel Waltner Goossen, *Women against the Good War: Conscientious Objection and Gender on the Home Front, 1941-1947* (Chapel Hill, N.C.: University of North Carolina Press, 1997).

9. Rachel Waltner Goossen, *Conscientious Objection and Gender: Women in Civilian Public Service during the Second World War* (Ph.D. diss., University of Kansas, 1993), 3.

10. Ibid., 536. See also Albert Keim, *The CPS Story* (Intercourse, Pa.: Good Books, 1990).

11. Mabel Groh, *Gospel Herald,* December 16, 1926: "It is after all the hand that rocks the cradle, that rules the world. Women's greatest power is in line

with the [home] sphere in which God intended her to serve. . . . Motherhood will continue to be woman's sphere to the end of time" since "[t]he truly Christian home is the nearest representation of heaven that earth contains."

12. Kimberly Schmidt, "Transforming Tradition: The Effect of Religion and Economics on Women's Work in Two Rural Mennonite Communities, 1930-1990" (Ph.D. diss., SUNY Binghamton, 1994).

13. A. Grace Wenger, Interview by author, 15 April 1994, Lititz, Pa. Tape recording in author's possession.

14. "Field Notes," *Gospel Herald* 38, September 21, 1945.

15. Olive Wyse, "Home Economics in the Mennonite School," in *The Proceedings of the Conference on Mennonite Cultural Problems, 1944* (Goshen, Ind.: Goshen College, 1947), 11.

16. Melvin Gingerich, "The Mennonite Family Census of 1963" [photocopy], 5. Vertical file, Lancaster Mennonite Historical Library, Lancaster, PA.

17. Ruth K. Lehman, "The One Thing Lacking . . . or the Status of Women Faculty at Eastern Mennonite College, 1917 to 1980" (M.A. thesis, James Madison University, 1981).

18. Donald Reiman Jacobs, "A Study of the Religious Life of the Mennonites in Lancaster Conference, Pa., 1890-1952" (Master's thesis, University of Maryland, 1954). See also Donald B. Kraybill, *Passing on the Faith: The Story of a Mennonite School* (Intercourse, Pa.: Good Books, 1991), 13.

19. Beulah Stauffer Hostetler, *American Mennonites and Protestant Movements* (Scottdale, Pa.: Herald Press, 1987), 264.

20. Nancy R. Heisey, "Race, Ethnicity and Gender in MCC Work."

21. Catherine Wessinger, ed, "Introduction," *Women's Leadership in Marginal Religions: Explorations Outside the Mainstream* (Urbana and Chicago: University of Illinois Press, 1993), 8.

22. Lucille Marr, "Ontario's Conference of Historic Peace Church Families and the 'Joy of Service,'" *The Mennonite Quarterly Review* 75/2 (April 2001), 18. See also Lucille Marr, *The Transforming Power of a Century: Mennonite Central Committee and Its Evolution in Ontario* (Kitchener, Ont.: Pandora Press, 2003).

23. Brekus, 18.

24. Lucille Marr, "The Time for the Distaff and Spindle: The Ontario Women's Sewing Circles and the Mennonite Central Committee," *Journal of Mennonite Studies* 17 (1999): 130-151.

25. Gloria Neufeld Redekop, *The Work Of Their Hands: Mennonite Women's Societies In Canada* (Waterloo, ON: Wilfrid Laurier University Press, 1996).

26. "A Less-Than-Central Irritant: The Report of the Gender Audit Project," prepared by Agnes Hubert, October 1997, 60.

27. Robert A. Orsi, *Between Heaven and Earth: The Religious World People Make and the Scholars Who Study Them,* (Princeton, N.J.: Princeton University Press, 2005) and David D. Hall, *Lived Religion in America: Toward a History of Practice* (Princeton, N.J.: Princeton University Press, 1997).

28. Steven M. Nolt, "Globalizing a Separate People: World Christianity and American Mennonites," Snowden Lecture, Young Center, Elizabethtown College, November 12, 2009.

29. Ibid.

30. Gerda Lerner, *The Majority Finds Its Past: Placing Women in History*

(Chapel Hill, N.C.: University of North Carolina Press, 1979).

31. Of course, prior to 1971, women were filed under their husband's first and last names, for example, as Mr. and Mrs. Peter Dyck.

32. Emily Will, "Witnessing 'Natural' Abuses of Power," *MCC Women's Concerns Report* No. 165 (Jan-Feb 2003): 10. The Institute for Women's Policy Research has consistently advocated for flex-time and on-site daycare as key for working women. See www.iwpr.org.

33. Luann Habegger Martin, "The 30th. Anniversary of the MCC Women's Concerns Committee," *Conrad Grebel Review* 23/1 (Winter 2005): 51-54.

34. Kathy Shantz, "Was it Me or Our Mandate?" *Women's Concerns Report* No. 165 (Jan-Feb 2003): 12.

35. Debra Simpson, "The Call to a New World Yet to Be: MCC Gender and Development Project," MCC Occasional Paper, No. 25, 1998.

36. "Questions to Ask: A Gender Guide," MCC Peace Office, Gender and Development Project, September 1998, 2.

37. Gwen Groff, "Compiler's Comments," *Women's Concerns Report* No. 165 (Jan-Feb 2003): 1.

38. "A Gender Guide," Appendix A, February 18, 2000, 10-11.

39. Bruce Guenther, "Analysis of MCC's Gender and Environmental Policies and Procedures for International Programs," September 25, 2006.

40. Scott, 27.

41. For example, see *Women's Concerns Report*, "Abuse Prevention and Recovery: History of MCC's Work" No. 166 (March-April 2003). One could also cite the MCC Washington Office, established in 1968 to monitor U.S. public policy and advocate for reform, and later the MCC United Nations Liaison Office, designed to "represent the voice of the powerless to the diplomats and civil servants," as examples of speaking truth to the powerful. Analyzing these offices in relation to gender—i.e. how our churches' peace position is gendered female, and what that means for the work of these offices—is outside the scope of this paper.

42. "Milestones, Materials, Meetings: Overview of MCC's Work Related to Women, Gender and Abuse," compiled by Linda Gehman Peachey, March 2010. See also "Looking Back: Women's Concerns Directors Reflect," *Women's Concerns Report* No. 165 (Jan-Feb 2003): 7.

43. Ibid.

44. Peggy Unruh Regehr, "Canadian Women's Concerns," *Conrad Grebel Review* 23/1 (Winter 2005): 80.

45. Ann Graber Hershberger, "Evaluation: MCC U.S. Women's Concerns Focus on Domestic Violence and Sexual Abuse," September 1995.

46. Dorothy Gish, "Women's Concerns Desk MCC U.S. Evaluation," 2002.

47. A 2007 survey of Women and Men in Mennonite Ministry by Pam Nath found that three times as many women as men (17.6%) had experienced sexual harassment, either from congregational members or from pastoral colleagues outside the congregation. This is down from 24% in the 1992 survey.

48. Jennifer deGroot, e-mail correspondence with author, April 23, 2010.

49. Groff, 1.

50. Heisey, 10.

51. Dorothy Yoder Nyce, "And So It Began: On Birthing an Organization," *Conrad Grebel Review* 23/1 (Winter 2005): 55-78.

260 A Table of Sharing

52. Ibid.

53. Ibid.

54. Global Anabaptist Mennonite Encyclopedia Online, "Mennonite Central Committee," *Global Anabaptist Mennonite Encyclopedia Online.* Web. Retrieved 29 April 2010. www.gameo.org.

55. Ibid.

56. "The rule—and it applies to outside higher education as well—the rule where women are concerned is simply this: The higher, the fewer. The higher in terms of level of education, the higher in terms of faculty rank, the higher in terms of recognized responsibility, the higher in terms of salary, prestige and status, the fewer are the women. . . ." Dr. Ann Sutherland Harris, quoted in "History Matters: The U.S. Survey Course on the Web, 'The Higher, the Fewer': Discrimination Against Women in Academia." Created by the American Social History Project/Center for Media and Learning (Graduate Center, CUNY) and the Center for History and New Media (George Mason University). http://historymatters.gmu.edu/d/6462.

57. Linda Schmidt, "Thinking Back," *Women's Concerns Report* No. 165 (January-February 2003): 6.

58. Briefing Paper, #C374, April 2010, "Are Women Now Half the Labor Force? The Truth about Women and Equal Participation in the Labor Force," by Ashley English, Heidi Hartmann, and Jeff Hayes, Institute for Women's Policy Research, 1.

59. Currently the Governance Council of Mennonite Church USA, made up of the executive director, director of churchwide operations, agency directors, agency board chairpersons, the moderator, and moderator elects has 10 men and one woman. See Joanna Shenk, "Survey: More Women in Leadership But Still Not Enough," *The Mennonite* (March 2010): 46-48. According to U.S. Bureau of Labor Statistics, the percentage of "managerial, professional, and related positions in the U.S. Labor Force held by women" in 2009 was 51.4 percent; thus in middle management, MCC is comparable nationally. But women in upper management positions lag far behind. According to data compiled by Catalyst, board seats held by women in Fortune 500 companies were 15.2 percent. Bureau of Labor Statistics, "Employed Persons by Detailed Occupation, Sex, Race, and Hispanic or Latino Ethnicity" (various years). Data reproduced by the nonprofit research organization, Catalyst. See www.catalyst.org/publication/207/women-in-management-in-the-united-states-1950-present and www.catalyst.org/publication/207/women-in-management-in-the-united-states-1950-present. Founded in 1962, Catalyst is the leading nonprofit membership and research organization working to expand opportunities for women in business.

60. Will, 9.

61. Regehr, *Conrad Grebel Review,* 81.

62. Confidential Interview, 8-25-2000, transcription in hands of author.

63. Memo from Lynette Meck to John A. Lapp, October 6, 1995, copy in author's possession.

64. Ibid.

65. Concerns about gender and women in leadership can be obscured by the language of choice. In fact, Mennonite Church USA conducted a Women in Leadership Audit in 2009 designed to explore why women said no to

church leadership. See Joanne Shenk, 46-48. Joan Williams notes that choice rhetoric veils the powerful pressures of domesticity in the language of self-fulfillment and obscures the reality of how jobs are structured in ways that may exclude mother's workforce participation: inaccessible or unaffordable day care options, lack of flex time, mandatory overtime, excessive travel, the lack of an at-home spouse to handle domestic responsibilities, etc. See *Unbending Gender: Why Family and Work Conflict and What to do About It* (Oxford: Oxford University Press, 2000). Writer Ann Crittenden goes so far as to say that women without children have achieved near-parity with men in the workforce. It is now motherhood, not gender, which determines inequality. Crittenden calls this the "mommy tax." See *The Price of Motherhood: Why the Most Important Job in the World is Still the Least Valued* (New York: Holt Paperbacks, 2002).

66. In their book, *Women and Men at Work*, 2nd. ed. (Thousand Oaks, Calif.: Sage, 2002), Irene Padavic and Barbara Reskin discuss the influence, often unacknowledged, of gender stereotypes in the workplace. They write, "Employers often have a particular sex in mind when they create new jobs, set pay levels, and organize how work is to be done and under what conditions" (11). At MCC, consider who we think of as appropriate to fill such positions as meat canner, material resources manager, dining hall supervisor, or mid-level manager, and at what level we would expect to compensate them. According to Joan Williams, people tend to remember stereotype-confirming behavior better than counter-stereotypical behavior and to assume that stereotype-confirming behavior will be repeated (*Unbending Gender*, 250).

67. *Women's Concerns Report* No. 161 "Barriers to Women in Leadership" (May-June 2002): 8.

68. Eloise Hiebert Meneses, "Doing Our Best: An Informal Analysis of the Cultural Context of Mennonite Central Committee," 1988, cited in "A Chronology of Studies/Conclusions on MCC's Organizational Culture," compiled by Rick Derksen, April 27, 2007.

69. Iris de Leon-Hartshorn, "Barriers to Women of Color," *Women's Concerns Report* No. 161 (May-June 2002): 8.

70. "Mennonite Central Committee Human Resources, Joint HR Committee Culture Report," March 2005, by Maricela Bejar, Prem Dick, Carol Eby-Good, Kiersten Hoffman, Anna Reimer, Janelle Siemens, Sophie Tiessen-Eigbike, and Mary Ann Weber.

71. Arlie Russell Hochschild, *The Second Shift: Working Parents and the Revolution at Home* (New York: Viking Publishers, 1989).

72. *Women's Concern Report* (May/June 2002): 4.

73. Ibid., 4.

74. de Leon-Hartshorn, 9.

75. MCC U.S. Early Termination Analysis, May 6, 2009.

76. "1999 Organizational Report Card," by J. Nathan Corbitt, Jacob Christiansen, Dolores Lee McCabe, and Vivian Nix-Early, reported in "A Chronology of Studies/Conclusions on MCC's Organizational Culture," compiled by Rick Derksen, April 27, 2007.

77. The Rev. Joy Carroll Wallis, first women to be ordained into the priesthood of the Church of England writes, "we often believe we can think our way into a new way of living, but that's actually not the way it works. In real-

ity, it's more likely that we will live our way into a new way of thinking" (www.goshen.edu/news/pressarchive/04-30-07-commence-folo.html).

78. Maria Lugones, "Playfulness, World-Traveling and Loving Perception," *Hypatia* 2/2 (Summer 1987).

79. Isabelle R. Gunning, "Arrogant Perception, World-Traveling, and Multicultural Feminism: The Case of Female Genital Surgeries," *Columbia Human Rights Law Review* 23/2 (Summer 1992): 18-48.

80. Gerda Lerner, *Why History Matters: Life and Thought*, (Oxford University Press, 1997), 240.

Part IV
Birthing New Programs: MCC as Incubator of Pioneering Projects

Chapter 11

Business with a Mission: The Ongoing Role of Ten Thousand Villages within the Fair Trade Movement

JENNIFER A. KEAHEY, MARY A. LITTRELL,
AND DOUGLAS L. MURRAY

The fair trade movement has become increasingly influential in the global marketplace. With a growing population of conscious consumers demanding ethically produced items, fair trade has grown from relative obscurity into a powerful market-based mechanism for social change that includes an ever-widening range of commodities. As of 2007, fair trade recorded $2.65 billion in yearly sales across thirty-three countries, directly benefiting millions of producers throughout the Global South. Fair trade provides producers with a number of enhanced benefits, including but not limited to (1) payment of a fair price, (2) enhanced economic opportunities, (3) long-term trading relationships, (4) transparent and accountable trade processes, (5) safe and healthy working conditions, and (6) access to capacity building and community development initiatives.[1]

While the broader fair trade movement remains united in its focus on social justice, fair trade food and handicrafts have developed into two distinct market sectors with separate governance structures. Due to rapid growth and differing strategies, the movement faces a number of tensions and challenges. Although the divergent approaches of these two sectors are a source of tension, their stories also demonstrate the capacity of the movement to meet market challenges flexibly while maintaining emphasis on core ethical values.[2]

This chapter uses the case of Ten Thousand Villages (henceforth Villages) to examine current fair trade tensions, challenges, and opportunities. Growing out of the efforts of Mennonite fair traders, Villages became a pioneer in fair trade handicrafts. We highlight the challenges this organization has faced as it developed successful business practices while remaining true to ethical values. We note how their struggle mirrors broader movement tensions stemming from the necessity of operating within the marketplace as a means of transforming global commerce.

We begin with an overview of the fair trade food and handicraft sectors and outline their historical trajectories. Next, we follow Villages' development from a small-scale mission to an economically viable commercial enterprise. We then examine present fair trade tensions and opportunities, arguing that Villages' innovative trust-based practices may serve as a model for committed ethical enterprise. Finally, we discuss the role of Villages' leaders within global fair trade governance and explore their efforts to hold fair trade more accountable to its social justice concerns. We conclude by arguing that fair trade tensions represent a healthy dialectic between market realism and ethical idealism. As the food and handicraft sectors are increasingly working together to address these tensions, their differing insights provide the framework for movement revitalization in the decades to come.

HISTORICAL OVERVIEW:
THE FAIR TRADE MOVEMENT

Trading relations between the Global North and South have long been marked by inequalities deriving from historical colonial relations and contemporary neoliberal processes of globalization. Fair trade is a multifaceted movement that has emerged in response to increasing poverty within the Global South, ongoing inequitable trade processes, and the failure of aid-based development projects to provide sustainable livelihoods to southern producers.[3]

In the mid-twentieth century, religious groups in the Global North created Alternative Trade Organizations (ATOs) to link disadvantaged southern handicraft producers with northern consumers. Along with Quakers and the Church of the Brethren, Mennonites in the United States were centrally involved in the movement's inception.[4] Early fair trade practitioners were not exclusively focused on handicrafts. In 1973, the Dutch Catholic organization Fair Trade Organisatie introduced its solidarity coffee as the first food commodity in European markets.[5] During this period, Latin American Jesuits popularized the doctrine of liberation theology in the Global South, using the notion of spiritual deliverance to demand emancipation and social justice for the poor. Devotees developed trade linkages with European brethren to open markets for disadvantaged coffee producers.[6]

Secular activists also developed early fair trade networks. In the 1960s and 1970s, political dissidents fostered the World Shop movement to bring development issues to the attention of northern consumers, selling such items as sugar cane, Nicaraguan solidarity coffee, and handicrafts. In 1968 the United Nations Conference on Trade and Development (UNCTAD) promoted a "trade not aid" philosophy, calling for a change in conventional trade relations.[7] As the political movement expanded, organizations in North America strived to put this philosophy into practice.

In the 1980s Pueblo to People became active in the handicraft and clothing sectors, selling Latin American items to U.S. consumers. In 1986 Equal Exchange first introduced fair trade coffee into the U.S. market as well.[8] Thus the secular movement joined with the faith-based initiatives and with democratically run producer cooperatives in the Global South to develop an alternative trade system capable of linking marginalized producers to ethical buyers in the Global North. Many saw fair trade as a stepping stone to global trade regulation and engaged in political advocacy to realize this goal. By designating fair prices for producers and by developing a comprehensive set of labor and environmental standards, fair trade organizations sought not only to regulate themselves, but also hoped to provide the framework for a new economic order.[9]

While the fair trade handicraft and food sectors were united in fostering fair trading practices, they eventually separated. In the late 1980s, fair trade sales slumped and the expansion of neoliberal policies within international trade limited the potential for fair traders to stimulate more effective state regulation. As a result, some fair trade organizations began to shift their focus from market opposition toward market reform.[10] By the 1990s Fair Trade-certified food commodities had become organized under a market-oriented product labeling system governed by Fairtrade Labelling Organizations (FLO), while the fair trade handicraft sector (including Villages) remained under the governance of the International Federation for Alternative Trade, today known as the World Fair Trade Organization (WFTO).[11]

Under WFTO, participating organizations directly operate production and retail networks and maintain credibility through a system of trust-based trade relationships. With its focus on direct trading linkages and grassroots control, WFTO continues to position itself in opposition to mainstream markets. Conversely, FLO engages product labeling as a strategy for market reform and in recent years has actively pursued mainstreaming policies to better serve its rapidly growing producer base. As it seeks to integrate Fair Trade-certified products into mainstream retail networks, FLO increasingly operates in conjunction with non-fair trade enterprises. Whereas WFTO requires organizational commitment to fair trade throughout the product chain, under FLO, non-fair trade entities such as Starbucks and Walmart may sell Fair Trade-certified products alongside conventionally produced goods.[12]

FROM SELFHELP CRAFTS
TO TEN THOUSAND VILLAGES

In 1920, church members founded the Mennonite Central Committee (MCC) as the primary international relief agency for Mennonites and Brethren in Christ in the United States (and later in Canada). A primary MCC commitment has been "to critique all economic systems according to their impact on the poor."[13] Thus the Mennonite fair trade vision grew out of core spiritual values, including the Mennonite emphasis on voluntarism, communal support, and service to the poor. In 1946 MCC volunteer Edna Ruth Byler started SELFHELP Crafts of the World (SHC) by selling Puerto Rican and Jordanian handicrafts to U.S. church and women's groups. SHC was among the first in the world to develop alternative trade networks to help disadvantaged artisans.[14]

This organization remained the personal project of Edna Ruth Byler until the mid-1960s, when it formally became an MCC project operating through a close-knit network of Mennonite thrift shops.[15] In 1976, MCC appointed Paul Leatherman to lead SHC, and after meeting with Asian and Latin American suppliers he outlined core company policies, most of which remain in practice today. Thus SHC committed to guaranteeing (1) trust- and transparency-based trading arrangements, (2) good working conditions, and (3) fair prices for producers by meeting or going beyond the asking price. SHC also agreed to pay full costs before receiving the product, contradicting mainstream retail practices. Villages maintains this high standard among handicraft fair traders today, paying fifty percent to producers when placing an order and the remainder at time of shipment.[16]

To reach a broader consumer base, Leatherman also focused on expanding sales by wholesaling artisan goods, increasingly through a network of contract stores. As the organization grew, SHC depended upon local volunteers to help a small base of paid employees for staffing, promotions, and merchandizing within its contract stores. Stores also engaged community-based boards of directors that were deeply committed to promoting fair trade, often through educational programming. Because SHC wished to challenge the alienating effect of the global marketplace, it sought to reconnect consumers to producers. Thus it committed to telling artisan stories and provided such information for local and in-store promotions. These strategies underscored SHC's unique mission-based and community grassroots approach to retail development.[17] However, as discussed in the next section, such strategies have also contributed to further internal tensions.

The contract store approach proved effective, but 1980s sales growth led to tensions within the Mennonite community. When MCC debated changing the company's pricing strategy of low markup to stimulate further growth, leaders were not sure if it was ethically legitimate to generate company profit given Mennonite values. After much debate and initial attempts with artisan feedback, the organization decided to pursue profits to reinvest in growth to increase future product orders and better serve its artisan base. SHC raised retail prices from ten to one hundred percent of company cost, allowing it to expand store openings in advantageous locales and to hire more staff.[18]

Not all Mennonite members were comfortable with this expansion. Some argued that SHC was promoting consumerism, which contradicts MCC spiritual commitments.[19] The Mennonite focus on communal support and sharing means that practitioners have an uneasy relationship with several core capitalist values. There are a number of Mennonite entrepreneurs who have become millionaires, but in theory practitioners are opposed to the focus on individual self-interest and the drive to accumulate private wealth and property. As most Mennonites live in capitalist societies, the faith is concerned with the potential for succumbing to these values through the necessary involvement in economic life. This is most apparent in MCC calls for its constituency to critically examine the relationship between economic practices and poverty.[20] Thus SHC's growth fostered critical reflection within the Mennonite community and provided the impetus for leadership to seek solutions at the interface of market and ethical values.

In the 1990s, market concerns also drove organizational innovation. SHC's unique artisan goods found an open market during the 1980s, but by the early 1990s the increased influx of imported goods led to stagnating sales. As a result, the company decided to develop a branding strategy to refocus on sales. According to Paul Myers—CEO during this time period—SHC had carried its producer focus to the extreme by ignoring consumer demand. This limited the company's ability to provide artisans with a sustainable income. Thus SHC decided to refocus on price and quality and to explore capacity building initiatives that would help its producers become more successful in the U.S. and Canadian markets.[21]

As part of its branding strategy SHC changed its name to Ten Thousand Villages, giving it a visual identity from which to build brand recognition. The company chose its name from a quote by Mahatma Gandhi which emphasizes the importance of local villages as the focus for development. With its new name, leaders wished to emphasize the distinctive but interconnected nature of contemporary societies by using the metaphor of Ten Thousand Villages to represent the world. In designing its logo, the company reinforced this notion of global interconnectedness through its depiction of diverse rooftops drawn in a continuous line.[22]

Next, Villages shifted its focus from contract stores to developing company stores. While contract stores adhered to company standards and practices, local community boards maintained control over retailing. In contrast, company stores allowed Villages to more directly govern the retail decision-making process and enhance consumer recognition. These changes led to additional tensions and a small number of Mennonites chose to leave the company to pursue charity work. Further, as Villages gained in business savvy, some feared continuing growth would undermine its ability to maintain core ethical standards. Dissenters were concerned that the new emphasis on company stores might undermine the company's mission-based emphasis on voluntarism and grassroots control. Yet Villages' overall branding strategy enabled the company to successfully expand throughout the 1990s and ultimately to provide more retail space for its artisans.[23] Table 1 delineates company growth during these years of branding.

Table 1: Ten Thousand Villages Sales Growth 1993—2008[24]

Year	Total Annual Sales	Percent Change
1993	$ 5,900,000	18.0%
1997[a]	$ 6,800,000	15.3%
2001	$ 10,914,156	60.5%
2003	$ 14,624,475	34.0%
2005	$ 16,085,865	10.0%
2006[b]	$ 20,135,080	25.2%
2007	$ 23,487,984	16.7%
2008	$ 25,513,297	8.6%

Notes: a. In 1996, SELFHELP Crafts of the World becomes Ten Thousand Villages which opens company stores in 1997; b. Myers retires with Craig Schloneger becoming new CEO. Villages expands branding.

VILLAGES TODAY: THE BUSINESS WITH A MISSION

Table 2: Ten Thousand Villages Producer Countries as of 2009[25]

Latin America	Africa	Middle East	South Asia	East Asia
Bolivia	Benin	Egypt	Bangladesh	Cambodia
Chile	Burkina	West Bank	India	Indonesia
Ecuador	Faso		Nepal	Laos
El Salvador	Cameroon		Pakistan	Philippines
Guatemala	Congo		Sri Lanka	Thailand
Haiti	Ghana			Vietnam
Honduras	Kenya			
Mexico	Niger			
Nicaragua	Nigeria			
Peru	South Africa			
	Tanzania			
	Uganda			

Table 2 highlights the thirty-five countries from which Villages sources its merchandise. The company is currently the largest fair trade retailer of handicrafts in the world, yet its Mennonite principles remain the central framework for company practices. As Leatherman states, "When I took over as Director, we were a mission trying to do business . . . we have now turned into a business with a mission."[26] This approach has enabled Villages to develop creative solutions to market requirements. Whereas mainstream corporations often rely

upon cheap labor and lax worker regulations as part of a profit generation and expansion strategy, Villages engages in company growth to
meet its artisans' needs through fair wages and honorable worker
treatment.

Villages' market growth is largely dependent upon the successful branding strategies instituted by Paul Myers. Current CEO Craig
Schloneger states that ongoing branding merely represents an expansion of Myers' previous approach and that it does not require any
lapse in commitment to wider fair trade goals. Rather, this market
strategy is being employed in tandem with ethical values to provide
a stronger retail network for disadvantaged producers. According to
Schloneger, branding is more than a label because it offers Villages
the opportunity to demonstrate its ethical standards to consumers by
presenting the consumer with the company mission and by showcas-
ing artisanal groups.

Villages is striving to enhance consumer recognition by getting
its story into large publications; in both 2008 and 2009 Forbes magazine and the Ethisphere Institute formally recognized Villages as one
of the top ethical companies in the world.[27] Villages is streamlining
agreements with contract stores to require that they maintain eighty
percent of sales in company products (which for about half of the
stores represents a percentage increase) and follow a common set of
promotional strategies. Schloneger stresses that the company does
not wish to create cookie-cutter chain stores; he maintains that an
eighty rather than one hundred percent sales requirement will allow
individual contract stores to maintain distinctive differences by
sourcing products from other fair trade organizations. However, he
also argues that for ongoing branding to succeed, customers must be
able to recognize Villages' product base.[28]

This branding strategy is also linked to capacity building initiatives for Villages' producers. There are two types of producer groups
with whom Villages operates: Type A groups comprise Villages' top
sellers, whereas Type B groups require more capacity building to develop the same design, product development, and production capacity expertise as their cohorts. As contract stores tend to order Villages'
top-selling products, it becomes difficult to showcase the products
made by its Type B groups, yet the company remains committed to
long-term relationships with all its artisans. This creates a challenge,
and the company's decision to implement the eighty percent rule
with contract stores has been made to secure store space for all of its
members as well as to streamline the differing contract requirements
that Villages had historically developed with individual stores.[29]

This decision has generated a degree of tension within the Villages network as some contract store boards of directors are concerned that this requirement may be difficult to meet, particularly in periods of economic downturn.[30] Additionally, for those stores where boards of directors, staff, and volunteers have become actively engaged in their communities, a strong store culture of pride, ownership, and activism has evolved. Tension has emerged as these stores try to reconcile their unique local identity with what is viewed as greater centralized direction and control from Villages at the national level.

As a retailer, Villages' primary focus is not on artisan training. However, the company engages in capacity building initiatives with producer groups in a number of ways. First, artisans come to work at Villages headquarters in Akron, Pennsylvania, or at its company store in nearby Ephrata to gain business and retail skills. Company leadership is planning to expand these opportunities to its broader network of stores throughout Canada and the United States. Villages also offers permanent Ephrata store space to its Pakistani rug producer group, JAKCISS Oriental Rugs. These sales occur separately from Villages' regular sales, and JAKCISS maintains its own (largely American) sales staff on the floor. In the future, Villages hopes to turn more of its company store space in the United States and Canada into multiple shops that artisans will independently manage. Finally, in 2008, Villages hired an Artisan Development Specialist to develop partnerships with other fair trade and development organizations operating in the countries where its artisans are located. By doing so, the company hopes to link producers to the resources they require so they may expand their existing product base and build production capacity.[31]

Villages follows the Christian principle of demonstrating good works through practice. Rather than adopting the political advocacy routes taken by European fair trade organizations, it attempts to show through its own work that ethics, success, and business can co-exist. Villages' leaders do not see its values as incompatible with business acumen; instead, they view any difficulties posed by their business-mission model as a surmountable challenge. Schloneger states that if the company were required to sacrifice any of its values to expand, it would choose not to grow.[32] Not only does Villages' mindset enable it to maintain its respected position within the broader fair trade movement, but company market successes also demonstrate that closely held values do not have to be sacrificed in favor of business goals.

While ongoing internal tensions within the Villages network demonstrate the difficulty of synthesizing market requirements with fair trade values, including Villages' ethic of voluntarism and system of grassroots control, the company model has nevertheless proved successful and may serve as a framework for the broader movement as it navigates similar tensions. That said, some within the organization have been critical of Villages' advocacy-through-practice approach. Such critics argue that Villages, and more broadly MCC and the Mennonite faith, have unnecessarily limited their potential impact on global trading relations by not engaging in political advocacy alongside other fair trade organizations.[33] Indeed heightened advocacy will likely be necessary if fair trade is to effectively position itself as the global market norm.

THE FAIR TRADE MOVEMENT AND THE QUESTION OF ACCOUNTABILITY

Current tensions within the fair trade movement run parallel to challenges facing Villages and the broader corporate social responsibility (CSR) movement. As neoliberal strategies dominate state and international governance, regulatory regimes have retreated from their commitment to social and environmental protections. To meet this regulatory gap, non-governmental organizations are pursuing multiple private accountability mechanisms.

Yet the diversity of private mechanisms makes it difficult to separate hype from committed engagement. A number of corporate actors have responded to consumer demand for ethically traded products by engaging CSR rhetoric without making substantial changes to business practices. By depending upon internal rather than external inspection mechanisms, such firms have successfully privatized the notion of accountability, thereby undermining the potential for private regulation to wholly address social justice concerns.[34] Not all CSR initiatives, however, rely on internal inspection to ensure accountability. Within fair trade, both FLO and WFTO have developed third-party mechanisms to ensure that fair trade standards are being met within participating organizations and companies. That said, FLO and WFTO have diverged in their accountability approaches and these differences have generated a number of movement tensions.

FAIR TRADE CHALLENGES AND TENSIONS

The Italian philosopher Antonio Gramsci provides a useful analytical framework to better understand the political dynamic between corporate and fair trade actors. His work recognizes civil society as a critical force in the fight against the inequities and injustice that characterize global capitalism. In this sense capitalists and civil society activists are engaged in a war of position, whereby the hegemonic group maintains its dominance by coopting and transforming oppositional demand into mere public relations rhetoric.[35] For the purposes of our discussion, corporations have used CSR and even the fair trade movement as a tool to regain consumer trust while continuing to avoid regulation. A growing number of mainstream retailers have begun to heavily publicize their commitment to ethical principles by offering small quantities of Fair Trade-certified commodities in their stores while their overall sourcing practices have yet to change, a practice referred to by some as "fair washing."[36] One outcome of this process has been a critical investigation of corporate ethical claims.[37] Fair trade as a third-party certification system has remained relatively unscathed from such critiques, but these broader developments have exacerbated movement tensions that are historically grounded upon the differing governance strategies pursued by FLO and WFTO.

Numerous fair traders are disturbed by FLO's mainstreaming policies, claiming that this approach favors market share over ethical considerations. Some have begun to question whether fair trade serves to humanize international trade as it claims, or if it ultimately reinforces producer-consumer alienation because it works within existing market structures.[38] Others are concerned that the movement may not be able to hold its oppositional stance as it moves ever deeper within the market. These critics argue that by working with non-fair trade entities, FLO's efforts to maintain grassroots control and ensure overall accountability may be compromised.[39] Indeed, corporate actors may primarily engage fair trade as a traceability mechanism, thus undermining movement emphasis on producer-supplier partnerships.[40]

A consequence is that the movement has become divided between those seeking to broaden the fair trade movement through expanding sales and those attempting to deepen the movement by strengthening core ethical values.[41] As a result a growing base of dissenters are calling for total organizational devotion to fair trade principles and view product labeling as an incomplete attempt to instill ethics into global trade processes. In response, WFTO has launched an integrated supply chain system approach to enhance organizational accountability and to support the fair trade organizations willing to meet its strict standards. While FLO continues to work in conjunction with mainstream corporations, it too has attempted to address the question of fair washing by ensuring that such entities meet fair trade standards for their certified products and by stepping up political advocacy campaigns.[42]

Ultimately fair trade tensions derive from the movement's attempt to work against the market while operating within the market. Such tensions are similar to those that occurred within the Mennonite community when Villages transformed its practices to gain increased market share for its artisans. Yet unlike Villages, the global fair trade movement is not ultimately accountable to a religious constituency, and while FLO's labeling strategy ensures ethical production, it does not require retailers to uphold fair trade standards within their own organizational structure as does Villages.

While current tensions may be divisive, they also symbolize a dynamic movement as realists and idealists critically engage with each other in their attempt to transform global markets. Given that fair traders must necessarily work within the rubric of global capitalism, the rapid growth of fair trade food commodities demonstrates how savvy business strategies can generate success, and therefore meet the economic needs of an expanding producer base. Conversely, WFTO remains staunchly committed to formational values and serves as an ethical check on movement growth, much as the Mennonite constituency has done for Villages.

ADVOCACY THROUGH PRACTICE: VILLAGES' INFLUENCE WITHIN THE FAIR TRADE MOVEMENT

As a company, Villages will never be able to provide an outlet for the demands of all disadvantaged artisans. However, it can provide the movement with a model for success, and in this sense, its advocacy through practice strategy may inform other fair trade retailers who are struggling to maintain core standards while expanding their market presence. Company members who are involved in movement leadership may offer insight into current tensions and ensure that the drive for growth does not lead to diminished standards. While Villages and the broader Mennonite constituency have been criticized for not engaging in direct political advocacy alongside other fair trade organizations, Villages' leadership has nevertheless been active

in political debates occurring within the internal fair trade movement.

Long-standing Villages member Doug Dirks was appointed
chair of the Fair Trade Federation (FTF) in 2008.[43] Dirks also remains
with Villages, where he has held numerous positions since 1985,
through its transformation and more settled expansion. Dirks argues
that given its size, Villages has a responsibility to share information
and leadership. He views his role in FTF as one of helping to develop
guidelines that offer fair traders creative flexibility without reducing
standards.[44] Village members also have historical ties to WFTO since
Leatherman was an integral part of its initial inception as the International Federation for Alternative Trade (IFAT).[45] In 1989, Leatherman helped incorporate this organization and he served on its committee for four years. He was involved in forming policies as this organization began to grow, and Mennonite ethical values infused his
decision-making process.[46] Myers, who was responsible for introducing branding strategies into the Villages framework, now serves
as WFTO Chair. Moreover, he served as president from 1993-1999.
As Chair, Myers has been involved in pursuing structural changes in
an effort to challenge the use of fair trade for "fair washing" purposes.[47]

Just as SELFHELP Crafts morphed into Villages as part of a successful branding strategy, WFTO is using its new name as part of a
broader branding program. It has developed a broad agenda for
change, including (1) branding the WFTO logo as an organizational
mark; (2) retaining its position that fair trade is to focus on small and
marginalized producers; (3) strengthening efforts to make membership affordable to small producers who cannot access other fair
trade certifications; and (4) reviewing membership criteria to
strengthen overall accountability. The WFTO is using the concept of
organizational certification to ensure commitment to fair trade's
core ethical principles throughout the entirety of the commodity
chain.[48]

The WFTO's organizational logo is thus not a product label.
Rather, its purpose is to brand producer and retailing organizations
that demonstrate full commitment to fair trade principles. However,
WFTO is also in the process of developing a third-party certified
product label for producers of commodities (such as handicrafts)
that are not covered under the FLO product-labeling system. In a
larger sense, WFTO's multipronged strategy presents a global solution to current fair trade challenges, as it focuses on generating a
more complete "sustainable fair trade economy" by providing an or-

ganizational brand while also expanding product labeling to encompass a broader range of producers.[49]

TEN THOUSAND VILLAGES AND
FUTURE FAIR TRADE MOVEMENT PROSPECTS

Fair trade tensions may be viewed in two ways. Within the literature, scholars cite mainstream market development, bureaucratization, and potential loss of grassroots control within the fair trade product labeling strand as primary sources of movement tension.[50] However, conflict may also be viewed as a source of broader movement innovation. There appears to be a growing consensus among fair traders as FLO and WFTO have recently come together to develop a new charter for fair trade principles. This charter formally articulates two distinct approaches to fair trade: the product certification route and an integrated supply chain approach.[51] Whereas CSR has previously proven fertile ground for firms that engage in ethical rhetoric as a public relations measure, renewed fair trade solidarity will better position the movement to challenge such behavior. Conscious consumers appear to be welcoming more stringent ethical standards as well. Recent research has highlighted the growing role of consumption as a political strategy to address global social justice concerns. As consumers increasingly self-identify with ethical consumption, their purchasing patterns are transforming global business practices, and in certain product sectors ethical purchases have either met or outstripped their conventional counterparts.[52]

Myers states that recent movement changes are in part due to leader awareness that while fair trade offers real resistance to conventional market norms, the movement continues to face major obstacles. Thus, WFTO is seeking consistency and order by demonstrating its position as a "gold standard" organization. Over the long run, it will establish stronger standards and markets to help consumers seeking ethical items. As strong organizations emerge to become a central force within the movement, Myers believes they will demonstrate a new level of unity to provide committed leadership. By collaborating more closely, WFTO and FLO seek to reunify the food and handicraft arms while strengthening governance strategies.[53]

Movement solidarity may enable fair trade to more effectively position itself as the global leader in trade accountability as well. Myers believes fair trade individuals and organizations in the Global South will become increasingly prominent in political debates.[54] Within the transnational policy arena, Amartya Sen and Martha

Nussbaum are demanding alternate strategies for global poverty reduction, and they have outlined a human capabilities approach to
serve this purpose.[55] Scholars have begun to note the link between
fair trade practices and the human capabilities approach to poverty
reduction.[56] Fair traders may bolster their engagement with political
advocacy by drawing more explicitly upon this broader development strategy.

Recent economic events demonstrate the failure of unbridled
capitalism. With the collapse of financial institutions and the crisis in
housing markets, hedge funds, futures, and more, the failures of the
neoliberal strategy of deregulation are increasingly apparent and
point to the need for flexible but globally oriented social regulation.
The current economic crisis will certainly pose its own set of challenges to both Villages and the broader fair trade movement, but at
the time of writing it is still too early to anticipate their nature and
scope. That said, fair trade successes have demonstrated the potential
for socially just and economically viable global trade. While the fair
trade strategy of transforming global markets from within warrants
caution due to ongoing concerns over cooptation by dominant neoliberal economic processes, FLO and WFTO's reunified commitment to core ethical values may enhance the movement's potential to
engage these processes more effectively.

Yet at some point fair trade's vision must cease being one of a resistance movement and seek to become the market norm. If the fair
trade vision is to be fully realized, practitioners must continue to
demonstrate that the movement offers an economically viable strategy for global trade regulation. Given these considerations, current
fair trade tensions are not necessarily a negative phenomenon; rather,
recent movement developments suggest that these tensions have
provided the impetus for fair traders to reunify the movement and
adapt to complex challenges.

In many ways, fair trade's multifaceted approach to trade governance represents an alternate vision for North-South relations and
global development and the case of Villages demonstrates the ongoing convergence between ethical and market goals. While internal
tensions within the Villages network highlight the difficulty of navigating uncharted paths, these tensions will likely stimulate further
company innovation. Thus, Villages' *business with a mission* approach
may be seen as a positive model for the broader fair trade movement.
Villages' leaders have emerged as pivotal players within fair trade
governance. By maintaining their historical critique of "all economic
systems according to their impact on the poor," they are actively pur-

suing solutions to historical tensions in the fair trade movement as well as within the broader global economy.

NOTES

1. For a critical overview of fair trade aims, see Douglas L. Murray and Laura T. Raynolds, "Globalization and its Antinomies: Negotiating a Fair Trade Movement," in *Fair Trade: The Challenges of Transforming Globalization*, ed. L. T. Raynolds, D. L. Murray and J. Wilkinson (New York: Routledge, 2007), 3-14. See also publications from the World Fair Trade Organization (WFTO), *Trends, Facts, and Figures* (2007), available from http://www. wfto.com/index.php?option=com_docman&task=cat_view&gid=94&&Ite mid=109 and *10 Principles of Fair Trade* (2009), available from http:// www.wfto.com/index.php?option=com_content&task=view&id=2&Itemi d=12.

2. See Michael Conroy, *Branded: How the Certification Revolution is Transforming Global Corporations* (Gabriola Island, BC: New Society Publishers, 2007); Terry Newholm and Deirdre Shaw, "Studying the Ethical Consumer: A Review of Research," *Journal of Consumer Behaviour* 6 (2007): 253-270; and Laura T. Raynolds and Michael A. Long, "Fair/Alternative Trade: Historical and Empirical Dimensions," in *Fair Trade: The Challenges of Transforming Globalization*, ed. L. T. Raynolds, D. L. Murray, and J. Wilkinson (New York: Routledge, 2007), 15-32.

3. For discussions of the diverse character of the fair trade movement, see Murray and Raynolds "Globalization and its Antinomies" and Laura T. Raynolds and John Wilkinson, "Fair Trade in the Agriculture and Food Sector: Analytical Dimensions," in *Fair Trade: The Challenges of Transforming Globalization*, 33-47.

4. In addition to Raynolds and Long, "Fair/Alternative Trade," see Gavin Fridell, "The Fair Trade Network in Historical Perspective," *Canadian Journal of Development Studies* 25/3 (2004):411-428; and Mary Ann Littrell and Marsha Ann Dickson, *Social Responsibility in the Global Market: Fair Trade of Cultural Products* (Thousand Oaks, Calif.: Sage Publications, 1999).

5. William Low and Eileen Davenport, "Postcards from the Edge: Maintaining the 'Alternative' Character of Fair Trade," *Sustainable Development* 13 (2005): 143-153.

6. Liberation theology is a school of thought popularized by Catholic dissidents in Latin America and Africa in the 1970s and 1980s. It is primarily known as a philosophical blend of Christianity with socialism, and as such, its doctrine views Jesus Christ as the liberator of the oppressed. Liberation theologians promote political activism as a tool for bringing social justice to poor and oppressed populations. Christian Smith, *The Emergence of Liberation Theology: Radical Religion and Social Movement Theory* (Chicago: University of Chicago Press, 1991). For the connection between liberation theology and fair trade see Gavin Fridell, *Fair-Trade Coffee: The Prospects and Pitfalls of Market-Driven Social Justice* (Toronto: University of Toronto Press, 2007).

7. On UNCTAD and "trade not aid," see Raynolds and Long "Fair/Alternative Trade," along with Low and Davenport, "Postcards from the Edge."

8. Marsha Ann Dickson and Mary Ann Littrell, "Consumers of Clothing from Alternative Trading Organizations: Societal Attitudes and Purchase Evaluative Criteria," *Clothing and Textiles Research Journal* 15/1 (1997): 20-33 and Margaret Levi and April Linton, "Fair Trade: A Cup at a Time?" *Politics and Society* 31/3 (2003): 407-432.

9. For more on the global ambitions of the fair trade movement, see Littrell and Dickson, *Social Responsibility in the Global Market*; Low and Davenport, "Postcards from the Edge"; and Fridell, "The Fair Trade Movement in Historical Perspective."

10. Fridell, "The Fair Trade Movement in Historical Perspective."

11. According to convention, Fair Trade in capital letters denotes the arm of the movement that engages in FLO-certified Fair Trade food production, whereas fair trade in lower case letters refers to the broader fair trade movement.

12. WFTO guidelines on what constitutes fair trade can be found in WFTO, *Marks and Labels* (2009), available from http://www.wfto.com/index.php? option=com_content&task=view&id=904&Itemid=310 and WFTO, *About WFTO* (2009), available from http://www.wfto.com/index.php?opt ion=com_frontpage&Itemid=1. See also Gavin Fridell, *Fair Trade Coffee*.

13. Mennonite Central Committee, *A Commitment to Christ's Way of Peace* (2008) available from http://mcc.org/about/peacecommitment/commit ment.html.

14. See Littrell and Dickson, *Social Responsibility in the Global Market*, along with Mennonite Central Committee, *A Brief History of MCC* (2008), available from http://www.mcc.org/about/history/.

15. Byler remained Executive Director of SELFHELP Crafts until her retirement in 1970.

16. Interview by authors with Paul Leatherman, Akron, Pa., June 23, 2008.

17. Littrell and Dickson, *Social Responsibility in the Global Market*.

18. Interview with Paul Leatherman.

19. Ibid.

20. See MCC, *A Commitment to Christ's Way of Peace*, and Calvin W. Redekop, "Capitalism," *Global Anabaptist Mennonite Encyclopedia Online*, available from http://www.gameo.org/encyclopedia/contents/C4233ME.html.

21. Interview by authors with Paul Myers, Akron, Pa., June 26, 2008.

22. See Ten Thousand Villages, *About Us*, available at http://www.tent housandvillages.com/php/about.us/index.php.

23. Littrell and Dickson, *Social Responsibility in the Global Market*; interview with Paul Myers.

24. Tabular information compiled by authors based on Littrell and Dickson, *Social Responsibility in the Global Market*, and Ten Thousand Villages, *One Vision Annual Report 2007-2008*, (Akron, Pa.: Ten Thousand Villages, 2008).

25. Table compiled by authors based on Ten Thousand Villages, *Find Artisans by Region or Country*, available at http://www.tenthousandvillages. com/catalog/region.php.

26. Interview with Paul Leatherman.

27. Ethisphere, *2008 World's Most Ethical Companies*, available from http://ethisphere.com/wme2008/ and Ethisphere, *2009 World's Most Ethical Companies*, available from http://ethisphere.com/wme2009/. For Forbes

coverage of Villages' growth see Forbes Magazine, *Ten Thousand Villages Grows with Fair Trade*, http://www.forbes.com/forbes/2009/0907/creative-giving-ten-thousand-villages-grows-with-fair-trade.html.

28. Interview by authors with Craig Schloneger, Akron, Pa., June 26, 2008.

29. Interview by authors with Doug Lapp, Akron, Pa., June 25, 2008; interview with Craig Schloneger.

30. Interview by authors with Anonymous interviewee #1.

31. Interviews with Lapp and Schloneger.

32. Interview with Schloneger.

33. Interview by authors with Anonymous interviewee #2.

34. Jennifer Clapp, "Global Environmental Governance for Corporate Responsibility and Accountability," *Global Environmental Politics* 5/3 (2005): 23-34.

35. Robert W. Cox, "Gramsci, Hegemony and International Relations: An Essay in Method," *Journal of International Studies* 12/2 (1983): 162-175.

36. In addition to Fridell, *Fair Trade Coffee*, see J. J. McMurty, "Ethical Value-Added: Fair Trade and the Case of Café Femenino," *Journal of Business Ethics* 86/1 (2008): 27-49.

37. Krista Bondy, Dirk Matten, and Jeremy Moon, "Multinational Corporation Codes of Conduct: Governance Tools for Corporate Social Responsibility?" *Corporate Governance* 16/4 (2008): 294-305; and Dirk Matten and Jeremy Moon, "'Implicit' and 'Explicit' CSR: A Conceptual Framework for a Comparative Understanding of Corporate Social Responsibility," *Academy of Management Review* 33/2 (2008): 404-424.

38. Fridell, "Fair Trade Coffee and Commodity Fetishism: The Limits of Market-Driven Social Justice," *Historical Materialism* 15 (2007):79-104.

39. Marie-Christine Renard, "Quality Certification, Regulation and Power in Fair Trade," *Journal of Rural Studies* 21/4 (2005): 419-431.

40. For more on the issue of partnership versus traceability, see Laura T. Raynolds, "Mainstreaming Fair Trade Coffee: From Partnership to Traceability," *World Development* 37 (2009): 1083-1093.

41. For more information on the tensions between broadening and deepening the fair trade movement, see Douglas L. Murray, Laura T. Raynolds, and Peter L. Taylor, "The Future of Fair Trade Coffee: Dilemmas Facing Latin America's Small-scale Producers," *Development in Practice* 16 (2006): 179-182.

42. Interview with Myers; Murray, and Raynolds, "Globalization and its Antinomies." See also WFTO, *Marks and Labels*, and WFTO and Fairtrade Labelling Organizations-International (FLO-I), *A Charter of Fair Trade Principles* (January 2009), available at http://www.wfto.com/index.php?option=com_content&task=view&id=965&Itemid=314.

43. Fair Trade Federation is the North American trade network for organizations and businesses that are fully committed to fair trade. It is closely connected to WFTO, which performs a similar function at the global level.

44. Interview by authors with Doug Dirks, Akron, Pa., June 26, 2008.

45. IFAT changed its name to the WFTO in 2008.

46. Interview with Leatherman.

47. Interview with Myers.

48. Ibid.

49. WFTO, *Marks and Labels*, and WFTO, *10 Principles of Fair Trade*.

50. See Murray and Raynolds, "Globalization and its Antinomies"; Raynolds and Wilkinson, "Fair Trade in the Agriculture and Food Sector"; and Renard, "Quality Certification, Regulation, and Power in Fair Trade."

51. WFTO and FLO-I., *A Charter of Fair Trade Principles.*

52. In addition to Conroy, *Branded*, see Alex Nicholls and Charlotte Opal, *Fair Trade: Market-Driven Ethical Consumption* (Thousand Oaks, Calif.: Sage Publications, 2005) and Deirdre Shaw, "Modeling Consumer Decision Making in Fair Trade," in *The Ethical Consumer*, ed. R. Harrison, T. Newholm, and D. Shaw (Thousand Oaks, Calif.: Sage Publications, 2005).

53. Interview with Myers.

54. Ibid.

55. The human capabilities debate is complex, with key contributors Amartya Sen and Martha Nussbaum taking different approaches to developing this concept. Whereas Sen favors a grassroots development approach to designing capability indicators appropriate to individual communities, Nussbaum is striving to develop a universal set of indicators to guide international political policies. For further information see Martha Nussbaum, *Women and Human Development: The Capabilities Approach* (Cambridge: Cambridge University Press, 2000); Amartya Sen, *Development as Freedom* (New York: Knopf, 1999); and Nussbaum and Sen, ed. *The Quality of Life* (Oxford: Clarendon Press, 1993).

56. Fridell, *Fair Trade Coffee*; Marsha Ann Dickson and Mary Littrell, "Measuring Quality of Life of Apparel Workers in Mumbai India: Quantitative and Qualitative Data," in *Advances in Quality-of-Life Theory and Research*, ed. M. J. Sirgy, R. Rahtz, and A. C. Samli, (The Netherlands: Kluwer Academic Publishers, 2003); Mary Littrell and Marsha Ann Dickson, "Employment with a Socially Responsible Business: Worker Capabilities and quality of Life," *Clothing and Textiles Research Journal* 24/3 (2006): 192-206; and Susan Strawn and Mary Ann Littrell, "Beyond Capabilities: A Case Study of Three Artisan Enterprises in India," *Clothing and Textiles Research Journal* 24/3 (2006): 207-213.

Chapter 12

The Gifts of an Extended Theological Table: MCC's World Community Cookbooks as Organic Theology

MALINDA ELIZABETH BERRY

As cultural artifacts, cookbooks help subgroups define themselves within and even over-and-against dominant culture. The shelves of Mennonite kitchens are stacked with such artifacts. Behind each recipe there is a story, and many collections of recipes commemorate significant moments and groups of people: the fiftieth anniversary of a congregation, an extended family, or a community organization. Yet, as recent articles about Mennonite cookbooks by Matthew Bailey-Dick and Rebekah Trollinger observe, in our theologizing we have neglected to turn to these cultural artifacts as theological and ethical resources. Perhaps, as Bailey-Dick suggests, our neglect of these theological resources is based on the way we too often focus on the sociological conflation of culture and faith rather than exploring how "the cookbook . . . stands as a witness to the gospel and a mission partner for God's work in the world."[1]

From this perspective, I will focus on two of the eight observations about "cookbook discourse" Bailey-Dick's essay develops—simple living and the globalization of Mennonites—by giving most of my attention to the theme of simple living as an example of a theological commitment MCC calls its constituent denominations to make in light of the global partnerships that form the basis of its organizational identity.

I am part of what we might think of as the "More-with-Less Generation" of Mennonites. With her trusty copy of *More-with-Less* in hand, my mother chose to trade full-time work as a college professor for full-time homemaking during her first decade of motherhood. She and my father had heard and studied the good news as interpreted and shared by Longacre and the many people who contributed anecdotes, poetry, and prose (not to mention recipes!) to the cookbook and its companions, *Living More with Less* and *Living More With Less: Study/Action Guide*.[2] Choosing the pattern I wanted for my cloth napkin, sneaking a pinch of bread dough from the weekly baking, and helping my parents during their monthly shift at the Co-op are all childhood memories from the way our family lived more with less. In this way, my generation and I were nurtured by Christians who believed that they had a responsibility to live in the world in an unencumbered way.

Not until I began to rub shoulders with others outside my denominational faith community did I begin to realize how much my view of North American culture had been shaped *directly* by Longacre's *More-with-Less* and *indirectly* by John Howard Yoder's *The Politics of Jesus*![3] In shaping a generation, Longacre also shaped Anabaptist and Mennonite God-talk, discipleship, and congregational life. In making a case for theological speech and ethical formation at home in light of what happens far away, Longacre and MCC set the stage for thinking about peace theology both in terms of international relations and community-building table fellowship.

But we must remember that our cookbook discourse is not confined to private conversation around the dinner table. The many other voices and bodies that take part in "our" conversation and "our" food became very real for me one morning when I attended a chapel service at Union Theological Seminary in New York. I noticed on the order of worship that the day's theme was "Extending the Table," which made me think of the beloved cookbook by that name.[4] As it turned out, this phrasing was more than a coincidence. The worship leader, a professor visiting from Yale Divinity School, had chosen all the words for worship that day from the *Extending the Table* cookbook, edited by Joetta Handrich Schlabach as an MCC project published by Herald Press.

This experience revealed to me that this MCC tradition of cookbooks, a tradition to which I and others who have cooked and eaten those cookbooks' recipes belong, is not just a cultural and culinary tradition. Indeed, these books are also theological and ethical resources. But how are *More-with-Less, Extending the Table,* and *Simply in Season* theological resources?[5] I will answer that question by making a two-part argument. First, as Mennonite Central Committee's constituents who have made these cookbooks possible by contributing and using their recipes, we should understand ourselves as contributing to a trilogy of Anabaptist constructive, organic theology. Second, the organic theology embodied in the World Community Cookbook series contributes to the theology and ethics of simple living, a social movement that connects the politics of daily living with a concern for authentic connection with other people rather than with things.

THE TASK OF SYSTEMATIC/ CONSTRUCTIVE THEOLOGY

The term *systematic theology* usually conjures up examples of voluminous works of excruciating theological detail like Thomas Aquinas' *Summa Theologica* or Karl Barth's *Church Dogmatics.* Cookbooks never appear in the mind's eye when someone says, "systematic theology," yet I believe the term is applicable to the World Community Cookbook Series, albeit in unconventional—or to state it more positively, organic—ways.

A primary feature of conventional systematic theology follows from its primary task: offering a clear and coherent accounting of Christian faith using traditional doctrinal categories like revelation, Scripture, providence, Christology, pneumatology, ecclesiology, and so forth. In recent years, theologians have begun referring to systematic theology as "constructive theology" to reflect the fact that this branch of academic theology is not only defined by its use of doctrinal categories. Following in the tradition of pioneering German theologian Friederich Schleiermacher (1768–1834), a constructive approach to systematics focuses on several foundational principles or claims and then builds a theological system by demonstrating the centrality of those principles to correlating doctrines.

For example, rather than writing a book detailing the historical and rhetorical inter-relatedness of doctrines about the incarnation,

Christology, and ecclesiology, a theologian taking a more constructive approach to these themes might begin by describing a group of
knitters in a local congregation who make prayer shawls. Using the
knitters' words to describe how they feel connected to Jesus' expressions of compassion as they knit, the theologian would explain how
and why theological coherence can be found between the knitters'
testimonies about their experience and these doctrines. The theologians' constructive task is to explore and explain how and why it
makes sense that knitting shawls can become a form of Christian
ministry, expressing our hopes for healing in Jesus' name.

As a theologian, I can testify to the intellectually and even aes-
thetically satisfying quality of cogently catalogued theological concepts, the hallmark of systematic theologies. And yet, an inevitable
criticism of such theologizing arises: Conventional systematic/con-
structive theology can easily become more of an academic exercise
and more spiritually nourishing for professional theologians than for
"people in the pew." While I am sympathetic to this concern, I do not
believe that this divide is inevitable. Because authentic spirituality is
a vital part of one's faith, spirituality should also be theologically informed. Without a meaningful connection between systematic/con-
structive theology and spirituality, even our most earnest expressions of Christian faith run the risk of being distorted. Academic theology in its systematic/constructive form helps keep our thinking
clear. So the question is this: How do we connect the insights, experiences, and concerns of all our faith communities' members with the
practices of theological reflection as faith seeks understanding?

In light of these questions, I believe that conventional forms and
modes of theologizing can learn from the more organic model for theological reflection prominent among Latin American Christian communities in the 1970s and 1980s.[6] Before I summarize the Latin American model, an explanation of how I am using the terms *conventional*
and *organic* is in order.

CONVENTIONAL VERSUS ORGANIC THEOLOGY

In this age of environmental crisis, the words *green* and *organic*
are ubiquitous, and we must use them discerningly. As I use organic
in the remainder of this essay, I will be employing it in its broad definitions—I am not just referring to a rating or label placed on products
that conform to the U.S. Department of Agriculture's organic guidelines and standards. While a chemist dealing with (in)organic com-
pounds would nuance this more, at a basic level, something that is

"organic" is a carbon-based organism that lives, dies, and decays. Beyond this basic definition, we are familiar with the generic use of organic in terms of foods and products manufactured without chemical fertilizers, pesticides, or synthetic materials (i.e., USDA ratings). But organic also describes the relationship among different bits and pieces that somehow combine in a harmonious way: the disparate parts, once they join together, clearly form a unified whole. An example of organic in this sense might be a jigsaw puzzle or the ingredients that a cook combines to make apple crisp (see *More-with-Less*, pages 270 ff. for the recipe). Whether by design or through discovery, the pieces and ingredients fit together in deeply satisfying ways.

Similarly, organic theologizing is a kind of God-talk that emerges from the living, breathing, organic grassroots of a faith community. Ordinary people produce this God-talk when they speak from the heart and reflect on the everydayness of faith lived out in their corner of the world, what some Latin American theologians refer to as *lo cotidiano*.[7] In other words, this is theological speech that has not been treated with chemical fertilizers or pesticides. While it may be informed by sources like the Apostles' Creed or the Schleitheim Confession, organic theologizing does not begin with the assumption that it must conform to those sources. Organic God-talk describes the natural and essential aspects of faith which have not been engineered to be pest resistant and heresy-proof so there are more "imperfections" than in meticulously cultivated God-talk grown in the academy.

But "imperfections" of organically grown theologizing are not really imperfections. *The purpose of organic theology and homegrown God-talk is to help communities take stock of their shared experiences and consider what kind of fruit they are producing, rather than viewing church as a place where we shop for unblemished fruits and vegetables plucked from the produce aisles without getting our hands dirty.* What is your disposition when you behold the biggest, shiniest, reddest apples; the handiest bag of mini carrots (cleaned, cut, and ready to eat); or the firmest "vine-ripened" tomatoes this side of the border?

My advocacy for organic theology is based on my own conversion to the importance of homegrown God-talk through Delores Williams' doctoral seminars which I attended during my coursework at Union. Williams described the organic approach to theology analogically as she advocated for its authenticity vis-a-vis conventional theology.

Her analogy takes us back to the produce section of the grocery story I described above. Imagine that you are standing among crates, baskets, and refrigerated displays of vegetables and fruits. From peas to potatoes and apples to oranges, you read the signs telling you that you have the option of conventional produce or locally grown produce. The question facing you is this: Do you want the chemically altered and manipulated fruit or vegetable—the one upon which chemical warfare has been waged so that it could make the 2,000-mile journey to the display in front of you without looking worse for wear? Do you want the apple that was grown two miles from where you are standing because it ripened on the branch and never met a wax dip because it did not need to survive a trip from the Pacific Northwest to the center of Ohio where you are shopping? Which of the two is closer to the true essence of what God created an apple to be: the conventional or the homegrown version?

Williams identifies a corollary between this culinary and nutritional choice and the dynamics around theologizing. Scientists, with good intentions, have tinkered with the genetics of conventional apple seeds to make their produce more pest-resistant, juicier, bigger, bruise-resistant, and able to withstand miles of transport from field to processing plant to grocery store to table. If you have ever planted a garden in your own backyard, or plucked a piece of fruit from a neighbor's tree, you will know that there are real differences between the homegrown version of fruits and vegetables and what awaits you in the produce section of Walmart, Meijer, Kroger, Food Lion, Safeway, or even Whole Foods.

Like those scientists, we theologians with our good intentions have also tinkered with Christian doctrine to maintain church teachings' heresy-resistant and heterodox-immune qualities, often with a healthy dose of male-centered biases. What we did not pay attention to is that our conventional varieties of doctrine have taken on the characteristics of ideals—what our Christology *should* look and sound like—rather than cultivating christologies that *are*.

As Christians, many of us have treated church like a box store where we can go one-stop shopping and get the most bang for our buck. Rather than teaching each other how to tend, prune, and harvest the apples in our local orchards—that is, to speak authentically about Christ—we leave it up to others to do the cultivating of our literal and figurative food. We do not ask questions or wonder about the differences among Fujis, Jonathans, Honeycrisps, and Galas or high Christology, low Christology, and liberation Christology.

To summarize, while there are a variety of ways to systematize basic Christian beliefs and construct a persuasive outline of our faith, I believe it is important that we make deliberate choices about the resources we use as we develop our theology. If we rely solely on conventional ways of doing theology, then we risk losing touch with the authentic, homegrown experiences of Christian faith that grow in the soil of *our* everyday living, not only what tradition has authorized as "safe." The value of organic God-talk is that, by its very nature, it has been cultivated in our own backyards and neighborhoods, the places where God is present with us as we discern how what we experience fits together with our confession of faith.

LATIN AMERICAN LIBERATION THEOLOGY AS ORGANIC THEOLOGY

In their introduction to liberation theology from Latin American, the Boff brothers explain that while "the term 'liberation theology' conjures up the names of its best-known exponents. . . . liberation theology is a cultural and ecclesial phenomenon by no means restricted to a few professional theologians." They add, "It is a way of thinking that embraces most of the membership of the church, especially in the Third World."[8] This last affirmation certainly resonates with MCC's commitment to global partnerships, antiracism work, and domestic legislative lobbying efforts, understanding that North Americans' view of the church must be shaped by the worldwide communion of Anabaptists through bodies like Mennonite World Conference.

Indeed, through partnerships with Latin American Anabaptists across the decades, North American Mennonites have continued to ask critical questions about where and how justice-oriented social analysis impacts peace theology. In addition to this resonance with a globalized ecclesiology, the three levels of theologizing within the church the Boffs describe using the metaphor of a tree help us "root" academic theological discourse and reflection in the church.

The three levels of theological reflection correspond to three modes or levels of discourse, practice, and method simultaneously at work in the church, namely, the popular, pastoral, and professional modes. Moving their model of church from the abstract to the metaphorical and analogical, the Boffs observe that "liberation theology could be compared to a tree." When I look at a tree, whether it is a sapling or hundreds of years old, I am amazed by both the complexity and simplicity of a tree's life. Roots, trunk, and branches all work together to maintain the health and integrity of this organism even as it provides food, shade, and shelter to other creatures in its ecosystem. One of the church's major responsibilities is to maintain the health and integrity of its witness to God's good news. By integrating popular, pastoral, and professional voices, experiences, and reflection the faith community takes steps to produce healthy, nourishing fruit as well as adequate shade and shelter for other parts of creation, evidence of the tree's strength and vigor.

The tree metaphor is not coincidental for the Boffs. Working with Antonio Gramsci's concept of the organic intellectual, the Boffs explain: "Those who see only professional theologians at work in [liberation theology] see only the branches of the tree. They fail to see the trunk . . . let alone the roots beneath the soil that hold the whole tree—trunk and branches—in place."[9] In other words, professional theologians who have committed to pursuing their scholarship within the liberationist tradition have also committed to being organically linked to the network of roots that nurtured them, thereby participating in a collective struggle to interpret and live out Christian faith and practices when confronted with sin and evil in the form of systemic, socio-economic inequality and oppression.[10]

It is not hard to see what liberation theology is when one starts at its roots—that is, by examining what the base communities do when they read the Bible and compare it with the oppression and long for liberation in their own lives. But this is just what professional liberation theology is doing: it is simply doing it in a more sophisticated way. On the middle level, pastoral theology uses a language and approach that draw on both the ground level (concreteness, communicability, etc.) and the scholarly level (critical, systematic analysis, and synthesis).[11]

While the three levels are easily distinguished based on the tasks, educational levels, and roles different individuals fill, the Boffs are quick to point out that integration happens at every level. Professionally trained theologians are still teaching Sunday school to elementary school-aged children. Business owners compose hymns and write prayers for their faith communities. Retirees take seminary classes. Or in the case of the World Community Cookbook series, a home economist and dietitian who took some seminary classes authored an integrated, comprehensive curriculum for responding theologically and ethically as the church to the world food crisis that broke open in the 1970s and continues to this day.[12]

DORIS JANZEN LONGACRE AS ORGANIC THEOLOGIAN: THE PRINCIPLES AND STANDARDS OF MORE-WITH-LESS

Like the integrating and collaborative approach of the liberationist model above, *More-with-Less Cookbook, Extending the Table,* and

Simply in Season gather together theological reflections from all three levels: root, trunk, and branches. Anabaptist organic theology, as we have created it communally through this trilogy, is less concerned with producing conventional fruit compared to the scholarly endeavors of professional, branch theologians like me. And yet, the people who have overseen the book projects that we often think of simply as cultural artifacts are women who have integrated "faith and reason" in ways that allow their particular educational and professional backgrounds to empower them to speak and feed their community as theologians and ethicists to all who would listen and eat. In being the catalyst for organic theological method, MCC has chosen to shape theology in a way that opens pathways for conversation and community building within and beyond MCC's constituency and supporting denominations. Doris Janzen Longacre has been one of the most powerful theological figures in blazing those trails, starting those conversations, naming those activities that connect us to each other, and inviting others to join us.

Longacre's baptism into the prophetic ministry of teaching her faith community about simple living and global food issues was a product of many factors. In addition to her roles as parent and spouse, trained as a dietitian, studied at seminary, and worked with MCC in Vietnam and Indonesia. In keeping with the uneasiness that prophecy can create, when the idea for this particular cookbook arose, so did deep ambivalence. Because MCC was not in the business of book publishing, it approached Herald Press, the publishing house of the Mennonite Church.

Project participants recall that Herald Press was somewhat reluctant to take on the publication because in its experience, cookbooks without a cake on the front did not sell. The *More-with-Less Cookbook* was most certainly *not* going to be a cookbook that featured cakes! Herald Press accordingly limited the number of first-run copies to 1,000. Despite concerns about book sales and profitability, MCC stood by its commission to respond to the world's food crisis and with Ken Hiebert's interpretation of MCC's logo using Swiss cheese, black-eyed peas, and wheat.[13] The "suggestions by Mennonites on how to eat better and consume less of the world's limited food resources" expanded like the yeast in a loaf of Honey Whole Wheat bread (see *More-with-Less Cookbook*, p. 57). This yeast-like expansion continued four years later, with Herald Press adding *Living More with Less* to the bookshelf, a supplementary volume to the cookbook containing simple living suggestions related to money, clothing, housekeeping, transportation, celebrations, recreation, and more. Taken together, the two volumes both reflected and spurred on simple living as a robust movement and expression of Christian faith.

Describing Mennonites as good cooks who also care about the world's hungry in the preface to *More-with-Less*, Longacre deftly recasts this cultural heritage in spiritual terms: "We are looking for ways to live more simply and joyfully, ways that grow out of our tradition but take their shape from living faith and the demands of our hungry world."[14] Part 1 of *Living More with Less* provides us with Longacre's biblical, theological, and ethical foundations for putting our new consciousness about the world into action. She outlines five principles or standards that guide our theological reflection:

1. Do justice;
2. Learn from the world community;
3. Cherish the natural order;
4. Nurture people;
5. Nonconform freely.[15]

While these principles seem obvious to many, the next question Longacre addressed added considerable complexity, asking how these theological norms become concrete action. When MCC asked its constituent households to eat and spend ten percent less on food resources than what North Americans were averaging, there was a response of "holy frustration": "'We want to use less,' they say. 'How do we begin? How do we maintain motivation in our affluent society?'"[16] This desire to turn away from rampant consumerism allowed Longacre to take an innovative approach to compiling the cookbook. As Mary Emma Showalter Eby, author of the beloved *Mennonite Community Cookbook,* observed in the introduction to *More-with-Less*: "This cookbook will appeal most to young homemakers whose lifestyles are more open to change, and whose desire for variety and creativity will lend enchantment for trying new recipes." She added: "Perhaps this is as it should be since they are most responsible for the food habits of the next generation."[17] Eby's observation is radical in the sense of "relating to the root." Beginning with the basic unit of our social fabric, the household, MCC called Mennonites—and many others—to live a connected life from our roots, through the trunk, and into our branches.

As she prepared the content of the cookbook and its companion, Longacre understood herself to be blending prophetic witness and pastoral concern for her neighbors around the world. The work of justice is an inescapable foundation of Christian faith, for when we do justice, we show that we love kindness and invite God's love to abide in us (Mic. 6:8; 1 John 3:17). Delivering a prophetic message to

North Americans, Longacre proclaimed that eating differently be-comes a political act, but she also stressed that such political acts bring rewards as well. In the spirit of invitation, she wrote,

> [C]onserving resources at home and taking on economic and political issues . . . are as inseparable as the yolk and white of a scrambled egg. It never works to say, "I'll stop using paper tow-els and driving a big car, but I won't take this world hunger thing past my own doorpost." Once an egg yolk breaks into the white, there's no way to remove every tiny gold fleck. Just so, once you walk into a supermarket or pull up to a gas pump, you are part of the economic and political sphere. Certainly your in-fluence is small. But whether you conserve or waste, it is real. *Many* people using or not using affects things in a *big* way. Gath-ering up the fragments of our waste—recycling, conserving, sharing—is a logical and authentic beginning. Such actions are the firstfruits of the harvest of justice. They are the promise of more to come.[18]

Page after page, Longacre focuses her readers' attention on the entire globe as a reminder that God does not live in North America. In this way, she locates Anabaptists' theological tree in a broader or-chard: ours is not the only faith community God cultivates so that it might bear good fruit. How do we "learn from the world commu-nity"? We can remember that affluence is not a form of intelligence or spiritual wisdom—having an abundance of financial resources does not make us wise. Citing Jesus' parable about the rich man and Lazarus, Longacre suggests that Lazarus acted as a missionary to the affluent, not the other way around. Responding to voices calling for liberation, Longacre stresses that "The best reason for listening to and learning from the poor is that this is one way God is revealed to us." She uses this organic theological insight to nourish our theological speech. "If we cannot learn from the poor [in our country and be-yond]," she implores, "why should we claim to follow one born in a barn and executed with thieves?"[19]

When we consider the meek and humble state of God's incarna-tion *and* God's awesome act of calling the cosmos into existence, we can see that God values nurture over exploitation, meaningfulness over meaninglessness. Asking how our actions bear out the hopes and desires we have for ourselves and our loved ones helps us nur-ture people. Longacre connects this care for one another with God's project of redemption that impacts all of creation. Isaiah 55 provides us with a vision of what the Earth will gain when we "eat what is good": The trees will clap their hands as the mountains and hills are alive with the sound of music. The covenant God makes with us is for all of creation: accordingly, we accept God's promises on behalf of the natural order. This means that we *represent* God's will and rule, not that we *are* God. Longacre's belief that we must reject notions of dominion over creation as sovereignty over creation led her to conclude that "faithful care of what actually belongs to God is the only biblical perspective," a claim which seems obvious today. But she wrote these words thirty years ago, before green had become a trendy color and before cherishing the natural order transformed into an imperative.

The fifth principle of *Living More with Less*—nonconform freely—brings Longacre into the thorny territory of a loaded theological concept, as she works to reclaim and perhaps redeem Paul's advice to the Roman church: "And be not conformed to this world: but be ye transformed by the renewing of your mind, that ye may prove what is that good, and acceptable, and perfect, will of God."[20] At the heart of nonconformity is the need for us Christians to avoid being defined by the priorities of broader culture that do not renew us or our communities. Longacre explains that nonconformity presents us with the option of a lifestyle based on simplicity and freedom compared to the enslaving forces of materialism and over-consumption: "simplicity is not restriction, sacrifice, or denial. It is emancipation. We are back to more with less."[21] From generation to generation, the external signs of nonconformity will look different because of the sociological shifts that take place in our lives. Regardless of our need to discern how we express our commitment to nonconformity, we will always need company: "If you head into unfamiliar woods, you had better find companions first; if you want to buck traffic, organize a convoy. To nonconform freely, we must strengthen each other."[22]

FROM THE ROOTS INTO THE BRANCHES

Organic theology that integrates justice, global consciousness, ecological awareness, nurture, and nonconformity has a great deal in common with Latin American liberation theology which always begins with the immediacy of context. To those who wonder where liberation theology is found, the Boffs write, "You will find it at the base. It is linked with a specific community and forms a vital part of it. Its service is in the theological enlightenment of the community on its pilgrim way." In this dynamic, the Boffs explain, liberation theologians are to be "vehicles of the Spirit" as they help their communities interpret God's good news in the face of society's oppressive systems and among its poorest people.[23] Longacre's interdisciplinary approach to theologizing clearly reflects this approach. As I have studied her work, I think the method and spirituality she articulates is truly prophetic and demands earnestness. Such earnestness can become wearisome even as it is necessary in the face of intensified cultural assimilation and economic patterns that are changing MCC's constituency. Even so, what Longacre began through organic theologizing with *More-with-Less Cookbook* and *Living More with Less* is still nourishing those of us who are her contemporaries, those of us who were raised with these values, and those of us whose introduction to Anabaptism came through the cookbook. As a series the cookbooks offer us a model for thinking critically about the alternative witness to and within culture that we can and do offer as Anabaptists. The theological resources within Longacre's, can, I contend, be discerned through a consideration of how one of her theological contemporaries, Duane Friesen, has carried forward her work.

Friesen's branch theologizing in this vein becomes another tool to help us consider how our Anabaptism might help us move more deeply into reading our context. While he is offering us an examination of culture and belief from the branches of the theological tree by using branch theologians like Yoder, Gordon Kaufman, and others, Friesen is clear that like Longacre, his vision of and for cultural engagement begins with cognitive dissonance at the root level.

> [T]heological reflection is generated and energized by the experience of deep conflicts that lie at the core of my being, tensions I find hard to put into words. . . . I am driven by a "fire in my bones" to be faithful to a vision of life that was passed on to me through my Mennonite heritage. This heritage passed on the conviction that at the center of the Christian life is the call to discipleship, the call to follow the way of Jesus Christ and to embody that way of life in an alternative community: the church. . . . I believe we need an orientation to life—a place to stand—that will make us an alien in our own country. At the same time we need to be aware of the relativity of that place where we stand that makes us no different than any of our fellow citizens.[24]

Both Friesen and Longacre respond to dissonant patterns that echo each other. They also find resolution in similar ways, demonstrating what Anabaptist organic theologizing looks like. For Friesen, we need to interpret the meaning of Christian faith in ways that connect the dots between biblical pacifism and public responsibility.[25]

Likewise, for Longacre the resource conservation she advocated is not an end in itself, based on scientific and sociological data. Instead, she claimed: "Our knowledge of others' needs and our guilt must resolve itself into a lasting attentiveness. This means being mindful, conscious, aware, so that never again can one make a decision about buying and using without thinking of the poor."[26] Both authors share a vision of community that is paying attention and responding to the world both in its brokenness and joy.

Using the language of "focal practices," Friesen describes how communities he has been part of have oriented their common life in accordance with God's *shalom*. "Focal practices," he explains, "are ways in which Christians embody or put into practice the virtues, those qualities of character that [identify] a Christian way of life." Interpreting this concept in organic terms, when such practices begin in the roots and their meaning and significance become more pronounced, trunk-level theologizing names these activities for the community, turning embedded habits into deliberate practices. In the branches, focal practices are theologized, further raising the community's consciousness about how its practices reflect identity and make meaning within broader culture.

Friesen calls for kinds of practices to our attention. First are "rituals of moral formation" such as baptism, communion, sabbath, prayer, and singing. Second, "process practices" that include dialogical discernment, reconciliation, and recognizing community members' gifts. Third are "pastoral care practices" that invite us to reflect on how our metaphorical view of community impacts our discipleship: household, body, sanctuary, healing balm, and so forth. Fourth, "practices of service to the wider community" involve our conception of the church's mission related to the world's needs at the macrolevel and hospitality at the micro-level, particularly by tending to both the symptoms of and larger structural dynamics that create injustice. No leap is required to connect the focal practices common among Anabaptist communities around moral formation, process, pastoral care, and service to the standards of *Living More-with-Less*.

BEARING GOOD ORGANIC
FRUIT MEANS IMPERFECTIONS

All of these practices speak with just as much evangelical spirit and fervor as a preacher at a tent revival. The experience of meeting fellow pilgrims whose spiritual autobiographies include the good news of simplicity and nonconformity as preached and interpreted by Longacre is not, many of us can attest, uncommon. Consider, for example, the testimony of David and Gail Heusinkveld about the transformative effect of the gospel according to *More-with-Less* on their lives:

> When Gail and I were in college together I was a religious stud-
> ies major, and part of those studies included church history. I
> found that the one group in church history I agreed with (or res-
> onated with) most was the Anabaptists. However I knew noth-
> ing of the Mennonite Church and assumed I needed to be like
> the Amish, horse and buggy and all that. . . .
>   After Gail and I were married a friend gave us a copy of the
> *More-with-Less Cookbook*. We liked the recipes, but most of all we
> were taken by the approach to life woven through the cook-
> book. It seemed to blend the way a Christian lives more com-
> pletely with what a Christian believes more completely and
> thoughtfully than anything we had seen before. Meals were one
> expression of Christian commitment, and we realized there
> were more ways of being Anabaptist than "horse and buggy."
> We decided to check out the Mennonite Church.
>   You should know we attended a Mennonite Church for a
> few years, then left because of the cultural barriers (we did not
> have a Mennonite name, we had no relatives who went to [Men-
> nonite colleges], etc.). It was not always easy, and only after
> some major life events did we return to the congregation and
> become members. You should also know that today you would
> find some convenience foods in our house, so the ideas in the
> *More-with-Less Cookbook* [are] not something we have been zeal-
> ous about. But we first entered the doors of a Mennonite Church
> because of the *More-with-Less Cookbook,* and we are still in the
> Mennonite Church in part because of how Mennonites connect
> faith and life.[27]

One of the things I appreciate about David's candor is the way he names the tensions between sociological dynamics surrounding ethnicity and culture, on the one hand, and theological-ethical projects of community formation, tensions which characterize every Men-
nonite faith community. In the closing sentence of his message, Heusinkveld does not use the pronoun "we" in conjunction with "Mennonites," indicating that the tension remains for him. Some of us flee the close(d)ness of ethnically bounded communities and congregations. Some of us recreate them in large cities. Some of us live in them as part of a commitment to "stay put."[28] Our awareness of the tension and how we respond to it are critical. Longacre calls us to

think of both our homes and tables as places where God is redeeming relationships because none of us is perfect.[29]

ONE COOKBOOK
BECOMES THREE: MORE THAN ONE EXPERT

A fight with cancer lasting just over three years ended Longacre's life in 1979. Evangelical theologian Ron Sider gratefully acknowledged Longacre's life and witness in his introduction to *Living More with Less*, the manuscript of which Longacre was working on when she died: "Doris deeply affected the lives of hundreds of thousands of people around the world with her widely influential *More-with-Less Cookbook*. *Living More with Less* is her last gift to the church, the poor, and the Lord she served." But, her husband Paul noted, just as Doris' manuscript was unfinished, so too is the work of simple living through responsible eating and living practices. He added, "The fact that others had to bring the book to completion is also symbolic. No one person is a final expert on the subject. We need help from each other."[30] I hear in his words a challenge and hope that all of us who identify with MCC share in the "More-with-Less" legacy. Indeed, Sider closes his introduction in a similar way: "May [*Living More with Less's*] powerful message stir us all to walk further along the path [Doris] carefully charted and joyfully trod." With the appearance of *Extending the Table*, which gathered together "recipes and stories in the spirit of *More-with-Less*" (1991), with "recipes that celebrate fresh, local foods in the spirit of *More-with-Less*" (2005), I feel certain that both the cookbook discourse and theological perspective on food that Longacre introduced into our faith communities is still at work as we continue to explore new pathways of understanding God more fully.

All three cookbooks work together theologically. As a series, the World Community Cookbooks operate with a set of very Anabaptist presuppositions about our theological identity as human beings. To be human means that we are able to recognize our own sinfulness in the way we neglect the deep connections among all life on the planet; accordingly, we have a responsibility to cherish the natural order. To be human also means that we have the chance to share in the triune God's promise of reconciliation which ends all enmity. Unlike other theological traditions that have shaped what we think of as mainline Christianity in North America, Anabaptism developed an understanding of our individual participation in the church that did not hold to a doctrine of original sin.[31] The Creator's grace works in our hearts as an agent of rebirth. As new men and women in Jesus Christ,

we are freed to live as his disciples. As new women and men, we testify to the Spirit's power as she leads us to discern how we live most
faithfully, freely, and simply as Christians when we are conscious of
the world as a community.

Our discerning attentiveness to the Spirit's movement through
"the priesthood of all believers" shakes up our complacency and
opens us beyond ourselves. It is why MCC's organizational identity
has steadily moved to an increasingly decentralized structure. It is
why the World Community Cookbooks are more than a collection of
recipes.

As Bailey-Dick helpfully points out, much Mennonite cookbook
discourse has a leveling effect compared to the academic discourse
that we often rely on to aid us in our interpretation and definition of
communal identity. He argues that "everyone has to eat and since
everyone has direct access to the forms and functions of Mennonite
cookery, a sort of 'kitchenhood of all believers' emerges in which all
those participating have the chance to become involved in the maintenance and renovation of boundaries vis-à-vis Mennonite culture
and theology."[32] Translated another way, our theological tradition as
North American Anabaptists lends itself to an organic approach to
dealing with basic questions about the meaning of Christian faith.
When we follow Longacre's lead and begin to understand ourselves
as vital parts of the church's work of proclaiming the good news
about the freedom that comes through socially engaged Christian
discipleship, we return to the root, the source of all life, and the
psalmist's affirmation: Everyone eats and so everyone has a place at
the welcome table to taste and see that God is good.[33]

FROM MORE-WITH-LESS
TO EXTENDING THE TABLE

Published in 1991, fifteen years after *More-with-Less*, *Extending
the Table* appeared as the sequel. This time, however, it was Herald
Press that approached MCC about collaborating on another cookbook. Joetta Handrich Schlabach served as project editor given her
background of a home economics degree, an MA in family economics
and management, an MCC voluntary service assignment with the
Food and Hunger Concerns Office in Akron, Pennsylvania, and a second MCC assignment in Nicaragua and Honduras. Having helped
MCC promote both *Living More with Less* and the action/study guide,
Schlabach was steeped in the questions and issues Longacre raised in
her work: eating lower on the food chain, paying attention to the

quantity of food we eat in North America, and simply using fewer resources to meet our dietary needs.

Schlabach noted that one of the criticisms of *More-with-Less* both then and now is that Longacre and the many contributors were being too preachy about simple living. But sometimes we need exhortatory sermons. I would also add that prophetic preaching, whether written or spoken, is a gift because regardless of how we receive its truth—by resisting mightily or experiencing conversion—the message changes us by working on our consciousness. Hardened hearts and righteous hearts sit side by side at church fellowship meals.

Encouraged by Herald Press's vision for an international cookbook, MCC developed the project in a way that maintained its commitment to all the standards of its predecessor but gave special attention to the second principle: learning from the world community. As voices from around the world shared their wisdom and experiences, a new message was also emerging for MCC. *Extending the Table*, Schlabach explained, became a way for MCC's constituents to better understand how, as North Americans, we are connected to the world community through MCC. Schlabach today notes that in our eagerness to share the resources we have with the poor, we have forgotten that the world is full of resources.[34]

By stressing the resources that exist among the world's peoples, Schlabach recasts the moral dimension of the practice of eating meals: Mealtime becomes a site of moral formation in which we North American Christians may open ourselves to connections with sisters and brothers around the globe.

> By reducing food to good, bad, fast, and affordable, people lose sight of the fact that food is first of all sacred—a precious gift of the earth to be enjoyed with others and shared by all. The intention of this book is to take us to the tables of people for whom food is the staff of life. This collection of recipes and stories invites us to sit with people we have never met, taste the flavors of their food, feel the warmth of their friendship, and learn from their experiences.[35]

The organic theology of *Extending the Table* begins with the book's title and intensifies through the storytelling that accompanies the recipes.

Over and over again, the practice of hospitality shines through in the stories of MCC workers and other contributors as they have experienced life in other cultures. Some of the most authentic expressions of hospitality are manifested in humility and simplicity. In this way, hospitality is markedly different from entertaining. When I read Longacre's caution that too quickly "serving guests becomes an ego trip, rather than a relaxed meeting of friends around that most common everyday experience of sharing food," I cry, "Amen!" in recognition of my own failing and admission that I have learned to confuse hospitality with entertaining from my mother even as we both aspire to keep things simple.

This is one of the reasons why Schlabach and her collaborators worked to keep *Extending the Table* from being a collection of international gourmet recipes. Simple living in a global sense is about sharing the food—its abundance and scarcity—of every day living throughout the world. In the third section of *Extending the Table*, Schlabach weaves together half-a-dozen stories about bread from the Hebrew Bible, the Christian Testament, modern-day Turkey, El Salvador, and the West Bank. Compared to these stories, "the bread aisles of modern supermarkets where factory-made bread likes in sterile wrap" are poor indeed! Are we North Americans ready and willing to relearn from our world community the deep and abiding truths of Christian faith through their bread-making practices and rituals, practices suffused with "the suffering of crushed grain, the hope of rising bread, and the liberation and reconciliation of broken bread shared with others"?[36] Again, Christian faith, through the practice of hospitality which is not reducible to entertaining comes into focus as eucharist, as the thanksgiving of table fellowship. The difference which prevents the collapse of hospitality into entertainment is in valuing what everyone around the table receives from God rather than providing others with the ultimate dining experience.

A NEW MORE-WITH-LESS
FOR A NEW GENERATION

Cathleen Hockman-Wert, co-editor of *Simply in Season* with Mary Beth Lind, takes a similar view of food and the spirituality of our eating practices. In a recent article titled "Preaching the Good News with Our Mouths Full," Hockman-Wert described herself as a food evangelist passionate about sharing the good news about basing our diet on "local, sustainably grown, and fairly traded food." This article also serves as a constructive theological statement that binds *Simply in Season* to *More-with-Less* and *Extending the Table.*[37] With her message focusing on food's spiritual significance and sacramental qualities, Hockman-Wert advances four theological claims about food:

1. Food is God's first gift to humans and other animals;

2. Food is a moral issue because not all foods are morally neutral;

3. Food is a gift for everyone throughout the world; and

4. Eating and shopping for food are spiritual disciplines.

Having also been morally formed by the standards and principles of Longacre's organic theology, Hockman-Wert's commitment to theological reflection about food inspired her involvement with the World Community Cookbook series, her desire to update *More-with-Less* to reflect the globalization of our North American eating practices. In the proposal that Hockman-Wert and Lind drafted for MCC, they explain their goals for *Simply in Season:*

> Our concept for a new book fits into the tradition established by *More-with-Less Cookbook* and *Extending the Table*: a tradition of gently, joyfully inviting people to understand the connections between the food on their tables and their global neighbors. Our focus builds on this tradition by also describing how our food choices impact our local neighbors and food security as well as the environment, drawing readers into economic justice and creation care issues already being discussed in MCC programs and publications.

Lind and Hockman-Wert described their target audience as MCC's constituency which has become incredibly diverse over the past several decades (moving far beyond Mennonites' Swiss, Dutch, and German ethnic lineages) as well as "anyone seeking meaning in their daily living." In speaking to this wide audience, the editors of *Simply in Season* had three goals:

1. to show the benefits of eating local, seasonal food and how eating this way promotes economic, environmental, communal, nutritional, and spiritual health;

2. to provide simple, tested, whole food recipes which help readers know how to use local, seasonal foods;

3. to offer hope, encouragement, and guidance to people seeking meaning in their lives [because] the choices we make about our food have spiritual implications as we rediscover our connections with God, with nature, and with those who produce our food.

While the editors were intent on keeping the practices related to simple living in view, they also sought to counter a message which ran through *More-with-Less* as an undercurrent, a message that sometimes equated inexpensiveness with moral superiority. We have to be cautious about this equation, Hockman-Wert explains:

> I felt that [*More-with-Less'*] emphasis on spending less could be

taken too far, putting people/myself into a "cheaper is always better" mindset, without looking at the bigger picture ... of why our food is so cheap and what that means for the environment and other people.

In this sense, *Simply in Season* is "a pendulum swing back the other direction, to invite people to consider spending more for some foods." She adds, "It's all still the same discussion of how our everyday actions reflect our values, in the particular time and place in which we live."[38]

This emphasis on what is local while being mindful of the global takes us back to the value of the homegrown. The trick is to remember that our North American backyards are not the only places where people are seeking faithful ways to understand the moral complexities of food and the life it nurtures. After all, Hockman-Wert points out, the main message of *More-with-Less* was for us to step and back and see our food in the larger context of God's world and our faith.

Used by permission of
Syracuse Cultural Workers

The depth of the community ethic at the heart of *More-with-Less Cookbook* and *Living More with Less* is part of what has made simple living in this mode a movement. Several years ago, as I was perusing a catalog from Syracuse Cultural Workers (SCW), a peace and justice publisher based in Syracuse, New York, I noticed the artwork and text of a poster entitled "Do Justice" and uttered an audible "Wow!" when I noticed the text was attributed to Doris Janzen Longacre. To see that the principles of doing justice, learning from the world community, cherishing the natural order, nurturing people, and nonconforming freely had caught the attention of a group of people beyond MCC's constituency both intrigued me and made me smile. Capturing the spirit of the *More-with-Less* mode of simple living in visual form, SCW's creative team reflected back to me the things my faith community has taught me to value reminding me of the revolutionary quality of this tradition of organic theologizing that I have inherited through Doris Janzen Longacre's work for MCC.

Intrigued by the poster, I contacted SCW's associate publisher Donna Tarbania to ask about how the poster had come about.[39] As SCW's Creative Team began discussing the ideas and images they wanted to offer the public, they found themselves mulling over globalization, food issues, the fair trade movement, questions about what justice looks like in both national and international settings, and living simply. Many book catalogs cross her desk, but from amongst all the titles, Longacre's books had caught Tarbania's attention.

SCW seeks to spread the message that despite the growth of multinational corporations, what really matters is the preservation of local communities; for Tarabania, this mission connected with how Mennonites have been theologizing the larger culture in which they find themselves. Tarbania noticed that Longacre's theological and cultural analysis had the depth and form that SCW was looking for. After all, Tarbania observes, if it is going to be more than a design aesthetic or fashion trend, simplicity needs an underlying purpose and ethic. In this way, the World Community Cookbooks are tools for shaping identity and even creating nonviolent social change. But more importantly, they are resources for cultivating theological reflection and spiritual wholeness in all kinds of communities. The question is, Are we as Anabaptists ready to use them that way on a broader scale?

Whatever answers we generate in response to this question, we must contend with the stereotypes and baggage each of us has about simple living as well as the need for self-critique of our communities. Some of us cringe at the sight of granola. Some of us have experienced the meanness of poverty. Some of us resent the meanness of our parents' frugality. Some of are frustrated by others' confusion of our choice for simplicity with a political agenda. Some of us do not want to be different from our neighbors. And yet we are all familiar with the stereotypes others have of us as Mennonites, Brethren, and Amish as "plain and simple folk" when the truth is today we are urban sophisticates and suburban "muppies." Students on our college campuses and in our high schools conform to fashion, technology, and other social trends. Just because you are Amish does not mean you are forbidden from having access to cell phones and fax machines. Placing the first editions of *More-with-Less Cookbook, Ex-*

tending the Table, and *Simply in Season* alongside each other and their redesigned versions tells the story of our communal transformation from what I shorthand as "rural simplicity" to "cosmopolitan simplicity," with a shift from basic earth tones to more vibrant colors. Even our MCC relief sales present us with layers of contradiction. Not only are we stuffing ourselves to feed others, but we are buying more things when MCC asks us to live with less. To raise money to support an organization that we celebrate for being cosmopolitan as it urges us to pay attention to globalization and international relations, we serve ourselves and our neighbors foods high on the food chain and steeped in ethnocentric nostalgia. We must ask ourselves yet another question: How do simplicity and sustainability translate into discipleship today, over thirty years after MCC invited us to embrace the freedom of simplicity and nonconformity as globally minded Christians?

Authentic Christian experience and discipleship are by definition organic and homegrown because they cannot be created in a lab, grown miles away, and then bought and consumed at bargain prices. As MCC's World Community Cookbooks remind us, it is a gift to be conscious of how what we eat, where we shop, the stories that accompany our food, allowing us to feast on the bread of life even as we butter a slice of Pilgrim's Bread. Need the recipe? See *More-with-Less,* page 58.

NOTES

1. Matthew Bailey-Dick, "The Kitchenhood of All Believers: A Journey into the Discourse of Mennonite Cookbooks," *The Mennonite Quarterly Review* 79/2 (April 2005): 153-178. See also Rebekah Trollinger, "Mennonite Cookbooks and the Pleasures of Habit," *The Mennonite Quarterly Review* 81/4 (October 2007): 531-47.

2. Doris Janzen Longacre, *Living More with Less* (Scottdale, Pa.: Herald Press, 1980); and Delores Histand Friesen, *Living More with Less: Study/Action Guide* (Scottdale, Pa.: Herald Press, 1981).

3. While I am sure it could be argued that Longacre's work was likely influenced by Yoder, considering that she had studied at Goshen Biblical Seminary after graduating from Goshen College in 1961, my point is that her work, in its practicality, simplicity, and spirituality had just as much, if not more, impact on those of us who were babes in arms as *The Politics of Jesus* began to appear on course syllabi and library shelves. Furthermore, arguably as many people, if not more, have come into the Mennonite fold via *More-with-Less* than via *The Politics of Jesus.* The two groundbreaking books can, of course, be viewed as complementary. For example, in the twenty-fifth anniversary edition of *More-with-Less,* June Mears Driedger explains that her entree into Anabaptism and Mennonitism came through both books. See Doris Janzen Lon-

gacre, *More-with-Less Cookbook* (Scottdale, Pa.: Herald Press, 2000), 199.

4. My affinity for *Extending the Table* comes from the two-fold introduction I had to the book. First, I have a vivid memory of a chapel presentation Joetta Handrich Schlabach made about the project while I was a student at Bethany Christian High School during the 1988-89 school year that left me with a sense that this was much more than a cookbook. Second, for several months my mother, a college friend of Doris Janzen Longacre and a *More-with-Less* fan, introduced dishes from the cookbook into our family's diet.

5. Doris Janzen Longacre, *More-with-Less Cookbook* (Scottdale, Pa.: Herald Press, 1998); Joetta Handrich Schlabach and Kristina Mast Burnett, *Extending the Table: A World Community Cookbook* (Scottdale, Pa.: Herald Press, 1991); and Mary Beth Lind and Cathleen Hockman-Wert, *Simply in Season: A World Community Cookbook* (Scottdale, Pa.: Herald Press, 2005).

6. While liberation theology led to a mighty sea change within Christian theology in its demand for practical and livable theology from the society's underside where Christians did not write dissertations because they were spending their days trying to meet their daily needs, it has also become a bit of a historical movement in light of both the dissolution of eastern European and Soviet-style-communism and the rise of Pentecostalism around the world.

7. Ada María Isasi-Diaz, *Mujerista Theology: A Theology for the Twenty-First Century* (Louisville, Ky.: Westminster John Knox Press, 1996), 66ff.; and Daniel H. Levine, *Popular Voices in Latin American Catholicism* (Princeton: Princeton University Press, 1992), 317.

8. Leonardo Boff and Clodovis Boff, *Introducing Liberation Theology*, trans. Paul Burns (Maryknoll, N.Y.: Orbis Books, 2006), 11.

9. Ibid., 14, 19.

10. Think of the forces of sin and oppression as diseases, fungi, or other pests that threaten the tree's life and well-being.

11. Boff and Boff, 14.

12. While terminology used by the UN and other humanitarian organizations has shifted from "food crisis" and "hunger" to "food security" and "food access," many of the issues remain the same.

13. My personal copy of *More-with-Less* indicates that by 1998 the cookbook had gone through forty-five printings, including six runs in 1979 alone. Herald Press data shows that the *More-with-Less Cookbook* has sold 865,000 copies. Levi Miller, e-mail message to author, July 23, 2009.

14. Longacre, *More-with-Less Cookbook*, 7.

15. Longacre, *Living More with Less*, 21ff. While Longacre described these "life standards" as her alternative way of speaking about "lifestyle," I am using the term *standard* interchangeably with *principle*. As Longacre writes, "Standard is a word that fits a way of life governed by more than fleeting taste. It is permanent and firm without being as tight as 'rules'" (16).

16. Longacre, *More-with-Less Cookbook*, 6.

17. Ibid., 9.

18. Longacre, *Living More with Less*, 26-27.

19. Ibid., 35.

20. Romans 12:2 (KJV).

21. Longacre, *Living More with Less*, 54.

22. Ibid., 55.

23. Boff and Boff, *Introducing Liberation Theology*, 19.

24. Duane K. Friesen, *Artists, Citizens, Philosophers: Seeking the Peace of the City—An Anabaptist Theology of Culture* (Scottdale, Pa.: Herald Press, 2000), 64-65. Beginning the process of theological reflection with cognitive dissonance is an age-old practice. The movement within theology for us to "own our context" invites theologians to name their dissonance. The term *cognitive dissonance* comes from Leon Festinger's work in psychology during the 1950s. The internal conflict we experience when something that challenges our view of reality that in turn moves us to find a place of resolution is how dissonance informs theological reflection. Greer Anne Wenh-In Ng, "Cognitive Dissonance," in *Dictionary of Feminist Theologies* , ed. Letty M. Russell and J. Shannon Clarkson (Louisville: Westminster John Knox Press, 1996), 49. We come face to face with the chasm between the way the world is and sense of what God intends for creation. The theological task that responds to this dissonance is two-fold: How do we explain why things are the way they are and then describe our vision for a better alternative?

25. Friesen, *Artists, Citizens, Philosophers*, 14.

26. Longacre, *Living More with Less*, 25-26.

27. David Heusinkveld, e-mail message to author, July 9, 2009.

28. This phrase comes from essayist Scott Russell Sanders' reflections on his choice to stand against societal trends related to mobility and put down roots and call a place and community home. See Scott Russell Sanders, *Staying Put: Making a Home in a Restless World* (Boston: Beacon Press, 1993).

29. Longacre, *Living More with Less*, 56.

30. Longacre, *Living More with Less*, 7, 11-12.

31. Specifically on this point Pilgram Marpeck contributed the notion of the counter-inheritance (*Gegenerb*). Marpeck did not believe that human beings lost their essential goodness when God expelled Adam and Eve from Eden. Rather, we have access to that goodness through redemption and our assurance of redemption is what constitutes this counter-inheritance which is in turn manifested by Christian love nurtured through discipleship (*Nachfolge*). This emphasis on recognizing sinfulness became the basis for Anabaptists' rejection of infant baptism. If original/human sin is not equated with our nature but with the self-conscious choice for evil rather than good, then redemption comes through baptism because baptism marks the choice to crucify sin and experience resurrection life in Christ. Given Marpeck's belief in *Gegenerb*, it is no surprise that he also disagreed with Protestant views of original sin and human nature that focused heavily on human depravity. While Anabaptists read the Bible in a way that readily accepted and acknowledged God's gifting human beings with free will, they could not accept the arguments for viewing human nature as inextricably bound to a defective will.

32. Bailey-Dick, "The Kitchenhood of All Believers," 163.

33. In another example of organic theologizing that resonates strongly with Longacre's work, June Alliman Yoder, Marlene Kropf, and Rebecca Slough build an Anabaptist paradigm of worship around the metaphor of meal preparation based in part on Psalm 34:8 in their book, *Preparing Sunday Dinner: A Collaborative Approach to Worship and Preaching* (Scottdale, Pa.: Herald Press, 2005).

34. Joetta Handrich Schlabach, interview by author, July 2, 2009.
35. Schlabach and Burnett, *Extending the Table*, 20. The writing-photogra-phy team of Faith D'Alusio and Peter Menzel have recently documented this continuing trend in their intriguing book that explores how families around the world spend their money on food: Peter Menzel and Faith D'Aluisio, *Hungry Planet: What the World Eats*, photo, Peter Menzel (Berkeley, Calif.: Ten Speed Press, 2005).
36. Schlabach and Burnett, *Extending the Table*, 45-46.
37. One noticeable difference between *Simply in Season* and its companions is the editors' choice to keep editorial commentary to a minimum with just a two-page preface limiting the organic theologizing to contributors' short sto-ries and reflections.
38. Cathleen Hockman-Wert, e-mail message to author, July 3, 2009.
39. Donna Tarbania, interview by author, June 24, 2009.

Chapter 13

A "Creative Tension": Mennonite Central Committee, Christian Peacemaker Teams, and the Justice Imperative, 1984-2006

PERRY BUSH

Following the Geneva Accords of 1954, hundreds of thousands of mostly Catholic Vietnamese civilians, fearing religious persecution from the new communist state in the north, began flooding into South Vietnam.[1] On a worldwide trip that summer, longtime MCC Executive Secretary Orie Miller found himself stranded in Saigon for four days and watched the crisis unfold from a ringside seat. "URGE MCC TEAM PROMPTEST POSSIBLE," Miller cabled MCC headquarters in Akron, Pennsylvania. "RELIEF NEEDS DESPERATE AND ACCUMULATING."[2] With the eager cooperation of officials from both U.S. foreign aid offices and the Vietnamese embassy, MCC began a longtime presence in Vietnam by quickly sending in a new team, led by a twenty-three-year-old Californian named Delbert Wiens, to "develop a consistently MCC pattern of service."[3] In line with the organizational culture of postwar MCC, this meant neutral service to stricken humanity, rendered simply—as a treasured phrase instructed—"in the name of Christ."[4]

However, within months of arriving in Vietnam, Wiens discovered that truly neutral service was impossible; the relief aid U.S. officials gave them to distribute primarily seemed to be for the purposes of political propaganda.[5] Do you really want us to cooperate with that agenda? he asked Akron. Miller hastened to reassure Wiens that "our workers since 1945, and in almost every country where we have located, have had to meet this in one way or another and come to what seemed right conclusions. . . ."[6]

As Miller, Wiens, and a host of other MCCers would discover, finding the "right conclusions" for this basic problem would become a good deal harder in the upcoming years. Through the 1950s and 1960s, for instance, MCC volunteers in Palestine obediently worked to demonstrate God's love through their organization's many aid programs. At the same time, they found themselves coming to identify with the Palestinian people they worked among, reacting emotionally and intellectually to the mass dispossession and deprivation experienced by Palestinian refugees prevented from returning to their homes, and questioning the appropriateness of traditional relief activities like clothing distribution.

Following the 1967 war, with the Israeli occupation of the West Bank and the Gaza Strip, such questioning would grow in volume and tenor among MCCers, as would their willingness to link peacemaking to a call for justice for their Palestinian partners.[7] Meanwhile, in Vietnam, the uncomfortable dilemma that Wiens had identified in 1955 only escalated in the ensuing years. Mennonite volunteers there discovered time and again that it was impossible to offer neutral service to the needy amid the inescapable pressures of a guerilla war. MCC's insistence that they continue to do so immersed scores of them in doubt, frustration, and deep personal moral confusion.[8]

Goshen College and Seminary graduate Gene Stoltzfus, for example, came to grips with the moral dilemmas of Vietnam in 1967 by publicly resigning his administrative position with International Voluntary Service there.[9] Afterward he returned home to organize against the war. To Stoltzfus, a central lesson of his Vietnam experience seemed quite clear. "In the context of war, injustice and oppression," he summarized later, "I felt that neutrality was morally suspect."[10]

In other words, in Palestine, Vietnam, and elsewhere, Mennonite service workers kept encountering what Mennonite theologian and

one-time Asia relief administrator J. Lawrence Burkholder identified
as the ambiguities of power. He argued that Mennonites had focused
on loving evildoers but had largely ignored the concept of justice, an
oversight which "had led to confusion as well as social apathy. It has
left Mennonites without a word to describe the vast majority of their
dealings with each other since justice is the basic norm of economic
life." It was time, Burkholder argued, for Mennonites to turn their attention to the pursuit of justice, for "love must take the form of justice
if it is to be effective."[11]

This was an agenda that especially seemed to draw the energies
of MCC in the post-1960s years. From the end of the Vietnam War
through the turn of the century, MCC would be further plunged into
an inescapable confrontation with the ambiguities of power that it
had first encountered in places like Vietnam and Palestine. Moreover,
these ambiguities would be a pushed on it in part by a new organization, Christian Peacemaker Teams (CPT).

In the end, partly through its developing relationship with CPT,
MCC would be transformed as an organization along the same lines
that its volunteers had been in Palestine, Vietnam, and elsewhere. No
longer could it imagine itself as a neutral balm for the wounds of war,
handing out a cup of cold water in the name of Christ without regard
to the underlying issues of justice.

"ISSUES OF JUSTICE ARE INTERTWINED WITH POSSIBILITIES FOR DEVELOPMENT"

The transformation of MCC and the birth of CPT would both
occur in a period of remarkably creative socio-political ferment
among North American Mennonites in the 1970s and 1980s. In these
years a fair number of Mennonites (not counting the Old Orders) had
begun to emerge from a complicated, half-century-long process of acculturation. This brought them face to face with the pain and injus-
tices of a burgeoning modern society which no longer lay outside the
borders of an isolated ethno-religious world.[12] By the later 1970s,
with the searing Mennonite experience in Vietnam having further
honed the urgency of such questions, rhetorically at least the major
Mennonite church bodies had begun to embrace radically new Mennonite positions on matters of justice and peacemaking. These were
stances that an older, traditional, two-kingdom theology which insisted on a firm distinction between Christ's kingdom, in which the
rule of nonresistant love held sway and the kingdom of the world
was marked by the rule of the sword, would have previously pro-

nounced anathema. For example, at a special joint meeting of the Mennonite and General Conference Mennonite Churches, in Bethlehem, Pennsylvania in 1983, delegates affirmed the legitimacy of nonviolent direct action against injustice.[13]

Meanwhile, Mennonite thinking on these and related issues was further developed and sharpened by an emerging new generation of activists who had come of age, politically, in the 1960s. Many of these were former MCC volunteers like Stoltzfus who had returned home determined to speak out publicly about the oppression they had witnessed overseas. Some threw themselves into organizing with church and secular activists on a variety of human rights and related campaigns, often in concert with agencies like Witness for Peace, one of a variety of newly emerging international justice groups created in these years as nonviolent means for resolving conflicts.[14] Within the Mennonite churches but for similar reasons, like-minded activists and academics like Ron Kraybill and John Paul Lederach worked at creating and institutionalizing new means of conflict mediation, efforts which resulted in groups like Mennonite Conciliation Service and International Conciliation Service.[15]

At the same time, a willingness to speak more proactively against injustice was reflected in the parallel plane of Mennonite development work. Beginning in the mid-1960s and continuing into the 1970s and 1980s, MCC volunteers rejected an older model of overseas service which portrayed MCC as volunteers, teachers, and givers while picturing local people as students and recipients. Instead, MCC asked its volunteers to function as learners from local people whom they accepted as true partners, a new relationship that stressed volunteers' fundamental accountability to host country needs and priorities.[16] As an influential 1994 evaluation of the Haiti program put it, "dignity is enhanced as host country persons become our teachers, supervisors and counselors. . . ."[17]

Accepting the agendas of local people meant that MCCers would focus on matters of justice. Longtime MCC Executive Secretary Ronald Mathies declared that MCCers were called to "an analysis of structures that are held responsible for the continuing destitution for the majority of the world's people." In so doing, they would engage in a kind of a "reverse mission" to change the policies of their own countries that had created such structures. Increasingly, these were activities which, according to Mathies, had "become deeply embedded in the mandate and program of MCC."[18]

In sum, as MCC's Latin American program administrator Linda Shelly phrased the fundamental lesson in 1994, "issues of justice are intertwined with possibilities for development."[19] Through the 1970s and 1980s, MCC programs the world over began to flesh out this recognition. In South Africa, for instance, volunteers made common cause with the growing anti-apartheid movement, led workshops in nonviolence, and periodically hid activists wanted by the police. In response, program directors Robert and Judy Zimmerman Herr were threatened with deportation by South African officials and Robert was once physically assaulted in the streets of Eastern Cape, probably as retaliation for this work.[20]

In Palestine in the 1970s and 1980s, MCC tried to work under the radar screen of the Israeli authorities so as to preserve the safety of its development programs. Yet it was also committed to working with its local Palestinian partners, partners who pressed MCC to speak out against the unjust practices of the Israeli military occupation. Gradually MCC raised the levels of its advocacy for a just peace in Israel/Palestine, and Israeli officials imposed a price. After country director Paul Quiring's 1977 testimony before the U.S. Congress on Israeli settlement expansion and incursions on Palestinian property rights, for instance, Israeli authorities labeled him "part of the PLO propaganda effort" and refused to renew his visa. Undaunted, MCC replaced Quiring with another volunteer with the same peacemaking portfolio. The work continued with such intensity that at one point, one official in Israeli Civil Administration threatened to "bring down" MCC.[21]

Likewise, MCC increasingly pressed the case for justice in Latin America (though, as with other international development groups, terribly belatedly), nurturing nonviolent resistance to the brutal dictatorships the U.S. had propped up throughout the continent.[22] As in Palestine, the organization preferred at times to push its advocacy from behind the scenes so as to not endanger its ongoing development programs. In Guatemala, MCC outsourced some of its confrontations by donating to Witness for Peace.[23]

Similarly, concerned about compromising the safety of its local partners in El Salvador, MCC funneled political information to "less-connected" groups, remembered one administrator, groups which "could speak out boldly and with less risk."[24] Instead of engaging in its own in-country activism, MCC encouraged returning volunteers to press the case for policy changes back home. MCC personnel on the ground struggled with the same dynamics that an earlier generation had faced in Vietnam. Even attending to simple human needs in the context of guerilla war, they discovered, took on inescapably political dimensions. But now, in Latin America, MCC responded more proactively, in 1985 launching a full program called the "Central American Peace Portfolio." This initiative placed an experienced peace worker, with a minimum of three years experience, in each MCC country in the region, where they threw themselves into conflict resolution efforts, nonviolence trainings, and other intentional aids to the ongoing regional peace process.[25]

In sum, by the mid-1980s, the Mennonite churches of Canada and the United States emerged from a long process of acculturation with a growing sense of responsibility for injustice, an obligation which began to be reflected in the on-the-ground actions of Mennonite development workers. About this time, however, a new group would emerge that would sharpen the dialogue about such matters within MCC and further push the edge of the development of Mennonite peacemaking—Christian Peacemaker Teams.

"WE MUST DO IT. WE WILL SCREW UP SOME-TIMES. THESE ARE EXPERIMENTS"

The origins of CPT have been laid out in intricate and voluminous detail elsewhere; only a brief summary is required here.[26] Following Ron Sider's monumental address at the 1984 Mennonite World Conference in Strasbourg, France, calling for the creation of a nonviolent peace intervention force, moderators of major American and Canadian Mennonite church bodies called on MCC's Peace Section to study the idea and bring back a proposal. The concept itself elicited immediate and widespread enthusiasm across the churches. Within months, over 6,000 people had written to request more information; by the eve of the initial organizing conference in the Chicago suburb of Techny, Illinois, in December, 1986, over 400 congregations had sent responses to MCC's initial study guide.[27]

Within MCC back channels, however, initial responses were more uncertain. The proposal produced "a lot of mixed feelings" at a September 1986 meeting of the MCC Executive Committee.[28] Privately, other MCC officials and volunteers thought the idea had potential but still harbored doubts. Longtime MCC hand Edgar Metzler, for instance, worried about the "strong sense of North American triumphalism" implicit in the CPT idea "that we can go to situations of international conflict and help provide an answer." MCC Canada officials Leona and Peter Penner found the proposal "somewhat patronizing and arrogant" for the same reason,[29] while the director of Canada's Mennonite Voluntary Service program articulated what became a standard critique of CPT, wondering if "combating (the) military with its own structural model (parachuting people into trouble spots) is the answer."[30]

So ambiguous were early MCC responses to the CPT proposal that, at a June 1988 meeting in Akron of senior MCC officials on the emerging new organization, Metzler reported to the CPT Steering Committee the group's consensus that "CPT likely will not and probably should not become an independent agency operating overseas."[31] But this, of course, is exactly what happened. The excitement grew at the Techny conference. Its atmosphere, remembered Paul Neufeld Weaver (who later served with both MCC and CPT) was "exciting, intense, expectant"; Stoltzfus recalled "vigorous" discussions.[32]

However, Stoltzfus, Carol Rose, and other activists could see the direction they were headed and actually held back a little. They were "careful not to push too hard," Stoltzfus said later, "because we knew we'd lose it all."[33] Instead, the activists got exactly what they wanted. An official CPT steering committee emerged from the meeting, with Stoltzfus hired as its coordinator (at first half-time) shortly afterward.[34] CPT was officially born, initially with legal existence under the Mennonite Church and with partial funding from MCC.[35]

For the first several years, the young group searched for direction, but some early convictions became foundational. Its guiding principles clearly established that it would be a "peacemaking body" which would "use only nonviolent methods grounded in an Anabaptist theology of the cross." In addition, CPT's founders declared they would not be "neutral on questions of injustice, poverty, hunger or oppression."[36] We would not be mediators in situations of injustice, longtime CPTer Art Gish said: "we stand on the side of whoever the gun is pointed at."[37] Propelled by such ideas, CPT emerged as an apt instrument to push the borders of a Mennonite peace witness which was clearly by then rejecting the stance of neutrality amid injustice. It would also be perfectly positioned to serve as a potent conversation partner for MCC.

The ongoing conversation between MCC and CPT surged and ebbed in various formats and venues through the mid-1990s. The intensity of the relationship seemed to peak in 1992 when, at the invitation of (then) MCC Peace Office heads Robert and Judy Zimmerman Herr, CPT Director Stoltzfus stopped by the agency's Akron, Pennsylvania, offices to meet with senior MCC officials in a long and evidently frank discussion. Stoltzfus acknowledged the potential for "chauvinism, nonviolent imperialism and triumphalism" in CPT's approach but still made the case for prophetic activism despite human frailties. "We must do it," he told MCC. "We will screw up sometimes. These are experiments."

MCC leaders like the Herrs and International Program Director Ray Brubacher agreed that "MCC does not want our caution to drain CPT's passionate energy," while also laying out a "disciplined, non-judgmental approach" to conflict, arguing that Christians were not called to be on any one side, but "on all sides, all the time." To Stoltzfus this smacked of a refusal to be "prophetic" ("which to him meant a refusal to be confrontational," the Herrs said later); altogether the CPT director was blunt in his critique of MCC as "valueless" and "lazy." "MCC," Stoltzfus said plainly, "has gone to seed."

That's not true, MCCers retorted. We do see the need to "confront the powers," but prefer to do it primarily in Canada and the United States, where "we know the rules" and "they are our own nation's powers rather than our host's." Major confrontations with the government of a host country could endanger MCC's ability to carry on development work. Since CPT did not plan to make the same long-term investment in various overseas locations, MCCers observed, it had less to lose when it "screws up."

It was an honest exchange of views but in other ways unhelpful; it seemed to leave a lasting residue in MCC. Staffers repeated Stoltzfus' tougher comments within MCC circles for some time afterward. As a result, the Herrs recalled, MCC Area Directors "did not go out to their way to engage CPT. . . . Opportunities were probably lost."[38]

In light of this growing distance between the two organizations, CPT's subsequent 1996 decision to incorporate and MCC's parallel decision to pursue legal separation seemed to follow as a matter of course. MCC largely ceased its funding of CPT about the same time.[39] The two organizations clearly proceeded from contrasting approaches to peacemaking, a point perfectly encapsulated in how MCC read CPT's decision to forgo work in the Sudan. In the mid-1990s, amid the context of the ongoing civil war in southern Sudan, the New Sudan Council of Churches—with which MCC had established a close working relationship—proposed a program in which international workers would accompany church leaders working in the region as a deterrent against their abduction by Sudanese government forces. MCC alerted CPT to this need and invited its participation.[40]

Stoltzfus recalls that CPT declined to get involved in Sudan simply because it was stretched thin and did not have the available personnel.[41] According to MCC officials, CPT refused to go to Sudan because CPT wanted to reserve the right to commit civil disobedience if it thought conditions there required it, regardless of the needs or wishes of the Sudanese church.[42] Because of this perception, the Sudanese churches withdrew their invitation to CPT. In other words, in MCC's mind, CPT would not operate in true accountability to local partners. Perhaps the real reason was a mixture of both perspectives.[43] Even so, at the same time Ray Brubacher recognized real potential for fruitful engagement, noting that "I think there is a healthy and creative tension between CPT and MCC."[44] Over the next fifteen years, that creative tension would be brought to boil as fulltime CPT workers finished their training and began heading out to the field.

"MCC IS MOVING IN THE DIRECTION OF CPT"

The first overseas setting for MCC-CPT interaction came in Haiti. Indicative, perhaps, of the potent cross-fertilization between the two organizations, much of the initial input for CPT's presence there came in 1988 from former Haiti MCCers, who gathered several times in Columbus, Ohio, to envision a CPT Haiti project. By 1993 CPT had sent several different peacemaker delegations to Haiti and had begun to lay the groundwork for its first long-term project.[45] Haiti certainly presented a compelling case for international intervention. Its unstable political situation—the military coup against newly elected President Aristide in 1990, with accompanying political repression and widespread human rights violations—rendered even basic development work profoundly difficult. In 1993 for example, ten years of MCC reforestation work was ruined in six months.[46]

While sometimes needing to evacuate key personnel back to the U.S., MCC steadfastly pushed on with its program, centered in a process called "animation," the development of Haitian community organizers.[47] A "model community development project," according to MCCer Paul Weaver, the animation program put a premium on working in close partnership with local people, bedrock MCC values which the 1994 Haiti program review reinforced with religious devotion.[48] Because of the intensifying political repression, the Haitian community organizers whom MCC had trained periodically needed to go into hiding, sometimes at the MCC guesthouse in Port-au-Prince.[49] Meanwhile, midway through 1993, CPT dispatched its first long-term volunteers to a seaside city with a reputation for violence called Jérémie. Without deep experience in the country (or even any Creole language capacity by most CPT volunteers) for contacts and logistical support, CPTers increasingly relied on MCC personnel, especially on MCCer Carla Bluntschli. Together with her husband Ron, Carla had served with MCC Haiti for nearly ten years, spoke Creole fluently, and had a deep grasp of conditions there, along with a genuine excitement for the mission of CPT.[50]

Because of their diverging philosophies and approaches, both organizations had taken pains to map out their relationship in Haiti before CPT even arrived. MCC Haiti country representative Gordon Zook readily agreed to provide a supportive role, though cautioning his superiors "that we need to keep it an arms-length relationship" because of CPT's "potential impact on our development work."[51] For his part, while clearly preserving CPT's freedom to do "something more gutsy than an MCC group can do during these volatile days," Stoltzfus conceded that MCC needed to "keep a distance" from CPT.[52] As CPT delegations arrived, Zook and other MCCers helped in their initial orientation to Haiti.[53]

Despite the careful preparations, however, the initial encounter of MCC and CPT in Haiti did not go well. When he arrived in Haiti as part CPT's first delegation, Paul Weaver found Zook "cool" and "cautious."[54] Carla Bluntschli's work became a particular flash point. Zook admired her intense and passionate devotion to the Haitian poor, but her political expression of it caused him problems. On her own, Carla organized a prayer vigil in front of the U.S. embassy on the one-year anniversary of the coup. This action stirred up criticism, she remembered later, from conservative missionaries and also from a visiting *New York Times* reporter.[55]

For his part, Zook saw such vigils as ineffective and misplaced, thinking instead that such protest was more appropriately expressed back home. As each arriving CPT delegation engaged in some kind of public vigil in Haiti, Zook passed word to all MCCers not to participate.[56] This directive reflected both the advice MCC had received from their Haitian partners, Bluntschli said,[57] and also longstanding MCC organizational culture with its distrust of in-country activism. CPTers arrived in Haiti "already knowing the problems and how to solve them," Zook told Akron, and seemed "more interested in confrontation than reconciliation."[58]

For their part, some CPTers distrusted Zook for several reasons, among them his minor administrative post with the U.S. Embassy.[59] Stoltzfus quietly admonished the CPT Haiti team for a careless press release which reinforced the misimpression "that we are knee-jerk leftists" and "loose cannons" which makes it "very hard to navigate in our church." Instead, he told them to just "cool off and then get on with the serious work of getting on with MCC."[60] Tensions eased when Carla Bluntschli finished her MCC term and stayed on in Haiti to do CPT logistical support, with partial funding from MCC.[61]

About the same time CPT closed down its efforts in Haiti, it cul-minated several years of delegation visits to Palestine by sending re-servists to begin what would become a long term presence there. CPTers encountered an MCC Palestine team with firmly established momentum in peacemaking, and the potential thus appeared for a fruitful relationship.

Things started off on a sour note in 1992 when a CPT delegation mounted a "peace walk" with some two hundred participants trying to march from Haifa to Jerusalem. This was apparently a moving event for the marchers, with much hymn-singing, sleeping outside in "shepherds' fields," and 113 of them arrested by Israeli authorities in a mass act of civil disobedience.[62] A CPT press release spoke of "warm welcomes extended" to the group of Palestinian families en route. But MCC's Middle East director presented a different picture. In actuality, he said, Palestinian families were aghast at what seemed to them the general "hippie" appearance and disturbing behavior of the marchers (men and women sleeping in close proximity outside on the ground). The reason they slept in shepherds' fields at all was because embarrassed local Palestinians, afraid they were carrying drugs, did not want them in their homes.[63]

In light of the vast cultural gaps that CPT would try to bridge in Palestine, as well as the evidently brewing tensions with MCC, it was surprising that the relationship between MCC and CPT unfolded with the warm collaboration it did. Already by 1993, MCCers had been pushing CPT to establish a team in Gaza.[64] Once CPT began its long-term presence with the arrival of an experienced team in He-bron in 1995, it quickly established a relationship with MCC which one volunteer there called "a healthy one and mutually beneficial." CPTers and MCCers regularly hosted visitors to each others' projects. CPTers came to the MCC office for their mail, while MCC helped CPT media interactions and performed other kinds of logistical support. They worshiped, socialized, and played card games together.[65]

More importantly, while MCC Country Representative Alain Epp Weaver at one point denied permission for two MCCers to en-gage in extensive nonviolent direct action with CPT, MCCers occa-sionally participated in nonviolent protests against Israeli military occupation.[66] Indeed, in an article Epp Weaver published in 2006, he referred to the two groups so interchangeably he seemed to conflate them.[67]

Back home, Daryl Byler and staffers with MCC's Washington Of-fice regularly arranged for congressional visits for returning CPTers. These were effective visits, he recalled, though the CPTers would at times "become a little more passionate and dramatic in their presentations." Byler recalled one instance when he took Art Gish to the office of an official at the U.S. State Department. Gish pulled some rubble from his pocket, set it on the official's desk, and told him, "These are the remains of the floor of a Palestinian home. . . . A few weeks ago I heard the laughter of children playing on this floor and then I heard their cry as the house was destroyed." In general, Byler reported, CPTers like Kathy Kern, Wendy Lehman, Rich Meyer, and others had a "broad understanding of the issues" and were not only passionate but carefully accurate.[68]

Several reasons explain the close MCC-CPT collaboration in Palestine. For one, CPT clearly had arrived in Palestine for the long term (as of this writing, they are still there), thus undermining any remaining stereotypes of arrogant Westerners parachuting into hotspots to bring peace. CPTers studied Arabic, absorbed local cultural mores, and in other ways learned from earlier mistakes (for instance, after the CPT Hebron team initially had women and men living in the same apartment, an affront to the religious sensibilities of the conservative Palestinian city, CPT later decided to separate women and men's living quarters).[69] In both Haiti and Hebron, Kern pointed out, "we expended much more emotional energy on cultural sensitivity issues than we ever did confronting violence."[70]

For its part, as MCC Palestine steadily expanded its peace advocacy, an internal transformation overtook many of its volunteers there. In the early 1970s, key MCC leaders in Palestine insisted on their volunteers taking a neutral position in the conflict between Israelis and Palestinians. Over the ensuing decades of work under military occupation, MCCers would find such a position morally untenable.[71] As their relationship deepened, noticed one MCC administrator, "CPT is moving in the direction of MCC, and MCC is moving in the direction of CPT."[72]

In the end the same kinds of collaborative relationships emerged between the two organizations in Mexico and Colombia, though not without a few rough patches, especially in Colombia. The prospects for smooth relations initially looked far slimmer in Mexico. By the time CPT delegations to the Chiapas region began arriving in 1995, MCC had been working elsewhere in Mexico for decades. In the mid-1990s MCC's program took shape around a variety of initiatives in health, education, and social services, and seemed especially centered on deepening relationships with the nearly dozen Mexican Mennonite churches and missions clustered primarily in Mexico City.[73] These churches were undergoing a deepened Anabaptist identity, a trend which MCC was especially eager to nourish (for example, as part of his MCC duties, Paul Weaver taught classes in peacemaking, service, and Anabaptist history at the Mennonite seminary in Mexico City). Still, many would have viewed many CPT activities with suspicion.[74]

In addition, MCC continued to nurture its delicate relationship with the conservative German-speaking Mennonite colonies in northern Mexico. Numbering about 50,000, these were the descendents of the migration of Old Colony Mennonites from Europe and Canada earlier in the century.[75] Still wedded to strict two-kingdom theological understandings, many of these German-speaking groups would have regarded anything faintly activist with alarm; it was "a stretch," Weaver said, for some of them to even relate to MCC. As CPT delegations arrived, Weaver remembered, MCC Country Director Dick Plett once informed the CPTers that they were not to use the word *Mennonite*. He also denied Weaver permission to assign a Bethel College (Kansas) student to work for a summer in Chiapas, where CPT was expanding its work.[76]

The potential for discord with MCC's partners in Mexico (and hence with MCC) also would have been exacerbated by the specific focus of CPT work in the country. Initially drawn to the Chiapas region by the expansion of Mexican military activity sparked by the Zapatista revolt (by the time CPT arrived, one reservist said, there was one soldier for every three civilians in the area), CPT had especially been horrified by the massacre of indigenous, nonviolent group called Las Abejas (or The Bees) by Mexican paramilitary groups at Acteal in late December 1997. Within eighteen months an increasing series of CPT delegations had culminated in the placement of a long-term team in Chiapas. The team threw itself into fasts, vigils, accompaniment, and other acts of solidarity with Las Abejas.[77] Weaver said CPT was "looking for confrontation," and found it in a challenge to Mexican immigration laws.[78]

CPT had arrived in Chiapas at the precise moment that the Mexican government, in an effort to intimidate outside groups flocking to Chiapas to support the Zapatista struggle, began to expel them for "interfering in the internal affairs of Mexico," in other words, for engaging in human rights work while on a tourist visa (the only visa CPTers and other international opponents of the government's military operations could legally acquire). Through this legal mechanism, in April 1997 Mexican authorities asked four members of a CPT delegation to leave the country, and then, in May, expelled a dozen Europeans.

When two members of CPT's long-term team were given expulsion orders, CPT decided to challenge this government policy by asking their supporters in Canada and the United States to flood local Mexican authorities with faxes. CPTers also refused to show their passports at military checkpoints.[79] In this manner, CPT's short-term interventions suddenly appeared an advantage rather than a liability. CPT could challenge immigration policies to the benefit of other international activist groups, and if its volunteers were expelled, they would not damage any deep ties to local people who had come to depend on them.[80] On the other hand, such confrontation conceivably entailed some risk to an organization that Mexican authorities might have connected to CPT, namely MCC. Within months, one source noted MCC's hesitation in even meeting with CPT because it "doesn't want workers to get kicked out."[81]

Given all the potential grounds for conflict, it was surprising that the relationship between the two organizations steadily deepened in Mexico once this initial crisis point had passed. Mexican immigration officials continued to issue citations to CPTers through 1999 but never did expel any CPT (or MCC) volunteers,[82] and tensions between MCC and CPT greatly eased.

New MCC Country Representatives arrived, Sara King and Marlin Yoder, who did not share in the German Colony Mennonites' instinctive fear of activism and were able to take a fresh look at CPT.[83] For instance, while "CPTers are seen as being a bit arrogant by some folks here," King wrote, after meeting with two of them, she found them "wonderful ambassadors in their listening skills and obvious care for all involved." In another letter asking CPT to be more careful to credit MCC in its press releases, she simply concluded by urging them to "Carry on with your good work!"[84]

Cooperative relationships were also forged by Paul Weaver, who has served as a CPT reservist and delegation leader from the time his MCC term ended in 1997, and also by a Mexican Mennonite named Eduardo "Lalo" Rodriguez. The one MCCer assigned to Chiapas, Rodriguez worked as a kind of "cultural broker," Weaver said, able to help CPT with logistical help and also interpret CPT work back to the Mexican Mennonite congregations.[85]

Much of the credit for closer CPT-MCC working relationships in Mexico was also due to decisions by CPTers to function, as MCC insisted, in partnership with local people. In 1999 MCC sponsored a tour of Chiapas by Mexican Mennonite pastors, some of whom returned to their congregations energized to involve their churches in sending supplies into Chiapas for relief.[86] CPTers regularly began visiting Mennonite congregations as they passed through Mexico City and cultivating relationships with Mexican Mennonite pastors, relationships which continued until CPT brought the Chiapas project to an end in 2001.[87] By that time, CPT concluded, the economic needs of people there had begun to outweigh the threat of violence. CPT's mandate, the agency reasoned, was to "get in the way" of violence, not to function as a development agency. Besides, it desperately needed Spanish-speaking reservists to head its expanding presence in Colombia.[88]

CPT came to Colombia because of an explicit invitation from the Colombian Mennonite Church.[89] The opening of the Colombia project seemed both a logical development—it would have been "irresponsible," Paul Weaver said, for CPT not to have gone to Colombia[90]—and one filled with tremendous potential for constructive nonviolent peacemaking in close conjunction with MCC. Like Haiti, Colombia was wracked by extensive and systemic violence, making it seem a promising venue for nonviolent reconciliation work. Warfare between a repressive government and leftist guerillas had raged there, on and off, since 1948; thousands of Colombians had been murdered by right-wing paramilitaries financed partly by the Colombian government and partly by drug money. In the late 1990s, as part of its war on the drug trade, the U.S. government began funneling over $1 billion in military aid to Colombia, money that, if anything, promised to intensify the violence.[91]

Yet, in contrast to Palestine, Haiti, Mexico, and nearly every other international situation where CPT had worked, Colombia offered a warmly supportive Mennonite church which for years had drunk deeply from the wells of prophetic Anabaptism. Beginning in the 1960s, Colombian Mennonites, aghast at the pervasive violence in their country, began to read Anabaptist history and apply it to their own context. Soon new leaders emerged, determined to orient the church along these lines, including attorney Ricardo Esquivia and Peter Stucky, a son of Mennonite missionaries. A product of a Mennonite boarding school, Esquivia had followed the revolutionary Colombian priest Camilo Torres during the 1960s. Twenty years later, Esquivia, by then an attorney, had decided that Anabaptism was profoundly revolutionary.

By the 1990s the Colombian Mennonite church, under the guidance of Esquivia, Stucky, and a host of others, initiated an array of activist Anabaptist ministries, ranging from peacebuilding programs in elementary schools, conflict mediation, nonviolence training workshops, human rights advocacy, and a legal campaign to win conscientious objector recognition from the Colombian government.[92] Because of this kind of Anabaptist profile in Colombia, MCC had not felt compelled to establish a program with personnel there until 2002, with strong support from the General Conference Commission on Overseas Mission. The church's vision and preparedness to respond in its context went beyond what MCC felt it could adequately support from a distance, and Colombian Mennonites were ready for MCC workers when MCC provided a volunteer named Bonnie Klassen to staff a new office in Bogotá.[93]

About the same time, the Colombian Mennonite Church invited CPT to send an exploratory team to the country to investigate sites for a long-term project. Several CPTers like Weaver and Richard Meyer carried private hopes for the agency's new project as the place, Weaver said, where MCC and CPT would "work more closely together."[94]

It was ironic, then, that in their first few years together in Colombia, the relationship between MCC and CPT was laden with tension. As in Haiti, the discord stemmed from the fundamental issues of CPT's degree of accountability to the local churches and also its willingness to push the edge of advocacy so far that it seemed to threaten MCC's ability to function. Tensions started with CPT's very entry into Colombia. The initial exploratory delegation visited three different locales, recalled Weaver (who was on the delegation), and recommended CPT begin work in one of them. Instead, CPT elected to put down roots in a fourth area, the city of Barrancabermeja and then later extended its activities up the nearby Opon River.[95]

The sites certainly seemed appropriate for CPT work. A hot, steamy oil-refining city about eight hours northwest of Bogota, Barrancabermeja had recently passed from control of guerillas to right-wing paramilitary groups intent on establishing control through intimidation and terror, with scores of local people abducted, tortured, and killed.[96] As CPTers headed up the Opon in long, motorized canoes, it would not be uncommon for them to come across the bodies of such victims, or body parts, floating in the water. On at least one occasion, CPTers accompanied a cadaver back to its grieving family.[97]

Long-term, Spanish-speaking CPT reservists plunged into the work with the same techniques of creative nonviolent intervention they had honed for years in Chiapas: public prayer vigils and fasts, networking with area human rights groups, extended conversations with soldiers at military checkpoints and paramilitary leaders to beg them to refrain from violence, and secret meetings with underground guerilla commanders where they pled for the same thing. They

loudly denounced paramilitaries, guerillas, and the Colombian government for human rights violations with such intensity to once trig-
ger a death threat from local paramilitaries.[98] Through such activities
CPTers saved local lives and modeled nonviolent intervention in dramatic and sacrificial ways, in a manner that angered Colombian officials but won praise from other observers, including MCC officials
back in Canada and the United States. Accompanying local refugees
back to their home communities seemed "an excellent use of CPT experience and time," wrote one with admiration.[99]

MCCers in Colombia, however, were less enamored. "The
Colombian mennonite church (sic) did not invite [CPT] or ask them
to work in Barranca," Klassen wrote home; "they actually asked
them not to work there," in part because there were no Mennonite
congregations in the area. CPTers did not regularly check in with
MCC when they passed through Bogotá; in one brief meeting with
her, Klassen recalled, Stoltzfus didn't seem as keen to listen as he was
to insist that "CPT needed to do whatever it saw best, regardless
what the Colombian Mennonite Church said."[100]

To an organization like MCC which stressed above all its accountability to local partners, the latter was the especially egregious
offense. It began to be accentuated by the complaints about CPT behavior that MCCers received from different Colombian Mennonites,
who seemed especially bothered by the way that CPTers did not adequately consult them about their activities and periodically disre-
garded security concerns.[101] CPTer actions may have been exemplars
of creative nonviolence, but some of them, both Klassen and Stoltzfus
knew, were patently illegal under Colombian law. The Colombian
government was certainly capable of acting in a high-handed manner, as it demonstrated in 2002 when it confiscated 2,700 school and
health kits Canadian and American Mennonites had sent, insisting
they represented a "black-market business deal."[102]

The tensions between MCC and CPT in Colombia suddenly escalated in late summer 2002, when several CPTers received expulsion
orders from the Colombian government; meanwhile, incoming
CPTers discovered they could not receive visas allowing them into
the country. This situation amounted to what Stoltzfus remembered
as a first-rate crisis for CPT. The few remaining CPTers worked themselves to near-exhaustion while CPT headquarters in Chicago, vow-
ing to keep the project going at all costs, searched for political levers
that could induce Colombian officials to lift the ban.[103]

Back in Bogotá, MCC's Klassen watched developments carefully.
So far, she wrote, Colombian officials seemed to be differentiating be-

tween CPT and other religious organizations.[104] Yet MCC knew this could change at any time, a point illustrated in August 2002, when the DAS, the Colombian secret security policy, called in Gustavo Angulo, the central administrator of the Colombian Mennonite Church, and demanded an account of all Mennonite-related activities in Colombia.[105] Suddenly here was a threat that seemed to validate MCC's central concern about CPT for the past dozen years. "What CPT does affects Mennonites in general," former MCC Latin American administrator Linda Shelly recognized.[106] Not just CPT but perhaps also MCC and other outside religious groups faced all kinds of potentially dire consequences: travel restrictions, no new visas for incoming volunteers, maybe even being asked to leave the country.[107]

In the end, none of the dire scenarios came to pass. Within a year CPT was able to obtain visas again through a volunteer service organization, and nothing came of the investigation. This change was due in part to CPT's ratcheting up of the political pressure back home (with much help from MCC's Washington Office)[108] and in part to a helpful conversation that the politically connected Esquivia was able to have with someone in the office of the Colombian vice-president.[109] In subsequent years, CPT cultivated an ever-deepening relationship with the Colombian Mennonite Church, to the extent of the local church helping in CPT orientations and a number of Colombians joining the CPT team. Perhaps in consequence, MCC and CPT relations in Colombia warmed as well.[110] Yet the entire episode illustrated that the potential remains for both conflict and collaboration between the two organizations.

"WE NEED EACH OTHER"

In 2006, in the wake of the long kidnapping of four CPT activists in Iraq and the tragic murder of Tom Fox, an executive with American Friends Service Committee wrote to MCC, wondering if MCC wanted to join with AFSC in approaching CPT with guidance as to the wisdom of placing its workers in dangerous situations. MCC officials caught the implicit condescension in the overture and would have none of it. "[W]e think it more helpful to engage CPT from the beginning as a mature organization that is an equal partner," Ed Martin wrote back.[111]

Perhaps that kind of perspective comes more naturally now to MCC than it had fifteen years earlier because the two organizations have grown much more alike. Certainly, as Robert and Judy Zimmerman Herr have observed, "as CPT matured" it became "more rooted in locations for the longer term . . . more responsive to the needs of local partners—and thus more like MCC."[112] Yet it should be clear from this study that the cross-fertilization worked the other way as well, a process which seems to have enriched both organizations, despite (and perhaps because of) their differences. "I've personally been grateful for these two complementary approaches that Mennonites take," MCC's Byler said. "Sometimes it seems to me that at MCC, we're too conservative and cautious and not wanting to rock the boat. Sometimes it feels to me that CPT maybe moves a little too quickly without getting enough information. But those are two ends that I think can be held in creative tension . . . we need each other."[113]

As Gene Stoltzfus pointed out, "a basic human need is peace."[114] The absence of conflict makes all other development work possible, a conviction MCC has acted on for decades. Yet especially in the past quarter century, MCC peace work has been increasingly accompanied by a willingness to press for justice for the victims of violence.[115] In concluding their survey of a half-century of MCC work in Palestine, Sonia and Alain Epp Weaver noted that MCCers there "found a studied neutrality impossible, realizing that a failure to speak out on behalf of the weaker party did not constitute neutrality but meant implicitly supporting the oppressive *status quo.*"[116] While MCC had already been moving this direction, it seems clear that this shift was partly also due to MCC's extended conversation with CPT.

NOTES

1. George Herring, *America's Longest War: The United States and Vietnam, 1950-1975* 2nd. ed. (Philadelphia: Temple University Press, 1986), 46; Stanley Karnow, *Vietnam: A History* (N.Y.: Viking Press, 1983), 222.

2. Orie O. Miller trip diary, June 2-September 10, 1954, 14; and Miller to Akron, August 17, 1954, both in MCC Correspondence, IX-6-3, "Miller, Orie O., Commissioner trip, 1954," Archives of the Mennonite Church, Goshen College, Goshen, Ind. (hereafter abbreviated as AMC).

3. William T. Snyder to Orie O. Miller, June 23, 1954 and July 21, 1954, both in MCC Correspondence, IX-6-3, "Miller, Orie O., Commissioner Trip, 1954," AMC. For a concise summary of these developments, see Luke S. Martin, "An Evaluation of a Generation of Mennonite Mission, Service and Peacemaking in Vietnam, 1954-1976," n.p., MCC/EMBMC, July, 1977, pp. 6-7; Wiens to Byler, November 11, 1954, MCC Correspondence, IX-6-3, "Wiens, Delbert," AMC; MCC Executive Meeting Minutes, "The 1955 Assignment and Planning," December 29-30, 1954, MCC Executive Meeting Minutes, IX-5-1, Box 3, AMC. For "consistently MCC pattern of service," see MCC Executive Meeting Minutes, "Memo of Understanding: Vietnam Unit," August 16, 1954, with Executive Committee minutes of September 23, 1954, MCC Executive Meeting Minutes, IX-5-1, Box 3, AMC.

4. So central was this phrasing to MCC self-identity that it became the title of the organization's first history. See John Unruh, *In the Name of Christ: A History of Mennonite Central Committee and its Service, 1920-1951* (Scottdale, Pa.: Herald Press, 1952).

5. Wiens to Byler, October 13, 1954, MCC Correspondence, IX-6-3, "Wiens, Delbert"; Wiens to Byler, November 25, December 28, 1954 and Feb. 5, 1955; and Wiens to Miller, Snyder, and Byler, March 30, 1955, all in MCC Correspondence, IX-6-3, "Indo-China Office, 1955," AMC.

6. Miller to Wiens, April 11, 1955, MCC Correspondence, IX-6-3, "Indo-China Office, 1955," AMC.

7. Alain Epp Weaver and Sonia K. Weaver, *Salt and Sign: Mennonite Central Committee in Palestine, 1949-1999* (Akron, Pa.: MCC, 1999), 77-87.

8. I developed these arguments in two overlapping articles: Perry Bush, "Vietnam and the Burden of Mennonite History," *The Conrad Grebel Review*, 17/2 (Spring 1999): 5-27; and Bush, "The Political Education of Vietnam Christian Service, 1954-1975," *Peace and Change*, 27/2 (April 2002): 198-224. For additional examples of the moral anguish induced by voluntary service in Vietnam, see the reflections by Mennonite Vietnam missionary James Metzler and longtime Vietnam MCCer Earl Martin: Metzler, "Vietnam: I Wouldn't Do It Again," in *Mission Focus: Current Issues*, ed. Wilbert Shenk (Scottdale, Pa.: Herald Press, 1980), 315-15, and Earl Martin, "Responses to Previous Issue," *The Conrad Grebel Review* 17/3 (Summer, 1999): 72-4.

9. For a good summary of IVS in Vietnam, with a particular focus on experiences of Mennonite volunteers like Gene Stoltzfus and Willie Meyers, see Paul A Rodell, "International Voluntary Services in Vietnam: War and the Birth of Activism, 1958-1967," *Peace and Change*, 27/2 (April 2002): 225-244.

10. Gene Stoltzfus, "Is Neutrality ever a Good Thing?" Sept. 25, 2008, in Stoltzfus' blog *PeaceProbe*, http://peaceprobe.wordpress.com/category/christian-peacemaker-teams/. Accessed June 24, 2009.

11. J. Lawrence Burkholder, "Autobiographical Reflections," in *The Limits of Perfection: A Conversation with J. Lawrence Burkholder*, ed. Rodney J. Sawatsky and Scott Holland (Waterloo, Ont.: Institute of Anabaptist-Mennonite Studies, Conrad Grebel College, 1993), 1-54, quoted 53.

12. This is a complex process that resists easy condensation here. I have unpacked it in *Two Kingdoms, Two Loyalties: Mennonite Pacifism in Modern America* (Baltimore: Johns Hopkins University Press, 1998), 90-220. Also see Leo Driedger and Donald Kraybill, *Mennonite Peacemaking: From Quietism to Activism* (Scottdale, Pa.: Herald Press, 1994), 53-59; and Paul Toews, *Mennonites in American Society: Modernity and the Persistence of Religious Community* (Scottdale, Pa.: Herald Press, 1996), 154-213, 238-66.

13. General Conference Mennonite Church and Mennonite Church General Assembly, *Justice and the Christian Witness*, (Newton, Kan.: Faith and Life Press, and Scottdale, Pa.: Mennonite Publishing House, 1985), 35-6.

14. Kathleen Kern, *In Harm's Way: A History of Christian Peacemaker Teams*, (Eugene, Ore.; Cascade Books, 2009), 3-4; Oral Interview, Perry Bush with Gene Stoltzfus, Bluffton, Oh., June 26, 2009. Stoltzfus also served as a volunteer with MCC in the Philippines for three years in the later 1970s. On the creation of Witness for Peace, Peace Brigades International, and a variety of nonviolent interposition groups, see Yeshua Moser-Puangsuwan and Thomas

330 A Table of Sharing

Weber, eds., *Nonviolent Intervention Across Borders: A Recurrent Vi*sion, (Honolulu, Hawai'i: Matsanuga Institute/University of Hawai'i Press, 2000).

15. Joseph Miller, "A History of Mennonite Conciliation Service, International Conciliation Service and Christian Peacemaker Teams," in *From the Ground Up: Mennonite Contributions to International Peacebuilding*, ed. Cynthia Sampson and John Paul Lederach (New York: Oxford University Press, 2000), 8-21.

16. Ronald J. R. Mathies, "Service as (Trans)formation: The Mennonite Central Committee as Educational Institution," *The Conrad Grebel Review* 13/2 (1995): 121-125.

17. Quoted in Mathies, "Service as (Trans)formation," 123. For the full program evaluation review, see "MCC-Haiti Program Review Team Report," Feb. 28-March 14, 1994, in MCC Executive Committee Minutes, April 1994, exhibits 16-17, Mennonite Central Committee Archives, Akron, Pa. (hereafter abbreviated MCCA).

18. Mathies, "Service as (Trans)formation," 126-32, quoted 126. Similarly, in these years, commented one MCCer working in Central America, he and his fellow volunteers learned that "doing community work could not be separated from the clear political and military realities of the region." See Mark Chupp, "Creating Space for Peace: The Central American Peace Portfolio," in Sampson and Lederach, *From the Ground Up*, 107.

19. Linda Shelly to Executive Committee Members, March 28, 1994, in MCC Executive Committee Minutes, April 1994, exhibits 16-17, MCCA.

20. Robert Herr and Judy Zimmer Herr, "Building Peace in South Africa: A Case Study of Mennonite Program," in Sampson and Lederach, *From the Ground Up*, 59-60, 63-76; personal email, Robert Herr and Judy Zimmerman Herr to Perry Bush, June 12, 2009, in author's possession.

21. Weaver and Weaver, *Salt and Sign*, 95-6, 103-108, quoted 106.

22. Gerald Schlabach, "Epilogue: More than One Task: North American Nonviolence and Latin American Liberation Struggle," in *Relentless Persistence: Nonviolent Action in Latin America*, ed. Gerald Schlabach and Philip McManus (Philadelphia: New Society Publishers, 1991), 255-57.

23. Linda Shelly to Gordon Zook, May 10, 1993, MCC Corr., microfilm roll 325, frame 1981, MCCA.

24. Linda Shelly to Gwen Groff and Ray Brubacher, Jan. 12, 1993, MCC Corr., microfilm roll 325, frame 2023, MCCA. "For the riskiest advocacy work," Shelly said, "I remember seeking out churches or new organizations that had no natural counterpart in El Salvador that would bear the repercussions . . . . It's one thing to take risks ourselves. It's quite another to put others at risk, unless it is by their choice"; personal email, Linda Shelly to Perry Bush, June 6, 2009, in author's possession.

25. Chupp, "Creating Space for Peace," in Sampson and Lederach, *From the Ground Up*, 104-108.

26. On the origins of CPT, see Kern, *In Harm's Way*, 1-11 and Miller, "A History of Mennonite Conciliation Service . . ." in Sampson and Lederach, *From the Ground Up*, 25-7.

27. Kern, *In Harm's Way*, 8; Miller, "A History of Mennonite Conciliation Service," 26. Likewise, in his summary of one set of responses from across the church, MCC Peace Section consultant Atlee Beechy reported "practically a

unanimous expression of enthusiasm for Sider's call . . . ." See Beechy, "Summary of 32 responses to the Sider Proposal," CPT Papers, IX-56, Box 1, file 9, AMC.

28. MCC Executive Committee Meeting Minutes, September, 1986, MCCA.

29. Edgar Metzler to Urbane Peachey, Jan. 20, 1986, CPT Papers, IX-56, box 1, file 9; Leona and Peter Penner to Christian Peacemaker Teams, July 14, 1986, CPT Papers, IX-56, box 1, file 2, AMC. For similar and other initial, thoughtful critiques, also see responses from Edgar Stoesz, July 24, 1986; Joetta Handrich Schlabach, Sept. 3, 1986; Paul Longacre, Sept. 27, 1986; and Joseph Liechty, Oct. 13, 1986, all in same file.

30. Joan Barkman to Edgar Metzler, Nov. 18, 1987, CPT Papers, IX-56, box 1, file 7, AMC. The critical phrase "parachuting people into trouble spots" (or some variant thereof) emerged into a standard put-down of CPT and it clearly rankled CPT people. Kern takes pains to rebut the charge (see Kathleen Kern, "From Haiti to Hebron with a Brief Stop in Washington, D.C.: The CPT Experiment," in Sampson and Lederach, *From the Ground Up*, 198). In my interview with him, Gene Stoltzfus referred to the phrase repeatedly, always holding up two fingers on each hand to accentuate the quotation marks; Stoltzfus interview, June 26, 2009.

31. Metzler to CPT Steering Committee, June 13, 1988, CPT Papers, IX-56, box 2, file 15, AMC.

32. Oral interview, Perry Bush with Paul Neufeld Weaver, May 19, 2009, notes in author's possession; Stoltzfus interview, June 26, 2009.

33. Stoltzfus interview with author, June 26, 2009.

34. Kern, *In Harm's Way*, 8-11; Steven Shenk, "Christian Peacemaker Teams approved in revised form," *Gospel Herald* (Jan. 6, 1987): 8-9. For another key document on the early emergence of CPT, see MCC's *Peace Section Newsletter* 17/4 (July-August, 1987).

35. Robert Herr to Monica Scheifele, April 12, 2006, MCC archive document, Http://nts1.mcc.org/filing/peaceofc.nsf/854bf79fce95d6085257465, MCCA.

36. Miller, "A History of Mennonite Conciliation Service," in Sampson and Lederach, *From the Ground Up*, 25; Kern, *In Harm's Way*, 5, CPT founding principles quoted 8-9.

37. Art Gish, *Hebron Journal: Stories of Nonviolent Peacemaking* (Scottdale, Pa.: Herald Press, 2001), 16. For a detailed analysis of CPT principles and theology, see James Satterwhite, "Christian Peacemaker Teams as an Alternative to 'Redemptive Violence,'" *Peace and Change* 31/2 (April 2006): 222-43.

38. Gwen Groff to Ray Brubacher, Sept. 25, 1992, "Subject: Overseas Dept. Meeting with Gene Stoltzfus, CPT Staff Person," MCC Corr. 1992, microfilm reel 309, frames 1619-1619, MCCA; Zimmerman Herr email to author, June 12, 2009. The quotes "chauvinism . . . triumphalism," "MCC does not want . . ." , "disciplined, nonjudgmental," and "they are our own nations'" were Groff's summary of the discussion; she placed the other quotes in quotation marks and were evidently direct transcriptions of the conversation. "MCC has gone to seed" and "not confrontational" are from Herr email, as is the data on the impact of Stoltzfus' remarks.

39. A number of considerations fed these decisions, which again came

from two differing perspectives. In MCC's thinking, since CPT was demonstrating a decreasing willingness to be accountable to either MCC or its partners in international settings, legal separation made sense as a means of reducing MCC's legal liability. On this see Berry Friesen to Brubacher, April 12, 1995; Groff to Brubacher at al, "MCC/CPT Relationship," May 16, 1996; and Groff to Stoltzfus, June 12, 1996, all in MCC Office archives, "CPT, 1996," MCCA. Stoltzfus merely said that there were other legal opinions available with different readings on the liability question, and he didn't know why MCC chose this one reading. CPT incorporated at this time because of a request by the Mennonite Board of Congregational Ministries, simply because CPT's budget was getting too large for them to adequately handle; Stoltzfus interview with author, June 26, 2009. After CPT incorporation, a MCC representative no longer sat on CPT's steering committee and instead MCC assumed the status of a CPT "liaison;" Robert Herr to Monica Scheifele, April 12, 2006.

40. Herr email to author, June 12, 2009; Robert Herr email to Linda Shelly, June 8, 2000, MCC archive document, http://nts1.mcc.org/filing/peaceofc.nsf/609747d42fbdbb852574465, MCCA.

41. Stoltzfus interview, June 26, 2009.

42. Herr email to author, June 12, 2009; Robert Herr to Shelly, June 8, 2000.

43. Judy Zimmerman Herr to Jan Jenner, Oct. 27, 1995, MCC Corr. 1995, microfilm roll 359, frame 1791, MCCA; Eric Olfert to Gwen Groff, March 29, 1995, MCC Corr. 1995, microfilm reel 359, frame 1381, MCCA. Judy Zimmerman Herr summarized the basic grounds for disagreement well: ". . . [I]t's more important to work on building up local peacemaking capacity than to train westerners to come into a situation to make peace," she told Jenner. "This has been the root of much of the on-going discussion between MCC and CPT and the source of some uneasiness on our part. Our other concern has been . . . that CPT is eager to remain only loosely connected to local churches, and reserve the possibility of acts of civil disobedience. From an MCC point of view, that looks like not taking the context of partnerships seriously. From CPT's viewpoint, I would guess that MCC looks compromised and unable to be prophetic. I think we do have some fundamental philosophical differences between MCC and CPT." Herr to Jenner, Oct. 27, 1995.

44. Ray Brubacher to Groff, Jan. 8, 1993, MCC Corr. 1993, microfilm reel 325, frame 2028, MCCA.

45. Ruth Stoltzfus Jost to Rich Sider, Dec. 19, 1988, CPT Papers, IX-56, box 2, file 15, AMC; Kern, *In Harm's Way*, 23-4.

46. Kern, *In Harm's Way*, 21-l2; Linda Shelly to Executive Committee members, March 28, 1994, in MCC Executive Committee Minutes, April 1994, exhibits 16-17, MCCA; MCC executive Committee meeting minutes, Sept. 1994, MCCA (on reforestation work). Besides, Stoltzfus, said, Haiti was suitable for CPT's first project because it was relatively close, a significant consideration for a young organization perennially strapped for cash; Stoltzfus interview, June 26, 2009.

47. Telephone interview, Perry Bush with Gordon Zook, June 15, 2009.

48. Barry G. Bartel, "Animation in Haiti: MCC Haiti's Experience with Rural Community Development," *MCC Occasional Paper* no. 8 (Feb. 1989): 1-5, 14-23; Weaver interview. As an example of the kind of values expressed by

the evaluation, consider just once sentence from the executive summary. "We recommend," the report read, "that MCC-Haiti partner with Haitian brothers and sisters to develop a spirituality that is personally transforming." See Review Team Report of MCC-Haiti: Executive Summary, p.1, in MCC Executive Committee Minutes, April 1994, exhibits 16-17, MCCA.

49. Telephone interview, Perry Bush with Ron and Carla Bluntschli, July 2, 2009.

50. Kern, *In Harm's Way*, 23-4, 30-2; Bluntschli interview; Zook interview; Carla Bluntschli, "Supplemental Report, December-April, 92-93," MCC Corr. 1993, reel 325, frame 1985, MCCA.

51. Gordon Zook to Rich Sider, Dec. 4, 1991, MCC Corr. 1991, microfilm reel 227, frame 2100, AMC; Zook to Linda Shelly, Dec. 30, 1992, MCC Corr. 1992, reel 325, frame 2030, MCCA.

52. "Transcript of a phone call with Gordon Zook, Gwen Groff, Rich Sider and Gene Stoltzfus," Dec. 4, 1991, MCC Corr. 1991, microfilm reel 227, frame 2098, AMC.

53. Zook interview.

54. Weaver interview.

55. Zook interview; Bluntschli interview.

56. Zook to Shelly, May 10, 1993, MCC Corr. 1993, reel 325, frame 1979, MCCA.

57. Bluntschli interview.

58. Zook to Shelly, May 10, 1993, and April 28, 1993, reel 325, frame 1982, MCCA; Zook interview.

59. Kern, *In Harm's Way*, 58-9.

60. Stoltzfus email to Carla Bluntschli, Joanne Epp and Ari Nicolas, May 8, 1996, CPT Papers, IX-56, box 7, file 9, AMC.

61. Bluntschli and Zook interviews; Groff to Stoltzfus, "MCC's contribution to Carla Bluntschli's work in Haiti," Aug. 6, 1993, MCC Corr. 1993, reel 325, frame 1956, MCCA. It is possible to overstate the importance of the tension between MCC and CPT in Haiti, particularly since some of it seemed to devolve merely from CPT run-ins with Zook. CPT and MCC worked in very different parts of the country and in actuality didn't encounter each other much. Moreover, in light of Haiti's poor transportation and communication network, the CPT team in Jérémie was thus a very long way away from Bluntschli in Port au Prince and communication access to Stoltzfus. CPT work was also hampered by the extreme poverty of most Haitians, which Kern admitted generally "poisoned" their relationships with locals. In light of these kinds of bigger problems, Stoltzfus said, dealing with MCC was a pretty minor issue; Zook interview; Kern, *In Harm's Way*, 64-6; Stoltzfus interview June 26, 2009.

62. "Peacewalkers Arrested at Green Line," CPT Press Release, June 8, 1992, MCC Corr. 1992, reel 309, frame 1646, MCCA.

63. Ed Epp to Groff, "Christian Peacemaker Teams Jerusalem Walk," Aug. 25, 1992, MCC Corr. 1992, reel 309, frames 1625-29.

64. John F. Lapp to Stoltzfus, April 16 and May 15, 1993, MCC Corr. 1993, reel 325, frames 1997 and 1978, MCCA. As it turned out, the CPT team had a short stay in Gaza, due primarily to personality conflicts among its members; see Kern, *In Harm's Way*, 499-505, especially 503.

65. Patricia Shelly email to Robert Herr, April 15, 1997, MCC archive document   Http://nts1.mcc.org/middleeastfiling/.nsf/6dcb07dd600457318 5256f2, MCCA ("a healthy one"); personal email, Alain Epp Weaver to Perry Bush, Feb. 26, 2009, in author's possession.

66. Epp Weaver to Rick Janzen, Nov. 6, 2005, MCC Archive Document Http://nts1.mcc.org/middleeastfiling/.nsf/6dcb07dd6004573185256f2, MCCA; Shelly to Herr, April 15, 1997; Epp Weaver email to Bush.

67. Alain Epp Weaver, "Mennonite Witness, U.S. Power, and the Palestinian-Israeli Conflict," in *Exiles in the Empire: Believers Church Perspectives on Politics*, ed. Nathan E. Yoder and Carole A. Scheppard (Kitchener, Ont.: Pandora Press, 2006), 123-24.

68. Oral interview, Perry Bush with J. Daryl Byler, April 2, 2009.

69. Alain Epp Weaver email to Dale and Gann Herman, Aug. 19, 2005, MCC Archive Document Http://nts1.mcc.org/middleeastfiling/.nsf/6dcb07dd6004573185256f2, MCCA; Kern, *In Harm's Way*, 224-25.

70. Kern, "From Haiti to Hebron," 197.

71. Weaver and Weaver, *Salt and Sign*, 92, 133.

72. Ed Stamm Miller to Groff, April 13, 1994, MCC Corr., "CPT," MCCA.

73. See, for example the Mexico sections of the 1994 and 1995 MCC *Workbooks*, MCCA.

74. Neufeld Weaver interview; Linda Shelly email to Tim S. Pannabecker, Sept. 15, 2001, MCC Archive Document, http://nts1.mcc.org/latinam /.nsf/d3d07ba790bc8d852574650, MCCA.

75. 1995 MCC *Workbook*; Weaver interview. For a description of the profoundly conservative, anti-modern orientation of the German Mexican colonies, see Royden Loewen, *Diaspora in the Countryside: Two Mennonite Communities and Mid-Twentieth Century Rural Disjuncture* (Urbana: University of Illinois Press, 2006), 110-16.

76. Neufeld Weaver interview.

77. William Payne, "People of Faith Occupy a Military Base," in *Getting in the Way: Stories from Christian Peacemaker Teams*, ed. Tricia Gates Brown (Scottdale, Pa.: Herald Press), 114-15; Kern, *In Harm's Way*, 229-238.

78. Neufeld Weaver interview. As the Mexico MCCer assigned as liaison to CPT (and also as someone with abundant sympathies for CPT), Weaver was well positioned to observe these dynamics.

79. Paul Neufeld Weaver, "Restoring the Balance: Peace Teams and Violence Reduction in Chiapas, Mexico" (Ph.D. Diss., University of St. Thomas, 2002), 125-127; Kern, *In Harm's Way*, 241-3.

80. Kern, *In Harm's Way*, 239.

81. No identifiable author (but clearly a CPTer), "November, 1997—Notes from conversation with Paul Weaver re: Mexican Mennonite Leaders," CPT Papers, IX-63, box 3, file 22, AMC.

82. Weaver, "Restoring the Balance," 128-9; Kern, *In Harm's Way*, 243-4.

83. Neufeld Weaver interview.

84. Sara King email to Kryss (Chupp), June 8, 2000, MCC Archive Document http://nts1.mcc.org/latinam/.nsf/d3d07ba790bc8d852574650, MCCA; and King email to CPTnet editor, June 7, 2000, MCC Corr., file titled "Chiapas—recent correspondence," MCCA.

85. Neufeld Weaver interview; Judy Zimmerman Herr to Robert Herr,

March 21, 2001, MCC Archive Document , http://nts1.mcc.org/latinam/.nsf/d3d07ba790bc8d852574650, MCCA.

86. Mexico section in 1999 MCC Workbook, MCCA; Sara King email to "J Mark and Kirk," April 26, 2001, MCC Archive Document, http://nts1.mcc.org/latinam/.nsf/d3d07ba790bc8d852574650, MCCA.

87. Judy Zimmerman Herr to Robert Herr, March 21, 2001.

88. Kern, *In Harm's Way*, 271.

89. Kern, *In Harm's Way*, 363.

90. Neufeld Weaver interview.

91. Kern, *In Harm's Way*, 361-63.

92. Ricardo Esquivia with Peter Stucky, "Building Peace from Below and Inside: The Mennonite Experience in Colombia," in Sampson and Lederach, *From the Ground Up*, 122-140.

93. 2000 MCC Workbook, 74; email, Bonnie Klassen to Perry Bush, May 19, 2009, in author's possession.

94. Robert Herr email to Linda Shelly, June 8, 2000 and Shelly to Daryl Yoder-Bontrager, June 7, 2000 ("work more closely together"), both in MCC Archive Document, http://nts1.mcc.org/latinam/.nsf/d3d07ba790bc8d852574650, MCCA.

95. Neufeld Weaver interview; Kern, *In Harm's Way*, 363-65.

96. Gene Stoltzfus, "Report on Colombia Trip, August 1-12, 2001, with Robert Herr email to Darryl Yoder-Bontrager, Aug. 16, 2001," MCC Archive Document, http://nts1.mcc.org/filing/peaceofc.nsf/609747d42fbdbb852574465, MCCA; telephone interview, Stoltzfus with Perry Bush, July 15, 2009, notes in author's possession.

97. Kern, *In Harm's Way*, 365-68, 386; Stoltzfus interview, July 16, 2009. Kern says that the Red Cross refused to take the bodies for fear that doing so would make them targets of paramilitary violence; Kern 368.

98. Kern, *In Harm's Way*, 374-383; Stoltzfus interview, July 16, 2009; Robert Holmes, "Dispatches from the Front," in Brown, ed, *Getting in the Way*, 135-157.

99. Yoder-Bontrager email to "The CPT Team in Colombia," March 27, 2001, MCC Archive Document http://nts1.mcc.org/latinam/.nsf/d3d07ba790bc8d852574650, MCCA.

100. Klassen email to Rachelle Schlabach, undated but with Raul Murcia email to Ron Flaming, March 11, 2003; Murcia email to Schlabach, Oct. 22, 2003, both in MCC Archive Document, http://nts1.mcc.org/latinam/.nsf/d3d07ba790bc8d852574650, MCCA; Klassen email to author.

101. Klassen email to author; Murcia email to Jon Rudy, May 27, 2003, MCC Archive Document, http://nts1.mcc.org/latinam/.nsf/d3d07ba790bc8d852574650, MCCA. Also see Klassen email to "Dear CPT Colombia," Aug. 30, 2002, same file.

Here, once again we are dealing with two different narratives; CPT's take on such accounts was so widely at odds with MCC's account that the two seemed to be operating on different planes of reality. It was *not* the case, Stoltzfus insisted, that CPT had heard a clear and direct no from the Colombian Mennonite Church about working in Barrancabermeja. It was contrary to the wishes of *some* Colombian Mennonites, he said, but others thought the area was a great place for CPT to work; so did the local organizations and

336 A Table of Sharing

human rights groups who had invited CPT there. Moreover, CPT regularly consulted, he said, with the Colombian Mennonite Church. Peter Stucky was an old friend of his from their days in seminary together, and Esquivia—"a very good man and very politically smart"—was likewise encouraging. "Once we settled in," Stoltzfus recalled, "he gave us one hundred percent support"; Stoltzfus interview, July 15, 2009.

The discrepancy between the two accounts may be simply due to the fact that Colombian Mennonites did not tell CPT everything they said to MCC, and also to the fact that the Colombian church itself was divided in their responses, with some leaders favorable to CPT and others less so. See Murcia email to Yoder-Bontrager, Sept. 3, 2002 and Murcia email to Robert Herr, Aug. 28, 2002, both in MCC Archive Document, http://nts1.mcc.org/latinam/.nsf/d3d07ba790bc8d852574650, MCCA.

102. Stoltzfus interview, July 15, 2009; Klassen email to author; "Colombia" entry in 2002-03 MCC Workbook, p.86.

103. Stoltzfus interview, July 15, 2009; Kern, In Harms's Way, 383-88.

104. Klassen email to Schlabach, March 4, 2003, MCC Archive Document Http://nts1.mcc.org/latinam/.nsf/d3d07ba790bc8d852574650, MCCA.

105. Murcia email to Flaming, Aug. 26, 2002, MCC Archive Document Http://nts1.mcc.org/latinam/.nsf/d3d07ba790bc8d852574650, MCCA.

106. Shelly email to author, June 8, 2009.

107. Murcia email to Zimmerman Herr, Aug. 15, 2003 and to Rudy, May 27, 2003, both in MCC Archive Document, http://nts1.mcc.org/latinam/.nsf/d3d07ba790bc8d852574650, MCCA.

108. Stoltzfus interview, July 15, 2009; Kern, In Harm's Way, 388.

109. Klassen email to supporters, Sept. 2, 2002 and Murcia email to Flaming, Sept. 3, 2002, both in MCC Archive Document, http://nts1.mcc.org/latinam/.nsf/d3d07ba790bc8d852574650, MCCA.

110. Stoltzfus interview, July 15, 2009; Kern, In Harm's Way, 413-15; Klassen email to author.

111. Bill Pierre email to Ed Martin, Feb. 9, 2006, Robert Herr to Martin, Feb. 16, 2006; also see Alain Epp Weaver email to "Colleagues," Feb. 10, 2006, all in MCC Archive Document, http://nts1.mcc.org/middleeastfiling/.nsf/6dcb0 7dd6004573185256f2, MCCA.

112. Herr email to author.

113. Byler interview.

114. Stoltzfus interview, July 15, 2009.

115. Nor was this a development confined simply to Mennonite agencies. Since the 1960s, one analyst summarized recently, American pacifists across the board have increasingly linked peacemaking with advocacy for justice. See Patricia Applebaum, Kingdom to Commune: Protestant Pacifist Culture between World War I and the Vietnam Era (Chapel Hill, N.C.: University of North Carolina Press, 2002), 211-12.

116. Weaver and Weaver, Salt and Sign, 133. Likewise, his years of work with a Nicaraguan peace commission brought home to MCCer Mark Chupp the central recognition that "neutrality is rarely possible and often not desirable in mediation." See Chupp, "Creating Space for Peace," in Sampson and Lederach, From the Ground Up, 119.

Part V

The Challenges of the Humanitarian Industry

Chapter 14

MCC's Development Paradigm(s)

ROBB DAVIS

In this chapter I explore whether or not MCC, in both its international and North American work, is guided by a single, coherent development paradigm, with my working assumption being that it is not. If this assumption proves sound, the question next becomes what multiple presuppositions do underlie MCC's work.

I begin by summarizing sociologist Vernon Jantzi's chronological account of the rise and fall of various development paradigms. While Jantzi's is not the only taxonomy of development theory, it provides a useful summary of historical trends within the so-called "development industry" and helps define critical assumptions that, implicitly or explicitly, drive development work carried out by bilateral and multilateral agencies and non-governmental organizations (NGO) alike. After this summary I proceed to analyze how these paradigms play out across the broader work of MCC, evaluating how Canadian and American constituents, support staff, and program staff as three distinct groups all arguably subscribe to differing development paradigms even as they all embrace the work of MCC. I then conclude with an examination of critical theological themes that should help MCC either critique or affirm elements of the development paradigms laid out by Jantzi.

DEVELOPMENT PARADIGMS

Jantzi summarizes four distinct paradigms that have driven international development work in the post-World War II period, all of which, it could be argued, continue in one form or another among "development industry" practitioners to this day.[1] Thus, while the four emerged more or less one after the other in the half century following the end of the war, elements of all can be found in current development practice.

The first paradigm in Jantzi's periodization of development approaches emerges from the assumptions of *modernization theory*. According to this paradigm, which dominated development thinking in the 1950s and 1960s, development is stifled because societies are unable to generate sufficient capital, either because of a lack of cultural "know-how" or because these societies are bound to "traditional" worldviews that lack a sufficient "future-focused" orientation. The problem facing underdeveloped societies is internal to those societies themselves and is solved through the "modernization" of those societies, a process aided through the transfer of technology (knowledge and physical resources) and values to the societies in question. External financial assistance is critical to solving the problem in this model.

In the 1970s the modernization approach gives way to what Jantzi labels the *growth with equity* paradigm. For true development to occur, the benefits of economic growth must be distributed more equitably among the most marginalized members of society (acknowledging that such marginalized groups may, in fact, make up the majority of the world's population). Providing access to marginalized groups requires decentralized programming and appropriate technology and service delivery. The development problem is internal to underdeveloped societies, consisting of an infrastructure unable to reach and benefit the poorest. External assistance to organize widely dispersed programs and engage marginalized groups in appropriate development activities is the key to addressing underdevelopment, growth with equity proponents insist. Technology transfer is still critical but must be made appropriate to the local situation and developed with a high degree of participation of poor people. Jantzi suggests that these first two paradigms are "assimilative" in nature in that they seek to assimilate economically underdeveloped nations into a global economic and social system.

The late 1970s and the 1980s, meanwhile, witnessed the rise of the *liberation from dependence* paradigm. Unlike the previous two paradigms that defined the problem of underdevelopment as internal to poor nations, this approach to development, originating in Latin America, sees the source of the problem as external to "underdeveloped" countries; poverty in the Global South, from this perspective, is a byproduct of international economic and political structures that subordinate local needs to those of wealthy "developed" nations, structures that also benefit the minority of elites who rule the poorer countries. The extractive and oppressing structures that keep people poor are a leftover of the colonial era and the world economic order is merely a neo-colonial structure. Development cannot occur within the structural constraints of this system.

For development to occur liberation from the dominant neo-liberal economic order is necessary and can only be accomplished through a broad raising of consciousness ("conscientization") among the marginalized themselves. As the poor organize to restructure their societies, they must also link arms with brothers and sisters around the world to bring about new international structures that are responsive to their needs rather than the needs of elites of all nations. Jantzi also refers to this paradigm—in contrast to the assimilative approaches as being transformative in nature, in that it seeks the fundamental transformation of oppressive structures.

The fall of the Soviet Union discredited Marxist-inspired approaches in the eyes of many and dealt a blow to liberation from dependency models of development. With the onset of a new wave of globalizing forces (certainly not a novel phenomenon, but one that gained impetus in the post "Cold War" era), issues of poverty and welfare have since the late 1980s been increasingly seen to be everyone's concern.

From the perspective of this *global interdependence* paradigm,[2] the problem is a world that is so connected that everyone's actions risk affecting everyone else—be it environmental degradation, global financial structures, food production, energy, or debt. The source of the development problem can be found in a lack of coordination at a global scale and the solution is greater concerted action, greater market integration, and a need to lay aside ideological differences. Recent examples of the application of this paradigm include the large "global health partnerships" (Roll Back Malaria, Stop TB, the Global Fund, Global Vaccine Initiative, etc.), recent FAO-sponsored food "summits," the Kyoto and Copenhagen climate meetings, G8 and now G20 meetings to discuss international financial regulation, the emergence of the WTO, and the list could go on.

Jantzi observes that each of these paradigms seeks to answer a series of questions about development: 1) What is the problem that impedes development? 2) Where is the source of the problem located—internally or externally? 3) What is the general solution to the problem? and 4) Where is the source of the solution located? Furthermore, each successive paradigm evolved, to some extent, Jantzi contends, because of the failures of previous paradigms to describe what was happening (or perhaps *not happening*) in the field of development.

OTHER PERSPECTIVES ON DEVELOPMENT

The above taxonomy can be rightly criticized for not including some important recent innovations in development thinking such as "rights-based development"; Amartya Sen's "freedoms" motif; macro-level, largely econometric analyses such as those done by Paul Collier; those that challenge the importance of "aid"—declaring it of limited value relative to the overwhelming importance of "trade"; and the entire body of literature known collectively as "post-development" theory.[3] Space does not permit a full analysis of these alternative perspectives but a few words are in order.

Rights-based development

Rights-based development (or rights-based approaches—RBA—to development) is less a new development paradigm and more a way of naming: a) the ends of development (grounded in customary and formal laws, treaties, and declarations at local, national, and international levels) and b) the obligations of various actors to assure that these ends are achieved. In one sense, RBA is a handle or lever by which change can be promoted. In reading various articulations of RBA one is struck by their simultaneous appeal to modernization, growth with equity, and liberation paradigms.[4] None of this is meant to disparage or downplay the importance of RBA to current development discourse but rather to point out that it can be articulated while accepting various elements of several of the development paradigms surveyed above. The same might be said of Sen's "freedoms" model, which might adopt the approaches implied by several of the above summarized paradigms to accomplish its ends.

Aid-versus-trade

Other macro-level and aid-versus-trade studies and debates stand more as critiques of how aid-based development is done as opposed to offering an alternative paradigm of development. Again, these critiques are useful and, in some ways (perhaps counter-intuitively) support certain notions implied in the liberation approaches—especially the liberationists' insistence that poverty and exclusion are often produced by factors (macro-regional and global) outside the context in which the poor live. Their prescriptions are not at all in line with liberation approaches but tend to be more consonant with the global interdependence paradigm in terms of their reliance on global economic integration.

Post-development views

While some post-development thinkers might describe their views as articulating a new development paradigm, most critics view post-development more as a broad and inclusive critique of "development" in general. A useful summary of post-development views and critiques is Adam Shanko's *A Taste of One's Own Medicine: Assessing Post-Development*. Shanko notes: "The 'post-development' scholars, as they came to be called, sought to uncover the ways in which the notion of development as proffered by the global North through its various agents was a means of domination over the economies, politics, and peoples of the global South." Post-development thinkers adopt postmodern language analysis (how "discourse" is used to "define" the world) and conclude, according to Shanko, that "A discourse can thus be understood as a regime through which the powerful define social relationships so as to justify the exercise of their power over others."[5]

While the post-development approach might seem similar to the "liberation" paradigm described above, it goes beyond liberation thinking to call into question the very idea of development, arguing that even the concept of poverty is a construct that is neither a natural given nor a cultural universal but was instead created to define the relationship between the powerful elites over those without power and to impose a system of domination and dependence. While critics of post-development focus on its inability to articulate alternatives, post-development ideas are useful in forcing those engaged in development to examine how their use of language conditions or defines actions and relationships.

The foregoing provides a taste of the many directions that development thinking has evolved over time. It does not, however, directly address three distinctive elements of MCC's work, namely, relief, peacebuilding, and advocacy. These aspects of MCC work can be linked to the dominant development paradigms in multiple ways.

Relief

While the concept of relief (punctual, largely unplanned-for aid given during times of crisis or in an ongoing manner to highly vulnerable populations) is not explicit in the four paradigms discussed above, one could argue that it follows assumptions embodied in the "modernization" or "equity" position. It is a pure transfer of "technology" (knowledge or goods), is external to the situation and, because relief does *not* question the underlying causes of the crisis in question, it by definition accepts internal causes of underdevelopment as largely given. It matters little that the causes are natural disaster or war: the lack of articulation of an appreciation for structural factors which may have led to or exacerbated the crisis exclude consideration of a liberation approach. Indeed, the existence of a "material resources" network across the North American MCC system that functions as a material transfer mechanism demonstrates a commitment to ongoing external transfer in the belief that such transfer will improve people's lives. Relief, then, is closely aligned to modernization or equity concepts.

Peacebuilding

Jantzi and Jantzi have argued that various peacebuilding "change theories" actually "fit" within one or more of the first three paradigms. MCC's peacebuilding work around the world adopts—explicitly or implicitly—nearly all the change theories they address. MCC's peacebuilding work is varied, with some of it based on technology-transfer assumptions, and still other peacebuilding work fitting more closely with liberationist approaches.

Advocacy

MCC engages in advocacy work in a variety of ways but most notably through its Washington, D.C., Ottawa, and New York (United Nations) offices. Jantzi and Jantzi suggest that advocacy is not consistent with the liberation perspective because it takes the existing power structures as a given, seeking to speak into them rather than fundamentally alter them. While this may be true to some extent, there are ways of approaching advocacy that focus on "enlarging the table" or changing the dynamics of who is permitted to speak into policy issues. Such approaches would seem to fit into the liberation paradigm.[6] I would argue that some of MCC's advocacy work is about this very thing: bringing excluded voices to the table. Further, much of MCC's advocacy work is driven by "solidarity commitments," which means that MCC speaks as partners urge or instruct it to speak. This too would seem to be the result of successful "conscientization" processes at work in MCC programs around the world.

HOW THE PARADIGMS PLAY OUT WITHIN MCC

In general, all of the first three paradigms can be found guiding the work of parts of MCC, depending on whom one talks to within the broader MCC world in Canada and the United States. Given its history and evolution, MCC only rarely engages in acts that would indicate acceptance of the global interdependence paradigm (periodic attendance at the international AIDS conference being the only example that comes to mind), and thus it will not be further considered here.

To understand who holds to which paradigms, I propose an analysis of MCC constituents, support staff, and program staff as three broadly defined groups that subscribe to differing views of what MCC's development (including relief) work is all about. Of course, these three categories of MCC stakeholders are not mutually exclusive. In some situations, for example, constituents may hold views similar to those of programs staff, especially when said constituents served previously within MCC programs. These three categories of MCC stakeholders should also not be taken as homogeneous but rather understood as representing "ideal types."

Constituents

MCC constituents are most likely to hold to either a modernization or an equity paradigm as they reflect on the development work of MCC. Many constituents identify deeply with the relief efforts of MCC, responding with cash donations and to material disasters such as the 2004 tsunami and the 2010 Haitian earthquake and regularly donating a wide array of material aid. MCC's relief work assumes many of the elements of the modernization or equity paradigms. Indeed, some MCC constituents articulate a "discomfort" with development approaches they perceive to be more in line with the liberation paradigm. One hears such discomfort in statements like: "we don't want to get involved in that 'peace' stuff." Such comments, I suggest, reflect less a negative judgment about MCC's peacebuilding work and more a critique of approaches that name and seek to deal with structural oppression, particularly when such approaches issue in advocacy against government entities or policies.

In this sense, most constituents adopt, in an uncritical way, modernization theory's assumptions that underdevelopment should be addressed via the transfer goods and know-how from the north to the south and that most problems of underdevelopment are due to internal problems (including corruption, lack of infrastructure, and lack of education) within underdeveloped nations. Additionally, most constituents would probably feel most comfortable with the assumptions of the equity paradigm and are content that MCC seeks out the "least" and the most marginalized. They would express satisfaction that MCC uses participatory approaches, builds capacity of local organizations, and engages in relationships with them to enable them to "develop themselves."

Program staff

Because program staff experience firsthand the complexity of poverty and the various forces that cause it, most of them adopt ways of viewing development that fall between the equity and liberation paradigm or somehow blend the two into a hybrid approach. Indeed, in some countries the equity paradigm would dominate and the focus would be on enhancing participation of marginalized groups in their own development projects, thus responding to the internally generated constraints to development. One could argue that most of MCC's work in Canada and the United States (perhaps with a few exceptions, including immigration, anti-racism, and First Nations work) follows the equity paradigm's assumptions.

In some places (and in relation to some programs like First Nations work) program staff might gravitate toward more of a liberation view as they focus on the externally determined constraints to development—especially the role of powerful nation-states (the United States in particular) and/or large corporate entities. In such cases program staff seek to foster local conscientization efforts and to link MCC's local work to international advocacy and public education efforts. Program staff holding to a liberation paradigm are likely to feel a certain amount of frustration about MCC's inability to speak truth to reticent constituents. Those program staff operating within the equity paradigm, meanwhile, are likely to find their work much more acceptable to the broader organization.

Support Staff

Since support staff (resource generation, human resources, communications) are the public face of MCC's programming to constituent stakeholders in Canada and the United States, they typically find themselves in a place of tension, especially when asked to articulate a vision for liberation-type activities. Indeed, most would feel a need to downplay efforts that are based on liberation assumptions and focus more on rallying support for relief and development efforts that conform more to either the modernization, or more likely, the equity paradigms.

While the foregoing is a very rough sketch of tendencies that exist within MCC, it should provide a useful starting point for considering which assumptions dominate across the organization as a whole. It is important to note that board members (across the various MCC offices) could hold to a variety of assumptions given that they are either constituents or former program staff. It is also critical to note that it is extremely rare that philosophical assumptions about development are even raised within MCC, be it at program, support staff, or constituent levels. Like many organizations of its size and complexity, MCC seeks to maintain a large "tent" under which various paradigms can fit and tries to avoid the messiness of dealing with the natural tensions that exist when differences begin to emerge.

THEOLOGICAL THEMES
OF IMPORTANCE TO MCC

To close this paper I turn briefly to a limited number of theological themes that could help MCC either critique or affirm elements of different development paradigms—or perhaps even move beyond them to consider its unique role as an Anabaptist agency.

Christology

Anabaptists articulate a historical understanding of the importance of the incarnation for faith and practice. Because Jesus' life and teaching provide a normative social ethic for Anabaptists, the idea of Christ's "emptying" and choosing a life of poverty and service provides a critical example for Anabaptists to emulate. The image of Christ as one who came to live in "solidarity" with a broken world is a critical motif in this ethic. Key concepts that illustrate this commitment would be simplicity, empathy (in distinction from sympathy), identification with the suffering of others, walking with the oppressed, taking the side of the downtrodden, and welcoming the stranger. Further, Jesus' mission statement in Luke 4 represents a vision for how the church is to live as it anticipates the coming reign of Christ.

MCC should ask which of the above-described development paradigms enables it most faithfully to model an incarnational way of being. What does this mean in terms of understanding and addressing the structural causes of poverty and exclusion? What does the incarnation imply about the "ends" of development: are "socio-economic" considerations sufficient? In what ways could MCC appropriate and more formally adopt Jesus' mission as its own?

Ecclesiology

Anabaptist theologian John Howard Yoder wrote in *The Christian Witness to the State* that the church bears the inner meaning of history.[7] In Yoder this idea was tightly linked to a consideration of the role of the state versus the role of the church in the world and he concluded that the church does *not* present an ideal social program to the state but rather acts as an ongoing corrective to the state using language the state itself has adopted (his "middle axioms") to challenge it to do what God has "ordered" it to do. In this conceptualization the church takes very seriously its dual identity of "aliens and strangers" and "ambassadors of reconciliation." In these roles the church models and lives the coming kingdom ethic and calls the powerful to fulfill their role as providing for security, peace and care for the least.

As MCC evaluates development approaches, it should ask questions such as these: Which of the development paradigms makes space for MCC to live the dual identity? Should MCC more explicitly articulate its own understanding of the role of the state and of the church's role vis-à-vis the state? If so, how might clarity on this point change the way MCC works in Canada, the United States, and abroad? How can MCC move beyond considerations of ecclesiology from a narrow focus on governance considerations (that it, representational issues related to who should sit on board) to a broader consideration of how its understanding of ecclesiology might help form or re-form the way it works?

Eschatology

Though there is great variety in Anabaptist understandings of the "end," most Anabaptists hold tightly to a vision of God's work as ultimately being about the reconciliation of all things to God. This view of the end implies not a destruction of earth, its cultures and social realities, but rather a transformation of them to accomplish God's purposes for the world. In this way Anabaptists see God as using the church to participate in what might be called the great unwinding of the Fall. Various scriptural images—swords into plowshares, the healing of the nations, each person under his/her fig tree, jubilee, etc.—paint a picture of a collective future reality into which the church is invited to live today.

Which of the development paradigms best enables MCC to live into this vision of our collective future? Is it possible to use the visions of the kingdom to articulate a vision for ministry in the present? Given the idea that the kingdom functions as yeast does, working its way through a lump of dough, how should MCC think about results, scale, and impact?

The "Powers"

Anabaptists have been at the forefront of rediscovering and re-articulating a theology of the "powers."[8] In these (and other non-Anabaptist) writings on the powers one finds the idea that the powers—ordained for good, fallen, and in need of redemption—are embodied in states, institutions, and ideologies that enslave and dehumanize people created in God's image. This consideration of the powers leads to a recognition that the local, national, and international institutions that *should* serve the needs of the least of these find their purpose diverted and distorted in a way that leads them to participate in the oppression of the most vulnerable members of society. The church's role is to expose the powers for what they are and to work for their redemption so that they might fulfill the role that God intended them to play.

To what extent do various development paradigms acknowledge the role of oppressive power structures in perpetuating poverty and exclusion? What would it mean for MCC to "expose" the "deeds of darkness" of the powers? How might MCC better articulate its own understanding of the role of fallen powers in oppressing, marginalizing, and dehumanizing people created in God's image? What might such an understanding mean for the creation of deeper spiritual disciplines within MCC's work?

Evangelism

While many people in MCC would say that MCC is not an evangelistic organization—indeed many would not support MCC if they felt it was—their discomfort with the term is less about its true meaning and more about what it has come to mean in the contemporary Canadian and American contexts. The gospel is simply the announcement of good news, the good news of the reign of Christ. Evangelism is the announcement, in word and deed, of the reconciliation of all things, the restoration of God's "good" earth, and the reconciliation of broken relationships. This "good news" is possible because of the victorious Christ who overcame death, revealing the domination system's "justice" as unjust and oppressive.

Which of the development paradigms make space for the announcement of the good news of the change that God is bringing to
the world? Should MCC spend more time re-articulating the meaning of evangelism and then "owning" the moniker of being "an evangelistic organization?" What would it mean for MCC to see itself as
"an announcer of the good news of the reign of Christ?"

Pneumatology

Christ said that his followers would do greater things than he did
because he was going to the Father. He added that he was sending a
comforter—the Spirit of God—who would lead his church to truth
and bestow gifts on the church so it might bless the world. The early
church was overwhelmed by the power of God's Spirit, and it was
clear to everyone that what was happening was *not* the result of
human power but the outcome of the Spirit's work in and through a
band of (mostly) weak and unremarkable people.

In terms of "results," "outcomes," and "impacts," what would it
mean for MCC to articulate a commitment that acknowledges that results are God's work? How can MCC avoid communicating a sense
of complacency or lack of rigor as it articulates this acknowledgment
that the results of its work are ultimately attributable to God? What
would it mean for MCC to be "weak" so that God's power might be
manifest through it?

A FINAL QUESTION (OR TWO)

The foregoing discussion of development paradigms and how
they play out within MCC was developed under the overarching assumption that "development" is largely an economic question. Indeed, all the paradigms assume that underdevelopment (whatever
its cause) is essentially about a scarcity of goods and services considered important for the full realization of human potential. Another
way to say this is that the overarching assumption in all of the paradigms is that the poor and oppressed experience a "deficit" while
those in the global north live with an "excess." As Paul Farmer has
said of the broader development project of which MCC is a part: We
must move resources down a gradient of inequality from those who
have to those who do not. Jeffrey Sachs would concur.

And yet . . . this view of development sees it as, essentially, a
"one-way street." "We" have what the rest of the world needs and it
is incumbent upon us to assure they get it. But is this really so? Is "development" really about (even mostly about) economics? Is there re-

ally only *one* gradient of inequality? While it is true that better health-care, clean water, and transparent governance structures are impor-tant to enabling people to experience the kind of life that God in-tended, are they (and the other typical development priorities) *all* that matter? Are there other "poverties" and "oppressions" more common in the Global North that are not named in the typical dis-course on development?

These questions, perhaps, lead us back to some of the critiques of post-development theorists. But more than that they lead us back to our own understanding of the fallenness and brokenness of all peo-ple and the realization that there are multiple "lacks," failures, and deficits, many of which are not the object of development work. Until the Global North recognizes its own poverties of violence, anomie, social disintegration, and overconsumption (to name only a few), one must wonder how well it can ever be equipped to engage in activities of "development" elsewhere. One can hope that MCC will develop its own paradigm of development taking into account the bi-direc-tional nature of the "gradients of inequality" and that it will use its considerable resources to create relationships of mutual aid, account-ability, and liberation for a global church.

NOTES

1. See Vernon Jantzi, "Helping Developing Nations: Socio-Political Para-digms of Development," in *Christian Perspectives on Social Problems*, ed. Charles P. Desanto, et al. (Indianapolis, Ind.: Wesley Press, 1990), 60-79. Jantzi's taxonomy can also be found in R. A. Yoder, Calvin W. Redekop, and Vernon E. Jantzi, *Development to a Different Drummer: Anabaptist/Mennonite Experiences and Perspectives* (Intercourse, Pa., Good Books, 2004) and is up-dated in Terrence L. and Vernon E. Jantzi, "Development Paradigms and Peacebuilding Theories of Change: Analysing Embedded Assumptions in Development and Peacebuilding," *Journal of Peacebuilding and Development* 5/1 (2009): 65-80.

2. Jantzi has more recently moved away from this global interdependence as a separate paradigm, preferring instead examine how those operating within any of the first three paradigms are using the effects of globalization to advance their development approach. Thus, for example, we see even those who operate under the liberation from dependency paradigm developing global "people to people" networks—e.g. Via Campesina or "demobilized soldier" networks.

3. For Sen, see especially *Development as Freedom* (New York: Anchor, 2000). Collier's best-known work is *The Bottom Billion: Why the Poorest Coun-tries are Failing and What Can be Done About It* (New York: Oxford University Press, 2008). For critiques of aid efficacy, see Dambisa Moyo, *Dead Aid: Why Aid Is Not Working and How There Is a Better Way for Africa* (New York: Farrar, Strauss, and Giroux, 2010) and William Easterly, *The White Man's Burden: Why*

the West's Efforts to Aid the Rest Have Done So Much Ill and So Little Good (New York: Penguin, 2007).

4. For an excellent example of this from a faith-based perspective see *Rights-Based Development from a Faith-Based Perspective* by the "Rights and Development Group" (Bread for the World, Christian Aid, Church of Sweden, DanChurchAid, EED, ICCO, Norwegian Church Aid, and Lutheran World Federation).

5. See Shanko, *A Taste of One's Own Medicine*, 2-3. Available online at http://www.allacademic.com//meta/p_mla_apa_research_citation/0/9/8/0/9/pages98090/p98090-1.php.

6. See, in particular, L. VeneKlasen, V. L. Miller, et al., *A New Weave of Power, People, and Politics: The Action Guide for Advocacy and Citizen Participation* (Bourton-on-Dunsmore, Warwickshire, UK, Practical Action Pub., 2007) and G. Gordon, *Advocacy Toolkit: Understanding Advocacy.* (Teddington, UK: Tearfund, 2002).

7. John Howard Yoder, *The Christian Witness to the State* (Newton, Kan.: Faith and Life Press, 1964).

8. See especially *Transforming the Powers: Peace, Justice and the Domination System*, by Ray Gingerich and Ted Grimsrud (Minneapolis: Fortress, 2006) and Chapter 8 of John Howard Yoder's *The Politics of Jesus: Vicit Agnus Noster*, 2nd. ed. (Grand Rapids, Mich.: Wm. B. Eerdmans, 1994).

Chapter 15

Relationships, Rights, and "Relief": Ninety Years of MCC's Integrated Response to Humanitarian Crises

WILLIAM REIMER AND BRUCE N. GUENTHER

Every night one billion people—one-sixth of the world's population—go to bed hungry.[1] Due to high food prices and impacts of global recession, the number of undernourished has risen to 850 million. The Millennium Development Goal of halving the level of undernourishment by 2015 to 420 million seems increasingly out of reach. Furthermore, climate change is increasing the number of persons affected by disasters as a result of an increase in the intensity and frequency of natural hazards, including drought, flooding, and storm surges.[2] An estimated 250 million people are currently affected by climate-related hazards in a typical year; this number could grow by fifty percent to an estimated 375 million a year by 2015.[3] The Stern Report on the economic costs of climate change, meanwhile, estimates that up to 500 million could be displaced by climate-related disasters by 2050.[4]

At the same time, however, the number of persons affected by conflict over the course of the last few decades has dropped dramatically. The number of armed conflicts has declined globally by more than forty percent since the early 1990s with sixteen major active armed conflict recorded in 2008. The number of refugees also declined by forty-five percent from 1992 to 2003.[5] However, the nature of conflict has changed, with an increasing trend toward one-sided violent attacks against civilians (terrorism) and an increased "outsourcing" of conflict by governments to state-aligned militia groups.[6] The drop in the number of conflict-affected people has been accompanied by a diversification and fragmentation of armed actors.

Mennonite Central Committee (MCC) has a long history of feeding the hungry and of responding to the needs of those affected by disasters and conflict since its inception in 1920. In this essay we explore shifts and trends in MCC's humanitarian assistance over the course of the organization's ninety year history. While MCC is well-known for its efforts in humanitarian assistance and crisis response, the organization has from the beginning attempted to integrate short-term emergency response with longer-term community development and peacebuilding. In responding to humanitarian crises, MCC has placed a strong emphasis on "building relationships" and partnership. This relational approach has strengthened ecumenical cooperation and enhanced the local capacity of partner organizations.

However, the organization has also faced a shift from volunteerism to becoming a more professionalized humanitarian organization, demanding more accountability and equity in the distribution of humanitarian assistance. While MCC was originally founded on the premise of assisting Mennonites in the Soviet Union, the organization's mandate has extended beyond those within the Mennonite community. In situations of armed conflict and in complex emergencies, MCC has emphasized the need for impartiality of humanitarian actors and has increasingly attempted to integrate peacebuilding activities into relief responses.

This study is divided into four sections. The first section discusses how MCC has demonstrated an integrated response to humanitarian crises, rejecting sector specialization and fragmentation. In the second section, we explore MCC's emphasis on "relationships," pointing to MCC's contributions to ecumenical cooperation, to its commitment to building local capacity, and the unique contribution of MCC's material resources program. The third section highlights the increasing call for greater accountability within the humanitarian sector and the challenge in ensuring that all have the "right to protection." In the final section, we analyze MCC's approach in the context of conflict and complex emergencies, highlighting MCC's attempts to demonstrate a "love of enemies" and to seek opportunities for peacebuilding. The conclusion summarizes these shifts and trends, posing a vision for "MCC at 100."

NINETY YEARS OF "RELIEF": SYNERGIES IN RELIEF AND DEVELOPMENT

MCC is amongst the oldest international relief organizations in the world. In July 1920, in response to Russian Mennonites affected by famine and following the Russian Revolution, twelve representatives of American Mennonite Conferences met in Eklhart, Indiana, to coordinate a joint Mennonite response to the crisis.[7] Similarly in Canada, in October 1920, fourteen representatives of Canadian Mennonite church conferences met in Rosthern, Saskatchewan, to form the Canadian Central Committee, a body which was to work jointly and in cooperation with the efforts of the American Mennonites.[8]

MCC faced a triage situation in Russia as it worked to keep as many people alive as possible during the famine. Resources provided by the Mennonite Central Committee were not sufficient to meet the growing needs of the about 48,000 Mennonites affected by famine. At the peak of the crisis, an estimated 100 people were dying per week in the German and Catholic settlement adjoining the Molotschna Mennonite colony as a result of severe malnutrition.[9] Across the Soviet Union between 1921–1922, around nine million people died in the second largest famine of the twentieth century.[10] MCC established soup kitchens while local selection committees identified criteria for identifying beneficiaries. MCC-supported committees gave preference to vulnerable groups, such as children, the elderly, single women, the ill, pregnant women, and nursing mothers. From its earliest days, MCC thus confronted difficult decisions about how to prioritize need.

These early activities also reflected the complex character of MCC involvements. While MCC initially focused its resources on the provision of humanitarian assistance, MCC quickly became involved in what we would now call "development" and "advocacy" activities.[11] In Canada, the Mennonite Board of Colonization began negotiating with the Canadian government regarding the migration and resettlement of Mennonite refugees to Canada. While the Mennonite Central Committee in the United States had intended to disband following the completion of the relief program in 1925, its members reactivated the organization when the call came to aid several thousand Mennonite refugees who had fled to Germany in 1929. MCC then assisted with the resettlement of Mennonite refugees in Paraguay in 1930.

In his discussion on the evolution of non-governmental organizations (NGOs), David Korten points to four distinct stages or "generations" of NGO development: 1) Relief and Welfare; 2) Community Development; 3) Sustainable Systems Development; and 4) People's Movements.[12] Drawing on Korten's definitions and analysis, one can see that MCC (and its predecessor organizations in Canada) has actually been active in all stages, or "generations," from its inception. In the Soviet Union MCC provided immediate humanitarian relief (e.g. soup kitchens), furnished support for local community development initiatives (e.g. tractors and resettlement), lobbied government for the protection of refugees, and created a movement by catalyzing and coordinating Mennonite churches and service agencies in the U.S. and Canada.

The provision of humanitarian assistance continued to be the dominant driver of MCC's program but always created opportunities for broader interventions. In response to the devastation of World War II, MCC established the "War Sufferers Relief" program which included the distribution of food and clothing, the provision of community services, and peace education.[13] MCC also undertook a multi-pronged response to the food crisis of 1973–74 catalyzed by the Sahelian drought and the oil crisis. At its annual meeting in Kansas, the MCC board adopted the "Hillsboro Resolution" which called for the broadening and strengthening of MCC's rural development programs, changes in North American consumption habits, greater financial assistance to meet growing food needs, and public policy advocacy.[14] Innovative MCC programs grew out of the Hillsboro Resolution, including the More-with-Less cookbook and the MCC Food Bank (now the Canadian Foodgrains Bank).

Despite MCC's attempt to respond to humanitarian needs in an integrated fashion, a recent survey of MCC constituents reveals that MCC is largely recognized for and associated with its work in humanitarian relief activities.[15] MCC's re-visioning process (New Wine/New Wineskins) has also highlighted the importance of MCC's "disaster relief" role in the eyes of MCC's supporters and partners, with stakeholders also pointing toward MCC's peacebuilding niche. However, an integrated approach of "relief, development, and peace" has been the hallmark of MCC's activities from its beginning in 1920.

Like MCC, other international NGOs grew out of the humanitarian imperative to respond to those affected by war and hunger, particularly in response to World War II.[16] These organizations have "evolved," increasingly looking to "longer-term" issues of sustainable development, conflict prevention, advocacy, and public education. At the same time, relief and development organizations have tended to become more specialized in response to the particular passions and interests of their constituency. "To feed the hungry and clothe the naked" stood as MCC's slogan during its early years of work in the Soviet Union.[17] However, as late as the 1950s, some MCC supporters raised questions regarding how much MCC should be involved in development activities such as health and education.[18]

NGO particularism limits the scope of organizations to respond with flexibility and creativity to complex problems and opportunities.[19] The rise of complex emergencies, the growing hunger crisis, and the increasing impact of climate change requires an integrated approach using multiple modalities. For example, in response to increasing drought risk and chronic food insecurity in semi-arid regions of Kenya, MCC has assisted partners with the construction of sand dams. The construction of these dams has reduced water insecurity through water harvesting in seasonal river beds. Combined with terracing activities, sand dams have improved household agriculture output and helped diversify livelihood opportunities.[20] During times of acute food insecurity as a result of drought, these sand dams have been constructed through food-for-work activities smoothing consumption for at-risk households while at the same time mitigating against drought in the long-term.

During the Kenya drought of 2009, MCC partner organizations observed that communities which had benefited from mature sand dams were less affected by the drought and that sand dams had not only prevented increased desertification but had transformed the ecology and raised water tables in the region. Sand dams have proven so successful that MCC has helped in the transfer of sand dam technology to Mozambique and Tanzania, with further exploration in southern Sudan and pastoralist areas of Uganda.

Organizations like MCC must focus on reducing vulnerability to natural hazards and preventing conflict which lead to humanitarian crises. To do so effectively, MCC must continue to work at viewing program design wholistically. Sustainable livelihood, climate change adaptation, and disaster risk-reduction theories and approaches should all be considered in program design in order to build social resilience in the face of growing vulnerability and accelerating change.[21] MCC has embodied this multi-sectoral approach in the past and should continue to embrace this.

RELATIONSHIPS AND AID:
ECUMENISM, PARTNERSHIP, AND BLANKETS

Within MCC circles, people often claim that "MCC is about building relationships" or that "connecting people" and "relationships" are primary to the organization's approach or philosophy. Despite this strong relationships narrative, scant attention has been paid to why this is important in carrying out MCC's mission—it has become "MCC lore."[22] What is the character of these relationships and how do they impact MCC's program? Relationship-building with and for whom?

The twentieth-century Jewish philosopher, Martin Buber, claimed that "all actual life is encounter." In *I and Thou*, Buber articulated what the French sociologist Pierre Bordieu would later call the relational mode of thinking which "identifies the real not with substances but with relations."[23] Rosalind Eyben, meanwhile, argues that aid agencies tend to minimize the importance of social connections and relations, viewing aid through a "substantialist" and technocratic lens. She argues that aid is not a "thing" but is shaped by particular patterns of social relations, relations themselves molded by context-specific and historically conditioned patterns of power. To make sense of aid, we must see aid as "not a thing in itself—money and technical cooperation—but also as patterns of social relations that both shape and are shaped through the giving and receiving of money and people."[24]

In the realm of MCC's humanitarian assistance program, "relationship building" has been expressed through a number of channels, including: 1) ecumenical cooperation; 2) partnering with local agencies and civil society; and 3) individual "gift giving" through MCC's material resource program. Cooperation and ecumenism have become increasingly important for MCC in its humanitarian activities. John Unruh may have contended that in the beginning "MCC was created as a service organization and not as a kind of ecumenical movement."[25] In fact, since its inception, MCC has fostered inter-Mennonite and broader ecumenical cooperation.

One of MCC's greatest contributions to increased ecumenical cooperation has been its role in founding Canadian Foodgrains Bank (CFGB). Following MCC's Hillsboro Resolution, MCC created the MCC Food Bank in 1976 to provide timely food assistance for those affected by acute food insecurity, and to promote longer-term solutions to hunger. In July 1982 the MCC Food Bank was dissolved, giving way to the Canadian Foodgrains Bank. Formed in November 1982 following a meeting with denominations representing the

Roman Catholic, United, Lutheran, Baptist, Presbyterian, the Salvation Army, and the Christian and Missionary Alliance churches in Canada, CFGB was incorporated in 1983 and now includes fifteen member organizations with the Catholic and Anglican church agencies joining recently in 2007.[26]

The call for increased cooperation in the humanitarian sector has become louder in the wake of poor global information sharing and disorganized program implementation in humanitarian crises. Ecumenical collaboration through CFGB provides opportunities for MCC's constituency to respond to needs throughout the world, sometimes extending beyond the reach of MCC's existing program partners. This collaboration provides opportunities for program contributions with trusted and like-minded agencies.

Other church member agencies frequently contribute to MCC's program account, with MCC also contributing to the efforts of other members. Notable collaborative responses to humanitarian crises include Afghanistan, North Korea, Zimbabwe, and Darfur, Sudan. Over the past ten years, MCC has programmed an average of six to seven million Canadian dollars annually through its account at CFGB (including CIDA matching funds) and has recently increased to over 10 million. On the American side, MCC was a founding implementing member of the Foods Resource Bank (FRB), established in 2000 to support smallholder agriculture programs of its member agencies. Similar to CFGB, FRB's fifteen members contribute resources to the projects of other members.

Ecumenical cooperation characterized MCC's response to economic sanctions against Iraq and the 2003 invasion of that country. In the build up to the war, MCC joined with Church World Service, the National Council of Churches USA, Jubilee Partners, and Sojourners in a $1 million program to respond to the health needs of Iraqi children in a campaign entitled "All Our Children" (AOC). The program focused on providing humanitarian assistance in Iraq but also included an advocacy component, with donors writing letters to U.S. President George W. Bush and engaging in advocacy against the war's impact on children. MCC's participation in AOC gave MCC access to more partners in Iraq and access to more resources.

Relationships built over the years at CFGB have also led to a more coordinated Canadian response to disasters in the area of non-food items, livelihood rehabilitation, and reconstruction. Following the southeast Asian tsunami in December 2004, MCC joined with three other church agencies—Presbyterian World Service and Development (PWS&D), the United Church of Canada (UCC), and the Primate's World Relief and Development Fund (PWRDF)—to form "PUMA," a coalition which accessed $6 million worth of CIDA matching resources to respond to an Action by Churches Together (ACT) International appeal for reconstruction and rehabilitation in India. Working together through a joint steering committee, PUMA supported a longtime MCC ecumenical partner in India, Churches Auxiliary for Social Action (CASA), in livelihood rehabilitation, housing reconstruction, and disaster preparedness and mitigation.

This multi-level ecumenical partnership—through PUMA, ACT, and CASA—increased coordination and minimize duplication and disparities in the delivery of humanitarian assistance theory. Rempel concludes that the success of the program hinged on effective coordination and constructive north-south dialogue. Rempel argues that the PUMA steering committee engaged CASA in a way that attempted to minimize the donor-recipient power imbalance. The process fostered constructive debate allowing CASA the necessary flexibility to respond to the priorities of the local community.[27]

Following this successful partnership, the Pentecostal Assemblies of Canada (PAOC), the Christian Reformed World Relief Committee (CRWRC), and Canadian Lutheran World Relief joined the group under the acronym PPUMACC in response to the South Asia Earthquake which affected India and Pakistan. In 2007, these agencies signed a memorandum of understanding under the banner of Canadian Churches in Action (CCA), a coalition which has now successfully carried out joint responses to disasters in the Philippines, Bangladesh, Myanmar (Burma), and China, with MCC taking the lead with our local partners in Myanmar and China.

In addition to promoting humanitarian coordination and ecumenical cooperation in Canada and the U.S., MCC also has a history of participation in local cooperation and ecumenism in the South. In the 1980s and 1990s, the World Council of Churches sponsored country-specific roundtables where denominational agencies, both local and international, met jointly to discuss and support coordinated humanitarian relief and community development programs of national-level church councils. MCC participated in numerous such roundtables, notably in Sudan, Zimbabwe, and South Africa, and has been frequently asked to chair the roundtable of the Sudan Council of Churches. MCC's leadership was appreciated due to the fact that it had staff on the ground which frequently related to the national church councils.

Ecumenical coordination efforts such as MCC's participation in the Sudan Council of Churches, and the PUMA response to the Indian

Ocean tsunami, have been successful in developing common agenda in cooperation with Southern partners while also responding to the needs of northern donor agencies (and their back donors). Aside from coordination, MCC has placed an emphasis on working through local partner agencies. While in the past MCC workers often engaged in the hands-on delivery of humanitarian assistance, MCC has shifted to almost exclusively working with local partner organizations who manage project implementation. In many cases, MCC's reliance on and relationships with local partners has greatly increased MCC's level of humanitarian access. This approach recognizes that local organizations will be the ones who remain with the affected community and that increasing their capacity is fundamental to long-term development.

In the recent case of Cyclone Nargis in Myanmar (Burma), reaching the affected population was a key challenge for international NGOs in the early weeks of the emergency response. Despite government restrictions on foreign aid agencies, MCC worked with established local partners to respond within days. In the case of the Rwandan genocide in 1994, despite having no program activity in either Rwanda or Burundi, MCC responded to the genocide through L'Eglise du Christ au Congo, with whom MCC had a historical relationship. Similarly, in the Gaza Strip, following Israel's military bombardment in 2009, MCC operated through local partner organizations able to deliver food and material resources to those affected, despite the Israeli economic embargo and restrictions on movement.

Not only has MCC worked alongside local partners, MCC has also heavily invested in building the local capacity of partners. In fact, MCC has played a role in the creation of numerous civil society and relief agencies which are now MCC partners in humanitarian crises. These organizations include the Meserete Kristos Church Relief and Development Association in Ethiopia, the Brethren in Christ Church of Zambia's Compassionate Care Ministries, the Mennonite Christian Service Fellowship of India, the Indonesia Mennonite Diakonial Service, and Mennonite Disaster Service (in Canada and the U.S.).

MCC's emphasis on working with local partners has forced the organization to struggle with questions of power and partnership. Peter Walker highlights the large power imbalance between those who come with money and political power and those who bring the local knowledge so crucial for understanding and acting in the local context. These unequal relationships between international NGOs and local partner organizations often mean that accountability only runs in one direction: back to the donor. Despite these power imbalances, somehow a relationship of mutual trust, responsibility, and accountability must be created.[28] Seconding MCC service workers to partner organizations and "sticking with partners" over an extended time frame has pushed MCC to be increasingly partner-driven and strengthened relationships of mutual trust.

In addition to the promotion of ecumenical cooperation and local partnerships, the practice of physical "gift giving" through MCC's material resources program has created relationships between MCC's supporters and project participants (beneficiaries) around the world. Through these far-flung "encounters" of meat canning, stuffing relief kits, sewing quilts, or harvesting food grain, individuals, churches, and other groups from Canada and the U.S. have expressed their concern for the plight of the poor and marginalized around the globe. The recent Material Resources Program review highlights the importance of this grassroots participation as an important channel through which people engage MCC's mission and "connect" with communities affected by conflict, poverty, and disaster.[29]

The pitfalls of short-term material responses shipped from North America are obvious: The local purchase of material resources is more cost-effective and supports local economic development; shipping increases MCC's ecological footprint and delays the delivery of relief items; and, finally, it risks leaving donors with the impression that the problem is "solved" through a one-way exchange. However, beyond these pitfalls, the Material Resources Review also noted the appreciation for the high quality of goods that MCC ships.

MCC blankets, hand-sewn by many volunteers in Canada and the U.S., are a case in point. In Darfur, displaced persons asked to exchange their thin United Nations blankets for the colorful MCC, hand-sewn quilts. They noted that these "Mennonite" blankets were lovingly made by persons interested in their plight. These blankets have provided warmth and demonstrated kindness in hostile environments including Rwanda, North Korea, and Iraq. Partners who visit MCC Material Resource centers in Canada and the U.S. are often awestruck at the number of dedicated volunteers committed to the mission of MCC who function as the lifeblood of the organization. Many of these MR volunteers were themselves once assisted by MCC (particularly in the Soviet Union in the 1920s or in Europe during World War I).

The more personal, or perhaps "relational," connection of the material resource program "makes things more real" and can create opportunities for transformation. In the lead-up to the 2003 Iraq invasion, Canadian and American university students participated in purchasing relief kits for war victims in Iraq; accompanying information on the impact of the conflict and the promotion of peace provided unique opportunities for increasing awareness on justice and peacebuilding issues as well as mobilizing people for advocacy.

At the same time, as Rosalind Eyben rightfully notes, "the gift is at one and the same time a material expression of potentially mutually transformative solidarity *and* of oppressive adverse incorporation into an unfair world."[30] While MCC should continue to emphasize relationship building through increased cooperation, partnership, and opportunities for constituency engagement, the organization must continue to work toward relationships that foster transformation and build solidarity. The emergence of rights-based approaches further underscores the increasing demand for accountability to those affected by all actors including public, private, and nongovernmental organizations.

"CARING IN THE NAME OF CHRIST" AND THE RIGHT TO PROTECTION

One of the greatest shifts in how MCC caries out its humanitarian activities is the growing "professionalization" of humanitarian assistance, particularly over the last few decades.[31] MCC's humanitarian activities have been influenced by a greater demand for accountability from donors, local stakeholders, and the broader humanitarian community itself.

In one of the greatest humanitarian crises of the twentieth century, MCC joined 188 other international aid agencies in eastern Democratic Republic of Congo (then Zaire) in responding to huge influx of Rwandan refugees fleeing the conflict in 1994. For the most part, poor collaboration existed among these agencies, leading to vastly different levels of assistance being provided to the affected population. The experience in Rwanda led to a call from humanitarian organizations for increased collaboration and also the agreement to the formulation of minimum standards for the humanitarian community.

The Sphere Project was launched and has succeeded in setting out agreeable minimum standards for humanitarian practice in the areas of food assistance, nutrition, water and sanitation, health, shelter, and site selection. At the core of the Sphere Project is the Humanitarian Charter which highlights three core principles for humanitarian actors: the right to life with dignity, the distinction between combatants and non-combatants, and the principle of non-refoulement.[32]

Adherence to minimum standards over the past decade has led to a reduction in the level of morbidity in refugee camps.[33] In addition to ensuring minimum humanitarian standards, humanitarian organizations are now forced to think through numerous complexities in the delivery of humanitarian assistance, including how to promote gender equity; ensure the participation of those affected; reduce vulnerability to disasters; build local capacity; and minimize the use of aid as a weapon (the "Do No Harm" principle).

The emergence of results-based management (RBM) systems in the wake of the Paris Declaration on Aid Effectiveness has also changed the way MCC carries out its relief activities. The pressure from back donors (notably CIDA and CFGB) and the MCC constituency along with MCC's own desire to "manage for results" has also led to greater rigor in MCC's planning, monitoring, and evaluation (PME) activities. Many within the organization have resisted the introduction of results-based management, arguing that this "Western rational planning model" has been imposed on MCC and our partners and that it hinders relationship-building and participatory development.[34] They contend that accountability for results and building relationships are mutually exclusive objectives.[35] Rather, when conducted in the context of partnership, accompaniment, and local accountability, RBM can be a strong learning tool, increasing program impact. The challenge for MCC remains our ability to go beyond "filling in the boxes" toward becoming a learning organization, building our own capacity in current development practice, particularly in PME methodologies.

The management structures particular to MCC's humanitarian and disaster response operations have also undergone significant change. In response to Hurricane Mitch, numerous humanitarian organizations were forced to reevaluate their operating procedures and policy to ensure the necessary field capacity to carry out large-scale disaster responses. A review of MCC's operating procedures led to increased information sharing within the MCC system as well as strengthened local capacity for disaster management and coordination. Similarly, the overwhelming response of MCC's constituency to the 2004 Indian Ocean tsunami has also forced MCC and other NGOs to reevaluate its operating procedures and management structures in the face of large-scale disaster responses.[36]

MCC's response to the Indian Ocean tsunami in 2004 also highlights the great disparity in the allocation of humanitarian assistance. MCC was entrusted with US$23 million from constituency and government grants to respond to the destruction in Sri Lanka, India, Indonesia, and Somalia. In addition to immediate emergency relief, trauma healing, and livelihood rehabilitation, these resources allowed MCC to build disaster resistant housing for 106 households in India and Indonesia, as well as a number of schools and libraries.

This overwhelming response to the tsunami stands in stark contrast to other major disasters of this kind, where on average, MCC is only able to respond on a much smaller scale. Levels of humanitarian assistance are often driven by media attention and the corresponding interest from MCC constituents. While MCC often receives a large influx of donations for sudden-onset emergencies (earthquakes, hurricanes, and cyclones), slower-onset emergencies such as drought or protracted conflict receive minimal interest from MCC's donor constituency. For example, in the case of most major African droughts, MCC is fortunate if it manages to raise $200,000, even though millions are affected. Oxfam points to the lack of impartiality in the delivery of humanitarian assistance globally, highlighting that the 500,000 people affected by the Asian tsunami in 2004 received on average $1,241 each in official aid flows, while in the same year the response to the 700,000 people affected by conflict in Chad received an average of $23 per person.[37]

Climate change , combined with increasing and volatile commodity prices, threatens to put millions upon millions of people at risk. The prospect of increasing drought due to climate change is notable since slow-onset disasters have accounted for almost 87 percent of all natural hazard-related deaths between 1990 and 1999.[38] However, far from being "acts of God," famine or acute food insecurity is the result of human action and inaction, representing a failure of accountability of humanitarian and government actors.[39] One of the key drivers behind acute food insecurity is the predictable nature of seasonal hunger. During the annual "hungry season" and during cycles of drought, households are forced to take on difficult "coping strategies" including reducing consumption, migration, the selling of assets, and the sacrifice of other expenditures (e.g. school fees). Combating these "normal cycles" of seasonal hunger is instrumental not only in tackling chronic rural poverty but also crucial to famine prevention.[40]

In the specific case of Ethiopia, the government and international donors have recognized that despite the cycle of annual "emergency" appeals, the majority of the affected households are chronically hungry and face predictable seasonal hunger gaps. In recognition of this fact, the Ethiopian government along with international donors created the Productive Safety Net Program which targets about eight million chronically food insecure households. Households are provided with predictable food assistance (in the form of food aid or cash transfers) during the hungry season.

MCC partners with the Meserete Kristos Church Relief and Development Association in the implementation of the safety net program in twelve peasant associations in southern Ethiopia. After four years of implementation, the program has succeeded in improving food consumption, reducing the "distress selling" of assets (along with other harmful "coping strategies"), and has even led to an increase in household asset holdings through group saving circles.[41] Ethiopia's safety net program has proven that predictable access to food during the hungry season positively impacts short-term food security while also contributing to longer-term poverty reduction.

Through MCC's account at the Canadian Foodgrains Bank, MCC partners implement similar seasonal safety net programs in Burundi, Nepal, and India. In the face of growing climate uncertainty, these social protection programs will become increasingly important as a means to promote climate change adaptation and risk reduction more generally.[42]

How does MCC work with the constituency to ensure the right to humanitarian assistance for all? If MCC believes that "caring in the name of Christ" means that all have the right to protection—that, in fact, there is a universal social minimum which all people should enjoy—the organization will have to increase its ability to respond to "forgotten emergencies" and increase program emphasis on the reduction of vulnerability to disasters and crises.

"LOVING THE ENEMY": IMPARTIALITY AND PEACEBUILDING

Impartiality remains a key principle for humanitarianism. While MCC began its work targeting its efforts at Mennonite sisters and brothers, over the last ninety years MCC has broadened its efforts to include those beyond the confines of denominational affiliation and ethnicity. In the context of armed conflict, the biblical challenge to "love enemies" has been fundamental to MCC's humanitarian activities. However, the place of humanitarian actors has become increasingly complicated in "complex emergencies" as foreign and domestic governments attempt to coopt humanitarian activities to advance political and military objectives.

The case of MCC's humanitarian activities in Vietnam is still instructive as MCC continues to confront issues of "impartiality" in the context of complex emergencies. MCC began its efforts in Vietnam in 1954 with the primary objective of helping the Protestant refugees in Southern Vietnam; yet "MCC quickly expanded far beyond this narrow calling to aiding the people of Vietnam with respect to need, not religion."[43]

Initially MCC cooperated with the U.S. government, distributing U.S. food aid and operating in southern Vietnam; however, this close association with government and military quickly changed. MCC personnel increasingly questioned the alignment of MCC's operations (through the Vietnam Christian Service) with U.S. government objectives. MCC stopped distributing U.S. food aid and increasingly began to reach out and build relationships across "enemy lines" by providing food assistance in Northern Vietnam. The U.S. government also raised questions when MCC service workers developed relationships with the communist leaders, including the National Liberation Front (the southern insurgency group) and northern Vietnamese leaders. By 1976 MCC was the only agency with staff in the country after the fall of South Vietnam. In cooperation with an "enemy state," MCC began operations with the new communist government, including the approval of US$1 million in humanitarian assistance.[44]

MCC has maintained its commitment to impartiality by working on both sides during conflicts and in complex emergency contexts, including operations in Ethiopia, Afghanistan, and Sudan. While the Ethiopian government was at war with the Oromos, Eritreans, and Tigrayan forces from the mid 1980s to the mid-1990s, MCC provided food and material resources to those affected by the conflict while also maintaining program in non-government areas of Ethiopia. Despite its knowledge that MCC was assisting those in non-government controlled areas, the Ethiopian government allowed MCC to continue its operations. Similarly, during Sudan's protracted war with the Sudan People's Liberation Army (SPLA), MCC assisted civilians in government and non-government controlled areas. The same goes for MCC's efforts in Afghanistan between 1996 and 2001. There MCC, through partnership with Medair, assisted people affected by the conflict in both Taliban and non-Taliban controlled areas.

Some international humanitarian organizations have chosen a more activist approach in complex emergencies, publicly speaking out against atrocities. However, MCC has approached these situations differently, using a dual-track approach: supporting "quiet diplomacy" through local advocacy initiatives, while at the same time remaining engaged in humanitarian efforts. Choosing to operate "under the radar" by taking cues from local partners, MCC has been able maintain humanitarian access in very difficult and complex environments.

The case of MCC's involvement in the Democratic Peoples' Republic of Korea (DPRK, or North Korea) reflects MCC's emphasis on staying engaged. In 1997, MCC launched an appeal for North Korea in light of growing hunger in this politically isolated country. MCC's constituency enthusiastically supported this effort, doubling MCC's original appeal request of CDN$ 360,000. In cooperation with the DPRK government, MCC has provided material resources, canned meat, soy milk, and other humanitarian assistance. While some in MCC's constituency question MCC's involvement in the DPRK, MCC has viewed humanitarian and development activities as opportunities for engagement. MCC has sponsored agricultural exchanges in between DPRK officials and Mennonites in Canada and the U.S. to build relationships and understanding. While relatively small, these exchanges have opened "windows of compassion" as we attempt to welcome and embrace "the Other."[45]

MCC's ability to create this space for engagement and to respond impartially has come under threat in a post-9/11 world and the emergence of "humanitarian wars." The line between humanitarian actors and military operations has become blurred with the emergence of "The Responsibility to Protect" doctrine, which justifies the use of military force to protect human rights of those affected by crisis. The "whole-of-government," or "3D," approach attempts to combine defense, diplomatic, and development efforts into a seamless, complementary whole, sacrificing the humanitarian imperative in the name of an integrated approach to achieving long-term peace.

For MCC these new forms of political-military strategy pose difficult questions about its attempts to respond impartially to human need. One month before the 2003 invasion of Iraq, the U.S. government contacted MCC's Middle East department to inquire as to whether MCC would be willing to accept funds for development activities in Iraq. The U.S. government saw and continues to see humanitarian agencies as part of their war effort, "force multipliers" for their campaigns in Iraq and Afghanistan. In Afghanistan, the Canadian and U.S. military have actively sought NGO participation in Provincial Reconstruction Teams (PRTs) which would involve the delivery of relief and development activities along side military and security operations. The widespread perception that aid agencies merely serve as emissaries of the coalition forces has led to a mistrust of agencies and an increase in violence toward aid workers.

MCC has clearly rejected this 3D approach as inconsistent with MCC's commitment to nonviolence and the need for impartiality to help those on "all sides." By contrast, MCC has sought to integrate community-level peacebuilding activities into relief and rehabilitation efforts. In *Do No Harm,* Mary Anderson argues that relief agencies should not only attempt to prevent further harm and conflict as a result of their activities but that they should "help war to end by lessening intergroup tensions and strengthening intergroup connections."[46] MCC has accordingly sought to "mainstream" peacebuilding into its relief activities.

For example, in the pastoralist Karamojong region of northeast Uganda, MCC worked with local partners to deliver humanitarian help and increase inter-ethnic cooperation. A serious conflict between the government of Uganda and the Karamajong had led to the destruction of local settlements, or "manyatas." Karamojong leadership requested support from MCC to help displaced Karamojong with food, cooking utensils, and blankets. Concerned about transporting these good through insecure territory, MCC called on the support of local partners in the Iteso region, which borders Karamojong. The Iteso and the Karamjong have historically been in conflict, with Karamjong often moving into Iteso territory during the dry season and forcibly taking over grazing land and water. When MCC approached Iteso partners with the proposition of distributing assistance to displaced Karamojong, the Iteso were willing to help and successfully carried out the distribution despite security risks and the history of conflict. According to former MCC representative David Klassen, this small effort enhanced relationships between the two peoples and created opportunities for future cooperation.

Similarly in Rwanda, MCC supported group income generation activities which brought together both Tutsi and Hutu ethnic women in the wake of the Rwandan genocide. MCC-supported projects formed inter-ethnic youth groups to reconstruct homes. In response to the identity-based violence following the Kenya elections in 2007, MCC assisted local religious leaders from competing ethnic communities in the joint distribution of food and non-food items.

MCC's response to a severe earthquake Iran in 1990 proved to be an opportunity for MCC to increase its engagement with Islam and increase its focus on interfaith bridge-building. Following the collapse of the Berlin Wall, Islam was replacing communism as the new "enemy" and MCC was encouraged to explore of interfaith cooperation. MCC developed a strong relationship with the Iranian Red Crescent Society and this initial "relief" engagement in Iran led to a later partnership with the Imam Khomeini Education and Research Institute (IKERI) with an emphasis on interfaith dialogue. Most recently this relationship led to numerous talks between church leaders and the current President Mahmoud Ahmadinejad in the context of growing hostility toward the Republic of Iran.

MCC's humanitarian assistance program has provided the organization with a window or space to demonstrate compassion and to deconstruct the notion of Otherness, even among those who are supposed to be "enemies." Remaining impartial in delivery assistance is not only fundamental to humanitarian practice but also provides opportunities for peacebuilding and ongoing engagement.

LOOKING AHEAD: MCC AT 100

This chapter has explored the development of MCC humanitarian activity over the past ninety years. Given these shifts and trends explored above, where will MCC be at 100? Certain directions for MCC's humanitarian work seem clear:

- *Integrating "relief, development, and peace":* From the beginning, MCC has integrated peace and development activities as part of its humanitarian and disaster response. To build social resilience and prevent the vulnerability that leads to crisis, MCC should strengthen the interplay between the various aspects of the organization's work, particularly given MCC's strength in peacebuilding.
- *Deepening ecumenical cooperation:* MCC is increasingly focusing its partnerships on Anabaptist-related organizations. Strengthening the capacity of these Anabaptist agencies should serve as an entry point for further ecumenical and interfaith cooperation—cooperation which has proved important in responding to humanitarian crises.
- *Building local capacity and partnerships:* MCC has a strong history of walking alongside partner organizations. If MCC is serious about "capacity building," MCC must invest the necessary resources into strengthening the capacity of local partners in disaster preparedness and response.
- *Reducing vulnerability to disasters:* In light of growing vulnerability to climate change and increasing food insecurity, MCC should increase its focus on measures to reduce vulnerability to disasters. Current efforts in disaster risk reduction, climate change adaptation, and social protection represent a strong starting point.

- *Engaging "the enemy"*: While at times, MCC's engagement with DPRK, Vietnam, Iran, and Iraq have raised questions among MCC's supporters in Canada and the United States, MCC should continue to be open to opportunities to engage and build relationships with people and countries classified as "the enemy."
- *Realizing "the right to protection"*: At present, MCC's ability to respond to disasters is driven by levels of media and constituency engagement in the situation. MCC should find more creative ways to generate resources and awareness about "forgotten crises."

By moving in these directions, MCC will build on and prove faithful to the lessons it has learned over nine decades of humanitarian action.

NOTES

1. See *The State of Food Security in the World: Economic Crises—Impacts and Lessons Learned* (Rome: United Nations Food and Agriculture Organization, 2009).

2. See M. L. Parry, O. F. Canziani, J. P. Palutikof, P. J. van der Linden, and C. E. Hanson, *Climate Change 2007: Impacts, Adaptation and Vulnerability—Contribution of Working Group II to the Fourth Assessment Report of the Intergovernmental Panel on Climate Change* (Cambridge: Intergovernmental Panel on Climate Change, 2007).

3. *Right to Survive: The Humanitarian Challenge in the Twenty-First Century* (Oxford: Oxfam International, 2009).

4. *Stern Review on the Economics of Climate Change* (London: United Kingdom Treasury, 2005).

5. See the *Human Security Report* (New York: Oxford University Press, 2005) and Stockholm International Peace Research Institute, *SIPRI Yearbook 2009: Armaments, Disarmament and International Security* (Stockholm: SIPRI, 2009).

6. SIPRI, 2009.

7. For MCC's early history, see P. C. Hiebert and Orie O. Miller, *Feeding the Hungry: Russian Famine, 1919-1925: American Mennonite Relief Operations under the Auspices of Mennonite Central Committee* (Scottdale, Pa.: Mennonite Central Committee, 1929); M. C. Lehman, *The History and Principles of Mennonite Relief Work: An Introduction* (Akron, Pa.: Mennonite Central Committee, 1945); and John D. Unruh, *In the Name of Christ; A History of the Mennonite Central Committee and Its Service, 1920-1951* (Akron, Pa.:; Mennonite Central Committee, 1952).

8. See Esther Epp-Tiessen, Chapter 4 in this volume.

9. See Hiebert and Miller, 215.

10. S. Devereux, P. Vaitla, and S. Hauenstein Swan, *Seasons of Hunger: Fighting Cycles of Starvation among the World's Poor* (London: Pluto Press,

372 A Table of Sharing

2008).

11. Hiebert and Miller, 293.

12. David C. Korten, *Getting to the 21st. Century: Voluntary Action and the Global Agenda* (West Hartford, Conn.: 1990).

13. Unruh, 357.

14. This multi-faceted approach continues today: in response to dramatic food price increases in over the past two years, leading to the contemporary "hunger crisis," MCC has once again called for an increase to food assistance, agricultural development, public policy advocacy, and constituency education.

15. "Mennonite Central Committee Communications Survey Report," Barefoot Creative (2009).

16. See David C. Korten, *Getting to the 21st. Century: Voluntary Action and the Global Agenda* (Bloomfield: Kumarian Press, 1990); as well as Marc Lindenberg and Coralie Bryant, *Going Global: Transformting Relief and Development NGOs* (Bloomfield: Kumarian Press, 2001), for discussions of the growth of humanitarianism and the aftermath of the Second World War.

17. See Herta Krauss, *International Relief in Action, 1914-1943, Selected Records, with Notes*, sponsored by American Friends Service Committee, Brethren Service Committee, and MCC (Scottdale, Pa.: Herald Press, 1944).

18. Ibid.

19. See L. David Brown and Archana Kalegaonkar, *Nonprofit and Voluntary Sector Quarterly* 31 (2002): 231-258 for a discussion of NGO particularism.

20. See R. Lasage, J. Aerts, G. C. M. Mutiso, A. de Vries, "Potential for Community-Based Adaptation to Droughts: Sand Dams in Kitui, Kenya," *Physics and Chemistry of the Earth* 33 (2008): 67–73; as well as "Sand Dams in Kenya" case study as part of the Canadian Food Security Policy Group's "Pathways to Resilience: Smallholder Farmers and the Future of Agriculture," available online at http://www.foodgrainsbank.ca/resilience.aspx.

21. On integrated approaches to humanitarian work, see Mary B. Anderson and Peter J. Woodrow, *Rising from the Ashes: Development Strategies in Times of Disaster* (Boulder, Colo.: Lynne Rienner, 1998); Mark Davies, Bruce Guenther, Jennifer Leavy, Tom Mitchell and Thomas Tanner, "Climate Change Adaptation, Disaster Risk Reduction and Social Protection: Complementary Roles in Agriculture and Rural Growth?" IDS Working Paper No. 320 (Brighton: Institute of Development Studies, 2008); and Lisa Shipper and Mark Pelling, "Disaster Risk, Climate Change and International Development: Scope for, and Challenges to, Integration," *Disasters* 30/1 (2006): 19-38. 2006.

22. See Terry Jantzi, "A Theoretical Framework for Understanding MCC's Emphasis on Relationships," chapter 17 of this volume, for a discussion of relationships within MCC.

23. Pierre Bourdieu, "Social Space and Symbolic Power," *Sociological Theory* 7/1 (1989): 15

24. Rosalind Eyben "Power, Mutual Accountability and Responsibility in the Practice of International Aid: A Relational Approach" IDS Working Paper No. 305 (Brighton: Institute of Development Studies, 2008): 9.

25. Unruh, 37.

26. J. M. Klassen, *Jacob's Journey: From Zagradowka towards Zion: The Autobi-*

ography of J. M. Klassen (Canada, 2001). For a number of reasons the MCC Food Bank was seen to be in competition with MCC. Some within the organization saw the Bank as resource-driven, viewing funds raised by the Food Bank (which included a match from the Canadian International Development Agency of $3 to every dollar raised) as in competitions with other MCC priorities. There was also increased pressure on MCC to store and ship commodities and Food Bank board members would often travel to monitor program without consultation with MCC staff.

27. See Henry Rempel, 2009, *World Cannot Express Our Gratitude: The Rebuilding of Lives in Response to the Tsunami in Southern India*, unpublished manuscript.

28. See Peter Walker, "Complexity and Context," (Boston, Feinstein International Center, Tufts University, 2008). See also Alan Fowler, "Authentic NGDO Partnerships in the New Policy Agenda for International Aid: Dead End or Light Ahead?" *Development and Change* 29 (1998): 137-159.

29. Shirley B. Yoder, *Material Resources Program Review: An Integrated Report of Findings and Recommendations* (Akron, Pa.: Mennonite Central Committee).

30. Eyben, 20.

31. Larry Minear, *The Humanitarian Enterprise: Dilemmas and Discoveries* (Bloomfield, Conn.: Kumarian Press, 2002).

32. The protection of refugees from being returned to places where their lives are at risk and freedoms are at risk.

33. Salama, P. Spiegel, L. Talley, R. Waldman, "Lessons Learned from Complex Emergencies over the Past Decade," *Lancet* 364 (2004): 1801-13.

34. See Eyben and T. Wallace.

35. It is notable that this resistance has come primarily from MCC personnel, while partners have frequently expressed an eagerness for further learning and resources.

36. Allen Harder, *Consolidated Report: Evaluation of MCC's Tsunami Response* (Akron, Pa.: Mennonite Central Committee)

37. See Oxfam.

38. Ben Wisner, Piers Blaikie, Terry Cannon, and Ian Davis, *At Risk: Natural Hazards, People's Vulnerability and Disasters,* 2nd. ed. (London: Routledge, 2004).

39. Stephen Devereux, "Introduction: From 'Old Famines' to 'New Famines,'" *The New Famines: Why Famines Persist in an Era of Globalization,* ed. Stephen Devereux (London: Routledge, 2007).

40. Stephen Devereux, Bapu Vaitla, and Samuel Haustein Swan, *Seasons of Hunger: Fighting Cycles of Quiet Starvation Among the World's Rural Poor* (London: Pluto Press, 2008).

41. Bruce Guenther, "Cash-for-Work, Vulnerability and Social Resilience: A Case Study of Productive Safety Net Programme in Sidama Zone, Ethiopia," M.Phil. dissertation (Brighton: Institute of Development Studies, 2007).

42. See Davies et al.

43. Paul Shetler Fast, "The Value of People Centered Development: MCC's Sustained Relationship with Vietnam, 1954-Today," unpublished paper.

44. Ibid.

45. Miroslav Volf, *Exclusion and Embrace: A Theological Exploration of Identity, Otherness, and Reconciliation* (Nashville, Tenn.: Abingdon Press, 1996).

46. Mary B. Anderson, *Do No Harm: How Aid Can Support Peace—Or War* (London: Lynne Rienner, 1999),

Chapter 16

Pacifism and the Responsibility to Protect: MCC and Just Policing

THEODORE J. KOONTZ

From contexts ranging from the halls of the United Nations in New York to the jungles of eastern Congo, MCC frequently confronts questions about the use of military or police force to protect the innocent. These questions have come into sharper focus in recent years, perhaps best symbolized by an extensive MCC Peace Office project issuing in a major conference and a book centered around the question of whether or how "Mennonites should be prepared to take up the problems of security and participate in wider ecumenical, national, and international conversations about them."[1] Framing the issue as helping to provide security represents a shift in angle of vision on the question of what it means to love our neighbors and our enemies. Among many other questions, this framing of the issue raises questions about how we should think about policing and even armed interventions aimed at protecting the innocent, questions with which I will grapple in this chapter.

Mennonites vigorously disagree as to how Mennonite pacifist commitment relates to the perceived responsibility to protect the innocent, as the following snapshots of Mennonite reflections, most by MCCers or from MCC publications, on these matters show:

We will pray for and witness to those in authority over our countries. We recognize that governing authorities have an ordering role in society. Some of us may be called to ministries of reconciliation, relief of human need and protection of the environment through service within governmental institutions. . . . We offer our witness to the state, reminding those in authority that they are called by God to use their power in ways that are constructive and life-giving rather than violent and life-destroying. . . .

We will strive to show by our lives that war is an unacceptable way to solve human conflict. This calls us to refuse to support war, or to participate in military service. . . . We support ministries of conciliation which search for peaceful resolution of conflicts. . . .

We will resist evil and oppression in the nonviolent spirit of Jesus. Our stand against unjust treatment of people employs the "weapons" demonstrated by Jesus—love, truth, forgiveness and the willingness to suffer rather than inflict suffering. Our witness anticipates God's transformative power in human hearts and institutions. In loving resistance we will stand with people in their struggle against the power of sin, and proclaim the liberation and reconciliation which come with the rule of God. —*A Commitment to Christ's Way of Peace, adopted by Mennonite Central Committee, February 1993.*[2]

To be a good neighbor as the Bible portrays often means intervention—sometimes armed intervention. The possible resort to armed intervention implied by R2P [the Responsibility to Protect] is a thorn in the flesh for the Historic Peace Churches, as for many others. It is very likely that, under certain circumstances, protection that involves the use of force or the threat of it may be inevitable. I suggest that it may be more helpful to be principled in regard to the dignity of people and their safety than to let the pacifist perspective keep us from living our responsibility toward those who don't have a choice of their fate. Violence is always destructive. Yet our struggle for nonviolence and peace is not rooted simply in wanting to be pure and right, but rather in giving Glory to God through protecting human lives and stand [sic] for their dignity as created by God. The Decade to Overcome Violence challenges Christians and churches "to overcome the spirit, logic, and practice of violence; to relinquish any theological justification of violence; and to affirm anew the spirituality of reconciliation and active nonviolence." The notion and approach of the Responsibility to Protect is a significant step to actually doing that. —*Hansulrich Gerber, former MCC Europe*

Director and staff person for the World Council of Churches Decade to Overcome Violence.[3]

In calling on the international community to come to the aid of vulnerable people in extraordinary suffering and peril, churches are not prepared to say that it is never appropriate or never necessary to resort to the use of lethal force. This refusal in principle to preclude the use of force is not based on naïve belief that force can be relied on to solve otherwise intractable problems; rather, it is based on the certain knowledge that the primary consideration must be the welfare of people, especially those in situations of extreme vulnerability and who are utterly abandoned to the whims and prerogatives of their tormentors. . . .

So churches do not fudge or shrink from the issue of resort to force for protection purposes. They acknowledge that in some circumstances it will be the only available option—an option that cannot guarantee success, but that must be tried because the world has failed to find and continues to be at a loss to find any other means of coming to the aid of those in desperate situations. *—Ernie Regehr, Adjunct Professor of Peace and Conflict Studies, former President, Conrad Grebel University College, and founder of Project Plowshares.*[4]

Despite the helpful words about prevention (before intervention) and rebuilding (after intervention), when stripped to its bones, R2P is in essence a twenty-first century "just war" theory.

We must remember that Hitler invaded the Sudetenland in 1938 in a humanitarian intervention to protect the oppressed civilian population.

Scripture makes it very clear that we are our "brother's keepers" and we have a responsibility to protect all who are vulnerable. My problem with R2P is not the recognition of that responsibility, but the suggestion that when all else fails, war is the best solution.

In fulfilling our Responsibility to Protect, the means which we use must be consistent with the ends we hope to achieve. A cornerstone for understanding of this is one of the oldest binding contracts, which is still used in the medical profession today, the Hippocratic Oath (c.400BC) which can be summarized as "First, do no harm."

Since the results of our actions when trying to protect vulnerable populations whether using military force or the power of love and truth "can never reliably be predicted," the only thing that we can say for certain is that when love and truth are used, rather than armed force, no additional members of the vulnerable population will be hurt by our actions. Jesus clearly understood this when he asked his followers to abandon the old ways dealing with evil, and follow His new path of love and compassion. —*Doug Hostetter, MCC Liaison to the United Nations, former MCCer in Vietnam, and former Executive Secretary of the Fellowship of Reconciliation.*[5]

These discussions among Mennonites over Christian responsibility to protect the innocent have been significantly influenced by wider conversations on these issues, both in ecumenical circles and in the so-called "international community." Since the early 1990s several interrelated bodies of literature suggesting that Christians should participate in and support certain narrowly prescribed military/police interventions have been developing. One literature speaks of "just policing,"[6] another of the "responsibility to protect (R2P),"[7] and a third of "just peacemaking."[8]

These literatures collectively pose some new—and (mostly) some old—challenges to MCC's commitment to nonviolence. While each body of literature frames the issues in somewhat different ways, the fundamental questions that Mennonite pacifists need to deal with in response to these literatures are essentially the same.

As we begin, we should ponder why the R2P defense of military or police force in limited cases—armed force to save populations from atrocities—has generated more interest and support from some Mennonite thinkers and leaders than have previous appeals by just war proponents to support armed force. An important part of the answer is precisely that we have deeper engagement with people holding different views on the issue of war than we had a generation or two ago. Such engagement takes many forms, an important one being the call for church unity growing out of ecumenical contacts, a call to come to agreement on an important "church dividing" issue (pacifism/nonpacifism), with the hope that perhaps something like just policing or just peacemaking language can bridge the gap between pacifists and just war proponents.[9] Furthermore, many longtime MCC partners with whom MCC has worked closely for many years thanks to a shared sense of mission have come to support R2P-type armed interventions. Our friends, not only those with whom we often disagree, want us to support R2P.[10] These deeper contacts with others are good; yet they make the challenges pacifists have faced for centuries feel more acute.

Another reason why contemporary appeals to police or military force have gained ground is the increased awareness of genocide and other crimes against humanity that comes to us through the media. Precisely the same well publicized tragedies (Somalia, Rwanda, former Yugoslavia, Darfur) that have called forth a new way of thinking in the international community have shaped our consciousness as Mennonite people. Perhaps even more important is the experience of MCC workers who find themselves living with friends and partners suffering gross human rights abuses. Their experiences come to the rest of us through their storytelling and allow us to grieve with people who suffer, people with whom we would not otherwise have had connection.

This increased care for others is good; it also raises more sharply the question, "How should we intervene to help them?" An answer that includes advocacy for governmental and international action, in addition to planning our own responses, has become natural for MCCers. MCC has learned that systemic causes of poverty and oppression should be addressed at national and international policy-making levels as well as through MCC's smaller-scale work. In the face of gross human rights abuses, what should MCC do, and what should MCC say to the powers that be?

An additional factor causing some Mennonites to be attracted to arguments that favor military or police violence to protect endangered peoples is that it represents a theologically more attractive argument than the arguments for use of armed force that we have heard most frequently in our recent history. Much of the rhetoric we have heard in favor of use of force, especially in the United States, has been rooted in "national interest" or "self-defense" rationales. The notion that nations have an inherent right to sovereignty and territorial integrity, and the corollary right to self-defense (often interpreted expansively by major powers) is enshrined in the UN Charter.

R2P and just policing are different. They start by focusing explicitly, and narrowly, on care for "the least of these," rather than on a nation's right to self-defense. R2P, we might say, "enshrines" the rights of peoples to protection from genocide and other crimes against humanity.[11] This move appeals to MCCers, who have come to see care for poor and vulnerable "neighbors" as central to the meaning of Christ's gospel. It stands in sharp contrast to calls for support of wars of "self defense" to protect us, wars waged on the other side of the globe against a small and amorphous threat.[12] These factors condition Mennonites to take R2P and just policing seriously, and they point to the strong affinity MCC has with some core concerns embodied in R2P and just policing. In short, R2P and just policing have appeal partly because we have changed (in many respects for the good) and because they represent significant shifts (in many respects for the good) in how the place of military or police violence should be understood in international life.

WHY JUST POLICING?

Having described the context within which just policing arguments have become plausible to some Mennonites, we must seek to understand the moral force of the arguments calling for armed interventions in cases of gross human rights abuses.[13] Typical arguments advanced in defense of R2P and just policing include the following:

"Something must be done" to save innocent peoples from massive killings. While a strong presumption in favor of using preventive and nonviolent initiatives exists, at times only a sufficiently armed international force will be able to stop the killing and arrest the criminal. The innocent and defenseless must be protected from perpetrators, by force of arms if necessary. Failing to do so amounts to a morally perverse preference for the life of the guilty over the life of the innocent.

To protect such innocent and defenseless peoples, the international community has an obligation to intervene with a police force that has sufficient strength to end those violations. Such an intervening force should be required scrupulously to observe international law in the conduct of its operations and it should be conducted under international auspices. The "sovereignty" of a nation should be subject to limitation through armed force by the international community, not only when it threatens international peace (as under the old paradigm) but also when it fails to protect its population(s) against gross human rights abuses or when it perpetuates such abuses.

International institutions, international law, and the capacity for international law enforcement should be strengthened and legitimated. Preventing genocides and international war require this, and the term policing itself, used on a global level, demands it. This language only makes sense in a context where there is a widely (though not universally) agreed-upon legal framework within which police (in contrast to soldiers) operate. Policing language suggests that violators of international law should be viewed as criminals to be apprehended by police and tried in an impartial court for their crimes.[14] Policing language stands in contrast to a perspective in which war operates as the supreme arbiter of international affairs, where those who disrupt international peace are portrayed as enemies to be killed, or at least defeated and disempowered, not as criminals who have violated a commonly held moral and legal code.

A number of critics, including pacifists and near pacifists, of the Bush administration's response to 9/11 made this kind of argument: the United States should have called bin Laden an international criminal and argued for his capture and trial instead of calling for an international "war on terrorism." By doing so, the U.S. could have strengthened international law, enhanced its own standing in the eyes of other nations, and helped to delegitimize war as a proper response to aggression, while at the same time acknowledging the need for "force"—meaning the violence necessary to bring about the arrest of bin Laden.[15]

Just policing (and R2P) provides a more restrictive framework and language for thinking about the use of force in international relations. It does not differ from "just war," which has been the dominant Christian conceptual language in these discussions, in the commitment to do something to save innocents. But war language, despite the best efforts of just war theorists to narrow the morally acceptable grounds for war and the acceptable means of fighting, connotes largescale and frequently indiscriminate killing that may have little or nothing to do with protecting the innocent.

Policing language, in contrast, suggests operations targeted exclusively at guilty parties (criminals), using comparatively light arms and the least amount of force possible (preferably, simply presence). Police operate under clearer rules of engagement and are subject to stricter discipline for violating those rules than are soldiers. Police work within a community that has agreed to the laws which police enforce, laws enacted by the community's freely elected leaders. In this view, the function of police is not so much to exercise violence against threats to the peace as it is to remind us to follow through on our common commitments.

AFFIRMATIONS OF JUST POLICING AND R2P

In short, according to its proponents, just policing represents a step in the direction of delegitimizing war and its comparatively uncontrolled violence. Christian pacifists can and should affirm certain elements of the R2P/just policing agenda:

(1) Just policing rightly stresses that seeking to protect the innocent from harm forms an essential part of loving our neighbor. Averting our eyes, hearts, and lives when others are misused has been a besetting sin of many Mennonite pacifists. The most powerful argument against pacifism has been and continues to be that failing to protect innocent neighbors constitutes a failure of Christian love.

Pacifism dare not mean only refusing to kill (although I believe it must mean at least that). It must also mean active engagement to prevent abuses of neighbors and efforts to protect the innocent when such abuses occur.

(2) At least in theory, policing is a step in the direction of more restraint in the use of lethal force, a step toward narrowing just war constraints.[16]

(3) Just policing, R2P, and just peacemaking call attention to the problems caused by an anarchic world system (i.e., a system with no overarching legitimate political authority) and point toward the need to strengthen the international community. A society with a responsive, effective, and legitimate government is a more peaceful society than a society lacking such a government, and our global society lacks such a government. These literatures address this problem, although greater centralization of power is not trouble-free.

(4) Just policing, R2P, and especially just peacemaking stress, much more strongly than most just war theory has done, the need to explore nonviolent alternatives and the expectation that there will often be such alternatives. These recent literatures give a good deal of attention to exploring and developing alternatives that might make war or lethal violence unnecessary.[17] In this way they take the "last resort" criterion of just war theory seriously in a way that just war advocates frequently have not.

In light of these powerful arguments, should Mennonites fully embrace just policing and R2P, giving them our blessing? Should MCC advocacy offices promote and embrace just policing, R2P, and related approaches to challenges confronting international affairs? I say no. Why?

R2P, JUST POLICING, AND JUST WAR[18]

First, Christian pacifist arguments against accepting just policing or a "responsibility to protect" through military interventions on behalf of those suffering great violence are just as strong (and just as weak) as they have been from the time of Christ. Nothing essential has changed by the introduction of just policing or R2P language. The fundamental issues are the same as those that have been argued between pacifists and just war theorists for centuries.[19]

The first serious challenge to nonviolence as the Christian norm arose in the fourth century when Christianity became tolerated and later required for officials and soldiers in the Roman Empire. In this new context of Christian power, theologians such as Ambrose and

Augustine asked an essentially new question for Christians who, until then, had had little power (apart from the power of testimony and example). It is a question that can occur only to people who have access to coercive power: "Does the command to love our neighbors mean that we have a 'responsibility to protect,' with violence if 'necessary,' our neighbors if they are being attacked?" Ambrose argued that a Christian should not fight back if he personally was attacked but should fight to protect others.[20] Analogously, on the basis of love of neighbor, the Christian emperor had a responsibility to protect, with violence if "necessary," innocent neighbors from guilty neighbors (or enemy-neighbors). In this context we find the first explicit statements by major Christian leaders endorsing some wars.

In later centuries Christian (and secular) moral arguments supporting violent defense tended to shift from a basis in "love of neighbor" to a basis in "rights," and especially the "right to life," and its corollaries—the "right" of violent self-defense and the "right" to defend someone else whose "right" to life was threatened. Nevertheless, at the heart of the Christian argument for "just war" is the necessity of a just cause, specifically, the defense of the innocent. And underlying that is the conviction that love of neighbor implies a "responsibility to protect" violently. The recent literatures make this fundamental conviction more obvious again by separating it from self-interest and self-defense.

The point of this brief look at the origins of the Christian justifiable war tradition is that the essential moral argument then was identical with the essential moral argument today supporting just policing or a "responsibility to protect" by using violence. And it is not only at the beginning of the just war tradition that this fundamental moral argument has been posed against pacifists. The major challenges to pacifism in the last century have all had this same underlying shape, though with different guises, and accompanied by other arguments. World War II: was there not a moral responsibility—based in love of neighbor—to protect through war the innocent victims of Japanese and German slaughter? Wars of liberation or revolution: was/is there not a responsibility to protect innocent victims of "violent" international and national political/economic systems through violence when other means fail? So-called "humanitarian" interventions: should we not support, or even participate in, armed interventions to save Somalis from chaos and starvation or Rwandans from genocide? Don't we have a "responsibility to protect" in such cases, rooted in love of neighbor? Just policing and R2P, in this perspective, are the latest forms of the argument that we should kill some people to save others.

I have been addressing the core criterion of just war, "just cause," which calls upon us to protect the innocent, using violence if necessary. But other key elements of just war thought also appear in R2P and just policing discussions, especially "legitimate authority" (though now with an emphasis on that authority being international rather than national), "last resort" (though now, as noted above, this element is developed more fully), "discrimination" (though now seeking to aim even more narrowly at perpetrators and to avoid killing innocents), and use of only the minimum level of armed force necessary.

"Just policing" and "responsibility to protect" are thus simply the newest shape of the argument against pacifism. This is not to say it is a weak argument. Any pacifist Christian who has not struggled deeply with the force of the argument that love of neighbor implies a responsibility to protect, with violence if necessary, is morally obtuse. But this form of the argument is no more right than the other forms of it were when they were used against our pacifist forebears. If we now find it more persuasive, it is likely because we are more wealthy and influential—powerful and in control—than most generations of Mennonites before us. It has become easier for us to identify with those who have the ability to "make things happen" than with those who live on the margins. We are amid our own Constantinian shift.[21]

As noted earlier, one can identify important differences between policing and war, differences rightly stressed in the "just policing" literature, and differences that I acknowledge make a moral difference—some killing is clearly more morally reprehensible than other killing. Nevertheless, I see nothing in either the Mennonite tradition or in the gospel that suggests that the fundamental moral issue for followers of Jesus is between killing in certain very limited circumstances and killing more indiscriminately. In other words, the real differences between policing and war should not be decisive for Christians in terms of participating in one but not in the other.[22]

To show (as I hope I have done) that the arguments in the just policing and R2P literature do not change the fundamental theological and ethical issue does not end the discussion, of course. It is possible that Christian pacifists have wrongly understood the gospel and that just policing provides an important corrective. Have we been right in insisting that the gospel compels us to refuse participation in or support of killing, even to protect innocent peoples? This is a complex and vexing question, one which resists a definitive answer, but one with which I nevertheless struggle over the following pages.

THE BASIS FOR CHRISTIAN PACIFISM: WE DO SEE JESUS

One can begin by noting that Christian pacifism (at least the variety of it that I am interested in defending) does not start with the core question of just policing or (especially) of R2P: how can we protect the innocent from slaughter? Rather, the central questions for Christian pacifists are about Jesus. Is Jesus really our Lord? Do we believe that Jesus reveals to us God's will and way for humanity? If so, what does he reveal to us? And, will we follow what we see in Jesus, even when it seems hard, stupid, or even, to some, morally wrong?[23]

While the new literatures I refer to in this essay make powerful (if essentially familiar) arguments for exceptional resort to violence, they do not seriously address the basic Christian pacifist objection to such violence. This objection is, of course, partly and importantly based on the words and commands of Jesus, particularly, "love your enemies." But Christian pacifist objection to violence goes far deeper, into an understanding of Good News itself that cannot avoid seeing nonviolence as anything but essential for those who would follow Jesus. Christian pacifism, at least in this form, is no simple legalism or absolutism ("we should not kill because we are commanded not to kill"), no wooden following a moral rule.[24] It is not first and foremost that we are commanded to be nonviolent; it is that we are compelled (but not coerced), impelled, and wooed by God's love and God's way revealed in the life, death, and resurrection of Jesus to be nonviolent.

So compelled by God's love revealed definitively in Jesus Christ, Christians cannot help but refuse to participate in (or bless) killing. Our abstention from all killing is not for the sake of keeping pacifism pure[25] or of holding to an absolute rule[26] but for the sake of faithfulness to Jesus and for the sake of "effective" participation in God's work in history. To accept the Lordship of Christ is to affirm that he is Lord of *our* lives. This means obedience, doing what he teaches and models, even if it does not seem, in the world's frame of reference, to make sense. It means we can give allegiance to no other power that claims loyalty above him or to give obedience to any other power that asks us to contradict him.

Accepting the lordship of Christ is also to affirm that Jesus Christ is Lord of the *whole world*. The God of Jesus Christ is in charge, more powerful than any other power, and ultimately victorious over sin and death. We do not have to defend God with means contradicting God's teaching and modeling in Jesus. We do not have to calculate all the consequences of our actions but must rather do what Jesus teaches and shows us, knowing that our obedience to God's revealed will, not our human wisdom, is the path to "success." The relationship of effectiveness and faithfulness is an ultimately positive one: Faithfulness to God cannot help but be effective if God is indeed God.

Yet this connection between faithfulness and effectiveness is not always obvious if one does not know the "language" of faith, if one does not have "eyes to see." In fact, the effectiveness of the Christian way is often hidden—what is the cross except a terrible defeat from any perspective other than that of faith? We need to rely on faithfulness rather than our calculations of effectiveness precisely because we are not smart enough on the basis of our human calculations to see what effectiveness will really be.[27]

Christian pacifism is rooted in an understanding of a central meaning of the gospel itself: The good news is that evil is overcome by God through the cross and resurrection of Jesus Christ, not through exceptional resort to violence. God did not show us in Jesus that we should challenge evil nonviolently but then resort to violence in an extreme situation—like when Jesus' innocent life was at stake. Legions of angels were not called down to "protect." Rather, God "saves" through a miracle, something outside the purview of "common sense." One need not resolve the controverted question of whether *God* also might use violent means in dealing with evil[28] to be convinced that when we are instructed to take up our cross and follow Jesus, it means "don't kill, even to protect the innocent." We should continue to reject the view that participating in some kinds of killings (for example, "police" actions instead of wars) is a proper Christian calling.

All of this amounts to the conviction that our vocation as Christians is to begin living "as if" the reign of God has come among us, accepting the call to make our work in God's world the embodiment of the newness that Jesus revealed. Surely we do not do so fully; we live in the old (both around us and in us) as well as in the new. But there is something starkly incompatible between living into God's reign and killing.

BUT WHO SHOULD SAVE THE INNOCENT?

I have contended that Christians should never kill, even to save the innocent. This claim stands opposed to the literatures advocating

R2P and just policing. At the same time, Christian pacifists agree with just policing proposals that Christians should work diligently to protect the innocent. But in all likelihood gross human rights abuses will continue even if we become far more diligent in our nonviolent efforts to prevent and protect than we are. Who, then, saves the innocent, and how, in what sense?

On the deepest level the answer for Christians seems to me clear: God saves us, surely from our sins, but also from our enemies, including the last enemy, death. The prophets frequently condemned relying on horses and chariots for protection, seeing such reliance as a failure to trust in God for salvation. The story of Jesus is in continuity with this perspective. The truth of the claim that God saves the innocent or the defenseless from violence, however, is far from obvious. History and contemporary reality provide ample evidence of innocents who are not saved, in any evident way, by God or anyone else. Yet the claims that it is God who saves, not us, and that that salvation is real, even if it is not always what we want or expect, seem undeniably central to Christian faith.

There is a serious danger of "playing God" when one starts justifying killing some, even to protect others. Is not God the one who gives, and has the right to take, life? Does "policing" make us, rather than God, responsible for saving human beings?[29] How are we called to participate in God's work of salvation?

We do well to begin answering the question about protecting the innocent by remembering that God saves. Granted, there is surely truth in the saying "God has no hands but our hands." Watching the world go to hell in a handbasket is not authentic Christian behavior. We must care for the well-being and safety of neighbors. Yet perhaps it is not authentic Christian behavior to feel the need to figure out how we can provide security in every situation. Such a need might be a sign not of faith, but of atheism (or a messiah complex), a sign of our implicit conviction that we are the ones who must protect and save, because God cannot or will not. Do we really trust God for protection, or do we only trust God until we *really* find ourselves (or our neighbors or innocents abroad) threatened?

God saves us (endangered peoples included), and Christians should participate in God's work of salvation (including the work of saving endangered peoples) while following the nonviolent way revealed in Jesus. On these issues I am clear. It is also clear to me that God does work through the powers that be to provide protection. Our ordinary lives are enabled by systems of government that provide necessary services and protection. The absence of effective government is the source of enormous suffering, as Russian Mennonites who lived through the chaos after World War I can attest.[30] (Relatively) good government is one of God's gifts to humanity, and its function of preserving order (dependent on coercion, however immediately or however much in the background) is one of government's gifts to us in our fallen state. Even when governments seek to do evil, God can use them to serve God's purposes, for in everything God is working for the good. The fact that Christians are not called to the vocation of ruling by sword-bearing does not mean that the powers that be are somehow outside the realm of God's providence.

Granted, how to think about all this is not clear. The most perplexing question for me in thinking about just policing and R2P has to do with the role of "the powers that be" in God's work of saving endangered peoples and how Christians should relate to those powers that be. How should we Christian pacifists think about the use of such force by the powers that be and what counsel should we have for them? I see no obviously conclusive answer and can only offer the "benefit" of my unclarity.

BEYOND DUALISM AND MONISM: RETHINKING THE RELATIONSHIP OF PACIFISM AND THE STATE

One approach sharply distinguishes Christians from "the powers that be," claiming that while Christians should be nonviolent, the powers that be may rightly use violence in their particular role as an ordering of God which has the responsibility of protecting the good and punishing the guilty. Christians *should support* this violence by public authorities. From this perspective, there are two "right" actions that seem contradictory. It is right for the authorities to use lethal force as necessary, yet at the same time it is wrong for Christians to do so.[31]

Another approach is to claim that there can be only one "right" action, that nonviolence is the norm for everyone, the powers that be included, that there are always viable nonviolent options for public officials, and that if public officials choose violent options, Christians should insist that there are nonviolent policy options and *should condemn* their violent actions. This perspective also implies that there is no inherent reason why Christians should hesitate to hold public offices that might theoretically involve killing—because there will always be alternatives to killing. Here there is no contradiction between the best policy wisdom and the call of the gospel.

This approach is attractive in that it stretches us to imagine creative possibilities when we might see only dead ends. If the powers that be always hold open the option of violence, preparation for that violence will consume creative energies and not go to into preparing other options. As a result, violence as a last resort will, de facto, become violence as an early resort. Monist approaches reflect a conviction that God's world is not morally incoherent—we do not need to do (or support) evil so that good may come of it. Monism has the great advantage of being theologically and intellectually tidy. There is no awkward or embarrassing dualism here.

A third approach agrees with monism that there can be only one (really) "right" action, that nonviolence is the norm for everyone, the powers that be included. It agrees with strongly advocating the exploration and implementation of alternatives that will make it unnecessary to use violence to protect vulnerable populations. It agrees in condemning violence by the powers that be in a great many cases, because there are available nonviolent alternatives. It is, however, less hopeful that we, or the powers that be, can always find nonviolent alternatives when peoples are being slaughtered, tending to see more tragedy (cross) on the way to God's ultimate victory (resurrection).

This approach agrees with the first in distinguishing the Christian calling from that of the powers that be, accepting that these powers have a role in protecting the vulnerable that is different from ours. However, it *will never support* the violence of those powers, partly because there are frequently nonviolent or less violent alternatives available, and the quick or routine resort to violence to solve problems obscures better possibilities. It will press the powers to pursue less and less violent alternatives. It will actively *condemn*, speak out against, violent options that the powers pursue when there are realistic nonviolent or less violent alternatives. And even if we don't see available better nonviolent alternatives, we will continue to advocate and experiment with alternatives and work at prevention—refusing to support the increased violence of armed intervention.

This view recognizes that occasionally we cannot offer an immediate, viable, public policy alternative that is in keeping with our calling as disciples. We have no advice to offer on the immediate policy question, but we continue doing and advocating those (many) nonviolent things that make for peace. At the same time, however, in the absence of another available alternative, we *do not actively oppose* a policing intervention, for example.[32]

IMPLICATIONS FOR
MCC'S PROGRAMS AND WITNESS

After all this, my conviction that MCC should not give unqualified endorsement to just policing or R2P agendas should be clear. Nor should Christians participate in and support armed interventions as envisioned by R2P. Maintaining such a stance can be hard going for individual MCCers and for MCC offices, especially when trusted friends in sister organizations who are usually allies disagree. MCC advocacy offices in Washington, D.C., Ottawa, and New York work closely alongside ecumenical partners and trusted non-governmental organizations who understand R2P as a vital peacebuilding strategy, who advocate for better coordination among governmental efforts in development, diplomacy, and defense for the sake of peacemaking. Furthermore, from my limited experience as an MCC worker in the Philippines and from visits to MCC Burundi and Rwanda programs, I have developed an awareness of how difficult rejecting the just policing agenda can be when one is in a context where rescue from deadly threats seems possible only by armed means. The only "answer" in those immediate situations is walking with people and helping "save" them in creative nonviolent ways.[33]

At the same time, MCC should rejoice in the attentiveness to "the least of these" represented by these literatures and should encourage agencies at all levels to take seriously the calls for prevention of crises, for nonviolent interventions in crises, and for healing following crises.[34] The issue is "putting your money where your mouth is." Urging governmental and international bodies to drastically redirect resources from military and policing priorities to positive peacebuilding priorities is an important task if prevention rather than crisis response is to become the actual, operational norm.

Simply on the basis of "effective" witness to the powers that be, MCC should focus on encouraging prevention and nonviolent alternatives and not endorse armed interventions. MCC has been efficacious in its testimony to government because it gets noticed for its nonviolent activity around the world. Part of that effectiveness comes from having people on the ground and relating to local populations in ways that only its service orientation can achieve. But part also comes from the compatibility between means and ends—putting its pacifist money where its pacifist mouth is. It is hard to see how shifting to support of just policing or R2P could enhance the power of its witness.[35]

In terms of its programs, MCC should essentially continue doing what it is doing. The long, slow work of helping to provide jobs, education, health care, food, water, and more is foundational to caring for the least of these, including the least of these discussed in connection with R2P. While MCC's basic work is significant in preventing crises like those R2P addresses, it is important to recognize that a very small proportion of preventable human suffering is caused by the situations to which R2P is designed to respond. For example, addressing poverty remains central in preventing crises and in reducing the estimated 16,000 child deaths daily that are caused by hunger.[36] Dealing with the newsworthy slaughters that lead to calls for intervention is better than ignoring those slaughters. But they easily grab attention and cause us to miss "ordinary" misery—ordinary misery into which we can intervene with more hope of building the new than we can through R2P-type armed interventions.

One of the subtle problems with R2P is that it focuses great attention and resources on the human suffering caused by direct violence by perpetrators. By doing so, it (probably inadvertently) directs attention and resources away from much greater sources of human suffering like hunger and preventable diseases. Builders of the new will concentrate their primary energies at this level, not being too swayed by the latest crisis.

More immediately related to the just policing/R2P agenda, MCC should continue efforts to help peaceful resolution of conflicts at all levels. Genocides and other crimes against humanity grow out of long histories. Typically much time elapses before a crisis reaches the front page of *The New York Times,* time during which better understanding and possible resolution of tensions can be explored. And following a crisis, healing from trauma can be encouraged, as a way of averting yet another crisis.

Finally, in all its work with the poor, oppressed, and endangered, MCC should continue to embody the call of Jesus, "Come unto me, all ye who labor and are heavy laden, and I will give you rest." (Matt. 11:28, KJV). Christian faith, a gift to us and to others. Perhaps the best gift of all, a gift of hope and love in a hard world.

NOTES

1. "Tracing the Grain of the Universe: Project Overview," in *At Peace and Unafraid: Public Order, Security and the Wisdom of the Cross,* ed. Duane K. Friesen and Gerald W. Schlabach (Scottdale, Pa.: Herald Press, 2005): 21.

2. Available at http://mcc.org/about/peacecommitment/commitment.html. Accessed September 25, 2009.

3. "The Responsibility to Protect and the Decade to Overcome Violence (2001–2010)," *MCC Peace Office Newsletter* (October-December 2006): 11.

4. "Comments from Ernie Regehr," in,*The Responsibility to Protect: Ethical and Theological Reflections*, ed. Semegnish Asfaw, Guillermo Kerber, and Peter Weiderud (Geneva: World Council of Churches, 2005): 105-106. This wording found its way into the document adopted by the WCC Assembly in 2006 entitled "Vulnerable Populations at Risk: Statement on the Responsibility to Protect," accessed on September 25, 2009 at http://www.oikoumene.org/en/resources/documents/assembly/porto-alegre-2006/1-statements-documents-adopted/international-affairs/report-from-the-public-issues-committee/responsibility-to-protect.html

5. Doug Hostetter, "Responsibility to Protect: The Development of the Concept at the UN, and a Critique from Personal Experience and Christian Perspective," unpublished paper presented at a conference on *The Responsibility to Protect and Christian Nonviolence,* Ammerdown Centre, Bath, England, 18-20 July 2008.

6. Gerald Schlabach, Mennonite by origin, convert to Catholicism, and a self-described "Mennonite Catholic," is the main proponent of just policing. See especially *Just Policing, Not War: An Alternative Response to World Violence* (Collegeville, Minn.: Liturgical Press, 2007); his essay in *At Peace and Unafraid*, ed. Duane K Friesen and Gerald Schlabach; and his essays in *Just Policing: Mennonite-Catholic Theological Colloquium, 2002,* ed. Ivan J. Kauffman (Kitchener, Ont.: Pandora Press, 2004). Another major discussion among Mennonites on just policing appeared in *The Conrad Grebel Review*, although it focused mainly on domestic policing. See Andy Alexis Baker, "The Gospel or a Glock? Mennonites and the Police," Spring 2007, and the issue devoted entirely to Mennonites and Policing, Spring 2008. The essays in the Spring 2008 issue emerged from a conference organized by MCC Ontario on Christian understandings of policing.

7. The main documents related to R2P in the United Nations system are *The Responsibility to Protect* by the International Commission on Intervention and State Sovereignty (Ottawa, Canada: International Development Research Centre, 2001) accessed at http://www.iciss.ca/pdf/Commission-Report.pdf on September 26, 2009, which is the Canadian government supported study that developed the R2P concept, and the United Nations General Assembly *2005 World Summit Outcome,* sections 138-139, accessed September 26, 2009 at http://daccessdds.un.org/doc/UNDOC/GEN/N05/487/60/PDF/N0548760.pdf?OpenElement. The World Council of Churches endorsed the R2P language and approach in "Vulnerable Populations at Risk: Statement on the Responsibility to Protect."

8. See especially Glen Harold Stassen, *Just Peacemaking: Ten Practices for Abolishing War* (Cleveland, Oh.: Pilgrim Press, 2004). The WCC in its *Initial Statement towards an Ecumenical Declaration on Just Peace*, 89ff. seems to suggest that "just peacemaking" and "just policing" can overcome the pacifist/nonpacifists divide. Accessed September 26, 2009 at http://www.overcomingviolence.org/en/resources/documents/declarations-on-just-peace/drafting-group/initial-statement.html .

Another older term used to discuss the same set of issues is "humanitarian intervention." By shortly after the turn of the century, this language had largely been abandoned in favor of these newer languages.

9. This is an important theme, however, in Schlabach's writing and in the

WCC documents noted above.

10. So, for example, the MCC Washington, D.C., Office increasingly finds itself in coalitions in which R2P or 3D (the coordination and sometimes integration of development, diplomacy, and defense initiatives) approaches are taken for granted, and as a result sometimes finds itself having to abstain from signing on to joint declarations by church advocacy offices, given the inclusion of support for forms of armed intervention in those declarations.

11. See Doug Hostetter, "Responsibility to Protect," for a fine brief description of the shift in UN circles on this matter of national sovereignty and the responsibility to protect.

12. This discussion relates closely to different understandings of the underlying rationales for permitting war with the justifiable war tradition which will be discussed later. Here it is sufficient to note that the former is far more compelling to Mennonite theological/ethical sensibilities than the latter.

13. I focus here especially on just policing language. While there are differences in these various literatures, they share commonalities on the points most relevant to our discussion. Just policing deals not only with the need for armed interventions in situations such as those described above; it also addresses domestic policing. International armed intervention is, however, the subject of this essay.

14. See for example Gerald Schlabach, *Just Policing: Mennonite-Catholic Theological Colloquium*, 2002, 57-59.

15. See, for example, Jim Wallis, "Hard Questions for Peacemakers," *Sojourners* (January-February 2002): 29-33. Wallis also claims, without documentation, that John Howard Yoder near the end of his life "was asking whether those committed to nonviolence might support the kind of necessary force utilized by police, because it is (or is designed to be) much more constrained, controlled, and circumscribed by the rule of law than is the violence of war, which knows few real boundaries" (32). It is easy to believe, on the basis of Yoder's life work, that he would be "supportive" of policing as preferable to war, just as he supported "strict constructionist" just war thought compared to what he called "just war without teeth." [Yoder, "How Many Ways Are There to Think Morally about War?" *The Journal of Law and Religion* 11/1 (1994): 83-107.] That did not mean he accepted a strict constructionist just war stance as the right Christian posture, and I have seen no evidence that the differences he rightly saw between policing and war meant that he viewed the first as a faithful Christian vocation (unless, perhaps, policing is redefined so as to rule out the readiness to kill if "necessary"). For a survey of Yoder's writing on the subject of policing see Andy Alexis-Baker, "Unbinding Yoder from Just Policing," in *Power and Practices: Engaging the Work of John Howard Yoder*, ed. Jeremy Bergen and Anthony Siegrist (Scottdale, Pa.: Herald Press, 2009): 147-165.

16. While I continue to accept this claim of just policing as being true, at least in situations like genocide, Nathan Colborne has raised serious objections to "policing" as a language to replace "warring" language. He argues, roughly, that viewing conflicts in societies or in the global community as a struggle of police versus criminals short-circuits debate because it assumes that the police are legitimate and criminals are illegitimate, when in both pol-

itics and in war the question of who is legitimate is precisely what is at stake. War, we might say, is a form of politics; policing is not. See Colborne, "A Peace Crueler than War? Just Policing in a Foucauldian Perspective," *The Mennonite Quarterly Review* 84/2 (April 2010): 249-266.

17. This is also true in the World Council of Churches documents *Vulnerable Populations at Risk* and *Initial Statement towards an Ecumenical Declaration on Just Peace*, cited above.

18. I am choosing in this essay not to speak to practical objections to R2P and just policing, focusing instead primarily on theological issues. However, I believe that some of these practical objections pose significant issues that should give pause to supporting armed interventions, theological convictions aside. Among these questions are the following.

1. Would an effective system of "just policing" be a good thing?

a. Can we safely assume that the global system would be just, and the police used justly?

b. What about sin? How can we know that the police will only defend the good? What is meant by "the international community" and who is, in fact, included, particularly when R2P actions can only be authorized by the Security Council and when the five permanent members can veto Council actions? Is this again a "community" that excludes the weak?

c. Can international interventions be like "community policing"?

2. Practical questions about implementation in the global political system

a. What is policing really like? How different are policing and war?

b. Is it possible to develop effective policing, policing that includes policing of big powers, not only of small powers? If not, then is not just policing simply another cover for domination of the weak by the strong?

c. Will just policing or the responsibility to protect simply lead to more justifications for more wars based on the "right" to interfere in the internal affairs of other states because of alleged human rights violations? Might the acceptance of these frameworks open the door to justifications of war that older theories allowing only "self-defense" prohibited?

d. How can just policing be confined or restrained as the theory suggests it will be? What is to keep just policing from becoming just (or unjust) war? What kind of serious (and very different) training would be needed for just policing interventions?

e. Can just policing be effective in protecting the innocent if it is limited by constraints on the use of force? Would just policing accept the possibility of surrender? If so, would this mean that big criminals would escape interventions? If not, how would just policing avoid becoming war?

19. Much of the argument in this section is taken from "Caring for the Least of These," *Canadian Mennonite* (April 14, 2008): 7-8. This feature article included views of several people, including Ernie Regehr, who disagreed with my assessment of the link between R2P and just war.

20. E.g., Ambrose quoted in Louis J. Swift, *The Early Fathers on War and Military Service* (Washington, Del.: Michael Glazier, Inc., 1983): 100-102.

21. MCC is, of course, an important part of this shift. It is, after all, MCC that taught us to speak with our political authorities through (although not only through) offices in Ottawa, New York, and Washington, DC. This shift is not inherently bad. The issue is whether we become more like Constantine, or

whether Constantine is prodded to become more Christ-like.

22. On the point of whether the difference between policing and war makes a difference concerning the appropriateness of Christian participation, it seems Schlabach disagrees. See, for example, *Just Policing: Mennonite-Catholic Theological Colloquium, 2002,* 23ff.

23. Here there is a vivid contrast with Ernie Regehr's contention quoted in the introduction: "This refusal in principle to preclude the use of force . . . is based on the certain knowledge that the primary consideration must be the welfare of people, especially those in situations of extreme vulnerability and who are utterly abandoned to the whims and prerogatives of their tormentors." This is a rather different starting point than the "certain knowledge" that we should follow Jesus.

24. As I am writing this there is much in the news about CIA torture and threats against enemies captured in the "war on terror." I am grateful for the moral outrage that many express against such actions. Yet I am mystified by this question: Why is it so awful in the eyes of many (most?) Americans when enemies are tortured and threatened in order to get information that might save many lives, but many of the same Americans would have no qualms if these same enemies were killed in an air strike or an assassination? Why is "absolutism" good in the case of rejecting torture (I agree that it is), but bad in the case of rejecting killing? Most (moral) people have some absolutes; it is not, therefore, an automatically negative thing if pacifists are "absolutists"— even though this isn't the fundamental basis of pacifism as I understand it.

25. As Hansulrich Gerber suggests above, and as Gerald Schlabach puts it somewhat differently: "My plea is that Mennonites not reject the just policing agenda simply to protect their pacifist identity for its own sake." See "Just Policing and the Christian Call to Nonviolence" in *At Peace and Unafraid,* 419-420.

26. As David Cortright suggests in rejecting "absolute pacifism" in favor of "pragmatic pacifism." See Cortright, *Peace: A History of Movements and Ideas* (Cambridge, UK: Cambridge University Press, 2008).

27. See my essay, "Thinking Theologically about War against Iraq," *The Mennonite Quarterly Review* 78/1 (January 2003): 100.

28. The issue of God's judgment and God's nature (i.e., is God a pacifist?) goes beyond both my topic here and my capability.

29. It is good to call to mind here the maxim "do no harm" underscored by Doug Hostetter, an important reminder for us as fallible human creatures who are not God. This is not a call to inaction, but, as I read it, a call to actions that are themselves not harmful. It is a caution against "doing evil that good may come of it." It also points to a morally significant distinction between doing something evil oneself and refusing to do evil in order to prevent others from doing a (presumed) greater evil.

30. They can also attest, of course, to the horrors of government power run amuck.

31. My essay, "Mennonites and the State: Preliminary Reflections" in *Essays on Peace Theology and Witness,* Occasional Papers No. 12, ed. Willard M. Swartley (Elkhart, Ind.: Institute of Mennonite Studies, 1988) makes an argument for a position somewhat similar to this. I hope it is more nuanced, critical, and limited than some versions of this perspective, partly because it ar-

gues that Christians should seek to hold government accountable to a standard of "least possible violence," while "dualistic" views often seem to give governments a blank check to do what they want. To be fair, most "dualistic" perspectives would claim that ultimately God's will for all of humanity is one—nonviolence. Differences in moral callings which mean it might be "right" penultimately for government to kill arise because of government's particular/peculiar function in a fallen world.

32. A view very similar to that developed here is reflected in the summary of one MCC Peace Committee meeting where these issues were debated April 11-12, 1997: "We will not call for humanitarian military intervention. We appreciate that there may be tragic situations where we have no alternative course of action to suggest. This could be either because our understanding is incomplete or because we cannot see a possible nonviolent solution. In situations like these, we may choose to publicly neither oppose nor support an international intervention. We would remain silent, not to disengage or to avoid action or to legitimate violence, but in recognition of the tragic and ambiguous nature of the situation.

"Governments, however . . . are required to act. Part of our responsibility at such times is to stretch the imaginations of both those who must act and those who can choose whether to act or not. In this light, we will frequently comment on humanitarian military interventions that governments or international bodies decide to take. We acknowledge that such interventions can, in some situations, save lives."

33. See Doug Hostetter's essay, above, for some examples. Also many issues of the MCC *Peace Office Newsletter* address these matters, including most recently the April-June and July-September 2009 issues on Rwanda and Burundi and on trauma healing, respectively.

34. I find these articulated especially well in the WCC documents.

35. I thank Theron Schlabach for this point.

36. "Hunger Facts: International," Bread for the World. Accessed October 4, 2009 at http://www.bread.org/learn/hunger-basics/hunger-facts-international.html.

Chapter 17

A Theoretical Framework for Understanding MCC's Emphasis on Relationships

TERRENCE JANTZI

But relationships are the most important part of our work. . . . As a former MCC worker who has intermittently worked with MCC over the past 20 years, I routinely have encountered statements stressing the importance of building relationships. Orientation sessions in Akron would discuss their significance. Country directors would affirm their centrality to new MCC service workers. Storytelling excursions by returned MCC workers would highlight the key role played by relationships in their work. Books on MCC celebrated MCC's diverse relationships.

However, despite the general acknowledgement that building relationships is an important organizational value, there has always been some difficulty within MCC in defining exactly *why* relationships are important. For the most part, development-focused efforts at justifying relationships within MCC have been pragmatic allusions to enhancing program efficiency, taking the form of claims such as, "If we build relationships, we will be better able truly to ascertain community needs," or "If we build relationships then people will be more willing to participate in our programs or adopt our innovations." However, this pragmatic emphasis does not reflect, at least not fully, the importance that building relationships occupies within MCC lore. Enhanced program efficiency would not explain why a country director might tell a new service worker that "it doesn't matter what you actually do in the community, so long as you build relationships while doing it."

An MCC Board member once commented to me, "You know, what MCC needs is a theoretical framework for relationship building." A good theoretical framework should be able to articulate a rationale for the intrinsic value MCC lore places on relationships and provide a means for analyzing MCC's non-program impact in community development. An articulated framework could also provide a mechanism for incorporating relationship building into program planning and program design.

This chapter should be considered an initial foray into developing such a framework. The essay is largely based on my doctoral research in MCC Bolivia in summer 2000. However, I will also draw on anecdotal experiences as a former MCC worker in Nicaragua, Lesotho, Bolivia, and Somalia and more recently as an MCC consultant to Colombia, Haiti, Uganda, and Bolivia for insight regarding the role of relationships in MCC and trends in MCC programming.

Two major constructs are presented as part of the analysis: social density and social capital. Emile Durkheim's model of *social density* emerged in the nineteenth century and has not normally been applied to community development work, but some elements in this model provide insights into the connection between relationships and development. The second construct, *social capital*, is a relatively recent phenomenon that only became widely applied to community development about fifteen years ago. Although social capital is the more contemporary construct, this narrative will first briefly cover Durkheim's concept of social density because it serves as the intellectual progenitor to the subsequent social capital literature.

DURKHEIM, SOCIAL DENSITY, AND DEVELOPMENT

Emile Durkheim, a French sociologist of the late nineteenth century and one of the greatest sociological theorists ever, developed models of society that have influenced generations of researchers within disparate fields, including international development, where his models served as the foundation for modernization theory, one of the principle paradigms of development.[1] Durkheim developed the concept of *social density* as a model to explain variations in societies.[2] He posited that certain societal characteristics could be deduced from the shape of social networks. Durkheim considered a society's social density to be a measure of the frequency and diversity of the social interactions within a given space. In Durkheim's framework, a social interaction was a moment of focused, ritualized interaction between two individuals or among a group of individuals. These interactions could range from relatively informal and simple greeting rituals ("Hi, how are you?") to more elaborate occasional ceremonies such as weddings or funerals, as well as simple everyday activities such as cooking together or farming together. The key element in all was a moment of shared interaction. These moments of shared interactions create a relationship bond ranging from slight and tenuous to deeper and longer lasting. A collection of social interactions within a group over time will build a sense of solidarity and cohesion between and among individuals.

Table 1: Societal Characteristics in High and Low Social Density

Low Social Density	High Social Density
• Generalist • Concrete forms of thought • Use of context-specific language • A religion based on a personal relationship to a deity • Intolerant • Slow rates of change • Strong sense of individual identity • Strong emphasis on community	• Specialist • Abstract forms of thought • Use of context-neutral language • A religion based on an abstract concept of deity (the divine life force, "that of God in all of us", etc.) • Tolerant • Rapid rates of change • Weak sense of individual identity • Strong emphasis on individual freedom

However, these social interactions do more than create a relationship bond; they also embed ideas. Durkheim posited that any ritualized interaction, no matter how informal or brief, contained implicit ideas or values planted within the participating individuals. The more an individual engages in a particular social interaction, the stronger the implicit values become embedded in the individual.

Durkheim contended that individuals in a low social density context would share similar characteristics including being generalists, using a concrete, simplified language, and having a strong sense of identity. In contrast, individuals in a context of high social density would be more specialized, use a more abstract language, and have a weaker sense of identity.[3] Subsequent theorists throughout the late 1800s and early 1900s applied Durkheim's ideas of social density to a range of phenomena from religion to economics to social change. The graph above depicts some of the societal characteristics ascribed to low and high social density contexts.[4]

Community development is a field devoted to intentional social change, facilitating the acceptance of new ideas in a context, and encouraging individuals to think creatively about solutions to community-based issues. In addition, initiatives such as micro-enterprise and alternative agriculture are based on encouraging individuals to find economic "niches" that they can occupy to increase household income.[5] Drawing on the social density model, one could say that the community development worker is trying to create a higher social density context—one that would see a more rapid rate of change, greater tolerance of diversity, an ability to think abstractly, and an emphasis on economic specialization. It follows then that changes in a community that create a higher social density— changes that increase the frequency and diversity of social interactions—should have consequences for development beyond specific programs.

Consider then the hypothetical scenario of a North American development worker sent to a country like Bolivia and placed in a relatively isolated rural community. The presence of this worker represents an automatic increase in the diversity found in the community. As they engage in the life of the community, such workers must perforce engage in social interactions with the community members around them—i.e., relationship building. If one steps back from the scene and measures the social density of the community, one could argue that the presence of a foreign worker will slightly increase the social density of the community through a slight increase in the frequency and a slight increase in the diversity of social interactions within the context. According to Durkheim, this slight increase in social density should also be accompanied by a slight increase in tolerance, a higher rate of change, and more creativity—regardless of what the worker actually does in the community.

There are some caveats to this conclusion. The presence of diversity in a community does not automatically imply an increase in community social density. Actual social interactions have to take place across this diversity. Durkheim's models allowed for pockets of relatively higher and lower social density in a region. Individuals who engage in more frequent and more diverse social interactions will occupy a higher level of social density than individuals who do not.

One can use this social density framework to interpret the impact of a community development worker's relationship building. If workers choose to disengage from the community and simply focus on their project work ("I only drill wells"), they will limit the frequency of their social interactions in the community and thus have less influence on community social density. If a worker only interacts with one segment of the community, then the benefit of social interaction diversity will only accrue to that segment of the community, meaning that one part of the community may experience a slight increase in social density but that the rest of the community will maintain its old level. Finally, if a worker is traveling throughout a wide region and has only infrequent social interactions, then the impact of these interactions is diminished, as Durkheim's models require repetitive social interactions to build higher social density.

SOCIAL DENSITY AND
MCC RELATIONSHIP BUILDING

In my research of MCC community development efforts in Bolivia, I focused on the positive and negative *unintended* consequences of an MCC worker presence. One of the common patterns that emerged confirmed the correlation of positive unintended consequences with higher social density. When MCC workers focused their time on a single community, intentionally engaged in a broad range of village life, and worked to build relationships with all sectors of a community, social density and positive unintended consequences emerged. In contrast, negative unintended consequences were most often correlated with MCC workers choosing to focus on their work to the exclusion of community life, trying to cover a broad zone or region, and focusing on a single sector of a community.[6]

The social density model can be brought to bear on the debated question of whether MCC should focus on placing international workers or on hiring local national workers to undertake community development work. From a transfer of technology perspective, hiring local national workers would make sense. They should already be familiar with the context, should have had training relevant to the needs of the community, and should already be able to speak the language. Everett Roger's work on the diffusion of innovations contended that change agent *homophily*—meaning how similar they were to the target population—was an important factor for whether a new innovation became widely adopted.[7] From this perspective, hiring a local national worker should create greater program effectiveness.

However, a foreign worker should have a greater impact on social density since one of the measures of increasing social density is the diversity of social interactions found in a context. A foreign worker will represent greater social diversity than a local national and their social interactions should lead to higher social density than an equivalent national worker. Hiring local national workers might increase program effectiveness, but placing international MCC workers should have greater unintended consequences because of their greater influence on community social density.

This local national versus international worker debate became particularly acrimonious in MCC Africa several years ago but has surfaced periodically in all regions. Applying the social density model to the debate suggests that the debate is between enhancing program effectiveness, on the one hand, and maximizing positive unintended consequences, on the other. Since these two models address very different dimensions of development work, this debate not surprisingly can become heated and has probably been exacerbated precisely because MCC lacks a relationship model for unintended consequences to incorporate alongside its program effectiveness models.

SOCIAL CAPITAL AND
COMMUNITY DEVELOPMENT

Social capital is a relatively recent model located within the Durkheimian intellectual tradition.[8] Although theorists and researchers had been studying the effects of social networks for decades, social capital literally roared onto the community development scene in the early 1990s, popularized by a series of articles by Robert Putnam culminating in his essay, "Bowling Alone: The Decline of Social Capital in America."[9] Community development researchers turning their energies to the task of understanding the role of social capital within community development generated literally thousands of articles during the latter half of the 1990s.[10] Social capital is now considered to be an integral component of community development and has provided a useful framework for understanding the unintended positive and negative consequences of NGOs working in community development.[11]

Social capital has generally been defined as "the features of social organization, such as social networks, norms, and values which help coordination and cooperation for mutual benefit."[12] Social capital is the facilitating agent that allows for rapid citizen mobilization and has a multiplier effect on other forms of community capital development.[13]

Putnam described four types of capital inherent in all communities: natural resource, infrastructural, human, and social capital.[14] He contended that a sustainable community would have all four of these capitals in balance. Putnam's framework gave community development workers a model for identifying what types of community development would be most appropriate in any given context. Where natural resource capital was degraded, environmental conservation efforts could be implemented, whereas if human capital was missing, skills training programs could be developed.

This community capital framework was later expanded and modified.[15] However, the role of social capital has most captured the imagination of researchers. It was an "invisible" capital—difficult to see by an outsider but nevertheless crucial for the well-being and sustainability of the community and necessary for the success of other development programs.

Numerous writers have stressed the contribution that dense and overlapping social networks make to a community's social capital. These networks can consist either of the formal associational networks found in civic groups or the informal social networks present in any community or region.[16] Both types of networks are important for social capital. These networks allow for the flow of information throughout a community, permit exchanges to occur, and provide a matrix within which to carry out community analysis, discussion, and consensus building.

Still, the mere existence of social networks does not imply a high level of social capital. Initial models contended that the patterns of organization in the social networks would yield different forms of social capital, not all healthy.[17] Butler Flora classified a community's social capital as horizontal, hierarchical, or non-existent based on the type of social networks present in the community[18].Social networks that are dense, overlapping, and promote egalitarian exchanges give rise to *horizontal social capital*—a positive force for development. In contrast, *hierarchical social capital* contained strong vertical networks

with weak or non-existent horizontal networks. Patron-client relationships or communities that depend upon a single industry typically exemplify hierarchical social capital.[19] This hierarchical type of
social structure was prevalent in areas of persistent poverty and was
an impediment to sustainable community development.[20] *Non-existent social capital* resulted from extreme isolation and the absence of
any social networks. Communities with non-existent social networks
are characterized by high rates of transition, high levels of crime and
delinquency, and low trust.[21]

Flora and Flora later refined the definition of social capital to include *bonding* and *bridging* components (see Table 2).[22] Bonding social
capital referred to the degree of internal cohesion and solidarity
within a group. Bridging social capital referred to the number of external connections outside of the group. Healthy communities would
contain both strong bonding capital and strong bridging capital. Un-
healthy communities would be weak in one or both of these dimensions.

Table 2: Bonding and Bridging Social Capital

Social capital does not consist solely of the network structures in
a community but also encompasses the set of norms embedded

	Low	**Bridging Social Capital**	*High*
		Individualism	*Regionalism*
Low **Bonding Social Capital**		Few connections between individuals. The wealthy tend to substitute economic capital for social capital (security, etc.) while the poor have few options.	Strong group identities, but little connection between groups. Region very resistant to change.
High		*Clientelism* Low sense of community identity, regional change promoted by connections to external interests	*Progressive Participation* Regional change driven by community needs and interests. Vital and healthy dynamics.

within these social relationships. According to the social density model, a specific social interaction in the networks will embed specific ideas. While these interactions may create a relationship bond, some types of social interaction can create negative complications. One such factor is the presence of power differentials.[23] Significant power differentials embedded in a social interaction can inhibit trust formation, limit the potential for reciprocal exchanges, and create one-way relationships leading to hierarchical social capital.[24] Theorists identified a set of norms important for strong social capital in a community—including trust, reciprocity, accountability, inclusiveness, and symbolic diversity—and proceeded to examine how interaction rituals may foster (or inhibit) the creation of these norms in a community.[25]

SOCIAL CAPITAL AND COMMUNITY DEVELOPMENT

The NGO Worker and Social Capital

Since social capital is the product of the social interactions and networks in a community, factors that impinge on these social networks will have an effect on social capital—intentional or not.[26] Most development organizations tend to emphasize technical, economic, or political development efforts rather than social capital. Nevertheless, these initiatives will affect social capital through the distortion or creation of social networks, the changing of values or norms, or the construction of new forms of interaction and leadership structures. In addition, the presence of NGO workers in a community or region will influence the social networks, norms, and values in the community as a byproduct of their presence and relationships.[27] In this analysis, four dimensions are important: trust, power, bonding/bridging capital, and informal networks.

Norms of Trust

NGO program plans are implemented through the actions and interactions of specific individuals (e.g., development officials, extension officers, or government representatives). The levels of trust embedded in these specific social relationships will influence not only the degree of community receptivity but also the social capital and norms present in the community. The more that NGO workers establish trust or engage in rituals that emphasize trust, the more they will increase social capital reserves in a community.

Power Differentials

As mentioned earlier, extreme power differentials are problematic for social capital. Power differentials embedded in the relationships between development personnel and community target populations can inhibit trust formation as well as creating hierarchical social networks. Although he does not use social capital vocabulary, Chambers' critique of the professional, mainstream development programs emphasizes the problems inherent in low social network integration and high power differentials.[28] Vergara argues that many NGOs create power differentials and hierarchical networks when they enter a community. When NGOs focus on a community's weaknesses, participants relate to NGOs as *beneficiaries*. Community members form relationships with the NGO personnel from a position of weakness and create patron-client networks.[29]

Bridging and Bonding Capital

Development workers in a community with weak bridging capital may find that they can be most effective in strengthening social capital by connecting community groups with each other (or to outside of the community). At the same time, development workers in a community with weak bonding capital may be able to create internal cohesion and solidarity through shared, collective activities. The relationships the NGO worker forms through shared activities will be an important factor influencing the quality of social capital in the community.[30]

Formal and Informal Interactions

While the social interactions generated by an NGO worker's formal development workshops and meetings are often documented, the informal interactions of the NGO worker are less systematized. Research findings consistently cite the importance of informal interpersonal interactions in promoting community development.[31] Most professional development programs attempt to create learning through formal interactions (e.g., workshops, seminars, or trainings) and in the process minimize the role of informal interactions. While there is a role for formal structures in community development, this bias underestimates the influence that informal interactions and long-term interactions can play in social learning and in creating this important bridging and bonding capital.[32]

The value of the social network integration of change agents, informal interactions, and trust-building are not necessarily new concepts within the field of development. However, interpreting these principles through the lens of social capital suggests that these elements have implications that reach beyond enhancing program effectiveness. An NGO program that negatively affects the social capital in a community can depress the potential of the community in other endeavors.

NGO programs may thus need to be evaluated not only in terms of whether they have accomplished their goals related to technology transfer or economic development but also in terms of whether they have positively or negatively affected social capital. Ironically, NGO projects labeled successes may actually reduce social capital and thereby depress community potential. Conversely, NGO projects labeled failures may actually enhance community development if they created greater levels of healthy social capital.

MCC AND SOCIAL CAPITAL: A BOLIVIA RESEARCH PROJECT

During the late 1990s my doctoral research on MCC examined how MCC workers affected community social capital. The project focused on a single region of Bolivia—the Yapacani Regional Development Program. The Yapacani colonization zone is located about 120 kilometers northwest of the city of Santa Cruz, where from 1990 to 1999 MCC operated an integrated development program.

The program contained two distinct components. First, an extension and rural development program based in the northern section of the Yapacani zone operated with personnel placed in local communities and carried out community development activities in these communities around agriculture, health, and education. Second, MCC personnel based in the region's central town promoted institutional strengthening among the Yapacani institutions and all the communities in the region. The research findings identified programmatic factors that enhanced and hurt community social capital.

MCC program elements that enhanced community social capital included low resource availability, worker placement in specific local communities, the practice of personal and program values that emphasized power devolution (e.g., servanthood values from a faith-based perspective or a simple living ethic), shared collaborative activities, and activities such as farmer-to-farmer visits that convened disparate groups together.

Low budget and minimal program resources

Economic wealth and status are one source of power. MCC generally operated with extremely low budgets. Programs usually allocated enough for the maintenance of program personnel, but with few, if any, additional resources for program infrastructure or funding projects. Having small budgets made community-based MCC personnel doing extension work more dependent on neighbors for carrying out program activities. This dynamic in turn encouraged reciprocal exchanges and reduced power differentials between the volunteers and the community. The minimal resources also encouraged more creative approaches to problem solving that drew on social capital reserves for successful implementation.

Placing personnel in communities

Assigning MCC workers to live in communities opened opportunities for forming relationships and for deep integration into rural social networks. Volunteer integration into community social networks helped network expansion and allowed for the volunteer perspectives and insights to be integrated into the community decision-making matrix (increasing social density). Placing volunteers in communities also reduced power differentials between the community members and the MCC staff, equalizing status and thus allowing horizontal relationships to form.

Values

MCC workers often possessed personal values or attitudes that motivated efforts to reduce power differentials between themselves and community members. For example, MCC recruits place a high priority on service and servanthood. Hence MCC personnel in Bolivia often intentionally sought to place themselves in positions of relatively low power in community dynamics; rather than arriving with an attitude of *"We are here to teach you"* they came with an attitude of *"We are here to serve you."* This value stance had the effect of helping to promote horizontal relationships and because of the specific social interactions involved, also embedded these servanthood values.

Egalitarian involvements

A former MCC country director once commented that "Relationships are built through shared activities." In this spirit volunteers thus worked alongside farmers harvesting their crops, clearing the land, or helping out with community-level projects. By working side-by-side with community members in shared activities rather than as supervisors or trainers, volunteers reduced power differentials between themselves and community members and promoted the creation of horizontal networks with the community members with greater trust embedded in the networks.

Ecumenical approaches

MCC volunteers tended to participate in the communities' religious life, an important social networking context.[33] The volunteers' willingness to participate in community spiritual life gave them greater credibility with community members and increased their acceptance among the people. Furthermore, in the interest of relating to all the community members and not appearing to take sides, MCC personnel living in communities usually adopted an ecumenical approach and supported any church denominations present. They also carried out community-wide activities (both secular and religious) that incorporated both church bodies. These ecumenical practices encouraged the creation of overlapping networks that crossed religious boundaries, fostered increased tolerance between members of different churches, and strengthened the norm of inclusiveness.

Farmer-to-farmer exchange programs

An evaluation of the Yapacani program found that farmer-to-farmer exchanges were frequently mentioned program highlights even though MCC viewed these as minor components to the program. When asked to elaborate, community interviews detailed that it was relatively rare for farmers to have a chance to visit non-family members in different communities. Farmer-to-farmer exchanges gave people opportunities to make connections and build relationships with others that they would not normally have met, promoting bridging social capital between groups.

Informal and long-term interactions versus the legitimization of presence

Placing volunteers in communities and emphasizing the importance of personal relationships helped volunteers integrate into the informal and long-term community networks where much collective learning occurs. This integration helped enhance community reflection and analysis on issues.

FACTORS REDUCING SOCIAL CAPITAL

Other aspects of the MCC program reduced social capital levels, reinforcing power differentials and inhibiting volunteer integration into community social networks. These included the following:

High resource availability

Persistent corruption in Bolivia has created an environment of suspicion and distrust surrounding any type of financial or material allocation.[34] Such suspicion has made it difficult for communities and NGOs to work together when large amounts of financial or material resources are at stake.

The MCC personnel in the Yapacani program reasoned that communities needed to take charge of their own development rather than rely on these NGOs of whom they were suspicious. This led them to develop a program where communities would write and submit their own projects for donor funding. Unfortunately, this move had negative unintended consequences; in spite MCC's intentions, communities were still dependent on an NGO in the process, namely, MCC. The fact that the program required MCC to act as a "gate-keeper" for access to international donor funds unintentionally created hierarchical networks between community members and MCC workers. Suspicions around possible embezzlement also eroded the levels of trust that MCC personnel had been able to establish with rural community members.

Zone-wide coverage

The region-wide component of the Yapacani program placed personnel in the central town to help operation across the zone. As a consequence, the volunteers living in town were not able to integrate very well into any social network. Communities did not get to know the volunteers and consequently did not trust them as much. Plus, the intermittent social interactions meant that the volunteers had relatively little influence on social density in any one place.

Overemphasis on formal workshops

In many communities, MCC involvement was limited to infrequent, high-intensity workshops with little or no outside interaction. Although the workshops did have a positive impact in some communities, the stand-alone, high-intensity format meant that the workshops did not necessarily contribute to increasing social density (the ideas and norms did not "embed" strongly) and the local social networks were not affected either.

Interchangeability of personnel
In some areas of the program a series of short-term personnel were used interchangeably to continue a process or program. The frequent transitions in MCC personnel inhibited relationship formation, trust building, and social network integration. Regular personnel turnover further resulted in minimizing the potential of MCC workers to strengthen social capital or to increase social density.

QUINCE AND CHALLAVITO: A TALE OF TWO COMMUNITIES

The contrasting experiences of MCC in two rural Yapacani communities highlight different connections among social capital, social density, and development. Quince and Challavito are neighboring communities in the northern section of the Yapacani zone. They have been settled for roughly the same length of time and have similar natural resource and economic capital. MCC worked in both communities for at least six years. However, the two communities demonstrated radically different responses to MCC programs. In Challavito MCC programs yielded encouraging results. The community took the initiative to design, develop, and implement several community-based projects. In contrast, Quince proved to be an extremely problematic experience for MCC workers. Tensions and frustration between MCC workers and community members eventually reached the point that MCC discontinued its work there.

This decision was particularly noteworthy because the Quince leaders were among the first community elder to lobby MCC to set up a rural development program in the Yapacani colonization zone, and early reports contained many positive references to Quince. In contrast, Challavito was an afterthought with little positive comments. The surprising divergence in the two communities can be attributed to two dimensions: first, existing internal social capital, and second, subtle differences in MCC's programming presence.

Community characteristics
The two communities possessed very different types of social capital. In Quince, a strong, authoritarian leader dominated the community, creating hierarchical social capital. The community also consisted of several relatively autonomous groups that had few connections with each other. Based on the social capital analysis presented earlier, these characteristics would indicate a fairly low level of community social capital dominated by a hierarchical form of social capi-

tal and located in the *clientelism* quadrant of the bridging/bonding table profiled earlier.

In contrast, Challavito was a smaller community that had overlapping horizontal networks with fewer distinct groups creating network gaps. The community had significant internal cohesion and was located in the *regionalism* quadrant of the bridging/bonding table profiled earlier. In addition, there was a tradition within the community of diverse leadership and strong norms related to rotating leadership roles. These factors contributed to a more horizontal form of social capital. The presence of this horizontal form of social capital was reflected in MCC worker reports noting that Challavito community members demonstrated both greater creative analysis during community workshops and were more likely to take advantage of available MCC technical resources.

Differences in MCC programming

The differences in social capital in the two communities may have been present at the beginning of the MCC presence in the region, but subtle differences in MCC programming also influenced the communities' social capital, enhancing the community social capital in Challavito and hurting it in Quince. One of these differences in programming was the relative continuity of the MCC personnel in each community and their integration into the social networks in the communities. MCC placed workers in both Quince and Challavito for the first six years of the Yapacani program. However, the volunteer presence in each community differed significantly.

In Quince, a succession of short-term volunteers lived in the community for periods of several months to one year. Eight different MCC workers worked successively in the community over a six-year period. The quantity of volunteers and the relatively short periods involved meant that it was difficult for trust to build between the community and the specific MCC workers, preventing service workers from integrating into the social networks of the community and reducing the frequency of social interactions (lowering social density). In addition, the two volunteers who did live in the community for relatively longer periods primarily engaged in zone-wide work, spending most of their time visiting other communities. Their continued absences made it difficult to sustain adequate follow-up in Quince and to spend time informally interacting with the community members.

In contrast, Challavito had more stable MCC personnel. Two MCC workers lived in succession in the community for three years each. The longer time frames allowed for greater trust and social integration to build. In addition, both three-year volunteers made a conscious decision to focus their work on Challavito and the immediate environs. Consequently, the volunteers in Challavito functioned in a manner most consistent with strengthening community social capital and building higher social density. They integrated into the social networks of the community, they interacted informally with the community members outside of the planned program activities, and they built greater levels of trust and cooperation between themselves and community members, enhancing social capital and increasing social density.

SOCIAL CAPITAL AND SOCIAL DENSITY: IMPLICATIONS FOR MCC AND RELATIONSHIPS

By now, the astute reader will have noted with some discomfort that many of the trends within MCC over the last decade are precisely those elements that might hurt social capital or reduce social density. MCC has shifted from the community-based development worker profiled in this research to a development model that emphasizes donor funding, seconding MCC workers to local organizations (where they usually live in a central town covering an entire zone), using more short-term personnel, and developing a central database for reporting that emphasizes formal programs and program effectiveness rather than unintended consequences and relationship building. While the surge in these directions has its genesis in a variety of complicated internal MCC politics, I would contend that this trend has been somewhat accelerated because of the lack of a good theoretical framework for understanding the unintended consequences of relationship building.

Although the shape of MCC program has changed, a theoretical framework for relationship building using the social capital and social density models still has relevance for MCC into the future. The principles of maximizing social capital and social density can still be applied to the "new" MCC because these principles are transferrable to other forms of social organization. Instead of communities, MCC's work is now with "the community" of local partner organizations. A recent program evaluation I led in MCC Uganda highlights how these principles can be applied to a contemporary MCC.

Partner and peer interviews commended MCC Uganda as being very successful in generating positive unintended consequences because although MCC functioned as a donor, it invested relatively small amounts of funding (following the "minimize external re-sources" principle from social capital). The country directors also worked tirelessly to establish close relationships with individuals in local partner organizations (slight increase in local partner social density and social networks) and worked to convene partners to-gether to discuss mutual issues (creating bridging social capital). MCC Uganda was also cited for its country director continuity. Only three country directors had served with MCC Uganda over the last twenty-one years (following the "long term personnel" principle from social capital). MCC Uganda representatives also engaged in in-formal social interactions and followed a "simple living" ethos (min-imizing power differences and creating horizontal relationships), seconded foreign workers to local organizations (following the "maximize diversity" principle in social density), and took care to en-sure that placements were not concentrated in any one place (dis-persing the impact on social density).

One of the challenges for the country directors was that while their relationship-building efforts were important, these efforts were not readily "seen" in the MCC programming document templates. These templates only "saw" a relationship when a seconded worker or a financial grant was involved. Fraternal organizational relation-ships (what might be considered the "informal relationships" for the donor-set) did not appear in program documentation, even though these occupied a significant percentage of country director time and energy and were crucial for building good social capital.

Creating bridging social capital between local partner organiza-tions can be an important relationship role for MCC in the future. In-stead of focusing on a set of single MCC-partner relationships (with subsequent vulnerabilities to creating a patron-client relationship), MCC might function to create a space where multiple partners can come together to discuss issues of mutual interest and make connec-tions with each other (the equivalent of farmer-to-farmer exchanges for local partners).

This convening role has been described by David Korten and others as a "fourth-generation" development model for international NGOs.[35] The international NGO functions as a connector rather than as a provider of funds or training. Convening local partner organiza-tions should enhance the bridging social capital among the commu-nity of local organizations. In addition, higher social density should occur because of greater network diversity which should then lead to more abstract thinking (and thus more creativity).

Table 3: Models and "Best Practices" for Relationship Building[36]

Social Density	Social Capital
• Maximize diversity in context • Engage in numerous social interactions • Engage in social interactions with numerous groups in context • Engage in repeated social interactions with groups of people • Engage in interaction rituals that highlight specific norms including horizontal relationships, trust, humility, creativity, and servanthood	• Minimize external resources • Facilitate connections between groups (such as farmer-to-farmer exchanges) • Engage in social interactions within groups that build cohesion and solidarity • Minimize power differentials • Engage in social interaction rituals that highlight specific norms such as trust and generalized reciprocity. • Be present in a context for an extended period of time. • Engage in multiple informal interactions in addition to formal NGO programming. • Avoid patron-client types of relationships • Practice ecumenical relationship building

While the unit of analysis and social organization may have shifted from a community focus to a local organization focus, the principles highlighted in this essay are still relevant for creating a theoretical framework of relationship building that can allow MCC to identify the positive and negative unintended consequences of its programs and informal actions. Table 3 summarizes the principles profiled in this essay for maximizing social density and social capital through relationships. Awareness of how social density and social capital are built, I contend, will be crucial for MCC as it reflects on its strategic reasons for working in a personnel-intensive manner and as it considers what relative weight it should place on relationship-building in its future programming.

NOTES

1. For an introduction to Durkheim's work, see John Macionis, *Society: The Basics* (Upper Saddle River, N.J.: Prentice Hall Press, 2006). On modernization theory, see David Ashley and David Orenstein, *Sociological Theory: Classical Statements,* 5th. ed. (Boston: Allyn and Bacon Press, 2001) and Andrew Webster, *An Introduction to the Sociology of Development,* 2nd. ed. (Atlantic Highlands, N.J.: Humanities Press International, 1984).

2. Randall Collins, *Four Sociological Traditions* (New York: Oxford Press, 1994).

3. Macionis, *Society.*

4. Collins, *Four Sociological Traditions.*

5. See Terrence and Vernon Jantzi, "Strengthening Civil Society for Rural Development: An Analysis of Social Capital Formation by a Christian NGO in Bolivia," in *Local Ownership, Global Change: Will Civil Society Save the World?* ed. Roland Hoksbergen and Lowell Ewert (Seattle: World Vision Publications, 2002).

6. Terrence Jantzi, "Local Program Theories and Social Capital: A Case Study of a Non-Governmental Organization in Eastern Bolivia," Ph.D. diss., Cornell University, 2000.

7. See, for example, Everett M. Rogers, *The Diffusion of Innovations,* 5th. ed. (New York: The Free Press, 2003).

8. For a discussion of social capital, see Collins, *Four Sociological Traditions.*

9. Robert D. Putnam, "Bowling Alone: America's Declining Social Capital," *Journal of Democracy* 6/1 (1995): 65-78.

10. E. Glaeser, L. Laibson, D. Scheinkman, J. Alexandre and C. Soutter, *What is Social Capital? The Determinants of Trust and Trustworthiness* (Cambridge, Mass.: National Bureau of Economic Research, 1999).

11. Jantzi and Jantzi, "Strengthening Civil Society for Rural Development."

12. Cornelia Butler Flora, "Social Capital and Sustainability: Agriculture and Communities in the Great Plains and the Corn Belt," *Research in Rural Sociology and Development: A Research Annual* 6 (1995): 3.

13. Jantzi, " Local Program Theories and Social Capital."

14. Robert D. Putnam, "The Prosperous Community: Social Capital and Public Life," *American Prospect* 13 (2005): 35-42.

15. Mary Emergy and Cornelia Flora, "Spiraling Up: Mapping Community Transformation with Community Capitals Framework," *Journal of the Community Development Society* 37/1 (2006): 19-36.

16. The literature on community social capital and social networks is extensive. Pertinent works include Coleman, *Foundations of Social Theory*; Putnam, "Bowling Alone"; Deepa Narayan, Deepa and Lant Pritchett, "Cents and Sociability: Household Income and Social Capital in Rural Tanzania, *Eco-*

nomic Development and Cultural Change 47/4 (1999): 871-897; Jan Flora, "Social Capital and Communities of Place," *Rural Sociology* 63/4 (1998): 481-506; Anthony Bebbington, "Sustaining the Andes: Social Capital and Policies for Rural Regeneration in Bolivia, *Mountain Research and Development* 18/2 (1998): 173-181; Ian Falk and Larry Harrison, "Community Learning and Social Capital: 'Just Having a Little Chat,'" *Journal of Vocational Education and Training* 50/4 (1998): 609-627; S. Green, "Community Practice: Opportunities for Community Building," *Social Work (Maatskaplike Werk)* 34/4 (1998): 362-369; and David J. O'Brien, Andrew Raedeke, and Edward W. Hassinger, "The Social Networks of Leaders in More or Less Viable Communities Six Years Later: A Research Note," *Rural Sociology* 63/1 (1998): 109-127.

17. In addition to Jan Flora, "Social Capital and Communities of Place," and Cornelia Butler Flora, "Social Capital and Sustainability," see Cynthia Duncan, "Understanding Persistent Poverty: Social Class Context in Rural Communities," *Journal of the Community Development Society* 37/1 (1996): 103-124.

18. See Butler Flora, "Social Capital and Sustainability."

19. See Duncan, "Understanding Persistent Poverty," and Alejandro Portes and Julia Sensenbrenner, "Embeddedness and Immigration: Notes on the Social Determinants of Economic Action," *American Journal of Sociology* 98/6 (1993): 1320-1350.

20. So contend Flora, "Social Capital and Communities of Place," and Duncan, "Understanding Persistent Poverty."

21. Edward S. Shihadeh and Nicole Flynn, "Segregation and Crime: The Effect of Black Social Isolation on the Rates of Black Urban Violence," *Social Forces* 74/4 (1996): 1325-1352; and Cornelia Butler Flora, Jan Flora, Jacqueline D. Spears, and Louis E. Swanson, *Rural Communities: Legacy and Change* (Boulder, Colo.: Westview Press, 1992).

22. Cornelia Flora and Jan Flora, *Rural Communities: Legacies and Change,* 2nd. ed. (Boulder, Colo.: Westview Press, 2008).

23. See A. L. Wilson, "Creating Identities of Dependency: Adult Education as a Knowledge-Power Regime," *International Journal of Lifelong Education* 18/2 (1999): 85-93; and John McKnight, *The Careless Society: Community and Its Counterfeits* (New York: Basic Books, 1995).

24. In addition to Duncan, "Understanding Persistent Poverty," see D. Matthews, "The Public's Disenchantment with Professionalism: Reasons for Rethinking Academe's Service to the Country," *Journal of Public Service and Outreach* 1/1 (1996): 21-28 and R. Eyben and S. Ladbury, "Popular Participation in Aid-Assisted Projects: Why More in Theory than Practice?" in *Power and Participatory Development*, ed. N. Nelson and S. Wright (London, England: Intermediate Technology Publications, 1995), 192-201.

25. For social capital and trust, see Francis Fukuyama, *Trust: The Social Virtues and The Creation of Prosperity* (New York: The Free Press, 1995); for reciprocity, see Putnam, "The Prosperous Community"; on accountability, see R. Vergara, "NGOs: Help or Hindrance for Community Development in Latin America?" *Community Development Journal* 29/4 (1995): 322-328; for inclusiveness, see Flora, "Social Capital and Communities of Place"; and on symbolic diversity, see Cornelia Butler Flora, "Building Social Capital: The Importance of Entrepreneurial Social Development," *Rural Development News*

21/2 (1997): 1-3.

26. See Flora, "Social Capital and Communities of Place" and Michael Woolcock, "Social Capital and Economic Development: Toward a Theoretical Synthesis and Policy Framework," *Theory and Society* 27 (1998): 151-208.

27. Ellen Wall, Gabriele Ferrazzi, and Frans Schryer, "Getting the Goods on Social Capital," *Rural Sociology* 63/2 (1998): 300-322.

28. Robert Chambers, *Challenging the Professions: Frontiers for Rural Development* (London: Intermediate Technology Publications, 1993).

29. Veraga, "NGOs: Help or Hindrance."

30. See Flora and Flora, *Rural Communities.*

31. Falk and Harrison, "Community Learning and Social Capital" and S. Green, "Community Practice."

32. In addition to Falk and Harrison, see C. Frankfort-Nachmias and J. P. Palen. "Neighborhood Revitalization and the Community Question," *Journal of the Community Development Society* 24/1 (1993): 1-14.

33. S. Salamon, "What Makes Rural Communities Tick?" *Rural Development Perspectives* 5/3 (1989): 19-24; Robert Wuthnow, *Sharing the Journey: Support Groups and America's New Quest for Community* (New York: The Free Press, 1994); and Peter Beyer, "The Global Environment as a Religious Issue: A Sociological Analysis," *Religion* 22/1 (1992): 1-19

34. D. Hertzler, "Settlers' Communities in the Bolivian Lowlands: Local Organizations, National Networks, and U.S. Intervention." Master's Thesis. University of Iowa, 1995.

35. See the discussion in Jantzi, "Local Program Theories and Social Capital."

36. Information taken from Jan Flora, "Social Capital and Communities of Place."

Conclusion:
The Church's Calling to
MCC for the Future

ARLI KLASSEN

MCC has been many things to many people since it was created in 1920 to bring coordination among various Mennonite relief committees in Canada and the United States. For some churches, MCC has become so successful in becoming *the* service agency of Canadian and United States Mennonite and BIC churches that there are many people who would like to see MCC open to incorporating any service initiative undertaken by any Mennonite congregation as part of MCC's program. There are other people who might say that this wide definition of MCC's mandate has hindered the ability of Mennonite congregations to be involved in missional service activity, because so much support and energy is given to supporting MCC's projects that energy is diverted away from the congregation's own engagements. Thus, the scope of MCC's mandate varies considerably from place to place and from time to time.

In some times and places, MCC has been primarily an inter-Mennonite organization, which is called to do whatever tasks the Mennonite churches have asked it to do. In this scenario, MCC's mandate is shaped primarily by the identity of those who do the asking, rather than by the tasks. In other times and places, MCC has been primarily

a Christian relief, development, and peace organization, which is
supported by Mennonite and Brethren in Christ churches. In this scenario, MCC's mandate is primarily shaped by the tasks to which
MCC has been called, rather than by those who do the calling. Balancing these two different ways of understanding MCC's calling and
mandate has been an ongoing challenge for MCC governance bodies.
MCC's focus on being locally driven has meant that MCC has looked
very different from place to place and from time to time. That is an
important variable that has led to MCC's success.

In a world of increasing competitiveness among relief, development, and peace organizations, and in a world of decreasing denominational loyalties, MCC has been pushed to define its identity and
calling more clearly. MCC can't be all things to all churches. The MCC
system itself has evolved into multiple governance structures where
each entity has begun defining MCC for itself. MCC has needed to
protect and clarify its mandate.

Similarly, in a world where there are more Anabaptists in the
Global South than there are in Canada and the United States, MCC
has been pushed to develop better structures for accountability to the
various Anabaptist churches in the countries where MCC is working.
The MCC system of multiple governance structures in Canada and
the United States, with no international accountability, has needed
revisions.

Thus, in 2008, MCC began a process of revisioning and restructuring called "New Wine/New Wineskins: Reshaping MCC for the
Twenty-First Century." This process engaged all MCC stakeholders
in discerning God's direction, listening to MCC's global stakeholders, unifying MCC, and increasing MCC's capacity for meaningful
impact. Three core questions guided the process:
- What task is God calling MCC to in the twenty-first century?
  (What is MCC's purpose?)
- Who is "the keeper of the MCC soul"? (To whom is MCC
  accountable?)
- What structures will ensure that MCC values and principles
  are effectively expressed at every level and drive exemplary
  programming? (How should MCC structure itself?)

A listening process, using the tool of "Appreciative Inquiry," was
set up, involving about 2,000 people in 60 meetings from 55 countries.
A leadership group of 34 people, the Inquiry Task Force, was created
to represent all of MCC's stakeholders, including Canadian and U.S.
denominational leaders, the 12 Canadian and US MCC entities, Mennonite World Conference, and international partners. Members of the

Inquiry Task Force participated in most of the appreciative inquiry meetings organized around the world. Their task was to listen: to listen to the people of God, and to listen to the voice of God, and to use their discernment to recommend a new vision, and a new structure for MCC in the future. Their recommendations were discussed, revised, and approved at a summit in June 2009 in Hillsboro Kansas, which brought together denominational leaders, the Inquiry Task Force, and six representatives from each of the 12 MCC jurisdictions.

The seven foundational identity and purpose statements that emerged from this summit give substantive clarity and direction to the whole MCC system for the coming years. They will become a unifying force that will shape and influence all parts of MCC, no matter how MCC is structured and governed. There will be plenty of room for discernment on how MCC will be locally responsive and locally shaped, within the context of commitments to a shared understanding of MCC. This is a historic shaping of MCC at this point in its history.

These foundational statements bring together both the identity and the task as important elements in defining MCC today and in the future. MCC has its identity in the Anabaptist churches that have called it into being and continue to shape and own MCC into the future. MCC has its identity in the tasks that focus on responding to basic human needs and working for peace and justice. MCC's values and faith convictions originate from the global Anabaptist communion of churches. It is only in holding all these pieces together that the strongest and clearest definition of MCC is visible. These foundational statements will seep through the MCC soul, and shape and unify all of MCC in the coming years.

MCC'S "NEW WINE" (NOVEMBER 2009)

Identity
Mennonite Central Committee is a worldwide ministry of Anabaptist churches.

Purpose
MCC shares God's love and compassion for all in the name of Christ by responding to basic human needs and working for peace and justice.

Vision

MCC envisions communities worldwide in right relationship with God, one another, and creation.

Priorities

MCC's priorities in carrying out its purpose and vision include each of the following:
• Justice and Peacebuilding
• Disaster Relief
• Sustainable Community Development

Approaches

MCC's approaches to our priorities include:
• Care for creation
• Address poverty, oppression, and injustice, including their systemic causes
• Accompany the church and our partners in a process of mutual transformation, accountability, and capacity building
• Build bridges to connect people and ideas across cultural, political, and economic divides

Values

• MCC values justice and peace. MCC seeks to live and serve nonviolently in response to the biblical call to justice and peace.
• MCC values just relationships. MCC seeks to serve justly and peacefully in each relationship and partnership, incorporating listening and learning, accountability and mutuality, transparency and integrity.

Convictions

MCC functions within the larger mission of the church. As such, MCC embraces the statement of "Shared Convictions" of global Anabaptists, as adopted by Mennonite World Conference General Council, March 2006. In these convictions we draw inspiration from Anabaptist forebears of the sixteenth century who modeled radical discipleship to Jesus Christ. We seek to walk in his name by the power of the Holy Spirit, as we confidently await Christ's return and the final fulfillment of God's kingdom.

MCC'S "NEW WINESKINS"

MCC's governance and management structures continue to evolve. For its first 24 years, MCC was governed by a single governing body and managed from a single office. In 1944, MCC opened its first "branch office" in Kitchener, Ontario, and in 1944 MCC changed its bylaws to ensure that MCC's governing body included both U.S. and Canadian representatives. Governance and management structures have continued to evolve over the decades, so that today, MCC has many offices in Canada, the United States, and about fifty countries around the world, as well as having twelve governing boards for both Canadian and U.S.-based MCC entities. Decisions that impact the whole MCC system need to be approved by consensus by all twelve MCC governing bodies.

Dissatisfaction has arisen over the complexities of making decisions that impact the entire MCC system, over the lack of accountability to any voices from the Global South, over the quality of relationships with Anabaptist denominations, and over the tensions between Canadian and U.S. approaches to international programming.

The Hillsboro Summit and the Inquiry Task Force developed four principles that are currently being used to reshape MCC's structures for the coming years. Design and implementation (in the short-term) are expected to be complete by 2012. The concepts included in these principles will continue to shape MCC for the long-term as MCC's structures continue to evolve.

Four Structure Principles (November 2009)

- MCC is seeking to become part of a global Anabaptist service entity, the shape and scope of which is still unknown. Mennonite World Conference is convening a consultation to carry these conversations into the future.
- MCC will create a central body to maintain the identity, purpose, and vision of an interdependent MCC system, and to provide leadership for the whole system.
- MCC Canada and the MCC in the United States will organize themselves internally within their country as they choose. Only MCC Canada and MCC U.S. will hold covenant relationships with the new central body.
- MCC's long-term goal is that many national/multi-nation Anabaptist-service entities will manage program within their own country of origin and beyond, committing to covenantal relationships with each other (likely without an MCC identity). MCC's short-term goal is to affirm the roles of MCC

Canada and MCC U.S. as distinct member entities, and to share management of MCC program beyond Canada and the U.S. between these two national entities.

The interpretation and implementation of these concepts will be worked on for years to come. It will be exciting to see these ideas develop and evolve over the coming decades.

Like any church or organization, MCC has seen many changes in the last 90 years. All organizations, including churches, pass through organizational life cycles. Our prayer is that new and renewed energy and vision will be created through this revisioning and restructuring work, carrying MCC with strength through the twenty-first century.

MCC has always been an inter-Mennonite organization—an arm of the gathered Anabaptist community in Canada and the United States. MCC has played a significant role in building linkages and relationships among all the different Anabaptist conferences and denominations in Canada and the United States. Some of those relationships come through sitting on MCC boards together, and some of those come through working side-by-side in a thrift shop, on the meat canner, at relief sales, in a material resources warehouse, and in service teams. MCC has the opportunity to expand its role in the church in building linkages and relationships among all the different Anabaptist conferences and denominations around the world. MCC was, is, and will be an arm of the global Anabaptist community, called by those churches to share God's love and compassion for all in the name of Christ, by responding to basic human needs and working for peace and justice.

The Index

R

Racial issues and MCC, 30, 61, 80,
164, 215-238, 254-257
Racism Awareness Program, MCC
U.S., 228
Refugees and displaced persons,
MCC work with, 26, 87, 172,
178
Amish support for, 141-142
Colombian, 326
improving circumstances, 354,
364
in Soviet Union, 356
Pakistan-India conflict, 34
Palestinian, 34, 38, 172, 311
Post-World War II, 89, 167, 176-
177, 184
in Germany, Holland and
Denmark, 33, 38, 179
MCC Commissioner for
Refugees, 33
Russian Mennonites to South
America, 32-33, 48, 88-89,
141, 181
to Canada, 44
Russian Mennonites, 33, 48, 88
with U.N. programs, 38
Yugoslavian, 33, 177-179
Russian Mennonites pre-World
War II, 32, 43, 88-90, 172-178,
355-356
Rwandan, 363
Somali, 177
Vietnamese, 172-178, 367
Regehr, Ernie, 377
Regehr, Peggy Unruh, 248, 253
Regier, H. H., 68, 70
Relief groups, early Mennonite
and Brethren in Christ, 27-29
Relief, MCC work in, 353-374, 422
and Mennonite World Confer-
ence, 88
and missions, 199-202
and Plain sect constituents, 135,
140-142, 150-152
and political neutrality, 310-312

at founding of MCC, 66-83, 172,
198
expanding internationally, 34-
38, 177
in development paradigms,
344-345
post-World War II, 32-33, 167-
184
with Canadian Mennonite relief
organizations, 42-61
women's service in, 240-243
Relief sales of MCC, 14-15, 132,
306
Anabaptist groups working together, 14-15, 30, 424
MCC income from, 146-147
Plain sect participation, 142,
146-153
women's contributions, 243
Rempel, C.J., 46-51
"Responsibility to protect" (R2P)
doctrine, 368, 375-396
Rodriguez, Eduardo "Lalo", 323
Roth, Lynn, 150-151
Russia, MCC work, *see* Union of
Soviet Socialist Republics,
MCC work
Russian Baptists, 37, 160
Russian Revolution, 31, 172, 355
Russlaender immigrants to
Canada, 43, 48-49, 52, 59
Rwanda, MCC work, 361-363, 369,
383

S

Schlabach, Gerald W., 209, 392
Schlabach, Joetta Handrich, 285-
286, 300-302
Schloneger, Craig, 271-273
Schmidt, Linda, 251
Schroeder, David, 50, 56-57
SELFHELP Crafts, *see* Ten Thou-
sand Villages
Sensenig, Ken, 150-151
Sewing Circle Committee, 46-47,
61

Breinigsville, PA USA
22 February 2011
256070BV00005B/2/P